Honour Among Nations?

Treaties and Agreements with Indigenous People

Marcia Langton, Maureen Tehan,
Lisa Palmer and Kathryn Shain (eds)

MELBOURNE UNIVERSITY PRESS

MELBOURNE UNIVERSITY PRESS
An imprint of Melbourne University Publishing Ltd (MUP Ltd)
PO Box 1167, Carlton, Victoria 3053, Australia
mup-info@unimelb.edu.au
www.mup.com.au

Typeset in 10 pt Meridien by J & M Typesetting, Australia

National Library of Australia Cataloguing-in-Publication entry

Honour among nations: treaties and agreements with indigenous people.

>   Includes index.
>   ISBN 0 522 85106 1 (paperback)
>   ISBN 0 522 85132 0 (e-book)

>   1. Indigenous peoples - Government relations.
>   2. Indigenous peoples - Legal status, laws, etc. 3. Treaties -
>   Interpretation and construction. I. Langton, Marcia.

>   323.11

'Ḻuku-Wäŋawuy Manikay (1788)'. Taken from the song 'Ḻuku-Wäŋawuy Manikay (1788)', composed by
Djencarra Galarrwuy Yunupiŋu (Mushroom Music Publishing).

The following figures are © Commonwealth of Australia and are reproduced by permission:

Figure 12.1:   South Australia, showing Native Title Claims as at 30 September 2003. Source: Geospatial
               Analysis & Mapping, NNTT.
Figure 13.1:   Areas of sea subject to claim as per Native Title Claimant Applications on the Register of
               Native Title Claims as at 30 June 2003. Source: Geospatial Analysis & Mapping, NNTT.
Figure 19.1:   Consolidated depiction of all Australian-Indonesian maritime boundaries after entry into
               force of the Treaty. Source: Geoscience Australia.

Publication of this work was assisted by grants from the Australian Research Council, the Aboriginal and
Torres Strait Islander Service, the University of Melbourne, the University's Faculty of Arts' Research and
Graduate Studies Committee, the School of Anthropology, Geography and Environmental Studies, and
Melbourne Law School.

The cover features *Nova Totivs Terrarvm Orbis Geographica Ac Hydrographica Tabvla* (c 1630) by Hendrik Hondius
Image courtesy of the University of Melbourne Library Map Collection, reproduced with permission.

'Luku-Wäŋawuy Manikay[1] (1788)'

by GalarrwuyYunupiŋu
as performed by Yothu Yindi on *Homeland Movement*[2]

My boys at ye olde Parliament, I raise a tale to relate
Now Balanda[3] say we lost our land in 1788

It seems that in that year of grace one Captain Phillip[4] landed
At a place in the east called Sydney Cove but he didn't come empty handed

For he put up a flag and said this land now belongs to George the Third[5]
and if anyone wants to challenge this then let his voice be heard

Oh haven't I told you often, my boy, that the land was all created
By Barama and the Djaŋ'kawu,[6] and then it was populated

By the Yirritja and the Dhuwa of the Yolŋu[7] at Yirrkala
By Rirratjiŋu, Gumatj, Dhalwaŋu[8] and the other *matha* and *mala*[9]

But there was no fight when the white man came, we welcomed him as a friend
But we never said he could have our land because that would be the end

For if Captain Phillip would have landed here and tried to take Yirrkala
It wouldn't have taken us very long to fix that English fellow

The *madayin* system[10] can only work if we own the land today
The older people are passing songs to the *djamarrkuli*'s[11] hands

The *buŋgul*,[12] land and the *manikay*[13] go hand in hand as one
As tomorrow calls we will decide a better destiny

Perhaps we should've known better boy, instead of the songs we sing[14]
To pledge allegiance to a white aristocracy

---

[1] Foundation-Site Song. Gumatj–English transcription and translation by Aaron Corn (2004).
[2] Yothu Yindi, *Homeland Movement* (Producer Leszek Karski, Mushroom Records, D19520, 1989, 15).
[3] Europeans.
[4] The first colonial Governor of NSW.
[5] British monarch (1760–1820).
[6] *Waŋarr* (ancestral progenitors) of the Yirritja and Dhuwa patri-moieties.
[7] People.
[8] Yolŋu patrifilial groups.
[9] Patrilects (literally, 'tongues') and patrifilial groups.
[10] Religious–legal system.
[11] Children's.
[12] Public ceremonial dances.
[13] Public song series.
[14] Manikay.

Contents

Part 1: Indigenous Agreement Making and Governance: An Historical Overview

Part 2: Recognition and Resolution in Treaty Making in Settler States

Bibliography available online at:
http://www.mup.unimelb.edu.au/ebooks/0-522-85132-0/bibliography.pdf

Abbreviations

ACC	Australian Copyright Council
ACCHS	Aboriginal Community Controlled Health Services
AFANT	Amateur Fisherman's Association of the Northern Territory
AHCA	Australian Health Care Agreement
AHDG	Aboriginal Health Development Group
AHMAC	Australian Health Ministers Advisory Council
AHMC	Australian Health Ministers Council
AIP	Agreement in Principle
ALA	*Aboriginal Land Act 1978* (NT)
ALRA	*Aboriginal Land Rights (Northern Territory) Act 1976* (Cth)
ALRM	Aboriginal Legal Rights Movement of South Australia
ATSIC	Aboriginal and Torres Strait Islander Commission
BCTC	British Columbia Treaty Commission
CAR	Council for Aboriginal Reconciliation
CERD	United Nations Committee on the Elimination of Racial Discrimination
COAG	Council of Australian Governments
CYLC	Cape York Land Council
HREOC	Human Rights and Equal Opportunity Commission
ICERD	International Convention on the Elimination of All Forms of Racial Discrimination
ICJ	International Court of Justice
ILO	International Labour Organization
ILUA	Indigenous Land Use Agreement
INAC	Indian and Northern Affairs Canada
JPDA	Joint Petroleum Development Area
NACCHO	National Aboriginal Community Controlled Health Organisation
NAHS	National Aboriginal Health Strategy
NATSIHC	National Aboriginal and Torres Strait Islander Health Council
NDP	New Democratic Party
NGO	Non-government organisation
NNTT	National Native Title Tribunal
NLC	Northern Land Council
NTA	*Native Title Act 1993* (Cth)
NTMC	Native Title Management Committee
OAS	Organization of American States
OSCE	Organization for Security and Co-operation in Europe
OTCS	Office of the Treaty Commission in Saskatchewan
PHCAP	Primary Health Care Access Program
PHOFA	Public Health Outcome Funding Agreement
RCAP	Royal Commission on Aboriginal Peoples 1996
RDA	*Racial Discrimination Act 1975* (Cth)
SACOME	South Australian Chamber of Mines and Energy
SAFF	South Australian Farmers Federation
SWALSC	South West Aboriginal Land and Sea Council
TLC	Tiwi Land Council
UEL	United Empire Loyalists
UNTAET	United Nations Transitional Administration in East Timor
USSC	United States Supreme Court
WCCCA	Western Cape Communities Co-existence Agreement
ZOC	Zone of Co-operation

Preface

The Hon Sir Anthony Mason AC KBE

This volume of essays presents various perspectives—legal, historical and humanistic—on a wide range of issues including such matters as sovereignty, treaty and agreement making, land rights, autonomy and self-determination. The essays seek to set these issues in a wider context. They deal with the evolution of international law as it expanded from a system of rules to govern the relations of European nation states *inter se* to a system of rules which sought also, however inadequately, to govern the acquisition of colonial territories in America, Africa, Asia and Australasia by the major European powers. International law is presently in the process of endeavouring to articulate the rights and interests of Indigenous peoples.

In this context, the essays highlight the difference between the treaty-making approach adopted in North America and New Zealand with the absence of such an approach in Australia. The reasons for the difference are discussed. They include the concept of *terra nullius* and the unconvincing distinction drawn between the degree of advancement of other Indigenous peoples and the Australian Aboriginal peoples for the purpose of denying the existence of rights of property, matters which were dealt with in the *Mabo (No. 2)* judgments of the High Court.

While the recognition of native land rights by statute and in *Mabo* has been seen as an important step forward, the difficulties of establishing Indigenous land rights are clearly acknowledged. The result has been to emphasise the virtues of resolution by agreement.

The essays, notably that by Noel Pearson, suggest that the High Court's interpretation of 'native title' in s 223(1) of the *Native Title Act* is unduly narrow and departs unjustifiably from the *Mabo* concept. One consequence is that the Australian concept of native title is more limited than that in North America and New Zealand, though there are other factors which contribute to that conclusion.

In the light of what has happened since, it can now be seen that the *Mabo* decision was not the threat to established land titles that some critics of the decision suggested. It may have played a significant part, however, in paving the way for the making of agreements whereby Indigenous peoples have achieved larger rights to the use and enjoyment of land.

One strong message conveyed by these essays is that the way forward to rectification of the injustice suffered by the Indigenous peoples is through the making of agreements. Another message is that the very process of negotiation reinforces the sense of community in the Indigenous peoples and in this way the process of negotiation strengthens their identity. The issues raised in the book are important. These essays will contribute to a better understanding of them into the future.

Prologue

Marcia Langton, Maureen Tehan, Lisa Palmer and Kathryn Shain

This collection is an important contribution to international debates on Indigenous peoples' rights, treaties and agreement making. The contributions in *Honour Among Nations?* describe and analyse a diversity of treaty and agreement-making instances between Indigenous peoples and others in settler states.

Drawing on a variety of academic disciplines, legal jurisdictions and contexts, the collection provides a comprehensive overview for readers interested in learning more about new directions in treaties, agreement making and Indigenous public policy and aspirations in settler states. The scope of the collection includes recent cases and historical analyses of past events. The main body of the collection consists of nineteen critical chapters grouped into four main sections. In addition, there is a general critical introduction, and four brief introductions that contextualise each of the volume's sections.

Many of the contributions in this collection were first presented as seminar papers in a seminar series titled 'Negotiating Settlements: Indigenous Peoples, Settler States and the Significance of Treaties and Agreements', convened in 2002 by The University of Melbourne's Professor Marcia Langton at the Institute of Postcolonial Studies in North Melbourne. The seminar papers were later revised by the authors for inclusion in this collection, while other papers were commissioned by the editors in 2003.

Both this collection and the 2002 seminar series are part of a broader Australian Research Council (ARC) and industry funded research project, 'Agreements, Treaties and Negotiated Settlements with Indigenous Peoples in Settler States: Their Role and Relevance for Indigenous and other Australians'. Beginning in 2002, outcomes of this project include the establishment of the Agreements, Treaties and Negotiated Settlements (ATNS) Project database. The ATNS database is an online gateway which links current information, historical detail and published material relating to agreements made between Indigenous peoples and others in Australia and other settler states. The ATNS database is designed for the use of Indigenous and other community organisations, researchers, government and industry bodies. It can be located at http://www.atns.net.au. This project also includes case studies of agreement making and the production of a series of legal issues papers.

This ARC Linkage project was awarded for 2002–2004 to Professor Marcia Langton, Foundation Chair of Australian Indigenous Studies at The University of Melbourne; Professor Larissa Behrendt, Faculty of Law and Jumbunna Indigenous House of Learning, The University of Technology Sydney; Ms Maureen Tehan, Faculty of Law, The University of Melbourne; and Dr Lisa Palmer, Postdoctoral Research Fellow, The University of Melbourne, to work in collaboration with the Aboriginal and Torres Strait Islander Commission, and continuing with the new Aboriginal and Torres Strait Islander Services as the project's industry partner. The Australian Institute of Aboriginal and Torres Strait Islander Studies has also supported this project.

Notes on Contributors

Mr Parry Agius is the Executive Officer, Native Title Unit, Aboriginal Legal Rights Movement, Adelaide and Honorary Associate, Department of Human Geography, Macquarie University, Sydney, Australia. He is a Narungga man, traditionally from the land and waters around Yorke Peninsula in South Australia.

Professor Ian Anderson is the Director of the Centre for the Study of Health and Society and Director of VicHealth Koori Health Research and Community Development Unit at The University of Melbourne, in Melbourne, Australia. He is also the Director of Research for the Cooperative Research Centre in Aboriginal Health. He is Koori and has a professional background in medicine and social sciences.

Professor Paul Chartrand is Professor of Law at the Faculty of the College of Law of the University of Saskatchewan, Canada. A member of the Indigenous Bar Association, he has been an advisor to various aboriginal and governmental organisations, including serving as a Commissioner on the Royal Commission on Aboriginal Peoples, the Aboriginal Justice Implementation Commission and on the Board of the Aboriginal Healing Foundation.

Dr Aaron Corn was a lecturer in Anthropology and Australian Indigenous Studies at The University of Melbourne, in Melbourne, Australia, in 2003. He was awarded an Australian Postdoctoral Fellowship by the Australian Research Council and is now at the Department of Music at the University of Sydney.

Dr Jocelyn Davies is a geographer based at the School of Earth and Environmental Sciences, University of Adelaide Roseworthy Campus, South Australia. She has worked on the South Australian statewide native title negotiations process as a seconded staff member to the Aboriginal Legal Rights Movement, Native Title Unit. She is a research theme co-leader in the Desert Knowledge Cooperative Research Centre, in the area of governance.

Dr Ravi de Costa is a Postdoctoral Fellow at the Institute on Globalization and the Human Condition, McMaster University, Ontario, Canada. He is currently co-ordinating a project called 'Globalization, Autonomy and Indigenous Peoples', which brings scholars from many disciplines together with Indigenous intellectuals, in order to assess Indigenous responses and resistance to globalisation.

Dr Julie Evans is an Australian Research Council Postdoctoral Fellow, in the Department of History at The University of Melbourne, in Melbourne, Australia.

Ms Michele Grossman is a Senior Lecturer in literary studies and professional writing in the Faculty of Arts at Victoria University in Melbourne, Australia. In 2002 she was a Visiting Fellow in the School of Anthropology, Geography and Environmental Studies at The University of Melbourne.

Mr Neparrŋa Gumbula is a Yolŋu elder and leader of the Daygurrgurr clan, Gupapuyŋu speaking people of the Yolŋu cultural bloc, northeast Arnhem Land, resident at Galwin'ku in the Northern Territory of Australia. He holds the inaugural Liya-Ṇaarra'mirri Visiting Fellowship at The University of Melbourne, in Melbourne, Australia.

Mr Bruce Harvey is the Chief Adviser Aboriginal and Community Relations for Rio Tinto Limited, in Melbourne, Australia.

Dr Richard Howitt is a human geographer in the Department of Human Geography at Macquarie University, Sydney, Australia. He worked as lead consultant to the Aboriginal Legal Rights Movement, Native Title Unit from 1999 to 2001 in South Australia.

Dr Sue Jackson is a geographer based at the CSIRO's Tropical Ecosystem Research Centre in Darwin, Northern Territory. She is a member of the National Reference Group of the Marine and Coastal Community Network and the Northern Territory's Coastal Policy Advisory Committee.

Ms Sandra Jarvis is an anthropologist working in the Native Title Unit, Aboriginal Legal Rights Movement in Adelaide, South Australia. During 2000 to 2003 she was acting Manager of the Native Title Unit, ILUA Statewide Section, with overall responsibility for co-ordination of the progress of the statewide negotiation strategy.

Professor Marcia Langton is the Inaugural Chair of Australian Indigenous Studies at The University of Melbourne in Melbourne, Australia. She is also a Chief Investigator with the research project on Agreements, Treaties and Negotiated Settlements. Marcia Langton is a descendant of the Yiman nation of central Queensland.

Ms Hannah McGlade is a Nyungar human rights lawyer and writer in the area of race discrimination law, in Perth, Western Australia. In 2003 she assisted the Western Australian State Government Inquiry into discrimination in the public housing sector.

Professor Bradford W. Morse of the Bar of Ontario is a Full Professor and a member of the Faculty of Law of the University of Ottawa, Canada.

Mr Graeme Neate is President of the National Native Title Tribunal in Brisbane, Australia. He is a Senior Fellow in the Law School at The University of Melbourne, in Melbourne, Australia.

Professor Ciaran O'Faircheallaigh is Professor and Head of the School of Politics and Public Policy at Griffith University, Brisbane, Australia.

Dr Lisa Palmer is an Australian Research Council Postdoctoral Fellow with the research project on Agreements, Treaties and Negotiated Settlements. She is based in the School of Anthropology, Geography and Environmental Studies, at The University of Melbourne, in Melbourne, Australia.

Mr Noel Pearson works in a voluntary capacity as Team Leader of Cape York Partnerships, in Cairns, Australia, a project negotiated between the Queensland Government and Aboriginal leaders of Cape York. Born in Cooktown, he is a Bama Bagaarrmugu of the Guuguwarrra Nation from Kalpowa and Jeannie River area in southeastern Cape York. The Lama Lama refer to his group as the Mbarimakarranma, or 'people from the little Red Flying Fox'.

Ms Kathryn Shain is a Research Fellow with the research project on Agreements, Treaties and Negotiated Settlements. She is based in the School of Anthropology, Geography and Environmental Studies at The University of Melbourne, in Melbourne, Australia.

Dr Lisa Strelein is a Research Fellow and the Manager of the Native Title Research Unit of the Australian Institute of Aboriginal and Torres Strait Islander Studies in Canberra, Australia.

Ms Maureen Tehan is a Senior Lecturer in the Law School at The University of Melbourne, in Melbourne, Australia. She is a Chief Investigator with the research project on Agreements, Treaties and Negotiated Settlements.

Professor Gillian Triggs is the Director of the Institute for Comparative and International Law at The University of Melbourne, in Melbourne, Australia.

Judge J.V. Williams, whose tribal affiliations are to the Ngäti Pukenga and Te Arawa (Waitaha, Tapuika), is the Chief Judge, Maori Land Court and the Acting Chairperson of the Waitangi Tribunal in Wellington, New Zealand.

Ms Rhiân Williams is a dispute management consultant based in Canberra, and an Honorary Associate in the Department of Human Geography, Macquarie University, Sydney, Australia. She is a Consultant Research Fellow with the Australian Institute of Aboriginal and Torres Strait Islander Studies, in the Indigenous Facilitation and Mediation Project. She has been a process adviser to the Aboriginal Legal Rights Movement, Native Title Unit in Adelaide, Australia.

Acknowledgements

Many people have contributed to the production of this edited collection. The editors acknowledge and thank all of the contributors who have given their time to researching and writing the chapters for this book.

This book is an important outcome of the Australian Research Council Linkage Project 'Agreements Treaties and Negotiated Settlements in Settler States: Their Role and Relevance for Indigenous and other Australians', and we especially acknowledge the assistance, by way of grant, of the Australian Research Council. We also acknowledge the continuing support of our industry partner, the Aboriginal and Torres Strait Islander Service. The support of The University of Melbourne, by way of a publication grant, is also acknowledged. In addition, publication has been supported by grants from the University's Faculty of Arts' Research and Graduate Studies Committee, the School of Anthropology, Geography and Environmental Studies, and Melbourne Law School.

We would like to thank Chandra Jayasuriya of the School of Anthropology, Geography and Environmental Studies at The University of Melbourne for her work in producing a number of maps for this publication. Fiona Finlayson of the School provided valuable administrative assistance for which we are grateful. We also thank Geoscience Australia, the National Native Title Tribunal and the Commonwealth Department of Communications, Information Technology and the Arts for permission to reproduce a number of maps, and the National Native Title Tribunal in Perth, for generous assistance with the preparation of others.

The collection has benefited from the work of a number of research assistants. We thank Odette Mazel, Catherine Burke, Willoh Sleeman Weiland, Prue Elletson, Haydie Gooder and David Llewellyn for their work in preparing draft chapters for publication. We thank Michele Grossman for her support and assistance during the proposal stage of this collection. We also thank Louise Adler, Amanda Finnis and Brian Ward of Melbourne University Publishing for their assistance with the publication of this book.

We would like to acknowledge the Institute of Postcolonial Studies in North Melbourne where, in 2002, we held the Negotiating Settlements: Indigenous peoples, settler states and the significance of treaties and agreements, Beyond the Frontier Seminar Series. The majority of chapters in this collection were first presented as seminar papers in that series.

Finally, we would like to thank Sir Anthony Mason for graciously agreeing to write the Preface for this collection.

Introduction

Marcia Langton, Maureen Tehan and
Lisa Palmer

Indigenous peoples, encapsulated by colonial regimes, and subsequently, settler states, have long attempted to negotiate for the recognition and redress of historical injustices. To varying degrees, they have also sought state recognition of their rights of sovereignty. Barkan[1] argues that these claims (whether by Indigenous peoples or others), based on injustice and the desire for recognition by the nation-state, are increasingly addressed by negotiating restitution.[2]

The power of this process of voluntary negotiations and agreements is that, while it goes some way towards making amends for past injustices, it also redefines future interactions between victims and perpetrators and attempts to negotiate improvements on existing social injustices. Moreover, restitution enables victimised groups to be recognised as groups, forcing a re-examination of the Enlightenment understanding of justice as exclusively the protection of individual human rights.

Indigenous peoples have brought to international attention the injustice of colonialism and the colonials' self-justifying claims to dominion. They have developed various models for the negotiated settlement of rights in their ancestral property and jurisdiction. Legal scholars have supported their rejection of the fantastic nature of settler states' claims to legitimacy and the alternative arrangements developed, such as treaties.[3]

The contributions in this book examine, among other things, the idea of recognition and restitution through the making of agreements, which

---

[1] Elazar Barkan, *The Guilt of Nations: Restitution and Negotiating Historical Injustices* (W.W. Norton & Company, New York, 2000).

[2] Ibid, xxvi. Barkan refers to restitution 'comprehensively to include the entire spectrum of attempts to rectify historical injustices' (ibid, xix). Restitution 'is thus not only a legal category but also a cultural concept' (ibid).

[3] James Anaya, *Indigenous Peoples in International Law* (Oxford University Press, New York, 1996); John Borrows, 'Sovereignty's Alchemy: An Analysis of *Delgamuukw v British Columbia*' (1999) 37 *Osgoode Hall Law Journal* 537; John Borrows 'Domesticating Doctrines: Aboriginal Peoples after the Royal Commission' (2001) 46 *McGill Law Journal* 615–661; Robert Williams *The American Indian in Western Legal Thought* (Oxford University Press, New York 1990); Garth Nettheim '"The Consent of the Natives": Mabo and Indigenous political rights' (1993) 15 *Sydney Law Review* 223–246; Paul McHugh 'The Common-Law Status of Colonies and Aboriginal "Rights": How Lawyers and Historians Treat the Past' (1998) 61 *Saskatchewan Law Review* 393.

has become the principal form of engagement between Indigenous nations and the modern nation-state. Building on their histories of engagement through treaty making (and breaking), in the United States of America, Canada and New Zealand, negotiated agreements have replaced treaties as the modern arrangement for engagement with Indigenous peoples with respect to resource use.[4]

Agreement making emerges in our historical analysis as an instrument of governance within and between the nation-state and Indigenous nations, or, as we sometimes refer to them, aboriginal polities. Particularly in settler nation-states that coincide with a number of aboriginal polities having their own customary law regimes, agreement making has evolved among these diverse entities as a means of engaging rationally in dealings in land access and use, resource distribution and governance. Such agreements eventuate in only the most opportune circumstances, however. The variation in outcomes from comprehensive settlements in Canada, such as the Nunavut Agreement,[5] to the agreement involving extinguishment or impairment of native title or other rights, such as in Australia, requires, at the very least, some explanation. Some of this explanation lies in history, and several contributions in this collection expand our understanding of the political

---

[4] Richard Bartlett, 'Canada: Indigenous Land Claims and Settlements', in Bryan Keon-Cohen (ed.), *Native Title in the New Millennium: A Selection of Papers from the Native Title Representative Bodies Legal Conference 16–20 April 2000, Melbourne* (Aboriginal Studies Press, Native Title Research Unit, Australian Institute of Aboriginal and Torres Strait Islander Studies (AIATSIS), Canberra, 2001); Shaunnagh Dorsett and Lee Godden, *A Guide to Overseas Precedents of Relevance to Native Title* (Native Title Research Unit, AIATSIS, Canberra, 1998); Michele Ivanitz, *The Emperor has No Clothes: Canadian Comprehensive Claims and their Relevance to Australia, Native Title Research Unit Discussion Papers, Regional Agreements No 4* (Native Title Research Unit, AIATSIS, Canberra, 1997); Marcia Langton, 'Dominion and Dishonour: A treaty between our nations' (2001) 4(1) *Postcolonial Studies* 13–26; Gary D. Meyers, Garth Nettheim and Donna Craig, *Indigenous Peoples and Governance Structures* (Aboriginal Studies Press, AIATSIS, Canberra, 2002); Margaret Stephenson, 'Negotiating Resource Development Agreements with Indigenous People: Comparative international lessons' in Bryan Horrigan and Simon Young (eds), *Commercial Implications of Native Title* (Federation Press, Leichardt, NSW, 1997); Canada, Royal Commission on Aboriginal People, *Report of the Royal Commission on Aboriginal Peoples: Restructuring the Relationship* vol. 2, part 1 (Supply and Services Canada, Ottawa, 1996); Gordon Christie, *Delgamuukw and Modern Treaties* (2000) Delgamuuk National Process http://www.delgamuukw.org/research/moderntreaties.pdf at 19 July 2000; John Borrows, 'Negotiating Treaties and Land Claims: The Impact of Diversity within First Nations' Property Interests' (1992) 12 *Windsor Yearbook of Access to Justice* 179–234; John Borrows, 'Nanabush Goes West: Title, Treaties and the Trickster in British Columbia', in John Borrows (ed.), *Recovering Canada: The Resurgence of Indigenous Law* (University of Toronto Press, Toronto, 2002); Deloria Vine, 'Reserving to Themselves: Treaties and the Powers of Indian Tribes' (1996) 38 *Arizona Law Review* 962–980.

[5] The Inuit of the Nunuvat settlement area and the Government of Canada, *Nunuvat Land Claims Agreement* (1993) Department of Indian and Northern Affairs: Canada http://www.ainc-inac.gc.ca/pr/agr/nunavut/index_e.html at 12 November 2003.

status of Indigenous peoples under colonialism and the practice of treaty making. Other chapters explain how the standing of Indigenous nations has been diminished, whether as a result of judicial decision or executive fiat. Others consider the ways in which recognition and substantive outcomes flow from agreement making, even in circumstances in which law has failed to accord formal recognition.

Indigenous people and human rights law

The twentieth-century paradigm of evolving Indigenous rights has involved a refining of human rights and law, with special reference to the circumstances of Indigenous peoples, as Morse explains.[6] There is no single concept of Indigenous rights, but rather an ever-growing body of law, opinion and practice, much of it developed during the twentieth century and arising from both the demands of Indigenous peoples themselves and from the concessions made by governments, international bodies and others to recognise various special rights and interests, and to accommodate them.

Moreover, as Morse observes,[7] the stature of Indigenous legal issues and the position of Indigenous peoples have grown dramatically in importance under both international and domestic law:

> In 1994, the Sub-Commission on the Prevention of Discrimination and Protection of Minorities adopted a *Draft Declaration on the Rights of Indigenous Peoples*, which had been under development by the Working Group on Indigenous Populations since 1982. This Draft Declaration is currently under exhaustive clause-by-clause review before the UN Human Rights Commission. … In 1994, the UN adopted the *Declaration on the Rights of Persons Belonging to National or Ethnic, Religious and Linguistic Minorities*, thus ensuring that it made advances for both indigenous and minority peoples. The International Labour Organization (ILO) overhauled *Convention 107* through the development in 1989 of the *Indigenous and Tribal Peoples Convention 169*, which has subsequently come into force, that concentrates upon a collective rights base approach and recognizes the continued existence of indigenous peoples as distinct peoples. More recently, the Organization of American States (OAS) has been consulting upon a proposed *American Declaration on the Rights of Indigenous Peoples* that could be adopted for the Western Hemisphere. In other regional fora, the European Council and the Organization for Security and Co-Operation in Europe (OSCE) have developed a series of international documents and institutions to recognize and protect the rights of minorities, which can provide

---

[6] Bradford Morse, 'Treaties, the Courts and Indigenous Rights' (Paper presented at the 13th Commonwealth Law Conference, Melbourne, Australia, 13–17 April 2003) 1–2.

[7] Ibid.

some advances for the indigenous peoples of that continent. ... Associations that are founded on shared history of colonialism, such as the Commonwealth and la Francophonie, have also begun to develop embryonic documents on human rights, as well as generate initial studies and rudimentary discussion on the rights of indigenous and minority peoples.

Simultaneously, many countries have chosen or been compelled to address the economic, political and legal situations of indigenous peoples within their domestic context. Constitutional recognition of indigenous peoples and their unique rights has occurred over the last two decades in a number of countries, while others have enacted fundamental changes through national legislation and policies. The highest appellate courts in a variety of countries have issued landmark decisions that have transformed the internal relationships between indigenous peoples and the nation states in which they live and fundamentally affected the political and legal landscape.[8]

Treaties and the development of international law

The period of the expansion of empires that led to the kinds of treaties, and the later forms of these pacts as modern agreements, is fertile terrain for understanding the several key concepts in the body of political thought and law on the nature of Indigenous rights. The history of treaty making in the 'New World' extended over 400 years for the British and French, and over 500 years for the Spanish, Dutch and Portuguese, with divergent outcomes throughout the colonies. Imperial powers found it necessary in various situations to justify acts of domination for juridical purposes.

The starting point for European expansion in the fifteenth century was the absence of formal relations between sovereigns with extra-European peoples, despite the legacy of the Roman Empire throughout Europe, and the trade relations that extended as far as China. The reach of the European powers into the 'New World' brought new peoples and civilisations within the ambit of a new international code of European regulation, and law developed *ad hoc* to justify conquest, trade, safe passage and other exigencies of imperialism. Thus, after initial contact had been established, the potential approaches of the imperial entities to regulate relations included all of those from unilateralism to reciprocity. Between these two extremes it was possible to find variants that expressed relations of ambiguous equality and inequality.[9]

---

[8] Ibid.

[9] Charles Henry Alexandrowicz, *An Introduction to the History of the Law of Nations in the East Indies 16th, 17th and 18th Centuries* (Clarendon Press, Oxford, 1967). See also Langton and Palmer, this volume.

The British have used treaties for the settlement of disputes since the thirteenth century. Treaties have been common practice between nations and states, either in the form we now know them at international law, or in different forms which stem from past customary law practices.[10] When the British and other European imperial powers entered the New World, treaties and agreements with Indigenous people ensued. Following the War of Independence in the colonies of America:

> Chief Justice Marshall of the United States Supreme Court explored the dilemma of the conflicting rights of settlers and Indigenous people, and adopted the compromise known as native title at common law. The Chief Justice reviewed the practice of Europe which developed after the 1537 Papal Bull, and declared that the 'rights of the original inhabitants were, in no instance entirely disregarded ... They were admitted to be the rightful occupants of the soil, with legal as well as just claims to retain possession of it'.[11]

Richard Bartlett, writing about *Johnson v McIntosh*, says that 'the equality declared by Chief Justice Marshall was tempered by a regard for pragmatic considerations'.[12] This decision was qualified to the extent that Chief Justice Marshall declared that, where the interests of settlers conflicted with the interests of Indigenous people, it was necessary to 'resort to some new and different rule, better adapted to the actual state of things' in recognising title to land. Thus, although 'Indians were recognised as the "rightful occupants of the soil", ...their title was "necessarily, to considerable extent, impaired"'.[13]

Such general justifications played a crucial role in European expansion overseas. They had inherent universal applicability and included such well-known terms as 'the right of conquest', and 'humanitarian' or 'civilising intervention'. Significantly, such justifications referred to rights that were specifically claimed by the European powers, such as the right to propagate the faith unhindered. Formally established juridical relations co-existed

---

[10] In the entry on 'treaty' in the *Oxford English Dictionary*, we find the claim that the first formal and written treaty made in England was in 1217 between Henry III and the Dauphin of France; John Simpson, and Edmund Weiner (eds), *Oxford English Dictionary* (Clarendon Press, Oxford, 2nd edn, 1989) vol. XVIII, 465.

[11] Richard H. Bartlett, *Native Title in Australia* (Butterworths, Sydney, 2000) 6; *Johnson v McIntosh*, 8 Wheat 543 (1823); 5 L Ed 681 (1823); 21 US 543 (1823). As Bartlett points out, the United States Supreme Court repeatedly affirmed the *Johnson v McIntosh* decision in *Cherokee Nation v Georgia*, 5 Pet 1 (1831); *Worcester v Georgia*, 6 Pet 515 (1832); *Mitchell v United States*, 34 US (9 pet) 711 (1835); *United States v Cook*, 86 US 591 (1873); *United States v Santa Fe Pacific Railroad Co*, 314 US 339 at 345 (1941).

[12] Bartlett, above n 11, 6.

[13] Ibid; *Johnson v McIntosh*, 8 Wheat 543 (1823) 574, 591, 599; 5 L Ed 681(1823) 688, 693, 695; as cited in ibid.

alongside claims to rights which the European powers never succeeded in securing in practice or which could only be secured at a much later stage.[14]

From the early nineteenth century, international law and its norms, elaborated by Europeans as an essential adjunct to their expansionist and colonialist activities around the globe, were taken to be universal. 'The bone of contention was determining who were the subjects of such a universal system of norms'.[15]

Colonial subjecthood

As Evans shows in Chapter 3 of Part 1, with her comparison of nineteenth-century settler manipulation of Indigenous peoples' political and legal subjecthood in Natal and Western Australia, the rule of law enabled the replication of the nation-state that evolved in Britain—'a nation-state which had itself been constituted through conquest, coercion and colonialism'.[16] As Evans argues, the rule of law operated ideologically throughout the nineteenth century as though the colonies were already the nation-states they would become, but with enduring and detrimental consequences for the Indigenous subjects, especially denial of equality before the law. In colonies of conquest, international law demanded the recognition of customary law and polities, while in settled colonies such as Australia (where the fiction of *terra nullius* was upheld), pre-existing laws and customs were not recognised. Rather, as British subjects, Indigenous peoples were theoretically entitled to the equal force and protection of British law. However, Evans argues that the British were able to circumvent their own legal standards by creating a separate system of criminal law which belied Aboriginal people's status as equal subjects. Evans's analysis places the scourge of racism, the hallmark of Enlightenment ideas that were fostered in Imperial expansion, at the centre of these developments. The colonial law effectively punished Aboriginal people, whose allegedly criminal offences inhibited settlement, and in this way criminalisation of native subjects went hand in hand with their dispossession.

In the 1830s, the Colonial Office in Britain had decreed that 'the new colonial constitutions should contain no discriminatory provisions on the basis of race, colour, class or creed'.[17] However, Evans notes that:

---

[14] Miguel Alfonso Martinez, *Report of the Special Rapporteur on Treaties, Agreements and Other Constructive Arrangements between States and Indigenous Populations: Second Progress Report*, UN ESCOR, Sub-Commission on Prevention of Discrimination and Protection of Minorities, 44th sess, Un Doc E/CN.4/Sub.2/1995/27 (1995).

[15] Ibid, para 167.

[16] Evans, this volume, 72.

[17] Ibid, 73.

the incommensurability of this theoretical commitment to liberty and equality with the economic aims of settlement—predicated on the need to subject and dispossess these same Indigenous peoples—together with prevailing notions of European superiority, meant that caveats were placed on the possibility of full equality for Indigenous peoples as British subjects at the outset.[18]

By example, the use of the British criterion of property qualifications for political rights in Natal was a powerful tool for disenfranchisement and disempowerment, while all the while appearing as the application of the rule of law. Such colonial foils, in the end, placed the issue of property and rights to land at the centre of the decolonisation agenda, and indeed, postcolonial history.

North America

During the same period, in the United States of America, despite the findings at law as to Indigenous nations being the 'rightful occupants of the soil', the doctrine of discovery was interpreted as an exercise of dominion that impaired the standing of these Indigenous nations. Nevertheless, the formal recognition of Indigenous peoples as entities with sovereign status, such as in the United States of America and New Zealand, had considerable advantages over the situation in Australia.

In North America, from the time of first settlement, in the years 1533 to 1789—that is, prior to independence and the Marshall cases—the administrators of British colonies treated Indian nations as equal sovereigns. They were relationships 'between sovereign nations' that 'accorded tribes an equivalent status to that of the colonial governments'.[19]

After independence, up until 1871, 'the United States government assumed the role of the British and Spanish governments and continued the earlier British policy of treating with the Indians as members of sovereign nations. These treaties were made under the authority of the federal treaty making power' enshrined in the United States' constitution.[20]

'In 1871, treaty making with the Indian tribes was discontinued as it was seen as an impediment to the assimilation of Indians into white society'.[21] After 1871:

---

[18] Ibid.

[19] Dorsett and Godden, above n 4, 2.

[20] Ibid; David Getches, Charles Wilkinson and Robert Williams Jnr, *Federal Indian Law: Cases and Materials* 3rd edn (West Publishing Co, St Paul, 1993) 2–6.

[21] Dorsett and Godden, above n 4, 4; *Appropriations Act 1871*, (25 USC § 71 [1976]), § 71: *Future Treaties with Indian Tribes*: No Indian nation or tribe within the territory of the United States shall be acknowledged or recognized as an independent nation, tribe or power with

'agreements' rather than 'treaties' were made with the Indians. Between 1911 and the 1970s, Congressional practice was to obtain some kind of consent from the Indians for any action it was considering which might affect them. Current practice is to use negotiated settlements as a means of dealing with complex issues.[22]

Dorsett and Godden suggest '[a]n example of this is the *Alaska Claims Settlement Act* (43 U.S.C. 1601–1629). Other subjects of negotiated settlements include child welfare and gaming on Indian reservations.'[23]

Treaties in Canada proceeded from a different basis from those in the United States of America. Almost forty treaties were negotiated between first nations and the British Crown during the period 1693 to 1862. The majority of these were peace and friendship treaties. However, Indian peoples were not considered to be sovereign powers. Post Confederation treaties, the numbered treaties, 'tended to follow a pattern of surrender of lands in return for particular rights, for example continued hunting and fishing rights, supplies or monetary payments', or smaller areas of Reserve land.[24]

In 1982, a new section, section 35, was inserted into the *Constitution Act*. It provides that 'the existing Aboriginal and treaty rights of the Aboriginal peoples of Canada are hereby recognised and affirmed'. Further, at sub-section 3, it includes land agreements as 'treaty rights' in order to achieve 'greater certainty'. In addition, section 25 of the Charter of Rights and Freedoms provides that 'the guarantee in this Charter of certain rights and freedoms shall not be construed so as to abrogate or derogate from any aboriginal, treaty or other rights or freedoms that pertain to the aboriginal peoples of Canada'.[25] The existing aboriginal and treaty rights include common law aboriginal rights and title. Together with the notion of the honour of the Crown and the Crown's fiduciary obligation to aboriginal peoples, these elements underpin agreement and treaty making in modern Canada.

The historical interplay between coloniser and aboriginal nations in North America and modern aspects of Canadian/aboriginal relations in the agreement-making process are explored by Morse in Chapter 2. A broad range of agreements exists in Canada today, including comprehensive land-claim settlements, some of which include self-government agreements;

---

whom the United States may contract by treaty; but no obligation of any treaty lawfully made and ratified with any such Indian nation or tribe prior to March 3, 1871, shall be hereby invalidated or impaired'.

[22] Dorsett and Godden, above n 4, 6.

[23] Ibid.

[24] Ibid, 22.

[25] Ibid, 23.

impact-benefit agreements; interim-management agreements; consultation agreements; local-service agreements; and many other types.[26] Some are legally enforceable; others are not.[27] The *Canadian Constitution Act 1982* protects some, while the status of others is uncertain. Some agreements are based on building long-term relationships; others involve only short-term, singular projects. However, Morse argues that the totality of these agreements demonstrate that Indigenous people are now engaging with others across the public and private spectrums in a manner that has become a normal part of business in Canada. It is an outcome that demonstrates that 'the unthinkable can in fact become commonplace'.[28]

The common law and constitutional tapestry woven by Morse provides a more optimistic backdrop for Chartrand, de Costa and Tehan in Part 2 (Chapters 6, 7 and 8, respectively), whose detailed analyses of the application of some of these principles present a more pessimistic view. For these authors, the pathway to modern, comprehensive agreements with aboriginal nations in Canada is strewn with obstacles, and in British Columbia at least, the unthinkable is not yet commonplace. Using the Royal Commission On Aboriginal Peoples as his guide, Chartrand points to serious anomalies in the modern Canadian treaty process, which excludes some aboriginal peoples such as the Métis,[29] and does not adequately extend recognition and self-governance principles within existing treaty negotiations. He identifies the failure of the common law to accord adequate modern recognition to all aboriginal nations and the reliance on nineteenth-century notions of recognition as central to the failure of the modern process to meet the standards set by the Royal Commission for 'nation-to-nation relationships institutionalised in treaties'[30] and a reconciliation of 'the national interest of each aboriginal treaty party with the interests of other Canadians'.[31] He proposes direct legislative recognition of all aboriginal nations as the first requirement for a realigned relationship on a nation-to-nation basis.

Both de Costa and Tehan add a further dimension to this critical analysis

---

[26] Bradford Morse, 'The Continuing Significance of Historic Treaties and Modern Treaty-Making: A Canadian and United States Perspective' (Seminar presented at Negotiating Settlements: Indigenous Peoples, Settler States and the Significance of Treaties and Agreements: Beyond the Frontier seminar series, Institute of Postcolonial Studies, Melbourne, Victoria, 22 July 2002).

[27] Ibid.

[28] Ibid.

[29] The need to incorporate the Métis in the modern agreement process may be accelerated by the recent Supreme Court of Canada decision in *R v Powley* [2003] SCC 43 (17 March, 2003, 19 September 2003) in which certain Métis rights to hunt were recognised as constitutionally protected rights under s35 of the *Constitution Act 1982*.

[30] Chartrand, this volume, 132.

[31] Ibid.

of the modern treaty process by focusing in detail on the operation of the process in the Province of British Columbia. Tehan takes up the theme of the inadequacy of the common law in relation to the modern treaty process in British Columbia, suggesting that common law recognition of aboriginal rights and title has failed to produce meaningful negotiations or agreement in the Province. She argues that while law may to some extent operate to transform attitudes, the inexorably political dimensions of negotiating agreements requires more than law to produce agreements that adequately protect aboriginal rights and title and engage the jurisdiction of aboriginal nations. Complementing this analysis, de Costa argues that the British Columbia Treaty Process is institutionally flawed in its structure, the content of negotiations and the attitudes of the federal and provincial governments. Resonating with Chartrand's broader analysis and Tehan's view of law's role, de Costa paints a bleak picture of the political processes surrounding treaty negotiations, and questions whether in this political and institutional moment in British Columbia there can be a rebalancing of the 'colonial relationship'.[32] Rather, he suggests that 'an incremental approach, even a permanent culture of negotiation'[33] may be preferable to final agreements, a view also taken up by Agius *et al.*[34]

New Zealand

The *Treaty of Waitangi*, signed in 1840 between the Maori and the British colonial government, 'is recognised as the founding document of New Zealand which resides in the constitutional field of its system of government.[35] The *Treaty* is in two versions: English and Maori. Because they vary in meaning quite substantially, there were problems of interpretation such that the English version had been privileged over the Maori. These differences between the versions have caused controversy in the interpretation of the *Treaty* and the application of treaty principles.[36]

The *Treaty* established the right of the Crown to govern in New Zealand and the terms of a peaceful settlement:

> In exchange Maori rights to their lands, resources and taonga [treasured things] were affirmed and Maori were granted the rights and privileges of

---

[32] de Costa, this volume, 146.
[33] Ibid.
[34] Agius *et al.*, this volume.
[35] Dorsett and Godden, above n 4, 32.
[36] Ibid, above n 4, 31–33; New *Zealand Maori Council v Attorney General [1987]* 1 NZLR 641 (*'Maori Land Council case'*).

'British citizenship'. As New Zealand became constitutionally independent from Britain the treaty obligations of the British Crown were transferred to the Crown in New Zealand.[37]

Unlike Australia, New Zealand has a unitary rather than federal structure of government, and while it is a constitutional monarchy it does not have a written constitution. The government's power to deal with Maori affairs derives not from a nominated head of power as under the Australian Commonwealth Constitution, but from the inherent plenary power arising from sovereignty itself.[38]

The *Treaty* provided that the Crown's right to govern was dependent upon it meeting its obligations to Maori people under articles of the *Treaty*. In recent times, the *Treaty* has been considered in a number of landmark cases dealing with Maori rights. In interpreting the *Treaty*, the courts have 'held it to be of no legal force, in itself, without incorporation into domestic New Zealand law'.[39] Dorsett and Godden explain that over the past ten years there has developed a significant body of case law that has clarified the *Treaty* obligation of the Crown:[40]

> Of particular importance in marking a change in the attitude of the Court was the *Maori Land Council Case* where the Court found that the *Treaty* should be interpreted in a broad manner and as an evolving instrument, taking account of international human rights norms. A number of treaty principles were elucidated in the course of that decision including: Sovereignty was exchanged for the protection of Rangatiratanga [full authority, chieftainship]; the treaty established a partnership imposing on the partners a duty to act reasonably and in good faith, and Maori are to retain Rangatiratanga over their resources and taonga [treasured things].[41]

As Williams says, the *Treaty* was 'an exchange of promises rather than a declaration of rights',[42] and it does not constrain the sovereign power of the New Zealand legislature.[43] However, that is not to say that the *Treaty* has no legal effect.

Williams simply and concisely locates the *Treaty* in the constitutional landscape of New Zealand, identifying its place as a relevant consideration in statutory interpretation.[44] Perhaps more significantly, Williams identifies

---

[37] Dorsett and Godden, above n 4, 33.
[38] Ibid, 31.
[39] Ibid, 34.
[40] Ibid, 35; *Maori Land Council case [1987]* 2 NZLR 641.
[41] Dorsett and Godden, above n 4, 35.
[42] Williams, this volume, 164.
[43] Ibid.
[44] Ibid, 165.

the raft of legislation in which treaty references now appear and that the *Treaty* now has a central place in legislation, bureaucracy and the scheme of New Zealand life.[45] Regardless of the lack of specific enforceability, the *Treaty* is entrenched in the political and legal processes, and will not 'go away'. Rather, Williams countenances the possibility of recognition of Maori jurisdiction and autonomy but within existing institutions. To this extent, the *Treaty* contrasts with the disparate approach to jurisdiction in Canada, and provides an alternative method by which to conceive Aboriginal sovereignty within the nation-state. Ultimately, Williams' contribution reinforces the fiercely regional and culturally specific nature of solutions to the issue of reconciliation of settler and Aboriginal sovereignty.

The idea of a treaty in Australia

Throughout Australian history, entrepreneurial, evangelical and humanitarian figures have attempted by various means, including attempts to make treaties, to resolve the hostile relationship between the Indigenous and settler Australians.[46] However, unlike in other settler societies, no treaty documents or treaty proposals were officially recognised. Judicial decisions declared Australia an uninhabited wasteland.[47] Consequently, the large body of treaty law centred upon developments in the United States of America and in Canada has not developed in Australia. This is despite numerous attempts at negotiated settlement and offers of settlement.

In his book, *Fate of a Free People*,[48] Henry Reynolds examines the evidence of treaty making during the early years of the first colonial settlement in Tasmania, when a treaty with the 'Chiefs' of the Aboriginal 'tribes' was discussed and considered. It was suggested that a treaty should have been entered into in order to restrain and prevent the extermination of Aboriginal people by the settlers. In Governor Arthur's correspondence, Reynolds finds explicit discussion of the need for treaties.[49] This is not surprising, given the international context of treaty making that we have just discussed. The missionary George Augustus Robinson was eventually commissioned to negotiate with the Aboriginal people.

Reynolds's evidence shows that 'treaty making was well understood among the Tasmanian tribes'.[50] He concedes that we may never know with

---

[45] Ibid.

[46] Langton, above n 4.

[47] *Cooper v Stuart (1889)* 14 App Cas 286.

[48] Henry Reynolds, *Fate of a Free People* (Penguin, Ringwood, Victoria, 1995).

[49] Ibid, 122.

[50] Ibid, 149.

any certainty whether or not George Augustus Robinson negotiated a treaty on behalf of the government; the conditions were not recorded. However, he does conclude that the evidence suggests that Robinson 'did reach an agreement similar to the treaties with tribes in North America', although the terms of the agreement were not honoured.[51] The ill-fated Batman treaty concerning an area of land, now encompassing Melbourne, met a similar fate. It was firmly rejected by Governor Bourke in 1835.[52]

Focussing on northern Australia, in Chapter 1 of Part 1, Langton and Palmer note that the Aboriginal societies along much of the northern coastline of Australia had traded with the seafaring peoples of the Indonesian archipelago, popularly known as the 'Macassans', from at least the seventeenth century till the early twentieth century, and concluded dealings with them which bear the hallmarks of the verbal treaties of North America and other colonies. They argue that Aboriginal peoples have continued this process of negotiation in their attempts to negotiate settlements with colonial authorities and the settler nation-state to the present day. Furthermore, they suggest that these negotiations, by, or with, Aboriginal people in northern Australia for settlements of trade and peace, have resulted in the extension of the jurisdiction of surviving Aboriginal customary polities, beyond their traditional boundaries into postcolonial commercial and legal domains. They observe, further, that modern agreement making affords recognition of Aboriginal customary polities that Australian statutes and common law have not. They draw our attention to the political terms of these contracts. Even though the Aboriginal parties must often negotiate under duress, consensus confers legitimacy on the state as it benefits from access to the Indigenous domain, while the Aboriginal parties have the opportunity to extend their customary jurisdictions into the modern economic and political spheres.

Unsettling sovereignties

It is not possible, as we have seen, to reduce the international relations between the Europeans and Indigenous peoples as a whole to a single pattern. For a long period a number of variants of international law co-existed and were employed by the Europeans, depending on the various circumstances and their diverse interests. While in their earlier engagements with non-European peoples the European interlocutors had

---

[51] Ibid, 156.
[52] Cecil Phillip Billot, *John Batman: The Story of John Batman and the Founding of Melbourne* (Hyland House, Melbourne, 1979) 97.

strategically negotiated treaties of peace, friendship and trade, with the rise of the positivist doctrine of the nation-state during the nineteenth century, the principles of the law of nations were taken by the Europeans to be universal, and these new European norms of governance were considered to be applicable to the whole world.[53] It was a doctrine that excluded any recognition of the alternative traditions of governance and sovereignty and increasingly provided the legal means for colonising states to consolidate territorial sovereignty over Indigenous lands.[54]

For the past two centuries, with the rise and decline of the 'blood and soil' doctrine of nation-state and sovereignty, the twinned ideas of nation-state and sovereignty have been challenged. As legal history scholar Joaquin Varela Suanzes has noted, Britain itself has not been free of serious challenges to the idea of sovereignty:

> On the other hand, there is no doubt that during the current century the principle of Parliamentary sovereignty has had to face new and very difficult challenges. Particularly three: firstly that faced by the 1937 Statute of Westminster, which compelled the reconsideration of the relationship between the British parliament and the Commonwealth; secondly that caused by Britain joining the European Economic Community in 1972, which put on the table the no less problematic relationship between the sovereignty of the British Parliament and the primacy of European Community Law; thirdly that implied by the approval in 1997 of the Autonomy polls in Wales and Scotland, which have compelled a redefinition of the role of the Parliament of Westminster and its relationship with the two new legislative assemblies. Such challenges have forced a reconsideration of the validity of Parliamentary sovereignty in Great Britain today where the debate regarding sovereignty has acquired great political importance and substantial academic interest...[55]

Recent literature on federalism draws attention to the way in which diversity is accommodated in constitutional and political arrangements in various state formations. Thomas Fleiner[56] has proposed that, in Europe at least, a number of different solutions have evolved in European nation-building, particularly expressed in European Constitutions with regard to their diversities. While the German constitution constructs the *volk*, or one-people, as the equivalent of the nation (conceived as a unity of people, territory, language and polity), Belgium, made up of three communities,

---

[53] Langton and Palmer, this volume, 38.

[54] Anaya, above n 3.

[55] Joaquin Varela Suanzes, *Sovereignty in British Legal Doctrine* (1999) 6 (3) *Murdoch University Electronic Journal of Law* http://www.murdoch.edu.au/elaw/indices/title/suanzes63_abstract.html at 3 December 2003.

[56] Thomas Fleiner 'Constitutions & Diverse Communities in the 21st Century' (Paper presented at the Institute for Comparative and International Law, The University of Melbourne, Victoria, 2001).

the French community, the Flemish community and the German-speaking community, recognises this diversity in its constitution. In the Serbian constitution, it is stated that '[p]ersons belonging to a national minority shall have special rights which they exercise individually or in community with others.' The Bosnian constitution asserts that it is the will of its various communities in the following: 'Bosniacs, Croats, and Serbs, as constituent peoples (along with Others), and citizens of Bosnia and Herzegovina hereby determine that the Constitution of Bosnia and Herzegovina is as follows'.[57] This rich diversity of communities of people caught up in several modern nation-state formations in Europe contrasts with the settler-state situation in Australia, in which unitary principles of nation-building have been, and remain, dominant in constitutional affairs. This has occurred notwithstanding the diversity of communities of interest inherent in the Australian Federation itself. Articulating this multilayered approach to sovereignty within the Australian nation-state may begin to prise open alternative ways of accommodating diverse communities.

In this respect, Chapter 5 by Corn and Gumbula is timely. It concerns an Aboriginal society with a history of asserting its customary rights in dealings with outsiders. The authors detail the depth, complexity and nuances of Yolŋu law and culture in their explanation of Yolŋu aspirations for full political rights in northeast Arnhem Land, in Australia's Northern Territory. They also present fascinating historical details of the events in Arnhem Land, many violent and brutal, that shaped their modern political aspirations. They clarify events so often misrepresented in the European accounts of those dealings.

In protest at the excision of their lands for bauxite mining by the Federal Government, the Yolŋu clan leaders prepared the famous Bark Petition in 1963, which was submitted to the Parliament in Canberra. The meetings of elders to prepare the petition was the precursor to their subsequent litigation in *Milirrpum and Others v Nabalco Pty Ltd and the Commonwealth of Australia*[58] and the Parliamentary Inquiry into the acquisition of the Yolŋu land for mining followed in 1964. Their case 'against the Swiss–Australian mining company, Nabalco, and the Commonwealth of Australia in the Supreme Court of the Northern Territory from 1970 to 1971 probed the complexities of Yolŋu law and its traditional provisions for managing property rights'.[59] Justice Blackburn, in 1971, 'ruled that Yolŋu proprietary interests in land

---

[57] Ibid.

[58] (1971) 17 FLR 141 ('*Milirrpum v Nabalco*').

[59] Corn and Gumbula, this volume, 105; see also Nancy Williams, *The Yolŋu and Their Land: A System of Land Tenure and the Fight for its Recognition* (Australian Institute of Aboriginal Studies, Canberra, 1986).

could not be recognised under Australian law'.[60] This was the first native title case in Australia, and its defeat was a source of dispute and protest until the decision of the High Court of Australia in *Mabo v Queensland (No 2)*.[61]

Historian Henry Reynolds has brought clarity to the issue of sovereignty in Australia. He observes:

> Aboriginal tribes were, in effect, small nations which had long traditions of complex 'international' relations. They made war and peace, negotiated treaties, settled conflicts, arranged marriages and organized access to resources and right of way across territories.[62]

In his study of Aboriginal sovereignty,[63] Reynolds clarifies the confusion in the conflation of two separate notions: nation and state. He distinguishes between them and examines the evidence for a conceptualisation of Aboriginal sovereignty. His conclusion is that sovereignty in Australia can be understood as residing within the distinct Indigenous and settler nations, and as such is compatible within the framework of the sovereign state. Such an arrangement need not be regarded as threatening the dismemberment of the existing state, or as separatism. As arrangements elsewhere in the world demonstrate, there is compatibility between a nation's sovereignty and a state's sovereignty. This is the essence of federalism.

Recognition, polities and agreement making in Australia

As we have already argued, negotiation and agreement making encourages the recognition of Aboriginal polities by government and other parties. Some of the contributions in this book examine the ways in which this is occurring in a variety of contexts. Negotiation and agreement making was not unknown prior to the High Court's recognition of native title in its famous *Mabo* decision.[64] Before 1992 statutory land rights schemes and, to a lesser extent, heritage legislation both provided a framework for some negotiation and agreement making.[65] However, native title is important in

---

[60] Corn and Gumbula, this volume, 105; see also *Milirrpum v Nabalco* (1971) 17 FLR 14.

[61] (1992) 175 CLR 1 ('*Mabo*').

[62] Reynolds, above n 48, 149.

[63] Henry Reynolds, *Aboriginal Sovereignty: Reflections on Race, State and Nation* (Allen & Unwin, NSW, 1996).

[64] (1992) 175 CLR 1.

[65] For examples, see Phillip Toyne and Daniel Vachon, *Growing Up the Country: The Pitjantjatjara Struggle for their Land* (Penguin Books, New York, 1984) 111–19; Yami Lester, *Yami: The Autobiography of Yami Lester* (Institute for Aboriginal Development, Alice Springs, Northern

our project because, for the first time, it engaged large groups of Aboriginal and Torres Strait Islander peoples in a process of recognition of their jurisdiction through negotiation and agreement making. It has provided a platform on which much negotiation, both native title and non-native title, has been built.

The common-law recognition of native title by the High Court established that customary rights to land had pre-existed and, under certain conditions, survived British sovereignty, giving rise to a customary title to land. The title survived in a range of circumstances in which it was not extinguished by valid acts of the Crown, such as valid grants of title to third parties or legislative acts which clearly intended to extinguish the title or limit the recognition of the title. The title was clearly outside the common law's tenurial system, but it encompassed rights that were recognised and protected by the common law, although those rights were not a part of the common law itself.[66] In fact, the title was said to be *sui generis* but the precise nature of the title and where it sat within the broader property system was unclear. It may be proprietary or merely a usufructuary right, or it might amount to a right to exclusive occupation, but it may be a lesser right. It was unclear what the right conceptually entailed.[67]

In reaching its decision, the Court in *Mabo* placed considerable reliance on the jurisprudence relating to common law aboriginal title in other

Territory, 1993) 158–9; Tony Press and David Lawrence, 'Kakadu National Park: Reconciling Competing Interests' in Tony Press *et al.* (eds), *Kakadu: Natural and Cultural Heritage Management* (Australian Nature Conservation Agency, Casuarina and North Australia Research Unit, Australian National University, Darwin, 1995) 1–14; Phillip Toyne, *The Reluctant Nation: Environment, Law and Politics in Australia* (ABC Books, Crows Nest, NSW, 1994) 48–64; Paul Kauffman, *Wik, Mining and Aborigines* (Allen & Unwin, St Leonards, NSW, 1998) 56–77, 81–96. See also Maureen Tehan, 'A Hope Disillusioned an Opportunity Lost? Reflections on Common Law Native Title and Ten Years of the *Native Title Act*' (2003) 27 (2) *Melbourne University Law Review* 523, 529–532.

66 Noel Pearson, 'The Concept of Native Title' in Galarrwuy Yunupingu (ed.), *Our Land Is Our Life: Land Rights Past, Present and Future* (University of Queensland Press, St Lucia, Queensland, 1997) 150, 155–6, 159.

67 The different conceptual approaches were considered in some detail in both the majority and minority decisions in the Full Federal Court decision in *Western Australia v Ward* (2000) 170 ALR 159. For detailed consideration of this issue, see also Katy Barnett, '*Western Australia v Ward*—One Step Forward and Two Steps Back: Native Title and the Bundle of Rights Analysis' (2000) 24 *Melbourne University Law Review* 462. In *Western Australia v Ward* ('*Ward*'), the High Court majority held that the title consisted of a number of separate rights in a bundle and could be extinguished one by one, but did not engage in any detailed analysis of the conceptual issues ((2002) 191 ALR 1, 35–6, 40 (Gleeson CJ, Gaudron, Gummow and Hayne JJ)). For a detailed discussion of the Canadian approach to this issue see Kent McNeil, *Common Law Aboriginal Title* (Clarendon Press, Oxford, 1989); *Delgamuukw v British Columbia* [1997] 3 SCR 1010 ('*Delgamuukw*'). See also Pearson, above n 66; Kent McNeil, 'The Relevance of Traditional Laws and Customs to the Existence and Content of Native Title at Common Law' in Kent McNeil (ed.), *Emerging Justice?: Essays on Indigenous rights in*

jurisdictions. *Johnson v McIntosh*[68] from the United States, the Canadian cases of *Calder v Attorney General of British Columbia,*[69] *Baker Lake (Hamlet) v Minister of Indian Affairs and Northern Development,*[70] *Guerin v The Queen*[71] and *R v Sparrow,*[72] *R v Symonds*[73] emanating from New Zealand, and *Amodu Tijani v Secretary Southern Nigeria*[74] were all crucial in providing jurisprudential and intellectual rigour to a decision that was bound to be controversial.

Since *Mabo*, three significant developments from our point of view have occurred. First, the *Native Title Act 1993* (Cth) (*NTA*) was passed and aimed, among other things, to resolve the retrospective effects of an underlying title which had the potential to invalidate land titles, including pastoral leases issued since annexation.[75] It also sought to codify the protection extended to the title through a regulatory scheme for decision making about land and resource use in the future act regime.[76] Subsequent amendments to the legislation in 1998 restricted the scope of the rights attaching to native title, both as a title to land and water and in relation to future uses of the land.[77]

Second, the High Court has gradually moved away from its engagements with the jurisprudence of common-law aboriginal title from other jurisdictions. The import of the common law in governing relations between aboriginal nations and the settler state in Canada are explored by both Morse and Tehan in Chapters 2 (Part 1) and 8 (Part 2), respectively. Whereas in Canada there has been development of the common law principles of recognition and protection of aboriginal rights through the notion of the honour of the Crown, the idea of a title to land based on prior occupation and limits on extinguishment, there has been little ongoing consideration of common-law principles in Australia. In the most recent trilogy of cases[78] there is little or no mention of any jurisprudential developments elsewhere. Where there is such a reference it is for the purpose of rejecting the jurisprudence, particularly any of the reasoning

---

Canada and Australia (University of Saskatchewan, Native Law Centre, Saskatoon, Canada, 2001) 416, 420–3, 435; Lisa Strelein, 'Conceptualising Native Title' (2001) 23 *Sydney Law Review* 95, 115; Pearson, this volume, 98.

[68] 8 Wheat 543 (1823); 5 L Ed 681 (1823) (*'Johnson v McIntosh'*).

[69] [1973] SCR 313 (*'Calder'*).

[70] [1980] 1 FC 518 (*'Baker Lake'*).

[71] [1984] 2 SCR 335 (*'Guerin'*).

[72] [1990] 1 SCR 1075 (*'Sparrow'*).

[73] [1847] NZPCC 387 (*'Symonds'*).

[74] [1921] 2 AC 399 (*'Amodu Tijani'*).

[75] Commonwealth, *Parliamentary Debates*, House of Representatives, 16 November 1993, 2878 (*Native Title Act 1993*: Preamble).

[76] *Native Title Act 1993* (Cth) Div 3.

[77] Richard Bartlett, above, n 11, 51–62.

[78] *Ward* (2002) 191 ALR 1; *Wilson v Anderson* (2002) 190 ALR 313; *Members of the Yorta Yorta Aboriginal Community v Victoria* (2002) 194 ALR 538 (*'Yorta Yorta'*).

in *Delgamuukw* relating to the idea of a robust aboriginal title to the land itself.[79] Similarly there was no mention of the approach of the Supreme Court of Canada to the treatment of oral evidence and to making findings of fact in cases involving aboriginal rights and title.[80] In fact, in this trilogy, the Court has retreated from the common law, treating the rights associated with native title as little more than statutory rights under the *NTA*.[81]

The third development has been a faltering, uneven but undoubted movement towards agreement making within the native title process which has now flowed beyond that increasingly complex and difficult jurisdiction.[82] Native title raised the *possibility*, for a brief period, of a realignment of power relations in land and resource allocation that challenged preconceived systems of decision making, and also the possibility of a new relationship between Indigenous and non-Indigenous people that went beyond land management to embrace fundamental issues of rights and status.[83] In Chapter 4 of Part 1, Pearson analyses the promise and disappointment of native title. What we have now, Pearson suggests, is an unfair denial of land justice resulting from the failure of the High Court to grasp the promise and meaning of *Mabo*. His exposition of this failure provides an alternative way to envisage native title rights as a fulsome title to land as recognised in other jurisdictions and provides for a principled re-appraisal of the native title regime. For the moment, however, native title is not only a diminished title but, as Pearson argues, is based on a reversion to the nineteenth-century principles of discrimination found in *Re Southern Rhodesia*.[84] This view resounds in a number of chapters in this volume, in which the substantive

---

[79] *Ward* (2002) 191 ALR 1; see Morse, this volume, 55; see Tehan, this volume, 149, 162.

[80] *Delgamuukw* [1997] 3 SCR 1010; *R v Van der Peet* [1996] 2 SCR 507.

[81] Tehan, above n 65, 558–63; Noel Pearson 'The High Court's Abandonment of "The Time Honoured Methodology of The Common Law" in its Interpretation of Native Title: Mirriuwung Gajerrong and Yorta Yorta' (Lecture delivered at the Sir Ninian Stephen Annual Lecture, University of Newcastle, New South Wales, 17 March 2003); and see Pearson this volume, 88.

[82] Tehan, above n 65, 564–70.

[83] Ibid, 537–8; Noel Pearson, '204 Years of Invisible Title—From the Most Vehement Denial' in Margaret Stephenson and Suri Ratnapala (eds), *Mabo, A Judicial Revolution: The Aboriginal Land Rights Decision and its Impact on Australian Law* (University of Queensland Press, St Lucia, Queensland, 1993) 80; Noel Pearson, 'From Remnant Title to Social Justice' (1993) 65(4) *Australian Quarterly* 179–81; Paul Keating, 'Australian Launch of the International Year for the World's Indigenous People' (1993) 3(61) *Aboriginal Law Bulletin* 4, 5. Writing seven years later, Justice McHugh has suggested that the decision in *Mabo* was an example of changes in 'political and ethical ideas' over time: Justice Michael McHugh, 'Judicial Method' (1999) 73 *Australian Law Journal* 37, 40–1. See also Alex Reilly, 'From a Jurisprudence of Regret to a Regrettable Jurisprudence: Shaping Native Title from *Mabo* to *Ward*' (2002) 9 (4) *E Law* Murdoch University Electronic Journal of Law [28] http://www.murdoch.edu. au/elaw/issues/v9n4/reilly94.html at 4 December 2003.

[84] [1919] AC 211.

content of agreement making rather than its legal context or reliance on strict legal rights or determinations of title is identified as the way forward.

What native title did stimulate was a culture of agreement making, and it is this culture, within and outside the native title process, that begins to engage Aboriginal polities and Aboriginal jurisdiction. We do not assert that this is always so or that there are not significant difficulties in both processes and outcomes. Agreements may not be negotiated in environments of equal bargaining power and resources.[85] As Jonas has posited:

> I must say that I do not share the optimism ... that agreement making processes under the *Native Title Act* offer a de facto treaty making process. This is too simplistic and fundamentally ignores the point that the native title system as structured is one that is not based on equality and non-discrimination. It does not facilitate the full and effective participation of Indigenous people. It is not a respectful system. Only when the native title system does provide real equality of opportunity—ranging from adequate, and equitable, resourcing of native title representatives through to the ability to negotiate over economic and development opportunities through to processes which facilitate Indigenous governance rather than imposed management structures—can it aim to fulfil this broader role.[86]

Agreements may fail to deliver promised benefits because of a lack of resources or a failure to address implementation issues,[87] or because the terms have been poorly negotiated.[88] In Chapter 18 of Part 4, O'Faircheallaigh explores key research questions and issues in relation to agreement outcomes and results, focusing on agreements between Indigenous groups and mineral resource companies. The paper contributes to the development of benchmarks, and identifies criteria for assessing the outcomes for Indigenous interests in relation to key issues commonly addressed in agreements.

---

[85] See especially Aboriginal and Torres Strait Islander Social Justice Commissioner, *Native Title Report 2001* (Aboriginal and Torres Strait Islander Social Justice, AHREOC, Sydney, 2001) ch 2; David Ritter, 'The Long Spoon: Reflections on Two Agreements with the State of Western Australia under the Court Government' (Paper presented at the Past and Future of Native Title and Land Rights Conference, Townsville, 29 August 2001).

[86] William Jonas, 'Reflections on the History of Indigenous People's Struggle for Human Rights in Australia: What Role could a Treaty Play' (Paper presented at the Treaty: Advancing Reconciliation Conference, Perth, 27 June 2002).

[87] Ciaran O'Faircheallaigh, *Implementing Agreements between Indigenous Peoples and Resource Developers in Australia and Canada* (Research Paper No 13, School of Politics and Public Policy, Griffith University, Queensland, 2003); Ciaran O'Faircheallaigh, *Negotiating a Better Deal for Indigenous Land Owners: Combining 'research' and 'community service'* (Research Paper No 11, School of Politics and Public Policy, Griffith University, Queensland, 2003).

[88] Michelle Riley, *'Winning' Native Title: The Experience of the Nharnuwangga, Wajarri and Ngarla People: Issues Paper No 19* (Aboriginal Studies Press, AITSIS, 2002) vol 2, 2; Frances Flanagan, *Pastoral Access Protocols: The Corrosion of Native Title by Contract: Issues Paper No 19* (Aboriginal Studies Press, AIATSIS, 2002) vol 2, 5.

In spite of these limitations in Chapter 10 of Part 3, Neate situates agreement making within the procedural maze of the native title scheme and the avenues for agreement this provides through native title consent determinations, Indigenous Land Use Agreements, the future act regimes and the right to negotiate. In so doing, he provides a cogent argument that the native title scheme ultimately endorses and promotes agreement making, whether in relation to the existence of native title in consent determinations or in relation to management of native title land and resources. Perhaps more importantly, Neate points to the capacity of the native title process to produce agreement on non-native title matters. Thus the process, while based in native title, has the capacity to and does go beyond native title processes and rights to produce agreed outcomes, even where no native title exists. This chapter presents negotiation between Aboriginal and Torres Strait Islander peoples and settlers as an established element of their continuing relationship.

Because of the *NTA* administrative regime, governments are being forced to treat Aboriginal people in a variety of ways. We thus find that by default Aboriginal people are, through the cumulative effect of native title determinations both by the Tribunal and by the Federal Court, being treated as peoples. The Aboriginal polity has emerged from the factors at work in the environment of dealing with native title holders in relation to economic and land use issues and resource distribution. By drawing on some specific examples Strelein (Chapter 11 of Part 3) points to the emerging paradox of narrowing native title rights and expanding ideas of Indigenous autonomy, authority and jurisdiction in agreement making; that is, a conflict between the 'legal conclusion' of native title and 'the idea' of native title. She identifies a similar paradox in governments at once opposing native title applications but engaging in and promoting agreement making, a paradox also identified by Tehan in the British Columbia Treaty Process. Exploring this tension allows an exposition of the significance of native title for both Indigenous and non-Indigenous Australians. Native title, she argues, is not limited to its strict legal parameters and the mired process accompanying it. It provides a framework for engagement between the state and Indigenous peoples and, as a result, goes beyond a form of title to a fundamental recognition of the distinct identity and special place of Indigenous peoples as first peoples.

The capacity to provide recognition through agreement making takes a variety of forms, although the scope, subject matter and legal context of agreements varies widely. Jackson (Chapter 13 of Part 3) provides an example of this in the context of agreements that ultimately recognise customary marine tenure. Most of the agreements that Jackson records are made outside of the native title process, although she emphasises that the *Croker Island*[89] decision has operated as an impetus to the more recent agreements. It is the variety of agreements that makes Jackson's contribution to this volume instructive. The agreements involve aquaculture and both commercial and recreational fishers, and generally arise out of a need for a land base from which to operate. However, the agreements herald a changed approach to management of marine resources. This approach allows Aboriginal people to have a say in their estates. By implication, this recognises an inherent aboriginal jurisdiction over marine resources and their management.

Bruce Harvey (Chapter 14 of Part 3), who has two decades of experience as a geologist and community relations expert in the mining industry, both in Australia and elsewhere, describes the process of cultural change in Rio Tinto Ltd that ultimately allowed the negotiation of the Western Cape Communities Co-existence Agreement in Cape York, northern Queensland. Backed in part by some nascent native title rights but equally covering large areas of land in which any native title rights had been extinguished, the negotiation of this ground-breaking agreement is detailed from the perspective of Rio Tinto Ltd. This story re-emphasises the twin points argued elsewhere in this volume that a willingness to move beyond strict legal rights and the recognition of the identity of the Wik, Wik Way, Thaayorre, Alngith and other peoples as polities with jurisdiction over land and resources were essential elements in reaching agreement. In a personal reflection on the process, Harvey suggests that globalisation played a major role in transforming the culture of Rio Tinto Ltd and producing the agreement. This discussion, perhaps presciently, builds on the argument we have made elsewhere in this Introduction that the transformation of the nation-state may accommodate broader treaty negotiations between Indigenous nations and the nation-state.

The experience of negotiating a broad-based, comprehensive agreement in South Australia, detailed by Agius *et al.* in Chapter 12 of Part 3 is one such example. The negotiations reflect the paradox identified by Strelein, of the South Australian Government at once arguing that native title did not exist in *De Rose Hill*[90] and engaging in the wide-ranging negotiations discussed here. Key elements identified in the process include the willingness of all parties to negotiate on identified issues and a recognition of the legitimacy

---

[89] *Commonwealth of Australia v Yarmirr* (2001) 208 CLR 1 ('*Croker Island case*').

[90] *De Rose v State of South Australia* [2002] FCA 1342. At the date of writing, the full Federal Court had heard the appeal in this case. The Court unanimously held that there were errors in the trial judge's reasoning, but it could not decide the matter without further submissions: *De Rose Hill v State of South Australia* [2003] FCAFC 286 (Wilcox, Sackville and Merkel JJ, 16 December 2003 Unreported).

of Aboriginal peoples' claims to property rights and concomitant governance rights as a basis for negotiations. A crucial element of transforming this recognition into reality, the authors argue, is to refocus attention on the process element and away from the expert-centered attention to substantive issues. In this, the authors are not arguing for the procedural maze that is the native title process, but rather, the human dimension of the process of negotiation and agreement. Thus intra-Indigenous decision making or the processes within the Aboriginal polity is a crucial element of successful negotiations.

One of the most pressing issues facing Aboriginal and Torres Strait Islander people in Australia today is that of health. In Chapter 15 of Part 4, Anderson says that until 1967 there was no Commonwealth health program for Indigenous Australians, and only in 1989 was the first National Aboriginal Health Strategy announced. He examines the history and development of the intergovernmental agreements known as the 'Framework Agreements' in Aboriginal and Torres Strait Islander health. These multi-sectoral agreements have become a key structural element of health delivery, allowing for co-ordinated strategies and collaboration in policy and planning in Australia's federally structured health system. They are process agreements which potentially suffer from a lack of central oversight and commitment to results. However, they are underpinned by the significant involvement of the Aboriginal and Torres Strait Islander community health sector. Anderson suggests that the effectiveness of these strategic agreements could be enhanced by moving beyond a sole focus on health-sector reform and developing better links to the whole-of-government decision-making processes as this relates to a range of other key social and economic indicators.

The moral claims for a treaty are considered by McGlade in Chapter 16 of Part 4, in which the opportunities to overcome racism provided by international covenants and conventions and domestic legislation and associated institutions are discussed. In this chapter, McGlade considers the political constraints and cultural biases which hinder the application of race-discrimination law in Australia. She argues that the exclusion of Indigenous people from both legislative responses and the institutions established to effect these responses leads to a loss of significant opportunities for change. It is suggested that a treaty or Bill of Rights pursued through constitutional amendment may provide more effective legal redress to counter the overt and veiled racism that continues to pervade the relationship between Indigenous and non-Indigenous Australians.

In Chapter 17 of Part 4, Grossman similarly raises the idea of a treaty to enshrine effective mechanisms for cultural protection for Indigenous cultural creators and authors. While there have been several important research investigations and publications on the issue of protecting Indigenous intellectual property in the arts and publishing,[91] Grossman notes that, for a variety of reasons, including entrenched cultural and historical biases, Australian publishing agreements 'have been slow to take up and explore the options' in their dealings with Indigenous cultural creators.[92] Recent government initiatives and the national debate concerning the usefulness of a treaty hold some promise for a better resolution of these issues. Grossman suggests that until publishing agreements are better equipped to deal with Indigenous concerns, Aboriginal and Torres Strait Islander people may wish to pursue a range of innovative strategies and mechanisms to circumvent the entrenched processes that currently take out of their control the reproduction and resale of their cultural creations.

A consistent theme in this collection is the intersection between pursuing the legal rights, international and domestic, of Indigenous people and pragmatic means for furthering Indigenous aspirations and goals outside of the formal legal conclusion of these rights. The negotiations over the *Timor Sea Treaty* exemplify this. Previously known as the *Timor Gap Treaty* between Australia and Indonesia,[93] the newly independent nation of East Timor was thrust into negotiations as a sovereign party with Australia soon after the United Nations Security Council declared its independence on 20 May 2002. For more than 350 years a Portuguese colony, East Timor became an internal colony from 1975, after the Indonesian invasion following the withdrawal of Portuguese troops. In Chapter 19 of Part 4, Triggs, writing on the new *Timor Sea Treaty* between Australia and East Timor, provides us with an example of a 'functional approach to international problem solving'[94] and argues that if parties are willing to set aside seemingly intractable disputes over sovereignty, then practical mechanisms and creative wording contained in skilfully negotiated treaties and agreements can allow the focus of negotiations to shift to defined and achievable goals of mutual concern while at the same time preserving each party's legal position. This focus on immediate or short-term priorities also provides a foundation from which to build firmer relationships of trust and confidence, a position from which parties may be able to better negotiate more difficult issues in the future. Triggs suggests that the outcome in this instance has been to the strategic advantage of both parties.

---

[91] See for example Terri Janke, *Our Culture, Our Future: Report on Australian Indigenous Cultural and Property Rights* (Michael Frankel and Company Solicitors, Sydney, 1998); Anita Heiss, *Dhuuluu Yala: To Talk Straight: Publishing Indigenous Literature* (Aboriginal Studies Press, Canberra, 2003) 83.

[92] Grossman, this volume, 301.

[93] Signed in 1989, ten years after Australia recognised Indonesia as the *de facto* and *de jure* sovereign over East Timor.

[94] Triggs, this volume, 330.

Conclusion

From its origins in imperial treaties, agreement making with Indigenous people has survived the end of Empire and infiltrated legal, constitutional and commercial institutions in settler states as a commonplace fact of modernity.

Consensus and contracts between Indigenous and settler state parties have avoided much unnecessary conflict, so that agreement making has become a preferred, sometimes unavoidable part of the political and economic landscapes of settler states in which Indigenous and local peoples have a case for restitution of their inherent rights as peoples. Regardless of the legal and political recognition, or lack of recognition, of Indigenous rights, agreement making is an important process through which people build relationships and carry forward the public recognition of Indigenous rights.

While Indigenous people may continue to be disadvantaged, even in apparently consensual arrangements, increasingly, the use of agreement-making tools by Indigenous peoples and settler states and their instrumentalities, described in this collection, are forging a new approach to governmental and Indigenous affairs that, to varying degrees, gives Indigenous people a genuine decision-making role in a range of issues affecting their lives and their territories. In this way, agreement making is an important means through which Indigenous people and nations can pursue recognition and restitution for historical and continuing injustices.

While we cannot claim that every instance or type of agreement discussed here results in justice or restoration of rights, we do contend that the works of the authors represent a significant contribution to the cause of justice in their careful expositions and comparisons of the situation across jurisdictions, particular statutes, treaties, agreements and cases. Dispossession and disruption, international and domestic laws, and the never-ending expansion of the market and modern urban settlement into Indigenous domains, have all had an impact on the capacity of Indigenous peoples to sustain ancient livelihoods and lifeways. This does not mean that Indigenous people are not willing to change. On the contrary, Indigenous peoples want to benefit from the economic projects that consume their resource base, and moreover want to develop economically in their own right.

Forearmed with studies of the historical origins of present-day institutions and modern-day innovations in this field, future negotiators and protagonists may be better equipped to tackle the bewildering complexity of issues that Indigenous people contend with in their dealings with states, commercial and corporate entities, courts and others.

We have not directly addressed the possibilities for a treaty in Australia as the means for addressing past injustice and grounding future relationships.

Professor Michael Dodson and others have done so elsewhere.[95] Whatever the possibilities and pathways for a treaty in Australia may be, they inevitably involve the need to redress past injustice and to accord recognition and protection to the distinctive rights and special status of Aboriginal and Torres Strait Islander peoples, based on prior occupation. Current negotiations and agreement making within the domestic Australian legal setting, in spite of their flaws, may be characterised as part of the process of recognition of Aboriginal and Torres Strait Islander polities and their accompanying jurisdiction. These developing processes and practices, and the existing institutions in a democratic federal state, then become the starting point for expanding possibilities for a new relationship.

---

[95] Richard Ah Mat, 'The Cape York View' (paper presented at the Treaty Conference, Murdoch University, Perth 26–28 June 2002) http://www.treaty.murdoch.edu.au/Conference%20Papers/ah%20mat%20speech.htm at 11 October 2002; Professor Larissa Behrendt, 'Practical Steps Towards a Treaty—Structures, Challenges and the Need for Flexibility' in *Treaty Let's Get it Right!* (Australian Institute of Aboriginal and Torres Strait Islander Studies, Canberra, 2003) 18–29; Fred Chaney, 'Eddie Mabo Memorial Lecture' in John Rickard and Vince Ross (eds) *Unfinished Business: Texts and Addresses from the Unfinished Business Conference* (Desbooks, Thornbury, 2002) 85–94; Michael Dodson, 'An Australian Indigenous Treaty: Issues of Concern' (paper presented at Limits and Possibilities of a Treaty Process in Australia, Australian Institute of Aboriginal and Torres Strait Islander Studies seminar series, 20 March 2001) http://www.aiatsis.gov.au/rsrch/smnrs/papers/dodson.htm at 18 December 2003; Michael Dodson 'Unfinished Business: A Shadow Across our Relationships' in *Treaty Let's Get it Right!*, 30–40; Patrick Dodson 'Until the Chains are Broken' (speech delivered at the Vincent Lingiari Lecture 1999 http://www.austlii.edu.au/au/other/IndigLRes/car/1999/2708.html at 18 December 2003; Patrick Dodson, 'Beyond the Mourning Gate—Dealing With Unfinished Business' (speech delivered at the Wentworth Lecture, 12 May 2000) http://www.antar.org.au/wentworth.pdf at 18 December 2003; Michael Mansell, 'Citizenship, Assimilation and a Treaty' in *Treaty Let's Get it Right!*, 5–17; Martin Nakata, 'Treaty and the Self-determination Agendas of Torres Strait Islanders: A Common Struggle', in *Treaty Let's Get it Right!*, 166–84; Tim Rowse, 'Treaty Talk 2002: Notes on Three Conferences', (2002–2003) 62 *Arena Magazine*, 30–7; Maureen Tehan, 'Talking Treaty: Responder' in John Rickard and Vince Ross (eds) *Unfinished Business*, 85–94; George Williams, 'Bills of Rights, the Republic and a Treaty: Strategies and Lessons for Reform' (paper presented at Limits and Possibilities of a Treaty Process in Australia, Australian Institute of Aboriginal and Torres Strait Islander Studies seminar series, 3 September 2001 http://www.aiatsis.gov.au/rsrch/smnrs/papers/williams.pdf at 18 December 2003; *Reconciliation: Australia's Challenge. Final Report of the Council for Aboriginal Reconciliation to the Prime Minister and the Commonwealth Parliament* (Council for Aboriginal Reconciliation, Canberra, 2000) ('*Reconciliation: Australia's Challenge*'); see generally *Treaty Let's Get it Right!*; See also National Treaty Conference (Canberra, 27–29 August 2002) http://www.antar.org.au/treaty_conf2.html at 18 December 2003; Murdoch University, *Treaty—Advancing Reconciliation* http://www.treaty.murdoch.edu.au/ at 18 December 2003; Australian Institute of Aboriginal and Torres Strait Islander Studies, *Treaty* http://www.aiatsis.gov.au/lbry/dig_prgm/treaty/contents.htm at 18 December 2003; University of New South Wales, Gilbert & Tobin Centre of Public Law, *Treaty Project* http://www.reconciliationaustralia.org/docs/speeches/chaney/treaty_conference.doc at 18 December 2003.

Indigenous Agreement Making and Governance: An Historical Overview

Introduction

Unsettling Sovereignties

Marcia Langton

Part 1 gathers several meticulous surveys of historical, legal and cultural issues involving the fate of Indigenous peoples in colonial and postcolonial periods. While international law, as the regulatory space of Empire and European global expansion, has dictated the terms of the existence of non-European nations that were captured by the colonial net, the subject peoples also had agency, and their assertion of their sovereignty and political rights has wrought profound changes in the course of historical events, as these essays show.

Social relations of the Indigenous domain and the global marketplace

Throughout history, transactions between large- and small-scale parties, whether involving commodity, gift, tribute, plunder or treaty, were inextricably linked with values that, although traditionally regarded as non-economic, were such that their social nature and effect were important to the contractual relationship or to subsequent relationships. Considered in this light, it is possible to understand the social relations of the Indigenous domain as well as of the marketplace or nation-state as determinants of the characteristics of the parties and the transactions. Aboriginal laws and customs have penetrated colonial relations, the postcolonial settler state and the global marketplace in various ways. This has been the case since the first ships from Europe ventured into the New World.

But this is not how the dominant—usually colonising—powers always viewed matters. International law grew from these types of relations, and *ex post facto* explained the nature of these social and economic contracts, formalising them as written documents, such as treaties, with enduring, although not always binding, effects. From the seventeenth century, the European idea that was deployed to exert dominance over the peoples of the New World was the notion of the absolute power of the sovereign; the vehicle of sovereignty was the emerging institution of the nation-state. Sovereignty, along with coeval ideas of racism, was fundamental to the European claims of supremacy over other peoples; claims which, however fantastic, led to the diminution of the power and status of peoples throughout the world. The outcomes were far from uniform, however.

Treaty making in context

The chapter by Bradford Morse on the continuing significance of historic treaties and modern treaty making in Canada and the United States of America details common-law developments and the relatively high standards of human rights that place the Indigenous nations of that region at the forefront of global developments in the recognition of Indigenous sovereignty and rights of self governance. In Canada, where the honour of the Crown is held to be a principle of interpretation of treaties, the legal rights of Indigenous peoples serve their interests well.

In Australia and other places, the existence of the original peoples of the territories was simply denied altogether. Langton and Palmer explain the historical circumstances of these developments, and explain how, despite the denial of their existence, Aboriginal groups in northern Australia have asserted their continuing customary polities by negotiating the terms of their co-existence in a range of agreements and treaty like events. This is in spite of the failure of the Australian courts to reinforce the opportunity presented by *Mabo*[1] to address 'historic grievance about land justice'.

Challenging the norm of sovereignty

Pearson's account of the courts' reliance on statute rather than common law in native-title decisions, and the declining capacity of native-title law to deliver outcomes to claimants, indicates that legal reform with respect to Indigenous people in Australia may be limited. That the Australian courts, in the later, post-*Mabo* decisions, did not look to other common-law jurisdictions, such as Canada, for precedent and interpretation, but increasingly

---

[1]   *Mabo v Queensland (No 2)* (1992) 175 CLR 1 ('*Mabo*').

turned to nineteenth-century concepts to justify denial of common-law rights, is an alarming trend.

In many parts of the world, a lack of sophistication in conceptualisations of the place of Indigenous peoples in modern nations hinders the development of Indigenous rights and institutions. Ironically, European political theory has as much relevance to Indigenous nations as to the new nations that have emerged after communism and the phenomenon of 'weak states'. Krasner observes that the norm of sovereignty at international law is challenged frequently by inconsistent principles, such as universal human rights. 'Sovereignty rules can be violated in inventive ways'.[2] He points out that since Jean Bodin and Thomas Hobbes 'first elaborated the notion sovereignty in the 16th and 17th centuries',[3] it has always been malleable in practice.

While principles such as state autonomy and independence, and the political authority to enter into international agreements, are the hallmarks of sovereign actors in international law, in practice these principles are fluid, contested and open to inventive interpretation. Historically, the practice of Customary International Law has operated on the notion that arrangements that bind parties to act according to certain principles and obligations will only be adhered to for as long as those principles and obligations remain mutually beneficial and expedient for the parties involved.[4] This has also been the case with treaties, and the application of the rule of law to the peoples of the colonial world. However, the scale of injustice involved in the project of colonisation has reverberated down the generations.

The nation-state and the sanctity of individual rights

While European intellectuals and leaders asserted the idea of the nation-state, which arose to meet the imagined ideal, they also propagated the idea of the sanctity of individual rights. Where they impaired the existence of sovereign nations in the New World, they also ambiguously applied the new doctrine of individual rights among these peoples to subject them to an imposed rule of law which aimed to dispossess and indenture them.

Evans's fascinating study of the British imposition of an impaired subjecthood on the people of nineteenth-century Natal and Western Australia

---

[2] Stephen D. Krasner, 'Sovereignty' (January 2001) *Foreign Policy* 20, 28.

[3] Ibid, 21.

[4] J.L. Goldsmith, and E.A. Posner, 'Understanding the Resemblance Between Modern and Traditional Customary International Law' (2000) 4 *Virginia Journal of International Law* 672.

exposes the double manoeuvre that was perpetrated in the name of the rule of law: a purported respect for the rights of individual, but a subterfuge that terminated their rights as peoples and ultimately worked to dispossess them.

Colonialism ruptured not just nations, or peoples, but communities and families, and denied subsequent generations their patrimony. When people have the political resources to transform the injustice of the past into restoration of their rights, they may be able to overcome, or set to rights, the impact that drastic interference in community life has on the lifetime-transcending interests that people would wish to transmit to their descendants.[5] Habermas,[6] Walzer[7] and Thompson[8] agree on the nature of the 'community life' that emerges in the modern manifestation of ethnic integration following colonial or historical disruption to their ways of life. Walzer stated: 'The idea of communal integrity derives its moral and political force from the rights of contemporary men and women to live as members of a historic community and to express their inherited culture through political forms worked out among themselves.'[9]

What is a nation?

Habermas proposes that a group's sense of a collective past is the foundation of a 'moral identity';[10] 'Our answer to that often asked question ... is that it is a group of people who feel they are ancestrally related.'[11] For Habermas,

> ... nations would differ from other ethnic communities only in their degree of complexity and scope: 'It is the largest group that can command a person's loyalty because of felt kinship ties; it is, from this perspective, the fully extended family.'[12]

Although Habermas is concerned with Europe, his ideas can be applied elsewhere. An instance of the communities of interests that form effective polities among the Yolŋu is provided in the chapter by Aaron Corn and

---

[5] See Janna Thompson, *Taking Responsibility for the Past: Reparation and Historical Justice* (Polity Press in association with Blackwell Publishers, Cambridge, UK, 2002).

[6] Jürgen Habermas, *The Inclusion of the Other: Studies in Political Theory*, (Ciaran Cronin and Pablo de Greiff, eds) (The MIT Press, Cambridge, Massachusetts, 1998) 148.

[7] Michael Walzer, 'The Moral Standing of States' (1980) 9 *Philosophy and Public Affairs*, 209.

[8] Thompson, above n 5.

[9] Walzer, above n 7, 211; see also Michael Walzer, *Just and Unjust Wars. A Moral Argument with Historical Illustrations* (Basic Books, New York, 1977).

[10] Habermas, above n 6, 129.

[11] W. Connor, *Ethnonationalism* (Princetown, NJ, 1994) 202, cited in Habermas, above n 6, 279.

[12] Habermas, above n 6, 130; citing Connor, above n 11.

Neparrŋa Gumbula, who specify, with attention to details of the land-tenure system, philosophy, religion and ceremonial life, the cultural underpinnings of Yolŋu aspirations for full political rights in northeastern Arnhem Land in Australia's Northern Territory.

While it might be expected that the common-law jurisdictions would share a uniformity of rights and institutions with respect to their Indigenous peoples, these papers show that this is far from the case. Unique temporal, geographic and cultural circumstances must be taken into account. But the administrators and officers of the law in the colonies, thousands of miles away from the European centres of power, were powerful men, and in practice barely accountable for their actions and decisions. Their role must surely rank with the peculiar ideas that international law developed to justify colonialism as a chief cause of generations of injustice. The contributors also demonstrate that, while the tradition of expedience for the sake of power endures, the agency of Indigenous people in pursuing their political rights also caused great changes, contributing to international law and the legal systems of modern nations, and in so doing, destabilising the ideals of European supremacy over many diverse native polities and nations.

Chapter 1

Treaties, Agreement Making and the Recognition of Indigenous Customary Polities

Marcia Langton and Lisa Palmer

Introduction

Treaty and agreement making between Indigenous people and others during pre-colonial, colonial and modern times has, to varied extents, required the recognition of Indigenous customary polities. In this chapter we investigate some instances of treaty and agreement making between Indigenous people and others, with the purpose of discussing critically the modern-day relevance of customary authority and legitimacy in modern Aboriginal political formations within the Australian nation-state. Some recent studies in history, and in legal and political thought apposite to the problem of contested sovereignty and governmental arrangements, have drawn our attention to inventive ways of considering colonial and postcolonial relationships and expressions of legitimate authority beyond the nine-teenth-century confines of the nation-state doctrine.[1] The Nunavut Final Agreement, concluded between Inuit people and the Canadian government in 1993[2] and other similar agreements that delegate self-government rights

---

[1] Miguel Alfonso Martinez, *Report of the Special Rapporteur on Treaties, Agreements and Other Constructive Arrangements Between States and Indigenous Populations; Second Progress Report*, UN ESCOR, Sub-Commission on Prevention of Discrimination and Protection of Minorities, 44th sess, Un Doc E/CN.4/Sub.2 (1992); Garth Nettheim, Gary Meyers and Donna Craig, *Indigenous Peoples and Governance Structures: A Comparative Analysis of land and Resource Management Rights* (Aboriginal Studies Press, Australian Institute of Aboriginal and Torres Strait Islander Studies, Canberra, 2002); Henry Reynolds, *Aboriginal Sovereignty* (Allen & Unwin, NSW, 1996); Stephen D. Krasner, 'Sovereignty' (2001) January, *Foreign Policy*, 20–31.

[2] Canadian Department of Indian and Northern Affairs, *Nunavut Land Claims Agreement*

to Indigenous peoples[3] provide new models for distributing rights of political legitimacy and governance. The potential for the application of such arrangements in the Aboriginal domain of Australia has been the subject of recent debate.[4] In Australia, Aboriginal political formations that extend and test the Western liberal traditions of absorption of culturally diverse peoples, particularly Indigenous peoples in Australia, have resulted from the application and development of native-title law and the outcomes of native-title agreements and policy based negotiations.

Kingsbury, in his examination of Indigenous people's claims in international law, notes that '[t]reaties between Indigenous peoples and colonizing or trading states made over several centuries commonly were premised on the capacity of both parties to act'.[5] To enter into treaty arrangements is to negotiate the terms of a relationship with a person or peoples. These terms may be subsequently defined and formalised by a treaty or agreement which gives rise to mutually binding obligations.[6] Treaty making between colonial entities and Indigenous peoples, despite the complex and opportunistic legal and political process involved, and the diverse circumstances and interests, has constituted an instrument of establishing and formalising relations. For the Indigenous protagonists, treaty making has enabled postcolonial forms of political jurisdiction and governance, even though the differential power relations mitigated against favourable terms for the colonised.

We first examine mercantile treaties between Europeans and the peoples they encountered in the Far East from the sixteenth to the eighteenth century, a period during which European powers were forced to negotiate trade with East Indies sovereigns already embroiled in their own systems of international law. We then turn to an examination of the ambivalent treaty making of colonialists in the new settler nation-states as they sought from the nineteenth century onwards to entrench their power over the Indigenous peoples of those lands. This summation is not intended in any way to describe the complex and contested historical patterns of that

(1993) Government of Canada http://www.ainc-inac.gc.ca/pr/agr/nunavut/index_e.html at 12 November 2003; see also Agreements, Treaties and Negotiated Settlements (ATNS) Project database, http:www.atns.net.au/biogs/A001503b.htm.

[3] See Canadian Department of Indian and Northern Affairs, *Self Government Agreements* (2003) Government of Canada http://www.ainc-inac.gc.ca/pr/agr/index_e.html#Self-GovernmentAgreements at 12 November 2003.

[4] Nettheim, Meyers and Craig, above n 1.

[5] Benedict Kingsbury, 'Reconciling Five Competing Conceptual Structures of Indigenous People's Claims in International and Comparative Law' (2001) 34(1) *New York University Journal of International Law and Politics* 234.

[6] Michael Dodson, 'An Australian Indigenous Treaty: Issues of Concern' (paper presented at *Limits and Possibilities of a Treaty Process in Australia,* Australian Institute of Aboriginal and Torres Strait Islander Studies seminar series, 20 March 2001), at http://www.aiatsis.gov.au/rsrch/smnrs/papers/dodson.htm at 18 December 2003.

period; nor ways that European imperial powers behaved towards the peoples they encountered in the Far East or the New World; nor, indeed how
they behaved towards each other. Nor do we contend in any detailed way
with the religious and ideological motivations that might have guided their
behaviour, or the technological, scientific and other changes during that
period. Our narrow concern is with some of the effects of developing international law and strategic considerations in those encounters.

In the second part of the chapter we discuss the history of Indigenous–
colonial relations and the absence of formally recognised treaties in
Australia. Based on the literature and our own fieldwork experience, we
draw attention to a number of attempts by Indigenous Australians to negotiate terms of settlement with those who visited, used or otherwise occupied their lands.[7] The evidence shows that, despite the legal fiction of *terra
nullius* and the absence of treaties with Indigenous peoples in Australia,
ample evidence for the Aboriginal capacity to establish intergovernmental
relations existed. Even if, as Reynolds[8] argues, there is a clear distinction to
be made between the states and nations, or even if national sovereignty is
an accretive and divisible bundle of things, the question remains: what of
Aboriginal customary authority and forms of governance, and the modern-
day adaptations of those traditions and customs in new political formations?
How are they expressed and how do they mediate between the state and
Indigenous jurisdictions? In concluding the chapter, we discuss the expression of Aboriginal governance in agreement making concerning land access
and use and resource distribution.

Mercantile treaties in the East Indies

As European nations set out across the oceans to the New World from the
sixteenth century onwards, seeking trade and riches, they actively engaged
in treaty making with those they encountered and, by making treaties,
bestowed recognition of their treaty partners' sovereign status. During this
time European states were themselves undergoing nascent political forms
of statehood and, as Miguel Alfonso Martinez, United Nations Special
Rapporteur on Indigenous Peoples, observes, the Europeans 'did not require
a particular form of societal political organization as *conditio sine qua non*

---

[7]   See Henry Reynolds, *Fate of a Free People* (Penguin, Ringwood, Victoria, 1995); see also
Ian McIntosh, *Can We Be Equal in Your Eyes?: A Perspective on Reconciliation from North-East
Arnhem Land* (PhD Thesis, Northern Territory University, 1996); Marcia Langton, 'Dominion
and Dishonour: A Treaty Between Our Nations' (2001) 4(1) *Postcolonial Studies* 13–26.

[8]   Reynolds, above n 1.

for considering a political entity as a sovereign actor in international relations'.[9] In Europe itself, along with 'empires, kingdoms, republics and
principalities', entities also considered to be sovereign actors included
certain 'towns, religious orders, duchies, provinces, cities, a bishopric and a
number of "demi-sovereign entities" ruled by the electors of the Germanic
Empire'.[10] In their encounters in Asia, the European visitors were forced to
contend with societies already adept in the practice of international diplomacy and trade. As Alexandrowicz writes:

> Though the Europeans had sailed to the East Indies since the end of the
> fifteenth century equipped with legal titles of a unilateral character and though
> they had at first intended to discover and occupy lands, and where necessary,
> to establish their territorial possessions by conquest, they had in practice to fall
> back on negotiation and treaty making in preference to resorting to war. In
> fact they found themselves in the middle of a network of States and inter-State
> relations based on traditions which were more ancient than their own and in
> no way inferior to notions of European civilisation.[11]

By the seventeenth century, the initial reluctance of the European powers,
under the sway of canonical law to make treaties with non-Christians and
infidels, was wholly tempered by the realpolitik of finding trade and political
niches in a region dominated by long autochthonous traditions of inter-state
trade, and the practice of treaty making soon became common practice on the
part of the European interlocutors. Commerce was, despite cultural and other
differences, reason enough to enter into treaty arrangements. Alexandrowicz
contends that, during this period of expanding world trade, beginning in the
sixteenth century, 'European–Asian relations developed to a considerable
extent on a footing of equality'.[12] In this development the cross-pollination
of principles based in the respective Eastern and Western legal traditions led
to the development of mutually agreed principles of international law. The
details of these are found in the texts of the mercantile treaties themselves
and the documents relating to their conclusion.[13]

However, while the ensuing treaty arrangements between local sovereigns and the European powers were initiated by the treaty partners in the
spirit of good faith, common interest and equality, this changed as the politics
and economies in the East came increasingly under the influence of inter-
European power rivalries based on the establishment of trade monopolies.

---

[9] Martinez, above n 1, para 146.
[10] Ibid.
[11] Charles H. Alexandrowicz, *An Introduction to the History of the Law of Nations in the East Indies: 16th, 17th and 18th Centuries* (Clarendon Press, Oxford, 1967) 224.
[12] Ibid, 1.
[13] Ibid, 2.

The previously concluded treaties then became instruments of inequality. This process caused severe detriment to the exercise of sovereignty by East Indies rulers:

> The relevant commercial privileges granted by the Rulers to the Europeans were at first not conceived as irrevocable or derogatory to their sovereignty. But as in the case of capitulations, the position of many Rulers tended to deteriorate in the course of time and revocability gave way to irrevocability and to inequality of status. The more contracting Rulers found themselves isolated from the outside world, the more their powers of resistance and independent action were bound to decline, resulting in their increasing dependence on one or another European sovereign.[14]

In the nineteenth century this led, in part, to the dissolution of the East Indies Companies and the division of the Asian region into colonial spheres of interest. However, the contribution of these three centuries of treaty making to the developing international principles of the law of nations was not insignificant. Legal principles such as the law of shipwreck, *droit d'aubaine*[15] and the abolition of slavery were themselves linked to the provisions of particular East Indies treaties; and legal principles adhered to by East Indies rulers, such as binding agreements, valid tests of sovereignty and the inter-Sovereign level as the basis for negotiating and concluding agreements all had an impact on the secularisation and evolution of the law of nations.[16] Moreover, international law itself was used by East Indies rulers to promulgate 'certain ancient customs, such as those relating to the treatment of foreigners ("capitulations") and the respect for the sovereign status of the ruler (absence of *debellatio*[17])'.[18]

However, as Alexandrowicz concludes:

> This process of law making came to end at the beginning of the nineteenth century. By that time the law of nations was for all practical purposes a complete discipline. Paradoxical as it may seem, it then started contracting into a regional (purely European) legal system, abandoning its centuries old tradition of universality based on the natural law doctrine. While European–Asian trade was still expanding, European egocentricity left the Sovereigns of the East Indies, which had largely contributed to the prosperity of the European economy, outside of the confines of European 'civilisation' and international law shrank to regional dimensions though it still carried the label of universality.[19]

---

[14] Ibid, 129.

[15] The ruler's right to claim the land of foreigners who died in their territory.

[16] Alexandrowicz, above n 11, 176-7, chapter 2.

[17] Footnote added: Conquest and subjugation.

[18] Alexandrowicz, above n 11, 177.

[19] Ibid, 2.

The positivist approach to international law

International law had by the nineteenth century come under the sway of a positivist approach to the law of nations, concerned primarily with the rights and duties of the nation-state. These ideas came to prominence through the writing of Emmerich de Vattel in *The Law of Nations, or The Principles of Natural Law* (1758).[20] This new doctrine exalted the entity of the nation-state and excluded any recognition of the alternative traditions of governance and sovereignty.[21]

Alexandrowicz found it difficult to state with any certainty which phenomenon came first: doctrinal change or the demise of the practical need for Europeans to engage in making treaties with those from whom they sought to gain commercial or territorial benefit in the 'New World'.[22] Martinez is in no doubt that Europeans began to dispense with treaty making with non-European peoples 'when they felt superior', unless a treaty was 'judged expedient or necessary', such as when the need arose to 'establish "rights" and priorities over competing European powers'.[23] Whatever the case, the positivist legal doctrine of civilised nations was soon to become the primary intellectual instrument of nineteenth-century colonialism.

Treaties as commercial contracts

In the 'New World', a similar pattern of treaty making occurred in the initial stages of contact with local Indigenous societies. Some of the treaties concluded were of a commercial nature, while others were treaties of peace and friendship. In both cases, the European parties were clear 'that they were indeed negotiating and entering into contractual relations with sovereign nations'.[24] However, in North America, treaty making quickly became a way for the colonists to legitimate 'their respective territorial claims in the "New World"' *vis à vis* other European powers, 'and in accordance with European standards' observed at the time which related to territorial acquisition and land cession.[25] Again, once the European interlocutors had cemented their

---

[20] Emmerich de Vattel, *The Law of Nations, or The Principles of Natural Law: Applied to the Conduct and to the Affairs of Nations and of Sovereigns* (Charles G. Fenwick trans., Carnegie Institution of Washington, Washington, 1916) [trans of: *Le droit des gens, ou, Principes de la Loi Naturelle / Appliques a la Conduite et Aux Affaires des Nations et des Souverains*, 1758].

[21] S James Anaya, *Indigenous Peoples in International Law* (Oxford University Press, New York, 1996).

[22] Alexandrowicz, above n 11, 156.

[23] Martinez, above n 1, para 109.

[24] Ibid, para 138. For examples, see Morse, this volume.

[25] Ibid, para 134.

place in the 'New World' as fully fledged nation-states, these new governments largely dispensed with the practice of treaty making, except where
matters relating to cession of land rights came to replace treaties of trade and
alliance. Native American groups by this stage had no choice but to engage in
such treaties with the colonial powers, and ceded considerable tracts of land
while always hoping that the new boundaries would be permanent ones,
quelling the settlers' desire for land.[26] Increasingly in this period, the positivist
doctrine 'provided the legal mechanism for consolidating territorial sovereignty over indigenous lands by the colonizing states'.[27] 'Indian' modes of
political organisation, so unlike the very recently developed formation of the
European nation-state, were deemed incapable of enjoying sovereign status
or rights in international law.

'By 1871 in the United States of America, treaty making with Indian
tribes was discontinued altogether, as it was seen as an impediment to the
assimilation of Indians into white society.[28] However, for the purposes of
this chapter it is significant to note that in the United States between 1871
and 1902, negotiated relations between the United States and Indigenous
governments were formalised as 'Agreements'. Morris posits that:

> [A]s a practical matter, particularly as regards American policy which
> continued to regard Native nations as sovereigns, the semantic difference
> between 'treaties' and 'agreements' was of limited importance. The change
> was an internal process alteration which affected the procedure in which non-
> Native Governments would interact with Native nations, but it did not alter
> the nature, nor the United States perception, of Native sovereignty.[29]

Treaties as agreements

An agreement is not necessarily considered to be of a different legal nature
to a treaty, particularly if the subject matter of the agreement relates to
'the notion and contents of sovereignty (such as territory/land and other
jurisdictional matters)'.[30] In such cases, both treaty and agreement are
settlements between parties having rights of dominion or possession.

---

[26] Martinez, above n 1, para 256.

[27] Anaya, above n 21, 22.

[28] Shaunnagh Darsett and Loe Godden, *A Guide to Overseas Precedents of Relevance to Native Title* (Native Title Research Unit, AIATSIS, Canberra, 1998) 4.

[29] G.T. Morris, 'In Support of the Right of Self-Determination of Indigenous Peoples in International Law' (1986) 29 *German Yearbook of International Law* 291–2., cited in Martinez, above n 1, para 330.

[30] Martinez, above n 1, para 333. However, Martinez notes that particularly where agreements are of a purely commercial nature and are conducted without the approval or ratification of the state, then an agreement may be considered to be merely a contract.

In 1840 in New Zealand, representatives of the British Crown nego-
tiated and signed the *Treaty of Waitangi* with a number of Maori chiefs.
In contrast to the absence of formally recognised treaty negotiations in
Australia, in New Zealand, 'negotiations over annexation were based on
the assumption that Maoris were a sovereign people'.[31] From the British
perspective, the *Treaty of Waitangi* transferred sovereignty to the British
Crown. Nevertheless, article two of the *Treaty* recognised and secured the
Maori right to 'the full exclusive and undisputed possession of their lands
and estates, forests, fisheries, and other properties' unless the Maori wished
to sell their land, in which case, under the terms of the *Treaty*, the Crown
had exclusive rights of pre-emption.[32]

In Australia, for reasons of expediency, various attempts by emis-
saries of colonial and post-Federation governments to engage formally and
establish agreements with particular Aboriginal leaders on the frontiers
failed because governments deemed them incapable of recognition at law.
Principally, because of ideological, political, demographic and geographical
considerations, it was more advantageous to regard Aboriginal people as
unworthy of treaty like arrangements than to make commitments that
might have become obstacles to the unfettered land appropriation in colonial Australia.[33]

In his book, *Race Relations Australia and New Zealand: A Comparative Survey
1770s–1970s,* Kerry Howe argues that the divergent colonial approaches
toward the Indigenous inhabitants of New Zealand and Australia can
be explained, in part, by the different initial responses to the arrival of
Europeans by Maori and Aboriginal peoples themselves. He writes:

> The richness and importance of artistic expression, mythology, ceremony
> and ritual to every aspect of Aboriginal life cannot be underestimated. Such
> features had major implications for contact with western man. Aboriginal
> society emphasised the status quo and emotional satisfaction derived from the
> Dreamtime. Aborigines were non-acquisitive. They had achieved a balance
> with their natural environment. Neither dominating, nor being dominated by
> it. They saw no need to change relationships with the world about them nor
> their fellow men. Life was conservative and repetitious. Values and priorities
> remained unchanged and unchallenged for tens of thousands of years ... Maori
> beliefs were far less entrenched in precedent. Thus if the new Christian god was
> as powerful and beneficent as the missionaries claimed then Maoris could add
> him to their own deities without too much trouble once they agreed to do so.

---

[31] Kerry Howe, *Race Relations Australia and New Zealand: A Comparative Survey 1770s–1970s*
(Methuen, Wellington, 1977) 25.

[32] See Williams, this volume.

[33] See for example, Howe, above n 31; Henry Reynolds, *The Law of the Land* (Penguin,
Ringwood, Victoria, 1992); Reynolds, above n 7.

Such a decision was unthinkable for Aborigines in the earlier years of contact for the new beliefs could in no way be reconciled with the all-embracing and complete values of the Dreamtime.[34]

Assertions about Aboriginal culture such as this have long permeated popular and academic discussion, and more recently, as we discuss elsewhere,[35] continue to attract attention in the findings of some members of the Australian judiciary who have interpreted traditional Aboriginal society as immutable and static. Yet they are assertions that are refuted by a substantial body of Australianist anthropological and historical literature that describes Aboriginal societies dealing with changing social realities, dynamically and pragmatically adapting to the constancy of changing material circumstances. While Aboriginal religion may be underpinned by an ideology of changelessness, both social discourse and beliefs in Aboriginal societies were in a continual state of flux long before the colonisation of Australia.[36]

The expansion of ancient jurisdictions and the resilience of customary polities

As should be expected, treaty making is also a practice common between native polities; for example, in North America in the security regime formed by the Iroquois in 1450.[37] In the light of this Indigenous history of treaty making, Martinez argues that more needs to be known about the reactions of Indigenous peoples to 'European overtures and politicking' in relation to treaty making, and that these historical encounters need to be (re)written 'from the point of view of Indigenous peoples' and from the perspective of Indigenous relations with foreigners.[38] He writes:

> . . . the following aspects merit a closer scrutiny: (a) questions of indigenous protocol regarding encounters and dealing with outsiders, which have rarely

---

[34] Howe, above n 28, 8–9.

[35] Marcia Langton and Lisa Palmer, 'Unsettling Sovereignties and Negotiating Treaties: The Re-emergence of Customary Exchange as Economic Relations' (Paper presented at the Peace and Reconciliation: International Perspectives Conference, Melbourne, 16 July 2003).

[36] See for example, Tony Swain, *A Place for Strangers. Towards a History of Australian Aboriginal Being* (Cambridge University Press, Cambridge, 1993); McIntosh, above n 7; Ian Keen, *Knowledge and Secrecy in an Aboriginal Religion* (Clarendon Press, Oxford, 1994).

[37] Known as the Iroquois League, it was a pact which recognised the 'sovereignty' of other Indian nations and enabled the negotiation of binding treaties between them; see Neta C. Crawford, 'A Security Regime Among Democracies: Cooperation among Iroquois nations' (1994) 48(3) *International Organization* 345–385.

[38] Martinez, above n 1, para 110, 111.

been addressed in detail (related to the formalities necessary for entering into relations with other entities); (b) indigenous modes of accommodating outsiders or newcomers; and (c) the concept of time in traditional cultures, especially the principles of fidelity to the past (in terms of indigenous fulfilment of duly established obligations).[39]

Peace making and the forming of alliances in Aboriginal Australia

In Australia, anthropologists have discussed inter-polity rituals of peace making and exchange, although largely as examples of religious behaviour.[40] Their political import has not attracted due attention, although the history of trading relationships and treaty and agreement making between the peoples of Arnhem Land and the Macasssan seafarers visiting their shores to collect *trepang* in pre-colonial times was tendered as crucial evidence by native title claimants in the Croker Island Native Title sea claim in 1998.[41] Similarly, the extension of these political and economic relationships to dealings with white settlers provides evidence of the initiatives of Indigenous polities and the perspectives of Indigenous parties in such matters; and they are of acute relevance to modern agreement making as a source of Aboriginal legal customs and traditions. A people do not desist from their political aspirations merely on the grounds of doctrinal denial of their existence or their capacity to engage politically with external entities. Treaty-like pacts which have continued to be negotiated and attempted by Yolŋu clans in Arnhem Land since the colonial period can be understood as a continuation and adaptation of Aboriginal perspectives on jurisdiction, exchange and international relationships in the region. For example, the literature on this subject documents a peace settlement negotiated by anthropologist Donald F. Thomson with Woŋgu, leader of the Djapu clan, in 1935.[42] In 1957, Yolŋu clan leaders expressed religious imperatives, political desires for territorial respect and economic reciprocity, when the Arnhem Land 'adjustment movement' was instigated by them at the mission at Elcho Island, where they revealed sacred *ringgitj* objects; in 1962 when clan leaders created the painted panels depicting sacred clan designs at the Yirrkala Methodist church; and in 1963, when the famous Bark Petition

---

[39] Ibid, para 106.

[40] See, for example, Stephen A. Wild (ed.), *Rom: An Aboriginal Ritual of Diplomacy* (Australian Institute of Aboriginal Studies, Canberra, 1986).

[41] *Mary Yarmirr & Ors v Northern Territory of Australia & Ors* (1998) 82 FCR 533.

[42] *Thomson of Arnhem Land* (video recording), New South Wales: A Film Australia National Interest Program in Association with John Moore Productions Pty Ltd, 2000.

by clan leaders, precursor to *Milirrpum v Nabalco*,[43] was submitted to the Parliament in Canberra.[44]

In the 1870s at the Fort Point Settlement (now known as Darwin), an alliance was negotiated between the colonisers and the Larrakia, a group whose property rights in the settled region were recognised by the Europeans as against other neighbouring Aboriginal groups, who at times expressed a varied degree of hostile intent toward the fledgling settlement. One of the reasons for the European decision to ally with the Larrakia was their need for a security or military alliance. According to Wells, 'This alliance was sought after and crucial to both parties and was based on the Larrakia, as the traditional owners of the Darwin region, asserting themselves and being recognised by the colonisers as the right group to negotiate an alliance with'.[45] Wells contends that:

> the Larrakia made pragmatic decisions about their initial interactions based on prior knowledge and experience of Europeans [gleaned in part from previous ill-fated settlements along the northern coastline], their weapons and their commodities ... the land the colonisers were intent on settling was Larrakia country and if Larrakia were determined to survive and stay about their country, then they had to negotiate how they would do it. This resulted in them forming an alliance with the colonisers.[46]

Wells locates the beginnings of this early political alliance between the Larrakia and the colonisers in the exchanges that took place as a result of bartering between the two groups.[47] She argues that, from a Larrakia perspective, these transactions both facilitated the acquisition of useful goods and provided a means for sorting out local cultural and political agendas, wherein bartering was 'a means of encouraging a more peaceful relationship', and a way of facilitating and expanding political interactions.[48] The parties in this alliance were at times friendly, and at other times hostile. Moreover, as Wells explains, 'it is also clear that this alliance was carried out in what was emerging as an unequal power relationship between the

---

[43] (1971) 17 FLR 141.

[44] See Ronald Murray Berndt, *An Adjustment Movement in Arnhem Land, Northern Territory of Australia* (Mouton, Paris, 1962); McIntosh, above n 7; Ian McIntosh, *The Whale and the Cross: Conversations with David Burrumarra MBE* (Historical Society of the Northern Territory, Darwin, 1994); John Cawte, *The Universe of the Warramirri: Art, Medicine and Religion in Arnhem Land* (NSW University Press, New South Wales, 1993); Langton, above n 7, 13–26.

[45] Samantha Wells, *Negotiating Place in Colonial Darwin: Interactions Between the Larrakia and Whites; 1869–1911* (PhD Thesis, Australian National University, 2003) ch 2, 101.

[46] Ibid, 100.

[47] Ibid, 85; see also Nicholas Thomas, *Entangled Objects: Exchange, Material Culture, and Colonialism in the Pacific* (Harvard University Press, Cambridge, Massachusetts, 1991).

[48] Wells, above n 45, 86.

colonisers and the Larrakia', a situation wherein an ever-increasing body of colonial laws were enforced to control and regulate both Aboriginal people and land use in the Darwin region.[49]

Present-day negotiated relationships

More than 130 years later, after decades of successive government policies aimed at dispossession and assimilation of the Larrakia, another phase in this history of negotiated relationships between the settler society and the Larrakia is occurring, in part as an outcome of a series of modern-day economic agreements. The Larrakia have arguably suffered greater dispossession of their land and lifestyle than Aboriginal people in some of the more remote areas of the Northern Territory. However, belated recognition of their rights through both the settlement in 2000 of the Kenbi Land Claim[50] on the Cox Peninsula (a claim lodged in 1979 under the *Aboriginal Land Rights (Northern Territory) Act 1976* (Cth)) and opportunities conferred by the recognition of native-title rights at common law[51] and the subsequent *Native Title Act 1993* (Cth) (*NTA*), has provided increasing legal recognition of the Larrakia's traditional interest in land in the Darwin region. This increasing recognition has forced, for reasons of legal and political expedience, both the Northern Territory government and the private sector to proceed with negotiations and agreement making with the Larrakia. This has meant that the Larrakia are now able to negotiate a significant financial stake in many of the commercial developments occurring on Crown land within the Darwin region.[52] At the same time, the growing involvement of the Larrakia people in regional economic and political life is promoting both Larrakia community development initiatives and broader community

---

49 Ibid, 101.
50 Office of the Aboriginal Land Commissioner, *The Kenbi (Cox Peninsula) Land Claim no 37; Report and Recommendation of the Former Aboriginal Land Commissioner, Justice Gray, to the Minister for Aboriginal and Torres Strait Islander Affairs and to the Administrator of the Northern Territory* (Aboriginal and Torres Strait Islander Commission, Canberra, 2000).
51 *Mabo v. Queensland* (No 2) (1992) 175 CLR 1 ('*Mabo*'). At the time of writing the Federal Court is hearing the Larrakia native title claim over the Darwin region, *William Maxwell Risk on Behalf of Larrakia People and Anor v Northern Territory of Australia and Ors (Darwin Part A)* D6033 Of 2001 FCA Northern Territory.
52 Northern Land Council, 'Landmark Native Title Agreement' (Press Release, 18 November 1999); Northern Land Council, 'Larrakia Set for $24m Urban Development Project' (2002) 4 (2) *Land Rights News 3;* Parliamentary Joint Committee on Native Title, Federal Parliament, *Northern Land Council: Submission to the Parliamentary Joint Committee on Native Title and the Aboriginal and Torres Strait Islander Land Fund, Inquiry into Indigenous Land Use Agreements* (2001) 8. See also the ATNS Project database, http://www.atns.net.au/biogs/A001163b.htm.

recognition of, and respect for, the rights and responsibilities of Darwin's traditional owners.[53]

A recent partnership arrangement between the Larrakia Nation Aboriginal Corporation, the Northern Territory government and fifty other organisations and agencies in the Northern Territory addresses the issues facing Indigenous 'itinerants' visiting Darwin from remote communities.[54] The Larrakia involvement in the 'Community Harmony Project' (formerly the 'Itinerants Project') is critical to the initiative's status and potential success, as the project is underpinned by an adherence to the principles of Larrakia law and cultural protocols which, as with other Aboriginal legal systems, require that visitors to Larrakia country show respect for the cultural authority of the traditional owners. The anti-social behaviour of many 'itinerants' in urban business and shopping precincts has been a perpetual grievance of the Northern Territory business community and 'itinerants' themselves have been subjected to denigration and demonisation in successive Territory government electoral campaigns. The irony is that, in order to move toward a resolution of this perpetual grievance, the settler state (now with a Labor government at the helm) has been forced to recognise and rely once again on the legal and cultural authority of the Larrakia traditional owners over the Darwin region, a situation not dissimilar to the security and brokerage alliance formed between the Larrakia and the colonisers in the 1870s.

Aboriginal corporate governance and authority

The changing political and legal landscape of agreement making is therefore a rich ground of inquiry in the context of the mediation of political relationships between Indigenous peoples and the nation-state in modern Australia. In the minimal form of Aboriginal land-holding corporation, the clan or some form of the clan-based corporation, we find that governance and dominion, such as those rights of possession asserted among Aboriginal groups in disputes over territory, are achieved both within and between such groups. As a result we find that there are transactions that may be construed as governance in a larger entity than the clan itself.

Authority is expressed regionally, as Aboriginal rules about permission

---

[53] Larrakia Nation, *Future Link* (2003), Larrakia Nation Aboriginal Corporation http://www.larrakia.com.future.html at 8 October 2002. See also the ATNS Project database, http://www.atns.net.au/biogs/A001163b.htm.

[54] Northern Land Council, 'Itinerants Project Up and Running' (2002) 4 (2) *Land Rights News* 20. See also the ATNS Project database, http://www.atns.net.au/biogs/A001504b.htm.

to enter estates demonstrate,[55] through geographically dispersed alliances of clan-based corporations (or language-based corporations) whose members' concern for the transmissibility of property, including resource rights, is expressed in their arrangements they conclude for the transmissibility of property rights to future generations. Such arrangements are achieved by institutional means, such as religious ceremonies,[56] adherence to marriage rules, and through the institution of elders who oversee the group's affairs to achieve outcomes deemed not inconsistent with a set of laws that supersede property tenure laws: these may be labelled territorial resource use laws, not entirely but substantially distinct from land-tenure laws. Elders ensure the transmissibility of not just property rights but a wide range of resource rights and incorporeal rights in the bio-geography of the region, as well as the other governing traditions and customs from which native title arises.[57]

Customary exchange and market considerations

The insertion of customary institutions and jurisdictions into the marketplace through agreement making, such as Aboriginal heritage management agreements, consultation protocols and intra-Indigenous agreements over boundaries of native title applications, is not mere syncretisation of tradition and modernity, but the transformation of relationships. These postcolonial forms of inter-polity engagement are underwritten by both customary exchange and market considerations.[58] Commercial agreements negotiated by Indigenous parties in the resource sector, state and regional-framework agreements relating to service delivery, and a comprehensive agreement-making approach negotiated as a result of rights conferred by the beneficial effects of *Mabo*[59] and subsequently, the *NTA*, are increasingly important in

---

[55] Fred Myers, 'Always Ask: Resource Use and Land Ownership Among Pintupi Aborigines of the Australian Western Desert', in Eugene Hunn and Nancy Williams (eds), *Resource Managers: North American and Australian Hunter-Gatherers* (Australian Institute of Aboriginal Studies, Canberra, 1982) 173–96; Nancy Williams, 'A Boundary is to Cross: Observations on Yolŋu Boundaries and Permission', in Eugene Hunn and Nancy Williams (eds), *Resource Managers: North American and Australian Hunter-Gatherers* (Australian Institute of Aboriginal Studies, Canberra, 1982) 131–54.

[56] See, for example, Wild, above n 40; Nancy Williams, *The Yolŋu and Their Land: A System of Land Tenure and the Fight for its Recognition* (Australian Institute of Aboriginal Studies, Canberra, 1986); Nancy Williams, *Two Laws: Managing Disputes in a Contemporary Aboriginal Community* (Australian Institute of Aboriginal Studies, Canberra, 1987); Keen, above n 36.

[57] Marcia Langton, 'Ancient Jurisdictions: Aboriginal Polities and Sovereignty' (Paper presented as a keynote address at the Australian History Association Conference, Challenging Histories Conference, State Library of Victoria, Melbourne, 5 October 2001).

[58] Langton and Palmer, above n 35.

[59] *Mabo* (1992) 175 CLR 1.

the political and legal landscape of agreement making in Australia. This chequered board of agreement-making processes and preferences is examined elsewhere.[60] Because, as Neate observes, 'a Court cannot and will not determine the consequences of a determination that native title exists,'[61] many of the issues that arise in dealings between native-title claimants and non-native title parties must be encompassed in agreements and negotiated settlements.[62] In this regard, the state and other parties are required to negotiate with Indigenous polities.

Through these agreement-making processes, the assertion of national sovereignty is contested by the assertion and exercise of Indigenous governance and customary authority. Indigenous forms of political legitimacy or jurisdiction compete both symbolically and politically with the declared nation-state sovereignty, which is often weakly exercised in the territory of the people, especially in remote areas. Some agreements in Australia today, while not treaties in the conventional sense of the term used in current international law, have effected mutual recognition of the respective jurisdictions of the Indigenous and settler parties, with the express purpose

---

[60] Marcia Langton and Lisa Palmer, 'Modern Agreement Making and Indigenous People in Australia: Issues and Trends'(2003) 8(1) *Australian Indigenous Law Reporter* 1–31.

[61] Graeme Neate 'Native Title Ten Years On: Getting on With the Job or Sitting on the Fence?' (Paper presented at the Native Title Update Forum: National Farmers' Federation, Carnarvon, Western Australia, 21 May 2002), online at National Native Title Tribunal (2002) http://www.nntt.gov.au/metacard/speeches.html at 20 October 2002.

[62] See Langton and Palmer, 'Modern Agreement Making', above n 56. We explain in this article the Indigenous Land Use Agreement provisions of the *NTA*:

> A pertinent example of an agreement-making scheme is the Indigenous Land Use Agreement (ILUA) provisions in the *NTA*. Agreements can be made under the terms of the *NTA*. The ILUA provisions replace the agreement-making process in s 21 of the unamended Act (which lacked statutory protection for agreements once they were made) and provide for legally binding negotiated agreements made voluntarily between people who hold, or claim to hold, native title and other people who have, or wish to gain, an interest in the area in question. Once it has been successfully negotiated, and after the procedural hurdles stipulated under the Act have been satisfied, an ILUA is registered as a statutory agreement under the *NTA* and is enforceable as a contract. In some circumstances, parties have agreed on an alternative framework external to the *NTA* procedures for negotiating such an agreement, and upon conclusion of the negotiations, sought to have the contract registered under the *NTA*. Native title parties are contractually bound and can be sued for any breach (14).

We also noted the numbers and types of ILUAs concluded:

> By October 2002, there were 54 ILUAs registered in Australia. These agreements covered a range of subject matter: access (6), consultation protocol (4), development (6), extinguishment (4), government (5), infrastructure (20), and mining (21). Many such native title claims, especially in Queensland (where 32 of the 54 ILUAs were registered), are proceeding through mediation to consent determination. The ILUAs in these instances form part of the package of documents that formalise the resolution of native title determination applications. Alternatively, ILUAs may be 'stand alone' agreements which deal with native-title issues independent of the native-title determination process (14).

of constituting jural, political and economic relationships based in an agreed distribution of public and private rights in land.[63]

Negotiating with the nation-state in Australia

In contrast, for example, to the Nunavut Final Agreement of 1993, which led to Nunavut self-government in Canada, or the 1996 *Te Runanga o Ngai Tahu Act*, through which the New Zealand government specifically recognised the legal personality and autonomy of Te Runanga o Ngai Tahu tribe, culminating in the 1998 Ngai Tahu Settlement,[64] Aboriginal groups in Australia are yet to receive overt legal recognition of their polities by the Crown. Nevertheless, Aboriginal peoples have partially restituted Indigenous forms of governance in the interface with the nation-state through negotiating their political rights, and thus their place in the nation-state, not merely as subjects or citizens, but as unique polities based in ancient jurisdictions and expanded by recently recognised statutory and common-law recognition.

The re-emergence of customary polities recognised under the rubric of 'Indigenous' rights and native title, and the expression of Aboriginal jurisdiction and governance in agreement making are a means for settling land access and use, resource distribution and the conditions under which these might occur. The settler state benefits (as usual) from the exploitation of land and resources in the Indigenous domain, while Indigenous people extend their customary jurisdictions, in which the incidents of native title or customary property rights originate, into the modern economic and political sphere.

---

[63] See Langton and Palmer, 'Modern Agreement Making', above n 60; and Harvey, this volume, 239.

[64] ATNS Project database, *Ngai Tahu Deed of Settlement* (1998) http://www.atns.net.au/biogs/A000661b.htm at 12 November 2002.

Chapter 2

Indigenous–Settler Treaty Making in Canada

Bradford W. Morse

Introduction

Treaties between Indian nations and European empires have served as the fundamental foundation upon which the official Indian–settler relationship has been built in the territories now called Canada and the United States of America since the 1600s. Treaty making was the approach preferred by both sides to sort out the essential terms of how colonists and their governments would relate to the original owners of the land. One of the critical historical, political and legal elements that distinguishes the North American experience from that of Australia is that there was a recognition from the early points of contact that pre-existing societies were completely sovereign. Before the arrival of Europeans in Oceania and in North America, there was little doubt that the Indigenous populations were sovereign self-governing peoples belonging to many distinct nations with their own legal, economic, and political systems, as well as possessing their own languages, cultures and religious beliefs.

Although European understanding of the Indigenous world of the Americas was minimal, there was nevertheless recognition that different societies were being encountered which had their own values and governmental structures, as had occurred previously in Africa and Asia. While Eurocentric presumptions of superiority existed among many early explorers and settlers, others marvelled at the health, prosperity and independence that existed within Indigenous societies. French, British, Dutch and Swedish representatives all accepted completely that Indigenous sovereignty existed such that formal intergovernmental relationships could be established on beneficial terms. The recognition that a treaty—and the process of treaty making—was the proper vehicle for forming such relationships between

European states and the nations of the so-called new world was quickly acknowledged by all.

Although Europeans clearly did not appreciate it at the time, Indigenous states in North America had a long history of treaty making before they ever encountered people from the other side of the Atlantic. A wide variety of treaty relationships existed among many of the Indian nations in North America, in some places extending over very long distances. Trade of natural resources and produced goods could occur over thousands of miles. Military alliances also were forged in opposition to common enemies, and military conflict was frequently resolved through creating new peace and friendship commitments through solemn treaty promises.[1]

Thus, from an Indian perspective, utilising treaties made sense as the primary peaceful method for dealing with newcomers—the only other alternatives being avoidance of contact or war, which were also pursued at various locales and times. However, the flood of migrants from overseas, coupled with their attractive trade goods, quickly led to the Indian nations along the Atlantic coast to conclude that peaceful relations was the preferred choice. Likewise, from the European perspective, treaties were a logical device to regulate future relationships, since that was how Europeans themselves attempted to organise their own internal relationships among competing states.

Treaty making, therefore, worked well as a common vehicle by which both sides could pursue the establishment of new relations based upon clear understandings. Each party was able to pursue its separate interests within a common construct. The pure act of negotiating out of self-interest brought together leading representatives in a context of equal status and a common objective of reaching agreement. Treaties became the best method by which to cement a relationship inspired by desires for peace and friendship, to encourage trading patterns that were economically beneficial to both sides, as well as to create potentially powerful military alliances against common enemies, either other European colonial powers or Indian nations.

It is also important to appreciate that control over treaty making on the European side rested exclusively with the Empire. That is, it was the Imperial government that possessed the sole prerogative to decide when to negotiate new treaties, with whom to seek such relationships and on what terms. Only the Crown could appoint representatives with a mandate to bind the government. The people on the ground—the colonists—could enter into private contracts of trade, but they had no authority whatsoever as private individuals or as communities to negotiate formal treaties or to acquire land directly from Indian nations.

---

[1] See, for example, Robert A Williams Jr, *Linking Arms Together: American Indian Treaty Visions of Law and Peace, 1600–1800* (Routledge, New York, 1999).

The place of treaties in modern Canada

The history of negotiating treaties, their political and legal significance up to the present day, as well as the many disputes which continue to arise regarding their meaning, create a situation that shares some similarities but is also markedly different in Canada from that in the United States of America, New Zealand or any other country with a coloniser–Indigenous treaty history. Understanding the place of treaties in modern Canada is only possible through appreciating the different types of treaties that have been signed, the history of treaty making that has occurred, the evolving legal importance that treaties have acquired over time, and the current practice of negotiating new treaties, land claim settlements and self-government agreements. It must also be recognised that first-nation perspectives on the function of treaties and the precise rights they contain have differed significantly from the views held by Canadian governments over the intervening decades, thereby causing considerable conflict, disappointment and frustration. Recent judicial interpretations,[2] along with the constitutional protection of treaty rights in 1982, have resurrected the importance of historic Indian treaties in Canada as well as the necessity for new treaties to be negotiated.

Since both Canada and the United States were predominantly established as British colonies with the same common-law legal system and the same initial approach by European settlers to dealing with the Indian nations, it is not surprising that both countries today share many of the same perceptions of treaty relationships. The United States case law, with its far greater volume and earlier vintage, has had considerable influence on the development of Canadian thinking in this regard.[3] In fact, some of the earliest treaties relating to Indian nations resident in Canada were actually negotiated in the United States' colonies. The border between the two countries also bisects the traditional territory of many Indian nations, from coast to coast.

The common law and official government policy of Great Britain in the 1600s was largely shaped by the emerging international law doctrines first enunciated by Spanish theologians and legal thinkers, especially Franciscus de Victoria, in the mid-sixteenth century.[4] After extensive debate and a

---

[2] See, for example, *Regina v Simon* [1985] 2 SCR 387; *Regina v Sioui* [1990] 1 SCR 1025; and *Regina v Badger* [1996] 1 SCR 771.

[3] In particular, the frequently called Marshall trilogy of *Johnson v McIntosh* 21 US 543 (1823); *Cherokee Nation v Georgia* 30 US 1 (1831); and *Worcester v Georgia* 31 US 515 (1832).

[4] For a fundamental work that analyses this period see Robert A. Williams Jr, *The American Indian in Western Legal Thought: The Discourses of Conquest* (Oxford University Press, New York, 1990).

period of controversy, international law came to recognise the Indigenous peoples of the so-called 'New World' as human beings with souls who were entitled to respect and to protection from physical violence. The developing theory of international law also recognised them as peoples who constituted sovereign nations.

Furthermore, the specific Indian nation that occupied a particular territory was viewed as the rightful owner of that soil in accordance with the terms of its own rules or laws. According to those laws, land was usually held with collective or communal title and could not be individually conveyed or sold. This meant that the 'discovering' European nation could not claim exclusive title to the 'new' lands, but merely the right, *vis à vis* other European countries, to enter into treaty relations regarding trade or military alliances, or to acquire land for settlement from a willing Indian nation. International law did, however, recognise a principle of conquest such that a victor in war obtained the legal right to seize territory and substitute its sovereignty for that of the defeated nation. While military conflict has occasionally been raised by the Canadian government in seeking to avoid treaty obligations, the Supreme Court of Canada has rejected such arguments to date, as there has been no clear or proven evidence of declarations of war or conquest.[5]

The evolution of treaty making in Canada

Canada has experienced four distinct eras in which treaties were negotiated:

1. from the earliest days of contact to the American Revolution
2. from 1790 to independence in 1867
3. from 1867 to 1930
4. the modern era from 1975 to the present.

Each period is considered briefly.

Peace and friendship treaties

The real thrust of treaty relations in the 1600s and 1700s, and the primary purpose of international or inter-governmental relationships generally among Europeans and Indian nations, was on trade, military alliances, and peaceful relations so as to permit colonies to flourish. Early agreements involved some small land conveyances for trading posts and forts while also establishing a pattern of gift giving. Offering gifts, which was to become a

---

[5]   See, *Regina v Simon* [1985] 2 SCR 387.

common element in almost all later treaties, made sense to Europeans as well as to Indigenous peoples in the Americas, as each was accustomed to presenting tokens of esteem and recognition on formal occasions.

The first formal treaty between the British Crown and the Iroquois Confederacy, the *Treaty of Albany* of 1664—also known as the 'Two Row Wampum'—typifies a number of these elements. The Iroquois (then consisting of five distinct nations but later increasing to six when the Tuscarora Nation joined early in the eighteenth century), who were a major military force and far more numerous than the British in the area, had previously been allies of the Dutch, who transferred their interest in New Netherland (renamed New York) to the British in 1664. The Iroquois were longstanding opponents of the Huron Nation, who were allied with the French colony of New France in the St Lawrence River Valley. Treaty negotiations extended over several days, resulting in separate agreements on 24 and 25 September 1664, consisting of the following key elements:

1. '... that the Indian Princes above named and their subjects, shall have all such wares and commodities from the English for the future, as heretofore they had from the Dutch.'
2. Each party pledged to capture and punish any fugitive committing any injury or violence to a person under the other's protection, so that all due satisfaction is given to the victim.
3. The English were mandated to 'make peace for the Indian Princes, with the Nations down the River'.
4. The English promised not to assist the three Nations of the Abenaki Confederacy and to provide accommodation to the Iroquois if they should 'be beaten' by those Nations.[6]

The Treaty was recorded in English, with an official version on parchment given to the Iroquois. The Treaty was also recorded on a *wampum* belt delivered to Colonel George Cartwright (on behalf of the Duke of York). The Iroquois method of recording the significance of important events involved the sewing together of beads made from shells on animal skins in pictorial patterns unique to that particular event. Thus, each party followed its traditional practice of acknowledging the import of the solemn occasion for all time in a way that fitted within its culture while making mutual assurances of fidelity to the promises made.

Treaty making quickly became the preferred strategy of Great Britain as it expanded its colonial and trading empire, directly through being welcomed by Indian nations into their territory, or through acquiring the

---

[6]   Edmund Bailey O'Callaghan (ed.), *Documents Relative to the Colonial History of the State of New York* (Weed, Parsons & Co, Albany, 1853–61) vol 3, 67–8.

European claims of its predecessors. A number of treaties were also negotiated with the Wabanaki Confederacy, (the Mi'kmaq, Maliseet, Penobscot and Passamaquoddy Nations) in northern New England and the Maritime colonies from 1678 until 1761. These treaties often followed political withdrawals by the Wabanaki's former ally, France. However, their purpose more generally was to have both partners commit to peace and friendship, free trade, non-molestation of citizens, respect for criminal and civil jurisdiction, release of prisoners and refusal to aid deserters.[7]

The early success of the treaty device (and the absence of an economically attractive alternative) caused it to be used over and over again to meet immediate needs as well as for long-term objectives, including to end any hostilities that may have arisen so as to restore peace and foster trade. Treaties were negotiated by Britain all along the Atlantic seaboard, from Georgia to Nova Scotia and as far west as the Appalachian Mountain range from 1664 onwards.

The emphasis upon Imperial control and the importance of treaty making was later confirmed by the Royal Proclamation issued by King George III on 7 October 1763. In addition to installing colonial governments for former French colonies in what became Quebec and Prince Edward Island and the Spanish colony of Florida, it also declared that Indian nations were to remain unmolested in their territories within British colonies unless they were willing to sell their lands to properly appointed Crown representatives, who would negotiate the purchase through public meetings, and resulting in formal treaty arrangements.

American independence to Canadian independence

The American Revolution changed everything for both the United States of America and for Canada. The land demands of colonists had been one of the driving forces underlying the American Revolution, so that the involvement of land speculators, including George Washington, was able to flourish without the Imperial constraints that had previously existed to honour prior treaty promises. Many of the Indian tribes had in that Revolution respected their military alliance with the British, such that they were now on the losing side without the continuing protection of the Crown or the existence of prior treaties.

The birth of the new country meant, of course, that all residents needed to decide where their future lay. Many of the colonists who had remained

---

[7] For extensive reviews of this experience, see Leslie F.S. Upton, *Micmacs and Colonists: Indian–White Relations in the Maritimes, 1713–1867* (University of British Columbia Press, Vancouver, 1979) and William C. Wicken, *Mi'kmaq Treaties on Trial: History, Land and Donald Marshall Junior* (University of Toronto Press, Toronto, 2002).

loyal to the British Empire, the so-called United Empire Loyalists (UELs), chose to flee the United States and move to what remained of British North America–Canada. They needed land on which to resettle, a factor that suddenly changed the pattern of the prior Indian–Crown relationship on the Canadian side of the border, where colonial settlement had been limited.

The American victory also forced a major relocation of many of the tribes from the east coast of the United States, moving westward and, in some cases, fleeing northward into Canada along with the UELs.

The victory also meant that the new United States of America was a vulnerable country, nervous about the solidity of its success in the Revolution without a guarantee against British invasion. Thus, it wanted to forge peaceful relations with outside powers and to stabilise its internal circumstances. In this regard, and wherever possible, it wisely decided to draw upon the benefit of the treaty relationships possessed by the British and to form new ones. The United States of America could not merely be a successor to existing British treaties, because that was part of the defeated empire, so it had to form new relationships of its own, which began with the *Treaties of Hopewell* with the Cherokee, Choctaw and Chickasaw Nations in 1785 and 1786.[8] Similarly, it did not wish formally to be seen to be following British policies, as it needed to demonstrate its independence; British decrees such as the Royal Proclamation of 1763 had to be modified and reborn as the *Non-Intercourse Act,* which was passed on 22 July 1790 by the United States Congress,[9] although the orientation was largely the same.

One of the obvious effects of the Revolution was an unleashing of demand for Indian land, thereby weakening the Indian nations that remained within the United States' borders in political as well as in economic and military terms. A by-product of the necessity for tribes to make peace with their far more-populous neighbour was to look to the United States court system as a vehicle for their continuing protection. Since they could no longer appeal to the British Crown as an ally, and in the face of their declining military and trading importance, the only option available was the United States court system.

This choice also presented serious challenges for Indian nations who saw themselves as fully sovereign. How could they invoke the protection of a foreign court operating in a totally different legal system and in a foreign language? This was not an attractive alternative, nor one that many Indian nations made, although a few did. What they discovered, not surprisingly,

---

[8] For an excellent discussion of the early United States policy, see Francis Paul Pucha, *American Indian Policy in the Formative Years: Indian Trade and Intercourse Acts, 1790–1834* (Harvard University Press, Cambridge, Massachusetts, 1962).

[9] 1 Stat 137 (1790).

was a United States court system that was itself relatively fragile as a new institution and primarily concerned about the vulnerability of this new country.

The United States Supreme Court (USSC), particularly under Chief Justice Marshall, through a series of cases in the 1820s and 1830s, sought to develop a principled foundation for what was essentially a political and legal compromise.[10] The options essentially presented to the court were either acceptance of the continuation of a full Indian nation sovereignty theory or a complete absorption of Indian people into the body politic. The former could threaten the United States' stability, as it would mean that Indian nations would continue to have the capacity to form treaties with European nations: this included the British to the north, whom they had just defeated, the French and the Spanish to the south, and potentially others. That possibility, obviously, was not attractive from a United States standpoint. On the other hand, denying all Indian sovereignty would contradict the treaty history that existed in North America as well as the initial efforts of the United States government, after the Revolution, to try and form peaceful, treaty based relationships with Indian nations. Such a legal position would also undermine the Federal government's own constitutional authority, as the division of powers with state governments had not precisely addressed the question of who possessed jurisdiction to engage in law-making and other aspects of non-commercial Indian affairs. Denying Indian sovereignty also could have the consequence that Indian people would be subjects, or potentially citizens with a right to vote.

Put another way, this legal interpretation would have meant that the United States government would not have had the authority over the important economic domain of Indian trade, of dealing with potential military threat, and of controlling vital revenue matters. One of the major ways of raising revenue in the days before income tax was through the sale of government land, and if the Federal government controlled the acquisition of land from Indian nations through treaties, then it would acquire the revenue from the re-sale of those lands to settlers.

Residual sovereignty

Therefore, the status of Indian nations and their treaty relationships held significant attractions for a federally created court intent on flexing its muscles in search of its own identity as the ultimate arbitrator of the United States Constitution and to seize a sizeable role for the Federal government as well as for the USSC itself. The response to these opportunities from

---

[10] *Johnson v McIntosh* 21 US 543 (1823); *Cherokee Nation v Georgia* 30 US 1 (1831); *Worcester v Georgia* 31 US 515 (1832).

Chief Justice Marshall was to develop a hybrid approach—neither full acceptance nor a full denial. Instead, he crafted a legal doctrine involving a transformation of former independent sovereignty into a continuing but internal variation, by developing a concept of domestic dependent nationhood. Indian nations are 'domestic' in the sense that they are declared to have lost international status or capacity to form relations with foreign countries. Their governments and their traditional territories are simply stated to be internal to the United States of America. They are deemed to be 'dependent' in that their authority is subject to some initially undefined power on the part of Congress and the executive branch to trench upon their autonomy.[11] Marshall also draws upon the imagery that Indian nations, by virtue of being dependent, are somehow like wards of state of the United States government as their protector or guardian.

The source of Marshall's thinking was largely his interpretation of the tides of history and a desire to draft a compromise that advanced Federal interests while respecting some recognition of the reality of Indian nations as distinct, self-governing peoples who were the rightful original owners of the soil. The theory indicates that Indian sovereignty remains but is circumscribed, so that what subsists from the formerly complete sovereignty is the residual sovereignty subject to further intrusions by the United States government in the future. This residual sovereignty includes the continuing power to negotiate treaties, but only with the United States of America, and to surrender territory for sale.

The landmark litigation before the USSC did not in fact protect the Cherokee Nation as they, among others, were forcibly dispossessed of their territory, and marched west of the Mississippi in the infamous Trail of Tears, on the orders of President Andrew Jackson.[12]

Land cession treaties in Canada

The Canadian experience during this same time period involved less drama; however, its consequences for many Indian nations was no less dramatic. The pressure for land to accommodate the arriving UELs and allied Indian nations required the emphasis in treaty making to switch from encouraging trade and peace to obtaining land on a massive scale for agriculture. Clearing the land for farming meant a drastic reduction in the wildlife population's capacity to support the traditional economy, and displaced the importance of the fur trade. The new wave of land cession treaties began in the late 1780s in southern Ontario, following the procedures of the Royal

---

[11] *Worcester v Georgia* 31 US 515 (1832).

[12] Rennard Strickland, *Fire and The Spirits: Cherokee Law from Clan to Court* (University of Oklahoma Press, Norman, 1975).

Proclamation of 1763, but with the focus upon acquiring clear legal title to land in a form of conveyance, in return for a lump-sum payment consisting of a combination of money and trade goods. Promises were made to reassure the Indian negotiators that they could continue to hunt and fish as before and would retain some of their lands, but little was said about how the influx of white colonists would reshape the country. By 1818, Imperial officials were complaining that the cost of such payments was becoming too onerous for the local colony to bear, leading to the substitution of annual payments (annuities). This effectively meant an instalment scheme was being used to pay Indian nations for their land with the money actually coming from the re-sale of Indian land to settlers and speculators, leaving the sizeable profits to subsidise colonial government costs.

The next key departure in the nature of treaties occurred through the negotiation of the *Robinson–Huron* and *Robinson–Superior Treaties* affecting the upper Great Lakes region. Not only did these two treaties operate on a far more massive scale (affecting more than twice the territory than all prior treaties combined), but they also introduced the concept of creating Indian reserves for individual communities out of small portions of the land surrendered under treaty. These reserves were set aside for exclusive use of individual Indian communities while the underlying title was held by the Crown. The *Robinson Treaties* effectively set the stage for all of the post-confederation treaties until 1975.

Treaties from 1867 to 1930

Canada was formally confirmed as a semi-independent country in 1867,[13] with Great Britain retaining ultimate control over all foreign affairs until the *Statute of Westminster 1931*[14] and over amendments to Canada's Constitution until 1982.[15] Canada expanded its territorial base considerably by acquiring western and northern lands held by the Imperial Crown and the Hudson's Bay Company under Royal Charter in 1870.[16] The Federal government immediately launched upon a campaign to negotiate treaties with the Indian nations in the southern portions of these areas, in order to enable agriculture, forestry and mining activities to occur on a large scale, along with the influx of settlers.

---

[13] *British North America Act, 1867* 30 & 31 Vict, c 3 (renamed in 1982 as the *Constitution Act, 1867*).

[14] 22 George V, c 4 (UK) (reprinted in RSC, 1985, App II, No 27).

[15] *Canada Act 1982* (UK) c 11.

[16] This massive territory was admitted through the *Rupert's Land Act 1868*, 31–2 Vict, c105 (UK) by Order in Council of 23 June 23 1870, effective 15 July 1870.

The number treaties

The so-called 'number treaties' (numbered from 1–11 as they were negoti-ated from 1871 to 1921, with adhesions to Treaty No 9 signed as late as 1930) followed the pattern set by the two *Robinson Treaties* of 1850. The written form, in English, of each treaty involved the surrender of vast tracts of land by Indian leaders on behalf of their populations to the Federal Crown. In return, they were given promises of annual payments, the setting aside of small parcels as exclusive Indian reserves for particular communities, guarantees of continued hunting and fishing rights and occasional other benefits (such as schools, farming implements, ammunition, medical supplies etc). The Indigenous version of the treaty negotiations and the oral promises made during the discussions is asserted, consistently, to differ dramatically from the 'official' text.[17] Many Indian elders have relayed stories of the negotiations as focusing on sharing the territory with the newcomers rather than surrendering the land absolutely. Many also allege that only the surface of the land ('to the depth of a plough') was being shared, but not the subsurface resources, and that the territory was to be left undamaged. Few of the Indian participants could anticipate the large-scale settlements that were to occur, or how the influx of farmers and foresters would fundamentally alter the landscape in a way that would virtually destroy the traditional economy in the southern portion of the Prairies in only a matter of a few years.

The advent of the residential school system, enforced vigorously through pass laws and the actions of police and government officials, cou-pled with the drastic reduction in game and trapping income, left many Indian communities devastated. The Métis nation was largely left even more destitute, as no communal land base was provided, while most Métis recipients of individual entitlements to blocks of land were defrauded under the scrip scheme that was imposed.[18]

Indian reserves

The passage of time led to a significant shift in Federal government attitudes, as Indian people were thought to face either extinction as a race (in part through the massive death toll from imported diseases) or complete absorp-tion into Canadian society as an underclass of farm workers and domestic labourers. Indian reserves became the vehicle to 'smooth the dying pillow'

---

[17] For examples of this differing perspective, see Treaty 7 Elders and Tribal Council with Walter Hildebrandt, Sarah Carter and Dorothy First Rider, *The True Spirit and Original Intent of Treaty 7* (McGill-Queen's University Press, Montreal, 1996); Richard Price (ed.), *The Spirit of the Alberta Indian Treaties* (Institute for Research on Public Policy, Montreal, 1979).

[18] Donald Purich, *The Métis* (James Lorimer & Company, Toronto, 1988).

or to serve as a laboratory for social re-engineering and assimilation. This perception was far removed from the days of viewing sovereign Indian nations as military allies and valuable trading partners. Treaties became anachronistic documents that had outlived their purpose and were neither to be renewed nor replicated elsewhere. All of this was to change, however, with the decision of the Supreme Court of Canada in *Calder v Attorney General of British Columbia*.[19]

The modern treaty era

The *Calder* case

The *Calder* case was launched by the Nisga'a nation of northwestern British Columbia as the latest salvo in their century long struggle to have their land rights recognised by the Crown. They went to court asserting their rights through the common law doctrine of aboriginal title over their traditional territory. Although they lost at trial, before the provincial court of appeal and ultimately before the Supreme Court of Canada, (on the procedural basis that they did not have the consent ('fiat') of the Crown in right of British Columbia to sue the government at a time when Crown immunity was still absolute), six of the seven judges concluded that the aboriginal title doctrine was still good law in Canada. While these six judges were evenly split on whether or not the aboriginal title of the Nisga'a had been effectively extinguished by general public lands legislation during the colonial era, they all were of the view that the Nisga'a had never surrendered their title by treaty or lost it through conquest. They were of the view that title could only have been extinguished by unilateral Crown action, with the judges differing on the level of explicitness required to meet the test for extinguishment. Even the leading judgment that ruled against continuing aboriginal title still stated:

> ... the fact is, that when the settlers came, the Indians were there, organized in societies and occupying the land as their forefathers had done for centuries.[20]

The aftermath of this landmark decision was enormous, as the Federal government completely recast its previous views and accepted that aboriginal title was likely still to exist in large parts of Canada where no historic treaty had previously been negotiated. The government issued a major policy pronouncement in August of 1973, in which it proposed to negotiate comprehensive land claims agreements based upon unextinguished aboriginal title in the form of modern treaties. Litigation immediately

---

[19] [1973] SCR 313 ('*Calder*').
[20] Ibid, per Judson J.

ensued in the Northwest Territories[21] and Quebec[22] to take advantage of this more favourable legal climate. An agreement-in-principle was reached on 15 November 1974 among the Grand Council of the Crees, the Northern Quebec Inuit Association, the Federal and provincial governments, Hydro-Quebec and the James Bay Development Corporation as the first major land claims agreement in the modern era. The parties concluded the final, 455-page agreement the following November.

Major agreements

Major modern land claim settlements have been negotiated between the government of Canada, the relevant provincial or territorial government and the aboriginal titleholders over the past quarter-century as follows:

- The James Bay and Northern Quebec Agreements (1975)
- The Northeastern Quebec Agreement (1978)
- The Inuvialuit Final Agreement (1984)
- The Gwich'in Agreement (1992)
- The Nunavut Land Claims Agreement (1993)
- The Sahtu Dene and Métis Agreement (1994)
- The Nisga'a Agreement (2000)
- Nine individual Yukon First Nation Final Agreements based on the Council for Yukon Indians-Canada-Yukon Umbrella Final Agreement (1993) starting in 1995 with the last one signed in 2003 (two more were initialled in 2003)
- The Tlicho (Dogrib) Land Claim (2003)
- The Labrador Inuit Land Claims Agreement (2003).

These settlements confirm exclusive land rights for the Indian, Inuit and Métis participants of the relevant agreements that exist in Quebec, British Columbia, Yukon, Northwest Territories, Nunavut Territory and Labrador, totaling over 600,000 kilometres. Many of them also include self-government jurisdiction. In addition, there are six large Métis settlements in Alberta that have been set aside for the exclusive use of those communities by the provincial government. As a result, almost 7 per cent of Canada is today recognised as being exclusively in aboriginal hands.

---

[21] *Paulette v Registrar of Titles (No 2)* (1973) 42 DLR (3D) 8 (NWTSC); reversed on other grounds, [1976] 2 WWR 193 (NWTCA); affirmed on other grounds [1979] 2 SCR 628.

[22] *Kanatewat v James Bay Development Corporation* (Unreported, Quebec SC, 15 November, 1973) (interlocutory injunction granted); reversed by Quebec CA (Unreported, Quebec CA, 22 November, 1973); leave to appeal dismissed (3–2), [1975] 1 SCR 48.

Current and future treaties

The process of treaty making is a long way from being finished in Canada. Aboriginal communities are continuing to gain recognition that more and more of their traditional territory remains in their exclusive hands. There are aboriginal title claims under negotiation in the Northwest Territories, the Yukon, Labrador, Quebec, as well as one in the Ottawa Valley and more than forty-five covering much of British Columbia. One can also anticipate that aboriginal title-based land claims will begin at some stage in the future in the rest of Atlantic Canada concerning first nations as well as the Labrador Métis. Negotiations are also at last underway concerning the continuing legal and political significance of the treaties of peace and friendship of the early eighteenth century between the Mik'maq and Malecite nations and the British Crown in the aftermath of the *Marshall* decision.[23]

The issue of Métis land rights, both regarding instances of extensive fraud under the nineteenth-century scrip system in the Prairies, as well as based on aboriginal title, has yet to find a sympathetic ear among non-aboriginal governments in Canada (other than the negotiations involving the South Slave Métis Tribal Council, Canada and the Government of the Northwest Territories).[24] The recent decision of the Supreme Court of Canada in *R v Powley*[25] may advance the thinking in this regard, although the existence of aboriginal title for the Métis has yet to make it to court.

Land claims are also vigorously pursued by most first nations that relate to unfulfilled treaty promises for the creation of reserves and other breaches of lawful obligations concerning reserve lands and first-nations' resources. As of 30 September 2001, there were 452 specific land claims currently under review by the Federal Departments of Indian and Northern Affairs and Justice. There are a further 118 specific claims that have been validated by the Federal Department of Justice that are now under negotiation, while an additional forty-seven specific claims that were rejected by the Department of Justice have been appealed to the Indian Specific Claims Commission. The Government of Canada has identified 227 specific claims as 'settled' as of 30 June 2001; however, a number of these have been resolved through administrative measures rather than through formal land claim settlements, while others have simply been closed. A total of 1153 specific claims had been lodged with the Federal government between 1970 and 30 June 2002, meaning that more than 300 claims are still in early

---

[23] *R v Marshall (No 1)* [1999] 2 SCR 456 ('*Marshall*').

[24] See, Government of Canada, *South Slave Metis Tribal Council Land and Resource Negotiations* (1997) Department of Indian and Northern Affairs http://www.ainc-inac.gc.ca/nt/pt/pdf/ssm01_e.pdf at 19 December 2003.

[25] [2003] 4 CNLR 321(SCC) ('*Powley*').

stages of the process, while estimates of 1000–2000 more claims have been suggested. Whereas comprehensive claims are based upon unextinguished aboriginal title, specific claims focus upon the loss of specific reserve lands, Federal maladministration of band funds and failure to honour treaty promises in a manner that could be considered to breach Canadian law or equity.

First-nation jurisdiction

A further reality is that Federal and provincial governments are slowly recognising that first nations are not only entitled to govern themselves but should be allowed to get on with doing so. Thus, first nations are confirming their jurisdiction with the agreement of Federal, provincial and territorial governments through self-government agreements in various parts of the country that can take the form of treaties. Perhaps the most well-known and controversial example in this regard has been through the *Nisga'a Treaty* in British Columbia, whose validity has been challenged in a number of lawsuits, including one unsuccessfully initiated in 1999 by the British Columbia Premier Gordon Campbell. There are also nine self-government agreements in place in the Yukon, with the last one signed on 18 October 2003. There are also agreements-in-principle or final agreements on self-government with the Meadow Lake Tribal Council in Saskatchewan, the Sioux Valley First Nation in Manitoba, and the United Anishnabeg Council in Ontario as well as a number of sectoral agreements with the Mohawks of Kahnawake.

Treaty negotiations have been heavily affected by the jurisprudence that has evolved over the past twenty years in several critical respects. As discussed below, the courts have articulated a clear set of principles that must guide all efforts in interpreting the proper meaning to be given to both historic as well as modern treaties. The Supreme Court has also definitively established the existence of a fiduciary relationship between the Crown and aboriginal peoples that has received constitutional elevation through section 35 of the *Constitution Act 1982*.[26] Each of these basic tenets is having a profound impact upon the way in which both federal and provincial governments must interrelate with Indian, Inuit and Métis communities.

Treaty interpretation principles

Although writing in dissent, McLachlin J (as she then was) in *Marshall* summarised the established principles of treaty interpretation to be followed, where she stated (at paragraph 78):

---

[26] *Constitution Act 1982*, being schedule B to the *Canada Act 1982* (UK) c 11.

This Court has set out the principles governing treaty interpretation on many occasions. They include the following:

1. Aboriginal treaties constitute a unique type of agreement and attract special principles of interpretation: *R v Sundown* [1999] 1 SCR 393, 24; *R v Badger* [1996] 1 SCR 771, 78; *R v Sioui* [1990] 1 SCR 1025, 1043; *Simon v The Queen* [1985] 2 SCR 387, 404. See also J. [Sákéj] Youngblood Henderson, 'Interpreting Sui Generis Treaties' (1997), 36 Alta L Rev 46; L.I. Rotman, 'Defining Parameters: Aboriginal rights, treaty rights, and the Sparrow Justificatory Test' (1997), 36 Alta L Rev 149.
2. Treaties should be liberally construed and ambiguities or doubtful expressions should be resolved in favour of the aboriginal signatories: *Simon*, supra, 402; *Sioui*, supra, 1035; *Badger*, supra, 52.
3. The goal of treaty interpretation is to choose from among the various possible interpretations of common intention the one which best reconciles the interests of both parties at the time the treaty was signed: *Sioui*, supra, 1068–69.
4. In searching for the common intention of the parties, the integrity and honour of the Crown is presumed: *Badger*, supra, at 41.
5. In determining the signatories' respective understanding and intentions, the court must be sensitive to the unique cultural and linguistic differences between the parties: *Badger*, supra, 52–54; *R v Horseman* [1990] 1 SCR 901, 907.
6. The words of the treaty must be given the sense which they would naturally have held for the parties at the time: *Badger*, supra, 53 *et seq.*; *Nowegijick v The Queen* [1983] 1 SCR 29, 36.
7. A technical or contractual interpretation of treaty wording should be avoided: *Badger*, supra, *Horseman*, supra; *Nowegijick*, supra.
8. While construing the language generously, courts cannot alter the terms of the treaty by exceeding what 'is possible on the language' or realistic: *Badger*, supra, 76; *Sioui*, supra, 1069; *Horseman*, supra, 908.
9. Treaty rights of aboriginal peoples must not be interpreted in a static or rigid way. They are not frozen at the date of signature. The interpreting court must update treaty rights to provide for their modern exercise. This involves determining what modern practices are reasonably incidental to the core treaty right in its modern context: *Sundown*, supra, 32; *Simon*, supra, 402.

It is important to note, however, that these principles may be subject to modification when interpreting a modern treaty in which the aboriginal party has received the full benefit of legal counsel and is negotiating highly detailed documents through a lengthy period of time in a language with which they are comfortable. Décary JA in *Eastmain Band v Canada (Federal Administrator)*,[27] stated at paras 21–22:

---

[27] [1993] 1 FC 501 (CA) ('*Eastmain*').

We must be careful, in construing a document as modern as the 1975 Agreement, that we do not blindly follow the principles laid down by the Supreme Court in analyzing treaties entered into in an earlier era. The principle that ambiguities must be construed in favour of the Aboriginals rests, in the case of historic treaties, on the unique vulnerability of the Aboriginal parties, who were not educated and were compelled to negotiate with parties who had a superior bargaining position, in languages and with legal concepts which were foreign to them and without adequate representation.

In this case, there was simply no such vulnerability. The Agreement is the product of a long and difficult process of negotiation. The benefits received and concessions made by the Aboriginal parties were received and given freely, after serious thought, in a situation which was, to use their counsel's expression, one of **give and take**. All of the details were explored by qualified legal counsel in a document which is, in English, 450 pages long. The scope of the negotiations was such that, in subsection 25.5 of the Agreement, Quebec undertook to pay to the James Bay Crees and the Inuit of Quebec, **as compensation in respect to the cost of the negotiations**, the sum of 3.5 million dollars [emphasis added and footnotes deleted].

This approach has been revised somewhat by the Quebec Court of Appeal's adoption of a hybrid approach in *Commission scolaire crie c Canada*.[28] In that case, the Court expressly quoted the nine principles as outlined in *Marshall* by Chief Justice McLachlin, cited above, while also accepting the appropriateness of the more traditional contract law approach in *Eastmain*. As a result, the Court suggested that modern treaties should be interpreted according to the intentions of all of the parties, rather than automatically assuming that any ambiguities will be resolved in favour of the aboriginal signatory. At the same time, the Court also noted the fundamental importance of the subject matter in that case—education—to the Cree. The Court concluded that a liberal, generous interpretation was warranted to the provisions concerning the participation of the Cree in discussions establishing the annual budget for the Cree School Board.

The jurisprudence thus indicates that the Crown and its representatives must adhere to the general treaty principles that have been elaborated by the courts over the past thirty-nine years since the decision of the British Columbia Court of Appeal in *R v White and Bob*[29] in dealing with all historic treaties. However in recent decades these principles have become somewhat modified, but only slightly, when seeking to ascertain the true meaning of the language used in modern treaties and other agreements reached between aboriginal peoples and federal or provincial governments.

---

[28] [2001] JQ no 3881. Leave to appeal dismissed on 24 October 2002.
[29] (1964) 50 DLR (2d) 193 (BCCA).

Fiduciary relationship

The existence of a fiduciary relationship between the Crown and aborig-inal peoples has not been in doubt since the Supreme Court delivered its judgment in *Guerin v The Queen*.[30] Over the intervening years this relation-ship has been extended beyond the context of the *Indian Act* to encompass Inuit and Métis communities. Similarly, the fiduciary is truly the Crown, as opposed to a particular government, such that it applies to both the Crown in right of Canada as well as in right of the province. While it is not certain as to the precise extent of the Crown's specific fiduciary obligations that may arise and how it must balance any such duties with its continuing responsibility to govern in the best interests of all Canadians, it is evident that the 'honour of the Crown' is always at stake whenever the Federal or provincial governments are interacting with Aboriginal peoples *qua* peoples or collectivities.

Negotiating new treaties or seeking the resolution of breaches of existing ones inevitably brings the honour of the Crown and its position as fiduciary in to play. These negotiations will consistently include factors of integral importance to the present and future well-being of aboriginal peoples, such as land, natural resources, governance, financial assets and essential public services. At the same time, the Crown also functions as the 'owner' of over 90 per cent of the country, and is the ultimate regulator of how all the terri-tory and its resources will be used. All levels of non-aboriginal government in Canada have had a tendency to go about their decision-making processes with little or no regard to aboriginal concerns. This behaviour has sparked a series of lawsuits[31] that have challenged the validity of Crown action for failing to consult effectively, or at all, with first nations who are potentially affected by decisions concerning natural resource allocations, park creation, road construction, environmental assessments and other matters.

Conclusion

Treaty and agreement making has been fully resurrected to once again form the cornerstone of the Indigenous-settler relationship in Canada.

---

[30] [1984] 2 SCR 335.

[31] See *Nunavik Inuit v Canada* [1998] 4 CNLR 85 (FCTD); *R v Jack* [1996] 2 CNLR 113 (BCCA); *Mikisew Cree First Nation v Canada (Minister of Canadian Heritage) et al.* (2001) 214 FTR 48 (TD); *Taku River Tlingit First Nation v Ringstad et al.*(2002) 211 DLR (4th) 89 (BCCA), leave to appeal granted; *Haida Nation v British Columbia (Minister of Forests)* (2002) 5 BCLR (4th) 33 (BCCA), leave to appeal granted; see Tehan, this volume.

While this approach may have largely disappeared in the United States, it is very much alive in Canada at the present time.[32] Major comprehensive land claims agreements have been reached through most northern regions and are starting to be achieved in British Columbia. The business of finally fulfilling outstanding treaty land entitlements in the three Prairie Provinces is near completion. Self-government agreements involving the recognition of significant governance powers for first nations and Inuit communities over both their territories and their members are slowly being reached in various parts of the country. The fiscal capacity to exercise governmental powers in a meaningful way is lagging behind; however, here too, there are examples of successful negotiations. The jurisprudence on what constitutes a treaty and the continuing significance of treaty rights has been far more progressive in recent decades. These developments have, of course, been encouraged to a significant degree by the entrenchment of aboriginal and treaty rights in the Canadian Constitution in 1982.

On the other hand, the aboriginal rights of the Métis have been almost completely ignored by the federal government and all provincial governments (with the exception of Alberta). The recent Supreme Court decision in the *Powley case*[33] may help to transform this picture, although the early indications are that the Federal government will continue to see the Métis as a provincial 'problem'.

It must also be recognised that the majority of first nations are not at a land-claims table that will result in a dramatic change to their territorial base or their economic conditions. While non-treaty first nations and the Inuit have benefited from judicial respect for aboriginal title over the past 30 years, the outlook for most first nations with historic treaties in Ontario and the Prairies remains grim until a more 'needs-based' approach is adopted by governments—or unless the courts further broaden treaty interpretation to restore the original Indian perception that treaties were to confirm the sharing of the country's bounty for the benefit of all. In my view, such a radical departure in the jurisprudence is unlikely until non-aboriginal Canadians come to appreciate that they have had treaty rights too, as the primary beneficiaries of historic Indian–Crown treaty relationships. One can only hope that this realisation will become more widespread in the future.

---

[32] See Chartrand, this volume.
[33] *Powley* [2003] 4 CNLR 321 (SCC).

Chapter 3

The Formulation of Privilege and Exclusion in Settler States: Land, Law, Political Rights and Indigenous Peoples in nineteenth-century Western Australia and Natal

Julie Evans[*]

Introduction

British settler colonies were characteristic of a very particular colonial forma-tion: that of settler colonialism. As distinct from franchise colonies such as India, or slave colonies such as in the Caribbean, where resource value was maximised through the extraction of surplus value of the labour of the colonised, economic interest in settler colonies was vested primarily in the land. Although Indigenous labour was certainly called upon, in purely structural terms, the primary objective was in securing permanent control of the land and converting it to alienable private property. Moreover, unlike in colonies of exploitation, the settlers had come to stay, literally seeking to **replace** the Indigenous inhabitants on the land. With reference to the Natal and Swan River colonies,[1] this discussion addresses the formulation

---

[*] My thanks to Patrick Wolfe, David Philips, Patricia Grimshaw, Maureen Tehan and Damen Ward for their critical commentary on an earlier version of this chapter. The opinions expressed here are my own.
[1] Southern Africa and Western Australia respectively.

of settler privilege and Indigenous peoples' exclusion within this type of colonial structure more generally.

Reconciling liberty and empire: the notion of individual equality before the law

The category 'British subject' provides a useful vehicle for analysing the historical foundations of the structural inequalities that continue to characterise settler states. The umbrella designation British subject signified Britain's theoretical commitment to upholding the rights and freedoms not only of British settlers but also of the Indigenous peoples they dispossessed, appearing to reconcile the classically incompatible ideas of liberty and empire.[2] The argument to follow demonstrates the pliability of the term, showing how it operated ideologically to encompass opposing interests through a notion of individual equality while practically facilitating the installation of privilege and exclusion from settlement to nationhood. In beginning to address the term's association with fundamental principles that characterise the rule of law,[3] the chapter adds a colonial dimension to historical and jurisprudential accounts of the development of this central pillar of liberal-democratic theory, which has traditionally been represented as a purely internal product of European historical processes.[4]

The discussion first considers settler manipulation of Indigenous peoples' political and legal subjecthood in order to achieve an exclusively white

---

[2] David Armitage, *The Ideological Origins of the British Empire* (Cambridge University Press, Cambridge, 2000) 8.

[3] The rule of law is the opposite of the rule of power, a legal counter to tyranny and the arbitrary use of force. The idea of the rule of law in both its procedural and rhetorical forms is to prevent and redress injustice. This paper is part of a broader project that reflects on the meaning of the rule of law as it was being formulated in British colonies in the nineteenth century, including how its instantiation was made possible by the very actions it abhors, as well as by the principles and values it defends. The analytical framework assumes the rule of law to be not simply an abstract ideal but, like the law itself, actively constitutive of the 'normal order' it presupposes, both at home and abroad. The complexities of some of the key concepts unable to be elaborated here are discussed in the monograph 'The Rule of Law in the Colonial Encounter: Its Meaning and Instantiation in the Lands of Others', Julie Evans, currently in preparation.

[4] For related scholarship, see Martin Chanock, *The Making of South African Legal Culture 1902–1936: Fear, Favour, and Prejudice* (Cambridge University Press, Cambridge, 2001); Bruce Kercher, *An Unruly Child: A History of Law in Australia* (Allen & Unwin, Sydney, 1995); David Neal, *The Rule of Law in a Penal Colony: Law and Power in Early New South Wales* (Cambridge University Press, Cambridge, 1991); Martin Krygier, 'The Grammar of Colonial Legality: Subjects, Objects, and the Australian Rule of Law' in Geoffrey Brennan and Francis G. Castles (eds), *Australia Reshaped: 200 Years of Institutional Transformation* (Cambridge University Press, Cambridge, 2002), 220–260; Peter Fitzpatrick (ed.), *Nationalism, Racism and the Rule of Law* (Dartmouth Publishing Co., Aldershot, 1995).

electorate in Natal. There was a dual legal system in colonial Natal whereby Africans, while formally British subjects and equally amenable to colonial law for criminal offences, remained subject to African law in civil matters. This legal pluralism reflected the conventions of international law, such that in colonies acquired through conquest, pre-existing laws should be recognised unless formally extinguished by the new sovereign.[5] I argue that the operation of a separate native law, while appearing to preserve and protect native interests, was deployed to control the Indigenous population in the interests of the colony. For current purposes, I discuss the ways in which Indigenous peoples' **legal** subjecthood under native law was deployed to diminish their **political** subjecthood, effectively excluding them from political power in Natal.

The discussion then turns to Western Australia, where as British subjects Indigenous peoples were also entitled to the equal force and protection of British law.[6] But in contrast with the situation in Southern Africa, the Australian colonies were categorised as colonies of settlement in which pre-existing laws and customs would not be recognised. Britain adhered to this mode of acquisition—implying a unitary system of law—despite challenges in colonial courts both as to the factual accuracy of the claim to peaceful settlement and to the morality of imposing British law on those who had not acknowledged subjection.[7] In view of comprehensive summary procedures adopted in the Swan River colony from the late 1840s, I argue, however, that despite the determinations of British law, Indigenous peoples were placed under a separate system of criminal law that belied their status as equal subjects.

---

[5] W. Blackstone, *Commentaries on the Laws of England* (Clarendon Press, Oxford, 1765–9) Introduction, 105–6.

[6] Faced with numerous reports of frontier violence, by the mid-1830s, the British Colonial Office was 'strongly affirming that Aborigines were to be treated as British subjects for all purposes'. See A. Castles, *An Introduction to Australian Legal History* (Law Book Co., Sydney, 1970) 522. In terms of both the actual treatment of Aborigines—such as that discussed here—and the formal challenges heard in local courts concerning their amenability, including in *inter se* cases, however, their position before the law remained indeterminate in some colonies until well into the middle of the century. See Castles, *An Introduction to Australian Legal History*, ch 18; see also Bruce Kercher, 'The Recognition of Aboriginal Status and Laws in the Supreme Court of New South Wales under Forbes CJ, 1824–1836' in A.R. Buck, J. McLaren and N.E. Wright (eds), *Land and Freedom: Law, Property Rights and the British Diaspora* (Ashgate/Dartmouth, Sydney, 2001) 83–102.

[7] For discussion of the effect of the mode of colonial acquisition in an Australian context, see Castles, *An Introduction to Australian Legal History*, above n 6, chs 1–2; see also John Hookey, 'Settlement and Sovereignty' in Peter Hanks and Bryan Keon-Cohen (eds) *Aborigines and the Law* (Allen & Unwin, Sydney, 1984) 1–18. Court cases addressing the amenability of Aboriginal people to British law for *inter se* offences (*R v Ballard* (1829); *R v Murrell* (1836) and the *Bon Jon* case (1841)) and Justice Cooper's 1840 determination that the Milmenrura people were not amenable to British law are also outlined in Kercher, *An Unruly Child*, above n 4.

While the colonial legal systems of Natal and Western Australia differed, they operated to produce similar discriminatory provisions that would secure settler privilege at the expense of Indigenous peoples. The analysis suggests, therefore, that the rule of law could be installed for settler subjects in these colonies in part through its abrogation in relation to Indigenous subjects as the land was being transferred. In effect, in establishing 'the normal order', the rule of law not only anticipated but enabled in the colonies the formation of the nation-state it had fostered in Britain—a nation-state which had itself been formed through conquest, coercion and colonialism.

The 'freeborn Englishman': the development of individual rights at home and abroad

Given Britain's theoretical commitment to equality between its subjects, discriminatory policies that maintained settler dominance in the colonies had to be skilfully worded in order to avoid disallowance by the Colonial Office. This careful manipulation was particularly apparent in relation to the recognition of Indigenous peoples' political rights.

What did it mean to be an **Indigenous** British subject in terms of political rights in Britain's settler colonies in the nineteenth century? Precise definitions of political subjecthood became more urgent in these colonies following adoption of the 1839 Durham report,[8] whereby Britain would grant first representative and then responsible government. The impetus for self-government had arisen as a result of serious unrest in 1837 in Upper and Lower Canada. With the loss of the American colonies clearly to the fore, the report outlined gradual political autonomy as a means of placating settler aspirations to democracy while maintaining their loyalty to empire. The report's recommendations were implemented throughout the British settlements in the decades that followed. In formulating these new constitutions, administrators in Britain and the colonies had to consider who would be included in the franchise.

Despite the political, social and economic inequalities that characterised Britain at the time, the notion of the 'freeborn Englishman' had managed to accrue significant ideological purchase.[9] The first *Reform Act 1832* (UK) had fortified the struggle for democratic rights and in the face of significant upheaval throughout the country, political privileges would be extended to

---

[8] John George Lambton, Earl of Durham, 'Report on the Affairs of British North America' [1839] CHIHM 32374 *Colonial Government Journals* (Otherwise referred to as 'Report of Lord Durham on the Affairs of British North America' [1839]).

[9] See E.P. Thompson, *The Making of the English Working Class* (Pelican, Harmondsworth, 1968) ch 4.

middle and working-class men as the century wore on.[10] Meanwhile, the influence of humanitarian and evangelical lobbies on colonial administration, particularly in the 1830s and 1840s, saw this rhetorical commitment to protecting and promoting individual rights held out to all British subjects in the colonies, whether settler or Indigenous.[11]

As far as the Colonial Office was concerned, the new colonial constitutions should contain no discriminatory provisions on the basis of race, colour, class or creed.[12] Significantly, though, the incommensurability of this theoretical commitment to liberty and equality with the economic aims of settlement—predicated on the need to subject and dispossess these same Indigenous peoples—together with prevailing notions of European superiority, meant that caveats were placed on the possibility of full equality for Indigenous peoples as British subjects at the outset.

Given the primacy of the need to convert communal land to private property, political rights, in the first instance, were pegged to a property qualification throughout the colonies. There was still a property franchise in Britain at this stage, of course, where landed ruling-class interests had yet to test their privilege in a more broadly based electorate. But, over time, in the colonies, particularly where successful assimilation policies produced increasing numbers of educated and propertied Indigenous men, class-based restrictions alone would not be sufficient to bolster settler control or to ensure that social distinctions would not be bridged no matter how 'European' non-Europeans became.[13] More broadly based exclusions had to be sought.

The case of Natal

'Without distinction of class or colour'

Natal was granted representative government in 1856, three years after the neighbouring Cape Colony. The Cape had adopted a 'colour-blind' franchise on a relatively low property qualification that preserved the principle, if not the substance, of equality—at least until the 1870s, when the

---

[10] Further reforms were granted in 1867 and 1884. Women were not enfranchised until well into the twentieth century.

[11] Following abolition of slavery, humanitarians had turned their attention to the condition of Indigenous peoples. In 1837, the Aborigines' Protection Society was formed and a Select Committee recommended ameliorative measures throughout the empire. See Julie Evans et al., *Equal Subjects, Unequal Rights: Indigenous Peoples in British Settler Colonies 1830s to 1910* (Manchester University Press, Manchester, 2003) introduction and ch 1.

[12] Both in Britain and its colonies, women's franchise was yet to be generally considered.

[13] H. Bhabha, 'Signs Taken for Wonders: Questions of Ambivalence and Authority under a Tree outside Delhi, May 1817' in H. Bhabha, *The Location of Culture* (Routledge, London, 1994) 102–122.

influx of Africans to the colony through territorial annexations prompted further legislative restrictions on their political privileges. Secretary of State Newcastle had insisted on this low qualification in 1853, stating that:

> It [was] the earnest desire of Her Majesty's Government that all Her subjects at the Cape without distinction of class or colour should be united by one bond of loyalty and a common interest and we believe that the exercise of political rights enjoyed by all alike will prove one of the best methods of attaining this object.[14]

In Natal, though, the demographic balance was far less favourable to the settlers, and the anxiety about being 'swamped' within a mixed electorate much more acute. Accordingly, despite observing Britain's instructions that there would be no explicitly discriminatory provisions in its charter, the terms of Natal's franchise qualifications were much more stringent from the outset. The property requirement was set at 50 pounds (or 10 pounds annual rent), twice that of the Cape. At this stage, few individual Africans could have qualified for the vote.

Ironically, over the following decades, Britain's 'civilising mission'— meant to ameliorate the worst effects of colonisation by training compliant subjects through education and conversion to Christianity—would encourage mission-educated Africans in Natal to aspire to the political power that settlers had no intention of sharing. Settler fear of the consequences of a significant African electorate was exacerbated by the military threat they continued to face from Zulu resistance. Consequently, by the 1860s, the local legislature had begun to seek a more comprehensive means of discriminating between the rights of Her Majesty's subjects than the individual property qualification would allow.

Buttressing settler hegemony

The solution would be found in creating a powerful link between the legal and political subjecthood of Indigenous peoples in Natal and in breaking, for Indigenous peoples alone, the nexus between property and the franchise. For, despite signalling their alignment with settler economic interests, the more Africans converted to private property, the more their potential political leverage threatened settler control. By 1862, a Natal Select Committee on land tenure argued against the automatic property qualification:

> The only real qualification of exercising political privileges must be sought in the knowledge and intelligence of the individual ... the freehold franchise

---

[14] Newcastle to Cathcart, no. 40, 14 March 1853, Public Record Office, London, Colonial Office (PRO CO) 48/337.

[is] simply ... a convenient tangible test for determining the existence of the mental and moral qualifications.[15]

As already observed, while class might work to stave off opposition within Britain, it was an insufficient safeguard in the colonies, which increasingly drew upon and produced racialised understandings of difference to buttress colonial interests.[16] But given continued Colonial Office sensitivity to outright discrimination, even after the waning of humanitarian influence, race had to be coded in other ways if colonial politicians were to avoid disallowance of their legislation. As Natal would not gain responsible government until 1893, when it no longer had to rely on British troops following the military defeat of the Zulu, discrimination had to be carefully managed, as categorical exclusion could not be seen to infringe Britain's commitment to equality between its subjects.

Natal had a useful structural precedent to draw on. The colony had already developed a system of indirect rule through the Shepstone system, by which Africans were placed in 'locations' and mission reserves.[17] In areas less attractive to settlers, Africans could cultivate land and live according to 'native law' under local leaders who were, in turn, responsible to a variety of colonial officials, and ultimately to the Lieutenant-Governor, who was declared the supreme African chief.

This legal pluralism claimed to preserve African cultural practices and insulate them from the immediate imposition of colonial law, at least in civil matters. But the system also facilitated the control of Africans as a group, through curfews and pass laws which resulted in extensive surveillance, primarily to control the movement of labour in and out of white areas, while contributing handsomely to colonial revenue through the imposition of hut taxes.

It was this separate legal system, which theoretically provided for a degree of African autonomy, that would produce an almost exclusively white electorate in Natal in a way that individual property qualifications never could.

Formulating privilege and exclusion

In 1865, the Natal legislature passed the *Native Franchise Act*, declaring that only Africans who were exempted from native law could qualify for the

---

[15] Scott to Newcastle, no. 104, 24 September, 1863, PRO CO 179/68.

[16] Patrick Wolfe, 'Land, Labor, and Difference: Elementary Structures of Race' (2003) 106(2) *American Historical Review* 866–905.

[17] See Leonard Thompson, *A History of South Africa* (Yale University Press, New Haven, 1995) 97–99.

vote. Africans could apply for such exemptions if they owned property, could read and write and took an oath of allegiance to the Crown. But in choosing to fall exclusively within the jurisdiction of the common law and thereby opening up the possibility of qualifying for the vote, Africans had also to turn their backs on their traditional laws and culture.[18]

Even if consenting to these uncompromising terms, few were successful in acquiring the franchise. The right to vote under exemption was further dependant upon fulfilling a twelve-year residential requirement, holding letters of exemption for seven years and gaining the approval of three white settlers and a magistrate. Even then, the Lieutenant-Governor had ultimate discretion in the matter and could take public objections into account. In responding to the legislation, the Colonial Office deferred to 'local experience', claiming that the colonial government would be 'the best able to judge upon the precise mode in which a gradual admission [to the franchise] should be effected'.[19]

Africans as a group were effectively excluded from the franchise. In the 1907 election, only six Africans had registered to vote in an electorate of 24,000.[20] While ostensibly upholding native interests, Natal's system of legal pluralism had been openly harnessed to settler concerns, effectively curtailing Indigenous peoples' political subjecthood.

The case of Australia

The rejection of legal pluralism

In the Australian colonies, on the other hand, the indeterminacy about the legal status of Aboriginal people that was apparent in the mid-nineteenth century would eventually give way to colonial as well as Imperial endorsement of a unitary system of law. This colonial reiteration that under *terra nullius* pre-existing laws would not be recognised, enshrined British law as exclusively authoritative, even in *inter se* matters.[21] But despite the obvious contrasts with the legal pluralism that characterised colonial Natal, comprehensive discrimination would be similarly produced in the Australian

---

[18] Significant parallels can be drawn with legislation known as the *Gradual Civilization Act 1857* and the *Gradual Enfranchisement Act 1869* in Canada.

[19] Newcastle to Scott, no 355, 5 December 1863, PRO CO 179/68.

[20] Evans et al., *Equal Subjects, Unequal Rights*, above n 11, ch 7.

[21] See above n 6. For critical discussion of the complexity of these issue, see Gerry Simpson, 'Mabo, International Law, Terra Nullius and the Stories of Settlement: An Unresolved Jurisprudence' (1993) 19 *Melbourne University Law Review*, 195–210; see also Kercher, 'The Recognition of Aboriginal Status', above n 6.

colonies through the strategic manipulation of group—as opposed to individual—amenability, within the overall commitment to equality before the law.

The individual and the law

The belief that Aboriginal people should be amenable both to the **protection** and to the **force** of British law called on prevailing British beliefs about the need to defend the right of the individual, especially against arbitrary prosecution and punishment. Although not formally laid down by Dicey until 1885,[22] this basic principle of the rule of law was significantly prefigured in discourse and, in applying notionally both to coloniser and colonised, became one of the major ideological tools in the justification of empire.[23]

The specific nature of this appeal to individual rights was particularly conducive to colonial concerns in Australia. Certain influential local officials had already stated that the success of the civilising mission would depend on 'breaking the stranglehold' of Australian Indigenous customs, which were cast as collectively cruel and degrading. The application of civilised and disinterested British law, on the other hand, was seen as safeguarding the rights of the individual 'victims' of such customs. Significantly, though, for enhancing colonial control of the Indigenous population as a whole, the sole application of British law also offered the attractive possibility of severing the control of elders over the young.[24] Given the structural imperatives of settlement, colonial interests in perceiving Aboriginal people as a group could co-exist with discursive appeals to their rights as individuals.

The right of the individual goes to the heart of the rule of law and to the free market economy it promotes. While far from secured in the metropole by the mid-nineteenth century, such individual rights were even more attenuated in the colonies, in which rhetorical commitments to equality had as little credibility as the assertion that markets would be free. In common with Enlightenment philosophy, more generally, in positing as universal the interests of a demographically narrow group of people, such classic liberal ideologies worked to facilitate exclusion.[25] Accordingly, attempts to classify people more broadly before the law—so that the law

---

[22] A.V. Dicey, *Introduction to the Study of the Law of the Constitution* ((first published 1885) Macmillan, London, 1961).

[23] A.W.B. Simpson, *Human Rights and the End of Empire: Britain and the Genesis of the European Convention* (Oxford University Press, Oxford, 2001) 22–6.

[24] The Colonial Office, for example, endorsed and distributed the views of George Grey. See Russell to Hutt, no 38, 8 October 1840, PRO CO 397/5.

[25] Bhabha, above n 13; Michel Foucault, 'The Eye of Power' in C. Gordon (ed.) *Power/ Knowledge: Selected Interviews and Other Writings* (Pantheon, New York, 1980).

relates to them as a group rather than as individuals, as we have seen in the case of Natal—simply expedited colonial interests in minimising disruption to development.

Group versus individual rights: discrimination, race and law

This powerful distinction, whereby one's fate at the hands of the law could be determined not simply by one's individual actions so much as by one's membership of a group, was particularly open to abuse in relation to the criminal law. The distinction was certainly not unknown in Britain,[26] but was more explicit and more comprehensive in the colonies, where race became deeply embedded in the practical operation of the law.

Susceptible to reduction to physical appearance alone, group membership rendered those who had committed no crime legally liable, at least to suspicion, with a very real possibility of prosecution, punishment and worse, simply on the basis of perceived identity rather than according to incontrovertible evidence of individual criminal actions adjudicated in a court of law. Conceived and executed in bodily terms, law could fortify the already formidable ideological power of race to naturalise discrimination. Indeed, in formulating what amounted to comprehensive regimes of exclusion, law could produce race in the colonies as much as be enacted under its influence.

For current purposes, this discussion concentrates on the association between law and race in Western Australia, when, from the 1850s, Aboriginal peoples as a group would be subject to comprehensive summary procedures for 'crimes' for which settlers would be brought before a court of law.[27] This demand for extraordinary procedures correlated with conflicts over dispossession, suggesting that the installation of the rule of law for the settlers—in terms of establishing 'the normal order'—was contingent upon the capacity to tolerate its abrogation in relation to Aboriginal peoples. In this sense, the suspension of the rule of law was intimately related to, rather than separate from, its regular operation.[28] Within this framework, what might otherwise be viewed as an aberration, or quite simply as unlawful or unjust, was actually constitutive of the rule of law itself. That is, in suspending itself, the rule of law maintained itself.

---

[26] See for example the *Vagrancy Act 1824* (UK).

[27] See Russell to Hutt, no 64, 30 April 1841, PRO CO 397/5; see also Paul Hasluck, *Black Australians: A Survey of Native Policy in Western Australia, 1829–1897* ((first published 1942) Melbourne University Press, Melbourne, 1970) 142.

[28] See G. Agamben, *Homer Sacer: Sovereign Power and Bare Life* (Stanford University Press, Stanford, 1998).

Formulating privilege and exclusion in the Swan River colony: embodying discrimination in law

In April 1841, British Secretary of State for War and the Colonies, Lord John Russell, disallowed a Bill originating from Swan River, now Western Australia, proposing special summary procedures against the Aboriginal population. Western Australia had been declared a separate colony some twelve years earlier and Governor Stirling had proclaimed the equality of Aborigines before the law.[29] But as pastoral expansion extended away from the original settlement near Perth to encroach on the outer regions, more and more so-called 'collisions' were taking place between settlers and Aboriginal peoples. The official correspondence states that these conflicts arose mainly in the form of attacks on settlers' stock or provisions.

In the context of widespread concern about settlers 'taking the law into their own hands', Governor Hutt had argued that adopting discriminatory summary provisions would allow a fairer and more efficient means of bringing Aboriginal peoples involved in these 'collisions' before British law. Under the proposed legislation, local magistrates, themselves prominent settlers and landowners, would have the power to charge and sentence Aboriginal people suspected of crimes other than murder, rape and arson to up to twelve months' imprisonment, with the option of hard labour and no more than three dozen lashes of the whip.

It is important to observe that the Bill's origins did not lie simply in settlers and administrators wanting legal recourse to outright coercion— although this was no doubt the case for some of them, especially as settlement expanded. In addition to serious colonial and metropolitan concern about unlawful settler violence, there was at least one other compelling argument that the absence of such procedures actually did discriminate against Aboriginal peoples. Given the vastness of the colony, being charged with an offence and being unable to raise bail would potentially subject Aboriginal people to several months' incarceration before their cases could be brought before the Quarter-sessions hearings.

In responding to the proposal, Secretary of State Lord Russell sympathised with the difficulty of Hutt's position and acknowledged his 'spirit of humanity and zeal for [Aboriginal] welfare' but regarded such discriminatory application of the law as 'dangerous in its tendency as well as faulty in principle':

> By thus establishing an inequality in the eye of the law itself between the two classes on the express ground of national origin, we foster prejudices, and give a countenance to bad passions which unfortunately need no such

---

[29] Stirling to Earl of Aberdeen no 53, 10 July 1835, PRO CO 18/15.

encouragement. It is wise to sacrifice some immediate convenience with a view to maintain the general principle of strict legal equality ...[30]

In not according with the ordinary procedures of the law, the exercise of such discriminatory summary power had then proved unacceptable to the Crown. For the time being, at least, the civilised and civilising principles of the rule of law would prevail over the desire of settlers and colonial administrators to secure a more efficient means of dealing with Aboriginal peoples whose criminalised behaviour was inhibiting settlement.

But by 1847, another Secretary of State, Earl Grey, approved the summary procedures Lord Russell had disallowed, with a reduction in the sentence to six months, and two rather than three dozen lashes of the whip.[31] With 'safeguards in the composition of the Bench',[32] the Aboriginal peoples of Western Australia, purely on the basis of belonging to the category Aboriginal rather than settler, were made legally subject to the arbitrary procedures of summary justice in place of the right to be brought before a court of law. Section VI of the Ordinance got to the heart of the matter, stating that convictions under these summary powers would stand:

> without setting forth the name of any witness, or the place where the offence was committed, and without setting forth any part of the evidence or stating the facts or the offence in any more particular manner than shall be necessary to shew that the offence was one triable under this Ordinance.[33]

The 1849 Ordinance introduced a much harsher period of colonial rule in Western Australia, and the Colonial Office's previous commitment to upholding strict equality of individuals under the rule of law gave way to tolerance of discriminatory provisions.[34] Tellingly, the maximum six-month penalty had grown to three years by 1859, and by 1874 the legislation was extended to those deemed 'half-caste'. By 1883, when the northern regions were being claimed, one justice alone could exercise summary power (if there was not another within 20 miles) and after the granting of responsible government, the penalty he could authorise had been extended to five years.[35] While settler subjects could also be tried summarily and, for some

---

[30] Russell to Hutt, above n 27

[31] Grey to Irwin, no 52, 12 September 1847, PRO CO 397/7.

[32] Hasluck, *Black Australians*, above n 27, 142

[33] *An Ordinance to Provide for the Summary Trial and Punishment of Aboriginal Native Offenders in Certain Cases*, 12 Victoria, no 18, 1849.

[34] Hasluck, *Black Australians*, above n 27, 140–2; see generally Elizabeth Ecclestone, *Fear, Favour or Affection: Aborigines and the Criminal Law in Victoria, South Australia and Western Australia* (Australia National University Press, Canberra, 1976); see also Enid Russell, *A History of the Law in Western Australia and its Development from 1829 to 1979* (University of Western Australia Press, Perth, 1980).

[35] Peter Biskup, *Not Slaves, Not Citizens: The Aboriginal Problem in Western Australia* (University of Queensland Press, St. Lucia, 1973) 22.

offences, might also be whipped, Aboriginal subjects could not elect to go before a jury; they had no right of appeal, the range of offences for which they could be tried under summary jurisdiction was far greater, and their penalties heavier.[36] Race, of course, elaborated the meaning and effects of these extraordinary procedures for Aboriginal people in ways that were completely unknown for settlers.

It is clear that Grey's endorsement of the summary provisions would be, as Russell had feared, the thin edge of the wedge. Grey was not unaware of the import of his decision, however, disclaiming any more general principle throughout the British dominions that native peoples would be subject to a different course of criminal procedure from other British subjects. 'Such a principle', he said, 'would ... contravene the plainest rules of justice'.[37]

In the case of Western Australia, summary procedures were administrated by a powerful alliance comprising local magistrates, the police and landowners, whose joint commitment to the transfer of the land and the entrenchment of middle-class values provided the framework within which they could perceive and exercise their summary powers.[38] Under this discriminatory legislation, Aboriginal people as a group were subjected to extraordinary procedures that could allow the punishment of those who had committed no crime but who could be suspected simply on the basis of their appearance alone. In this sense, and within the grim politics of the settler-colonial encounter, the possibility to rule by terror—by inducing general anxiety and alarm within a designated population and by opening the way for arbitrary prosecution—could operate in tandem with the rule of law as the nineteenth century wore on.[39]

Conclusion

In spanning the realms of law and politics throughout the period under consideration, the ideological significance of the term British subject would be both broad and enduring. By the end of the century, the term would be once again invoked as these colonies were preparing for nationhood. Natal's Prime Minister would declare the ordinary right of a British subject

---

[36] Hasluck, *Black Australians*, above n 27, 142.

[37] Grey to Fitzgerald, no 11, 2 June 1848, PRO CO 397/7.

[38] 'in the outback settlements the unavoidable fact is that when [an Aborigine] appears before local justices he appears before people who, as a class, have a very strong interest in his case and who may be the very persons he is alleged to have wronged.' Hasluck, *Black Australians*, above n 27, 142.

[39] See J. McGuire, 'Judicial Violence and the "Civilising Process": Race and the Transition from Public to Private Executions in Colonial Australia' (1998) 29 (3) *Australian Historical Studies*187–209.

the right to freedom and access to the protection of the law. The right to the franchise, on the other hand, was a 'race privilege' that only whites could exercise.[40] Although the *apartheid* regime was still to come, the seeds of its foundation were sown in such colonial soil. Similarly, in the decade preceding federation in Australia, Western Australian politicians would be foremost among those decrying any mention of the word citizen in the new federal constitution. 'Subject of the Queen' was a much safer term that could accord greater latitude to discriminate—and the term soon would countenance legislation to disenfranchise the nation's Indigenous peoples and would oversee the new century's race-based regulation and control.[41]

Antony Anghie has argued that 'the construction of the barbarian as within the reach of the law but outside its protection' was a powerful boon to the project of establishing European sovereignty abroad.[42] While Anghie is concerned to understand the operations of law and sovereignty in their international domains, the above analysis demonstrates that such a construction would be similarly useful domestically in naturalising the unequal application of British justice in relation to Indigenous peoples.

For while being legally determined under international law at the outset of settlement, sovereignty had still to be practically secured within the colonies, a task made both more difficult and more urgent where Europeans were outnumbered or where the land had yet to be comprehensively brought within colonial control.

The term British subject therefore both facilitated colonial governance and helped constitute the nation through its capacity to accommodate such strategic responses to settler concerns to establish their hegemony while at the same time upholding notions of justice and equality.

In using it to assist in charting the limits of the rule of law in the colonies, this study throws further light on these critical periods of colonial rule when settler privilege was being installed in the lands of others. The analysis demonstrates historically how the rule of law cannot prevail unless particular interests claimed as universal are able to prevail and clarifies its role in securing that predominance through normalising the interests of the settlers and by supporting the racialisation of those deemed to fall outside its full protection.

---

[40] Natal Legislative Council, extracts of debate on 2nd Reading of the *Franchise Law Amendment Bill* 20 June 1894, encl. in Hely-Hutchinson to High Commissioner, conf.,16 September 1895, PRO CO 119/92.

[41] See Julie Evans, 'Safer as Subjects than Citizens' in T. Banivanua-Mar and Julie Evans (eds), *Writing Colonial Histories: Comparative Perspectives* (RMIT Publishing, Melbourne, 2002): 165–83.

[42] Antony Anghie, 'Francisco de Vitoria and the Colonial Origins of International Law' in P. Fitzpatrick and K. Darian-Smith (eds), *Laws of the Postcolonial* (University of Michigan Press, Ann Abor, 1999) 89–107, 103.

Chapter 4

Land is Susceptible of Ownership

Noel Pearson

Introduction

Contrary to recent decisions of the High Court of Australia, the common law of native title recognises that Indigenous people in occupation of land are entitled to **possession** where the Crown has declined to expropriate their title by the act of State constituting the acquisition of sovereignty. McNeil's rigorous analysis in *Common Law Aboriginal Title*[1] was referred to by members of the Court in *Mabo v Queensland (No 2)*.[2] This chapter reiterates McNeil's analysis, with two amendments: first, that possessory title is not a claim to land separate from that of native or customary law title; and secondly, that Indigenous people have allodial possession rather than a fee simple on the presumption of a lost grant.

In its recent decisions in *Commonwealth v Yarmirr*,[3] *Western Australia v Ward*[4] and *Members of the Yorta Yorta Aboriginal Community v Victoria*,[5] the High Court has misinterpreted the definition of native title under the *Native Title Act 1993* (Cth) (*NTA*) and fundamentally misapplied the common law. Before turning to these two propositions, I will first set out the historic meaning of the High Court's decision in *Mabo*.

The three principles of native title

On 3 June 1992, the High Court finally illuminated the true legal history of the British colonisation of Australia. Properly understood, the law of the

---

[1] Kent McNeil, *Common Law Aboriginal Title* (Clarendon Press, Oxford, 1989).
[2] (1992) 175 CLR 1 (*'Mabo'*).
[3] (2001) 208 CLR 1 (*'Yarmirr'*).
[4] (2002) 191 ALR 1 (*'Ward'*).
[5] (2002) 194 ALR 538 (*'Yorta Yorta'*).

colonisers recognised a native entitlement to land from the time that sovereignty was first acquired. Contrary to the assumption that the land was *terra nullius*, the High Court confirmed that the common law of England, carried upon the shoulders of the colonists and falling upon Australian soil, included the doctrine of recognition of native title.[6]

The then-High Court had to contend with two compelling realities. First was the fact of original occupation and possession of Australia by its Indigenous peoples and the recognition of this by the imported common law. The second was that the recognition and protection of these original rights to the land did not occur until 204 years after sovereign acquisition, and the colonists and their descendants had acquired many titles and privileges over the course of the preceding two centuries. How was the fact that native title formed part of the common law of Australia, inherited from Britain, to be reconciled with the fact of colonial history and the accumulation of rights and titles on the part of the colonists and their descendants over 204 years?

In my view, the Mason and then Brennan Courts articulated three basic principles which set out a reconciliation of these two realities, and which should have formed the architecture for the final settlement of the longstanding and unresolved question of Indigenous land justice.

White land rights

The first principle was that non-Indigenous Australians who had accumulated rights and titles over two centuries could not be now disturbed in the enjoyment of their privileges, notwithstanding the circumstances by which they came to possess them. So the first principle of native title law in this country should be known to all Australians—though it is not—as the 'white land rights' principle: that the lands of the non-Indigenous people, including the lands alienated by the Crown for its own use, are indefeasible, and cannot now be disturbed by any claim to native title.

Leftover land title

The second principle was that, seeing as the whole country was once subject to native title, whatever lands were left unalienated after 204 years, was the entitlement of its traditional owners; and in all fairness title should be declared for their benefit forthwith.[7] In other words, the Indigenous people were entitled to whatever lands were left over. The remnant lands after

---

[6] *Mabo* (1992) 175 CLR 1, 58 (Brennan J), 109 (Deane and Gaudron JJ), 182 (Toohey J).
[7] Ibid, 70 (Brennan J).

two centuries were not substantial, the largest areas being in the desert and remote parts of the country.

Co-existence

The third principle, which was articulated in *Wik Peoples v Queensland*[8] in 1996, was that there were some larger tenures, such as pastoral leases and national parks, in which the Crown title could co-exist with native title, and in that co-existence the Crown-derived title prevailed over native title in the event of inconsistency.[9]

These three principles, if properly understood, and if faithfully followed, potentially laid the foundations for a just settlement of the historic grievance about land justice which lay unresolved between the old and new Australians.

Alas, it has not turned out this way. Ten years after *Mabo* we are engaged in expensive and time-consuming battles over whether remnant lands should now be declared in favour of Indigenous peoples and whether a subservient native title should co-exist with Crown titles where the latter always prevails over any native title.

What is not understood about native title claims after *Mabo*, and certainly after the *NTA*, is that it is simply not possible for non-Indigenous parties to lose any legal rights or title as a consequence of a native title finding. These land claims are not true litigations in the sense that either party may suffer loss as an outcome. Non-Indigenous parties to land claims can never lose any of their rights or titles, because these were either indefeasible under the common law—and if they were ever invalid, the *NTA* has now cured any invalidities.[10]

The only party that can truly lose in a native title claim is the Indigenous claimant. The non-Indigenous parties to claims—including the Crown— have nothing to lose on their own part, only an argument to the effect that the Indigenous people have no entitlement.

The travesty of the current native title system in Australia, and the reason the process is not delivering on the justice which the principles of *Mabo* set out, lies in the fact that non-Indigenous parties are allowed to oppose claims for native title even though they have no rights or interests that are vulnerable as a result of a native title finding.[11] These third parties

---

[8] (1996) 187 CLR 1 ('*Wik*').
[9] See, for example, ibid, 249 (Kirby J).
[10] See *Native Title Act* div 2, div 2A, div 2AA.
[11] More than 500 parties joined the *Yorta Yorta* litigation, alleging that they had interests that were affected by the claim. See further, Wayne Atkinson, '"Not One Iota" of Land Justice: Reflections on the *Yorta Yorta* Native Title Claim 1994–2001' (2001) 5 *Indigenous Law Bulletin* 19, 21–2.

are in an extraordinary position: all of their rights and interests are guaranteed by the common law and by validating legislation, and the Attorney-General pays for their legal costs—so they have nothing to lose by refusing to consent to native title determinations under the framework of legislation which was founded on the assumption that most claims could be settled by mediation and negotiation. If you can never ultimately lose, and the Attorney-General is paying your legal costs, you can resist native title until the cows come home. And, parliaments and the judicial system assume that you are a vulnerable party in the native title claims process, without actually understanding the clear truth: that non-Indigenous Australians are completely secure in their entitlements and can never lose a vested right, or even an expectation of a right as a result of the broadening of the definition of 'past acts'[12] in legislation.

The country forgets that, in April 1993, when Indigenous leaders met with Prime Minister Paul Keating to discuss impending legislation responding to *Mabo*, it was the Indigenous leadership that proposed support for legislation validating non-Indigenous titles that were uncertain as a consequence of the operation of the *Racial Discrimination Act 1975* (Cth). To the extent that non-Indigenous rights were uncertain after *Mabo* it was Indigenous people who proposed the validation of these uncertain titles.[13] This was a gracious concession on our part in 1993. But the position of other parties to native title over the past decade has essentially been this: not only do we want our own rights and titles to be secure, we will resist any claims for remnant native titles as well.

Let me now turn to the two propositions I alluded to in the beginning of this chapter. The first concerns the misinterpretation of s 223(1) of the *NTA*, namely, the very definition of native title.

---

12 *Native Title Act* s 228.
13 The document handed to the Prime Minister was called the 'Aboriginal Peace Plan'. An account of this document and this meeting between Indigenous leaders and the Prime Minister is set out in Aboriginal And Torres Strait Islander Social Justice Commission, *First Report*, 1993. Then Commissioner Dodson wrote:
The Aboriginal Peace Plan contained eight principles, including:
• protecting native title interest by requiring the titleholders to consent to any future dealings in native title land,
• expanding the basis of claims to include people who cannot claim traditional connection to land,
• ensuring future claims for native title could be made more simply,
• establishing a process for settlement of future claims.
In return, the Aboriginal Peace Plan proposed to accept the validation of interests granted over native title land which may have been invalid because of the *Racial Discrimination Act*. The validation proposal said that compensation should be negotiated, not decided upon by government.

The misinterpretation of the *NTA* s 223(1)

Section 223(1) reads:

> The expression **native title** or **native title rights and interests** means the communal, group or individual rights and interests of Aboriginal peoples or Torres Strait Islanders in relation to land or waters, where:
>
> (a)   the rights and interests are possessed under the traditional laws acknowledged, and the traditional customs observed, by the Aboriginal peoples or Torres Strait Islanders; and
>
> (b)   the Aboriginal peoples or Torres Strait Islanders, by those laws and customs, have a connection with the land or waters; and
>
> (c)   the rights and interests are recognised by the common law of Australia.

In my respectful view, the Court's decisions in *Yarmirr*, *Ward* and now *Yorta Yorta*, have yielded a complete misinterpretation of a fundamental provision of the *NTA*.[14] I am in respectful agreement with the judgment of his Honour, Justice McHugh, in *Yorta Yorta* in relation to s 223(1).[15] This definition was intended to make clear that native title was whatever the common law of Australia decided it was. Paragraphs (a) and (b) of s 223(1) were intended to faithfully reflect the key requirements of the common law as set out in the judgment of Justice Brennan, as he then was, in *Mabo*. They were not intended to supplant or in any way amend or supersede the definition of native title at common law.

And yet, the court has basically taken the view that the *NTA* has somehow 'transmogrified'[16] the common law meaning of native title; that the starting point—and ending point—for the definition of native title is

---

[14]   See Noel Pearson, 'The High Court's Abandonment of the Time-Honoured Methodology of the Common Law in its Interpretation of Native Title in *Mirriuwung Gajerrong* and *Yorta Yorta*' (Paper presented at the Sir Ninian Stephen Annual Lecture 2003, University of Newcastle, Newcastle, 17 March 2003), online at Cape York Partnerships http://www.capeyorkpartnerships.com at 4 December 2003.

[15]   *Yorta Yorta* (2002) 194 ALR 538, 571–3 (McHugh J).

[16]   While the judgments in *Yarmirr*, *Ward* and *Yorta Yorta* do not refer to the common law rights in *Mabo* being 'transmogrified' by the *NTA*, this seems to be the assumption on the part of all justices other than McHugh J and perhaps Callinan J. This underlying assumption was articulated most explicitly by Kirby J during the course of argument in *Ward* (Transcript of Proceedings, *Western Australia v Ward* (High Court of Australia, Kirby J, 6 March 2001)):
>   KIRBY J: You seem to be starting your submissions with the common law. You are going back to *Mabo* and to what Justice Brennan said and so on.
>   MR BARKER: Yes, I am, your Honour.
>   KIRBY J: Is not the starting point now, the river having moved on, the statute, because the people in Parliament have, as it were, taken another step? Recognition by the common law is one element in what Parliament has provided, but **the starting point now is surely the Act of the Federal Parliament** (emphasis added).
>   And later:

legislation that was intended to protect, not define, the title. As a result, in *Ward* and *Yorta Yorta*, the entire discussion of native title is treated as an exercise in statutory interpretation rather than an articulation of the common law. Important questions concerning the concept and nature of native title, its content, extinguishment and proof are dealt with, without any reference to the large body of common law of which Australian native title forms a part.

Even a circumspect party to the Australian native title story since *Mabo*, Justice French, the first President of the National Native Title Tribunal, makes clear that the High Court's interpretation of s 223(1) defied reasonable understandings and expectations:

> Most recently, in *Members of the Yorta Yorta Aboriginal Community v Victoria* ... the High Court again emphasised the statutory definition of native title as defining the criteria that had to be satisfied before a determination could be made. To that extent the Court appears to have moved away from the original concept of the Act as a vehicle for the development of the common law of native title.[17]

His Honour went on to say:

> The way in which [the High Court in *Yorta Yorta*] applies the words of ss 223(a) and (b) of the Act to the determination of native title rights and interests may have transformed the Act from a vessel for the development of the common law into a cage for its confinement.[18]

KIRBY J: ... At least on one view, the passage of the *Native Title Act* **transmogrified** the common law entitlements. It is an Act valid on the face of it, it has been enacted under the powers that are given by the Constitution to the Federal Parliament. It talks of 'title', and it provides for the recognition of native title as defined—that is in section 10—it provides for limits on extinguishment in section 11, and, at least in my view at the moment, **foraging around amongst what members of this Court said before the Federal Parliament within its constitutional power provided for native title, its recognition and limits on its extinguishment, is just misconceived. It is starting at the wrong place.**
We have title, we have native title, but we have it under an Act of the Federal Parliament, the validity of which is not challenged, and at least orthodox approaches would suggest that you then look into the Act with the benefit of the past, but not controlled by the past. You are giving meaning to what the Federal Parliament, within its constitutional power, has provided. It has talked of 'title' and therefore **you have to give content to an Act, not forage around amongst the predecessor provisions of the common law** (emphasis added).

[17] Justice Robert French, 'A Moment of Change—Personal Reflections on the National Native Title Tribunal 1994–1998', (2003) 27 (z) *Melbourne University Law Review* 488, 520; see also Maureen Tehan, 'A Hope Disillusioned, an Opportunity Lost? Reflections on Common Law Native Title and Ten Years of the *Native Title Act*', (2003) 27 (2) *Melbourne University Law Review* 523, 558–64.

[18] French, above n 17, 521.

A search of the cases cited in *Ward* and *Yorta Yorta* reveals that hardly any cases are canvassed in support of the Court's conclusions on the state of Australian law. There is absolutely no reference in either of these Australian cases to what is the seminal Canadian decision on native title, and in my view the most important decision on the subject since the High Court's decision in *Mabo*, namely the decision of the Supreme Court of Canada in *Delgamuukw v British Columbia*.[19] Given that *Delgamuukw* dealt with the very issues that were at issue in *Ward* and *Yorta Yorta*, it is startling that no reference[20] is made to it in Australian law. Indeed *Mabo* itself is only referred to for its place in the chronology of native title in Australian law, rather than for the purposes of discussing its articulation of the common law.[21]

In my respectful view, the Court has drawn a transparent and convenient line between the common law of native title up to the time of the passage of the *NTA*, and its subsequent articulation in Australian law, where the meaning of native title is treated as a question of statutory interpretation. This leaves Australian pronouncements on native title open to

---

[19] [1997] 3 SCR 1010 ('*Delgamuukw*').

[20] The only reference, in *Ward* (2002) 191 ALR 1 at 34, 36 and 177 is to Lambert J's judgment in the British Columbia Court of Appeal's decision in *Delgamuukw v British Columbia* (1993) 104 DLR (4th) 470. There is no reference in any of the cases to the Supreme Court's decision in *Delgamuukw*.

[21] In their joint judgment in, *Yorta Yorta* (2002) 194 ALR 538, 558, Gleeson CJ and Gummow and Hayne JJ almost dismiss the relevance of *Mabo* to the meaning of native title:

> The legal principles which the primary judge considered were to be applied to the facts found were principles which he correctly identified as being found in the *Native Title Act's* definition of native title. It is true to say that his Honour said that this definition of native title was 'consistent with' language in the reasons in *Mabo (No 2)* and that it was, in his Honour's view, necessary to understand the context in which the statutory definition was developed by reference to what was said in that case. **It may be that undue emphasis was given in the reasons to what was said in *Mabo (No 2)*, at the expense of recognising the principal, indeed determinative, place that should be given to the *Native Title Act*** (emphasis added).

In *Yarmirr* (2001) 208 CLR 1, 39, Gleeson CJ, Gaudron, Gummow and Hayne JJ had said that while the *NTA* should be the starting point of any inquiry, it should be understood as 'supplementing the rights and interest of native title holders under the common law of Australia'. Later in *Ward* (2002) 191 ALR 1, 16, Gleeson CJ, Gaudron, Gummow and Hayne JJ moved the emphasis decisively towards the legislation:

> No doubt account may be taken of what was decided and what was said in [*Mabo*] when considering the meaning and effect of the *NTA*. This especially is so when it is recognised that paras (a) and (b) of s 223(1) plainly are based on what was said by Brennan J in *Mabo (No 2)*. It is, however, of the very first importance to recognise two critical points: that s 11(1) of the *NTA* provides that native title is not able to be extinguished contrary to the *NTA* and **that the claims that gave rise to the present appeals are claims made under the *NTA* for rights that are defined in that statute** (emphasis added).

And later:

> Yet again it must be emphasised that **it is to the terms of the *NTA* that primary regard must be had, and not the decision in *Mabo (No 2)* or *Wik*.** The only present relevance of those decisions is for whatever light they cast on the *NTA* (emphasis added).

bare assertion, as the body of the common law dealing with native title is rendered irrelevant because the legislation is treated as having superseded the common law. That this is what has happened is readily evidenced by a perusal of the cases cited in *Ward* and *Yorta Yorta*.

It is not possible in this paper to set out a complete refutation of the High Court's reasons for completely ignoring the common law on what is called 'aboriginal title' in Canada, and which we call 'native title'. The High Court has not given 'reasons', as much as expressed bald assumptions, beginning with Justice Kirby's over-generalised dismissal of overseas precedents in his decision in *Fejo v Northern Territory*:

> Care must be exercised in the use of judicial authorities of other former colonies and territories of the Crown because of the peculiarities which exist in each of them arising out of historical and constitutional developments, the organisation of the indigenous peoples concerned and applicable geographical or social considerations ...[22]

This statement underlies the approach taken by all of the members of the High Court to overseas precedents. The approach is in stark contrast to the judgments in *Mabo*, which drew heavily from other common law jurisdictions (and, indeed, Justice Brennan had specifically rejected as discriminatory[23] the notion that what Justice Kirby refers to as 'the organisation of the Indigenous peoples concerned' should ever be a factor in determining whether their rights to land would be respected by the common law). During the course of argument in *Ward*, Justice Gummow said that the applicability of the Canadian law in the Australian context was 'an important question'.[24] It was a question that remained unanswered in all of the judgments in that case, and indeed in the subsequent *Yorta Yorta* case. If the court has not been derelict in its duty to the Indigenous peoples of Australia in failing to give sound reasons for refusing to grapple with overseas precedents that are at odds with its preferred views, it has certainly made its task easier by relying upon the legislation rather than engaging with two centuries of precedent developed throughout the English common law world.

---

[22] (1998) 195 CLR 96, 98 ('*Fejo*').

[23] *Mabo* (1992) 175 CLR 1, 41–2 (Brennan J).

[24] Transcript of Proceedings, *Western Australia v Ward* (High Court of Australia, Gummow J, 6 March 2001):

> BARKER: Yes. There is no doubt, your Honour, that *Delgamuukw* sets up a contrary proposition, that Justice Lee strongly relied on it and we, indeed, strongly rely on it here. **We do not accept that on any proper reading of Delgamuukw the constitutional provisions infect the reasoning in a way that makes it inapplicable in the Australian common law.**
> GUMMOW J: **That is an important question**, I guess.
> MR BARKER: It is an important question, and I would like to come back to that as well, if I could (emphasis added).

If the Court's interpretation of s 223(1) of the *NTA* is to be accepted as correct, then the Parliaments that passed the 1993 legislation and the amendments of 1998 were under grave misapprehension as to what they had done. Indeed, Indigenous leaders and Prime Minister Paul Keating had assumed that the legislation simply protected native title from hostile extinguishment—that what was being protected by the legislation was the common law right.[25]

It is not enough to say that it is a misnomer to talk of native title as a 'common law right'.[26] Native title is not a common law title, but it is a title recognised by the common law.[27] The point about the common law and native title was well made by Justice McHugh in *Yorta Yorta* when he reviewed the statements made in Parliament in respect of s 223:

> ... I remain unconvinced that the construction that this Court has placed on s 223 accords with what the Parliament intended ... They showed that the Parliament believed that, under the *Native Title Act*, the content of native title would depend on the developing common law.[28]

Upon reflection, it should be readily appreciated that the one agenda of the Indigenous parties to the 1993 arguments about native title legislation was the concern that the common law rights articulated in *Mabo* be protected. We were vigilant against any attempt to replace or transform the common law rights to any form of statutory creature. Our understanding of s 223(1) was consistent with that of the Commonwealth, namely that it was intended to be a faithful reflection of the common law—no more and no less.

Now that the High Court has contradicted this position, it would seem to me that the most urgent reform to the Australian law on native title is to amend the definition of native title to make clear that native title means whatever the common law of Australia says that it means. Native title should be illuminated, not by bare assertion in respect of statutory provisions enacted to protect native title from extinguishment, but by what Justice MacLachlin, as she then was, described in that elegant phrase in

---

[25] See, for example, Commonwealth, *Parliamentary Debates*, House of Representatives, 16 November 1993, 2877–83 (Paul Keating, Prime Minister); Commonwealth, *Parliamentary Debates*, House of Representatives, 9 March 1998, 781–8 (Daryl Williams, Attorney-General).

[26] *Yorta Yorta* (2002) 194 ALR 538, 560.

[27] *Mabo* (1992) 175 CLR 1, 59, Brennan J said as follows: 'Native title, though recognized by the common law, is not an institution of the common law and is not alienable by the common law.'
And also 61: 'native title, being recognized by the common law (though not as a common law tenure)'.

[28] *Yorta Yorta*, (2002) 194 ALR 538, 572, per McHugh J.

R v Van der Peet,[29] quoted by Justice Gummow in *Wik,*[30] 'the time-honoured methodology of the common law'.[31]

The misapplication of the common law

Let me now turn to the second allegation concerning the misapplication of the common law in relation to the concept of native title.

It is now settled law that provided that the Crown did not, by act of state, extinguish the rights of the Indigenous people, their rights would continue after annexation. This is consistent with the so-called 'doctrine of continuity'[32] and *Mabo* and the *Native Title Act Case*[33] confirmed that the acts of state establishing the colonies of Australia did not extinguish the rights of the Indigenous inhabitants. While the principle that rights continue after the change of sovereignty is clear, what is unclear is '**what** continues?'

In his seminal treatise, *Common Law Aboriginal Title,* the Canadian Professor Kent McNeil applied the English law on possession to the position of Indigenous inhabitants at the time the British Crown acquired sovereignty.[34] He concluded that the fact of Indigenous occupation of land gave rise to the right to possession.[35]

McNeil's treatise is the most rigorous examination of the English common law on possession as applied to the situation of Indigenous peoples. He concluded, and the one judge that discussed this thesis in *Mabo*, Toohey J, accepted, that Indigenous people would be entitled to a so-called possessory title to land.[36] Both McNeil and Toohey J assumed that possessory title and native title—what McNeil called 'customary title' and his Honour called 'traditional title'—were separate concepts, and separate bases of claim to land by Indigenous people.[37]

In my respectful view, this assumption was in error. Rather than possessory title being separate from native or customary title to land, my view is that the common law on possession **applies to native title**. The principles concerning occupation and possession apply to native title. Indeed, if we return to the foundational cases on native title in the common law

---

[29] [1996] 2 SCR 507 ('*Van der Peet*').

[30] *Wik* (1996) 187 CLR 1, 184.

[31] *Van der Peet* [1996] 2 SCR 507, 377.

[32] McNeil, above n 1, 171–4; *Mabo* (1992) 175 CLR 1, 183 per Toohey J.

[33] *Western Australia v Commonwealth* (1995) 183 CLR 373 ('*Native Title Act Case*').

[34] McNeil, above n 1; see also Kent McNeil, 'A Question of Title: Has the Common Law been Misapplied to Dispossess the Aboriginals' (1990) 16 *Monash University Law Review* 91.

[35] McNeil, above n 1, 205–8.

[36] Ibid; *Mabo* (1992) 175 CLR 1, 207–13 (Toohey J).

[37] McNeil, above n 1, 195, 300, 241; *Mabo* (1992) 175 CLR 1, 178 (Toohey J).

world—namely, the decisions of the United States Supreme Court under Chief Justice Marshall in the early decades of the nineteenth century: *Johnson v McIntosh*[38], *Worcester v Georgia*[39] and *Mitchell v United States*[40]—we find that Indian title was founded on the fact of occupation of land, not in a primary sense on their traditional laws and customs. Sure, the Native American Indians lived on their land in accordance with their traditional laws and customs which determined entitlement between them and governed their internal affairs—but the protection afforded by the common law arose from the fact of occupation of their homelands. After a very careful analysis of the early United States cases, McNeil concluded as follows:

> The Crown (and hence the States or the United States, as the case might be) ... acquired the 'naked fee', which it could grant, subject always to the Indian right of occupancy ... That right, it seems, is generally the same throughout the United States: **it depends not on the particular customs or laws of individual tribes** (the general existence of which has none the less been acknowledged) ... **but on their actual occupation of lands** from what has occasionally been said to be 'time immemorial'...[41]

The core misconception centres on our understanding of what happened at the time of sovereignty, when the rights of the Indigenous inhabitants to their homelands continued under the doctrine of continuity. What continues after annexation? The rights and interests established under traditional laws and customs, or the right to occupy and possess the land under authority of, and in accordance with, the traditional laws and customs of the Indigenous people?

It has been assumed throughout the Australian discussion[42] of native title and through some of the Canadian discussion[43] up to *Delgamuukw*—

---

[38] 21 US 543 (1823).

[39] 31 US 515 (1832).

[40] 34 US 711 (1835).

[41] McNeil, above n 1, 255 (emphasis added).

[42] See, for example, *Mabo* (1992) 175 CLR 1, 58–9 (Brennan J), 88 (Deane and Gaudron JJ).

[43] Lambert J's interpretation of the doctrine of continuity in the British Columbia Court of Appeal's decision in *Delgamuukw v British Columbia* (1993) 104 DLR (4th) 470 is based on the assumption that it is the rights established under Aboriginal laws and customs which continue after annexation, and which is the 'source' of Aboriginal title. This was in contrast to the emphasis on occupation (rather than traditional laws and customs) in earlier decisions of the Supreme Court of Canada (*Calder v Attorney-General of British Columbia* [1973] SCR 313 (*'Calder'*) and *Guerin v The Queen* [1984] 2 SCR 335, (*'Guerin'*). In *Calder* at 328 Judson J spoke on behalf of three of the seven justices when he described Aboriginal title as follows:

> ... the fact is that when the settlers came, the Indians were there, organized in societies and occupying the land as their forefathers had done for centuries. This is what Indian title means and it does not help one in the solution of this problem to call it a 'personal or usufructuary right'. What they are asserting in this action is that they had a right to continue to live on their lands as their forefathers had lived and that this right has never been lawfully extinguished.

including that of McNeil[44]—that it is the rights and interests established under traditional laws and customs that continue. In my respectful view, the correct answer is that it is **the right to occupy and possess the land** under the authority of, and in accordance with, the traditional laws and customs of the Indigenous people, that survives annexation. The distinction is subtle, but crucial.

This distinction underlines that the foundation of native title is possession arising from occupation—not the details of traditional laws and customs. These laws and customs determine who is entitled to the possession, and it governs the internal allocation of rights, interests and responsibilities among members of the native community—but they do not determine the content of the community's title, which is possession. Possession being what Justice Toohey described as a 'conclusion of law' arising from the fact of occupation.[45]

Instead, our Australian law has misconceived native title by focusing on the traditional laws and customs of the Indigenous people. The end result—now evident from the High Court's decision in *Yorta Yorta*—is that in order to establish native title today, Indigenous claimants are forced to prove the details of their traditional laws and customs at the time of

---

In *Guerin* at 376 Dickson J said that *Calder* 'recognized aboriginal title as a legal right derived from the Indians' historic occupation and possession of their tribal lands'.

[44] McNeil, above n 1, ch 6. Following the British Columbia Court of Appeal's decision in *Delgamuukw* and before the Supreme Court's decision on the appeal, Kent McNeil analysed the judgments of the Court of Appeal in 'The Meaning of Aboriginal Title' in Michael Asch (ed.), *Aboriginal and Treaty Rights in Canada* (UBC Press, Vancouver, 1997) 135, 137 and commented on the source of Aboriginal title as follows: 'The courts seem to be vacillating between two possible sources of Aboriginal title—Aboriginal occupation and Aboriginal laws—without pronouncing in favour of one or the other.'

It was this search for a single answer to the question of 'what is the *source* of native or Aboriginal title?'—which has been the subject of much of the circular commentary on native title over the years—that led to the misconception which this paper is directed at. It is not a question of **choosing** between Aboriginal occupation or Aboriginal laws as the source of Indigenous title—both are relevant, because Indigenous title is sourced in **the occupation of land by Indigenous peoples under the authority of their Aboriginal laws and customs**. Aboriginal law determines:

(i) **who** is entitled to the communal possession which the common law recognises as arising from the fact of occupation of the land by a native community and

(ii) the **allocation of rights, interests and responsibilities** that are 'carved out of' of the communal possession, within the community of titleholders

Aboriginal law also contributes evidence of:

(iii) the **territory** to which the native community is entitled to possession

(iv) the **descent** of this entitlement to possession from the predecessor native community that held the title at the time of annexation, to the successor native community which holds the contemporary entitlement.

For a summary of my views on this matter, see Noel Pearson, 'Principles of Communal Native Title' (2000) 5 *Indigenous Law Bulletin* 4.

[45] *Mabo* (1992) 175 CLR 1, 207 (Toohey J).

sovereignty, when the English common law of possession would only require that claimants prove occupancy which precluded the Crown from obtaining beneficial title. An horrendous burden of proof has been placed upon native claimants, purely through the misconception of title arising from the misapplication of the common law.

This explication, that communal native title is a right to possession arising from the occupation of land by the predecessor native community at the time of sovereignty, also explains the content of the title which arises from occupation. The content of communal native title is the title which occupation affords, namely possession. Properly understood, communal native titles across the continent are not determined by what his Honour Justice Gummow described in *Yanner v Eaton* as the 'idiosyncratic' laws and customs of the particular native community.[46] These idiosyncratic laws and customs do determine those native title rights and interests that are variously described as 'pendant upon',[47] 'parasitic upon',[48] 'privileges of'[49] or 'carved out of'[50] the communal title. But the title of the community as a whole, as against the world, is a mundane possession. Following 1788, all communal native titles in the acquired colonies were the same. They all amounted to a uniform possession. If there is variation between communal native titles today it is because they have suffered some form of specific derogation by valid act of the legislature or Crown—not because they were originally diverse and determined by idiosyncratic laws and customs.[51]

Pendant native title rights and interests should be understood as constituting any right or interest to which possession gives rise, as regulated

---

[46] (1999) 201 CLR 351, 384 (Gummow J) (*'Yanner'*).

[47] *Western Australia v Ward and Others* (2000) 170 ALR 159, 186, 189, per Beaumont and von Doussa JJ.

[48] *Delgamuukw* 3 SCR 1010, 1080 [111] per Lamer CJ.

[49] *Yanner* (1999) 201 CLR 351, 384 per Gummow J:

> The exercise of rights, or incidents, of an Indigenous community's native title, by subgroups and individuals within that community, is best described as the exercise of privileges of native title. The right, or incident, to hunt may be a component of the native title of a numerous community but the exercise by individuals of the privilege to hunt may be defined by the idiosyncratic laws and customs of that community.

[50] *Mabo* 175 CLR 1, 61–62 per Brennan J:

> ... where an Indigenous people (including a clan or group), as a community, are in possession or are entitled to possession of land under a proprietary native title, their possession may be protected or their entitlement to possession may be enforced by a representative action brought on behalf of the people or by a sub-group or individual who sues to protect or enforce rights or interests which are dependent on the communal native title. Those rights and interests are, so to speak, carved out of the communal native title. A sub-group or individual asserting a native title dependent on a communal native title has a sufficient interest to sue to enforce or protect the communal title ...

[51] With respect, I believe it is the failure to grasp this point which leads McNeil to error in his interpretation of *Wik*, to which I make reference in note 54 below.

by traditional law and custom, and of course today, subject to any valid derogation or regulation by valid act of the legislature or Crown. Traditional laws and customs regulate the exercise of any and all of the rights and interests that flow from possession. This is where evidence of traditional law and custom is relevant.

However, in the Australian law as it now stands, it is assumed that native titles are entirely constituted by reference to traditional laws and customs adduced as a matter of proof.

There are two further sources for this misconception. Firstly, the term 'native title' is subject to a confusing conflation—it is used indiscriminately in the sense of the communal native title and also in the sense of the rights and interests that are carved out of the communal title.[52] But there is critical difference between the communal title and the pendant rights and interests. Mr Yanner's entitlement to hunt crocodiles is a right which is carved out of the communal title of his people. The right to hunt crocodiles is an incident of possession and the traditional laws and customs of the Gangalida people regulate Mr Yanner's exercise of rights under the communal tenure.

The problem is that the judicial and academic discussion of native title switches (often unconsciously) between the discussion of native title in its communal sense, and its pendant rights and interests sense, thereby causing conceptual confusion. The principles which apply to both senses of native title are critical and different. This is why the oft-quoted statement of Justice Brennan in *Mabo* is the source of so much of the confusion into which the Australian law has fallen, where he said:

> Native title has its origin in and is given its content by the traditional laws acknowledged by and the traditional customs observed by the Indigenous inhabitants of a territory. The nature and incidents of native title must be ascertained as a matter of fact by reference to those laws and customs.[53]

This statement is correct in relation to the native title rights and interests that are carved out of the communal title. But it is apt to mislead in relation to the description of communal native title.[54] After all, the title of

---

[52] Section 223(1) of the *NTA* conflates the two forms of title by including in the same definition 'native title' and 'native title rights and interests'; expressions which are said to 'mean the communal, group or individual rights and interests of Aboriginal peoples or Torres Strait Islanders in relation to land or waters'.

[53] *Mabo* (1992) 175 CLR 1, 58.

[54] In a 1997 article, 'Aboriginal Title and Aboriginal Rights: What's the Connection?' (1997) 36 *Alberta Law Review* 117 at 138–142, McNeil set out the most coherent understanding of Brennan J's judgment in *Mabo*—which corrected the prevailing misinterpretation in the Australian judicial and academic commentary. Despite the availability of this excellent analysis, it has been completely ignored—both by the judgments and by the submissions put forward by practitioners representing native claimants in Australia. It is not possible in

the Meriam people in *Mabo* amounted to 'possession, occupation, use and enjoyment', 'as against the world'—concepts known to the common law and not comprising the details of Meriam law and custom.[55] It is elsewhere in his judgment that Justice Brennan articulated the approach to understanding the nature of communal native title when he said:

> If it be necessary to categorise an interest in land as proprietary in order that it survive a change in sovereignty, the interest possessed by a community that is in exclusive possession of land falls into that category. Whether or not land is owned by individual members of a community, a community which asserts and asserts effectively that none but its members has any right to occupy or use the land has an interest in the land that must be proprietary in nature: there is no other proprietor … The ownership of land within a territory in the exclusive occupation of a people must be vested in that people: land is susceptible of ownership and there are no other owners.[56]

His Honour went on to describe the relationship between the communal title and the pendant rights and interests when he referred to *Milirrpum v Nabalco Pty Ltd*:[57]

> The fact that individual members of the community, like the individual plaintiff Aborigines in *Milirrpum*, enjoy only usufructuary rights that are not proprietary in nature is no impediment to the recognition of a proprietary community title. Indeed, it is not possible to admit traditional usufructuary rights without admitting a traditional proprietary community title.[58]

There is a second source of misconception, and this is the failure to recognise that the term 'title'[59] has two senses that are related but distinct, one referring to the manner in which a right to real property is acquired and the other referring to the right itself. That is the first sense concerns 'entitling conditions' and the second concerns 'rights'. The two senses correspond respectively with conditions and consequences; the one causal, the other resultant.

In the term 'native title', the common law and Aboriginal law play different roles. Aboriginal law determines **who** is entitled to the rights

---

the space of this paper to set out my proposition that McNeil was, however, in error in his analysis of *Wik* at 142–3.

[55] *Mabo* (1992) 175 CLR 1, 76 (Brennan J).

[56] Ibid, 51 (Brennan J).

[57] [1972–3] ALR 65 ('*Milirrpum*').

[58] *Mabo* (1992) 175 CLR 1, 51 (Brennan J).

[59] This explanation follows McNeil, above n 1, 10. McNeil discusses the term 'title' as part of his introduction to possession and title to land in English law. He did not, as I have now done, apply this explication of the term 'title' to native title, or customary law title as he called it. The question of the meaning of 'native title' was fruitlessly discussed in argument before *Ward* (Transcript of Proceedings, *Western Australia v Ward* (High Court of Australia, Kirby J, 6 March 2001)).

recognised by the common law, arising from the occupation of land at the time of sovereignty (and, indeed, Aboriginal law recognises the descent of these rights to any contemporary claimant community). The form of the title is possession, which flows from occupation. The entitling condition is the occupation of land under authority of Aboriginal law and custom. The right afforded by the common law is possession.

Rather than appreciating that 'native title' incorporates the common law and Aboriginal law in its two different senses, the prevalent assumption is that native title is constituted by Aboriginal law alone.

Conclusions

I will conclude by amending McNeil's compelling thesis on possessory title in two respects. Firstly, as I have already said, in my respectful view, McNeil was incorrect to assume that possessory title is a separate basis of claim to that of customary law or native title. Rather, the law on possession applies to the law on native title. In my view, this position is already confirmed by the Supreme Court of Canada in its decision in *Delgamuukw*. Then Chief Justice Lamer said:

> ... prior occupation, however, is relevant in two different ways, both of which illustrate the *sui generis* nature of aboriginal title. The first **is the physical fact of occupation, which derives from the common law principle that occupation is proof of possession in law**: see McNeil, 'Common Law Aboriginal Title'[60]

and:

> **Under common law, the act of occupation or possession is sufficient to ground aboriginal title** and it is not necessary to prove that the land was a distinctive or integral part of the aboriginal society before the arrival of Europeans[61]

and:

> However the aboriginal perspective must be taken into account alongside the perspective of the common law. **Professor McNeil has convincingly argued that at common law, the fact of physical occupation is proof of possession at law, which in turn will ground title to the land: Common Law Aboriginal Title.**[62]

---

[60] *Delgamuukw* [1997] 3 SCR 1010, 1082 [114] (emphasis added).
[61] Ibid, 1098 [145] (emphasis added).
[62] Ibid, 1110–1 [149] (emphasis added).

So there we have it: the application of the English common law principles concerning possession to the law on native title.

The second respect in which I would amend McNeil's thesis concerns the question of the form of title to which possessory title gives rise. McNeil argued that the Indigenous occupants of land, holding possession, would be entitled to a fee simple on the basis of a presumed lost grant.[63] That is, the common law would apply in much the same way as it would to any possessor who could not show an actual grant from the Crown (in the case of England the presumed lost grant applied to a great many titles in that country). At least one commentator has baulked at piling fiction upon fiction.[64] In my respectful view, it is unnecessary to conclude that possessory title amounts to a fee simple on the fiction of a lost grant. Rather, the title should be taken as it truly is: it is a *sui generis* form of possession. It is *sui generis* in that it is an allodial possession and does not have its origin in the tenurial system, and secondly, it is subject to derogation by valid exercise of sovereign power.

By way of conclusion, let me revisit Lord Sumner's famous statement in *Re Southern Rhodesia*[65] where his Lordship described a now outdated approach to the recognition of native title by reference to where claimant peoples stood in relation to some 'Darwinian' scale of social organisation. The passage is as follows:

> The estimation of the rights of aboriginal tribes is always inherently difficult. Some tribes are so low in the scale of social organisation that their usages and conceptions of rights and duties are not to be reconciled with the institutions or the legal ideas of civilised society. Such a gulf cannot be bridged. It would be idle to impute to such people some shadow of the rights known to our law and then to transmute it into the substance of transferable rights of property as we know them.[66]

Justice Brennan, as he then was, said in *Mabo* that this kind of approach 'depended on a discriminatory denigration of inhabitants, their social organisation and customs', and he concluded that 'it is imperative in today's world that the common law should neither be, nor be seen to be, frozen in an age of racial discrimination'.[67]

The danger into which the Australian law on native title has fallen is that while the discriminatory approach inherent in *Re Southern Rhodesia* has

---

[63] McNeil, above n 1, 208, 242–3.

[64] Brendan Edgeworth, 'Tenure, Allodialism and Indigenous Rights at Common Law: English, United States and Australian Land Law Compared after *Mabo v Queensland*' (1994) 23 *Anglo-American Law Review* 397.

[65] [1919] AC 211.

[66] Ibid, 233–4.

[67] *Mabo* (1992) 175 CLR 1, 41–2 (Brennan J).

been rejected in respect of whether Indigenous rights in a settled colony survive annexation—no matter how peculiar the social organisation and customs of the people concerned might be—in relation to the question that follows, namely 'what rights survive annexation?', the prejudice of *Re Southern Rhodesia* is revived and Indigenous social organisation and customs are used to accord to Indigenous occupants of land a lesser form of possession than would be accorded to any other occupant by the common law. Indeed, the content of the title of an adverse possessor is not limited to what she can prove by reference to laws, customs, and social organisation—rather she is accorded possession because she is in factual occupation. Yet, the title of the Indigenous occupant is limited by proof of whatever traditional laws and customs may be adduced to a court, no matter how arcane they might be. Indigenous claimants can say to the High Court of Australia today: the common law only required that we prove occupation at the time of sovereignty, but *Yorta Yorta* now requires us to prove the details of the traditional laws and customs that existed more than two centuries ago.

This situation is not good. The situation is pregnant with the prospect that the opportunity which *Mabo* represented for the settlement of land grievance in accordance with the three principles I outlined at the beginning of this chapter, will ultimately be unfulfilled. In my view this situation can only be fixed if the definition of 'native title' in s 223(1) of the *NTA* is restored to its original intention by Parliament, and that the explication of native title be undertaken by the Australian courts in accordance with 'the time-honoured methodology of the common law'. This is the least that Indigenous peoples having faith in the common law heritage of this country could expect from the country's Parliament and High Court.

Chapter 5

'Now *Balanda* Say We Lost Our Land in 1788': Challenges to the Recognition of Yolŋu Law in Contemporary Australia

*Aaron Corn and Neparrŋa Gumbula**

Figure 5.1: Neparrŋa Gumbula traces the footsteps of Captain Arthur Phillip at Sydney Cove (now Circular Quay) only forty-one years after the direct contestation of Yolŋu sovereignty by an alien power (photo © Aaron Corn, 2003)

* As authors we have collaborated academically since our first meeting at Galiwin'ku in northeast Arnhem Land in 1997, and share a common passion for music and knowledge. In writing this chapter, we have pooled our shared experiences of community life in Arnhem Land, participating in the Ŋärra' Legal Forum at the Third Garma Festival of Traditional

Introduction

This chapter examines some of the cultural underpinnings of contemporary Yolŋu calls for the comprehensive recognition of their full political rights and legal jurisdiction over northeast Arnhem Land by Australian governments. Arnhem Land is an Aboriginal Land Trust that spans 96,786 square kilometres in the tropical northeast of Australia's Northern Territory (see Figure 5.2). It is currently home to some 11,000 Indigenous Australians— including around 7000 Yolŋu (People) in northeast Arnhem Land—whose hereditary ownership of land and marine estates in the region pre-dates European settlement in Australia from 1788 by scores of millennia.

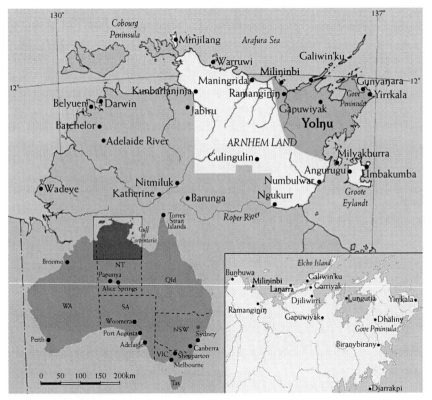

Figure 5.2: Arnhem Land (map © Aaron Corn, 2003)

Culture at Guḻkuḻa in 2001 and contributing to the Australian Indigenous Studies Program at the University of Melbourne. Gumbula brings to this collaboration his expertise as a *ḻiya-ŋära'mirri* (wise, learned) Yolŋu elder and legal specialist and experiences of working as a First Class Constable for the Northern Territory Police at Galiwin'ku from 1986–92, serving on the Galiwin'ku Town Council from 2000–2003 and in the Mala Elders Program in Darwin under the auspices of the Northern Land Council. Corn brings to the collaboration his understanding of music as a medium through which contemporary Arnhem Land people express their ancestrally-given identities.

After many of the early pastoral ventures that had been trialled in the region between 1870 and 1908 had failed financially, the Commonwealth Government zoned Arnhem Land as an Aboriginal Reserve where, ostensibly, local peoples would remain isolated and free to pursue their traditional lifestyles unhindered. However, in practice, Anglican and Methodist missionaries established small towns throughout the region from 1908–73. In the vast majority of cases they became the effective administrators of local peoples on behalf of the Northern Territory Administration, until these powers were ceded to more representative local governments following the abolition of the *Native Administration Ordinance 1940–64* (NT). In the mid-1970s, the Commonwealth Government passed the *Aboriginal Land Rights (Northern Territory) (ALRA)*,[1] under which inalienable freehold title to Arnhem Land was granted to an Aboriginal Land Trust that holds the title on behalf of Aboriginal people entitled by Aboriginal tradition to use or occupy that land.

The foundation contested

In 1989, a largely unknown band from a community named Yirrkala in remote northeast Arnhem Land had its debut album released by Mushroom Records. The name of this band was Yothu Yindi, and the album was called *Homeland Movement* (1989).[2] At the time, Mushroom Records was noted for its brave philanthropy in supporting a previously unsigned trio of Yolŋu musicians from the Northern Territory, whose first album was unprecedented in its juxtaposition of fairly conventional rock songs against traditional songs of the *manikay* genre.[3] *Homeland Movement* had been all but

---

[1] *Aboriginal Land Rights (Northern Territory) Act 1976* (Cth).

[2] Yothu Yindi, *Homeland Movement* (Producer Leszek Karski, Mushroom Records, D19520, 1989).

[3] Michael Gudinski, 'Formal Address' (Speech delivered at the Opening of the Yirrŋa Music Development Centre, Gunyaŋara, Northern Territory, 17 July 1999). *Manikay* are a sacred song series central to the performance of public (*garma*) Yolŋu ceremonies. They are among the most important hereditary properties owned by Yolŋu groups and, along with corresponding dances and designs, constitute a lasting record of the observations made by ancestors about the ecologies of their respective homelands. *Manikay* lyrics make extensive use of the sacred names that are possessed by each Yolŋu group, and can only be interpreted at the discretion of mature leaders who are *ḻiya-ŋärra'mirri* (learned, wise) in *rom* (law, culture, proper practice, the way). Other than this, a manikay series is most readily identifiable as the property of a particular Yolŋu group by the distinctive vocal pitches and melodic contours that are known as its *ḏämbu* (head). A consummate knowledge of the hereditary names, songs, dances and designs of one's group, and a demonstrated ability to direct their execution in ceremony are prerequisites for leadership in Yolŋu society. *Manikay* are conventionally performed by learned male singers who accompany themselves with *biḻma* (paired sticks), and are additionally accompanied by a male *yiḏaki* (didjeridu) player.

forgotten by the time that Yothu Yindi found eventual chart success with an unsolicited, yet extremely popular, remix of the track 'Treaty' from its second album, *Tribal Voice*.[4] However, among the numerous hidden treasures of *Homeland Movement* was the album's closing song, 'Luku-Wäṉawuy Manikay (1788)' (foundation site song).[5]

'Luku-Wäṉawuy Manikay (1788)' was composed in 1988 to mark the bicentenary of Australia's occupation by *Balanda* (Anglo-Australian) governments. It was composed by Galarrwuy Yunupiṉu—the eldest brother of Yothu Yindi's lead singer, Mandawuy, and current Chair of the Northern Land Council—and drew on his long experience of lobbying Australian governments for the recognition of his people's pre-existing legal jurisdiction and property rights over their hereditary estates. The first three couplets of this song parody a sitting of Parliament in which a Yolṉu leader explains to his peers that their hereditary land rights are being contested by *Balanda* interlopers who claim that they took possession of the entire Australian continent when their British forebears planted a Union Jack in the name of King George III at Sydney Cove in 1788.

Despite the intentional humour of 'Luku-Wäṉawuy Manikay (1788)', the history of struggle for land justice behind its composition is one of great sorrow and personal loss. Galarrwuy and Mandawuy Yunupiṉu's father, Mungurrawuy, was one of twelve Yolṉu leaders from Yirrkala who, in 1963, unsuccessfully petitioned the Federal House of Representatives to stop the development of a bauxite mine on their nearby hereditary lands.[6] Their ensuing legal case against the Swiss–Australian mining company Nabalco and the Commonwealth of Australia in the Supreme Court of the Northern

---

In ceremonial contexts, these musicians also lead the performance of corresponding dances by men, women and children. Above all, *manikay* celebrate the beauty of qualities vested in Yolṉu and their homelands by *waṉarr* (ancestral progenitors), and affirm the ancestrally given identities and values of the groups who perform them.

4   Yothu Yindi, 'Treaty' in *Tribal Voice: Extended Edition* (Producer Mark Moffatt and Filthy Lucre, Mushroom, TVD91017, 1991) track 2. The remix of 'Treaty' with which Yothu Yindi found its first chart success was produced by a studio in Melbourne called Filthy Lucre and released on the extended edition of *Tribal Voice*.

5   Yothu Yindi, 'Luku-Wä awuy Manikay (1788)' in *Homeland Movement* (Producer Leszek Karski, Mushroom Records, D19520, 1989) track 15.

6   Marika Milirrpum et al, 'Yirrkala Petition 1963' in Howard Morphy, *Aboriginal Art: Arts and Ideas* (Phaidon, London, 1998) 252–7; Bain Attwood and Andrew Markus, *The 1967 Referendum or When Aborigines Didn't Get the Vote* (Aboriginal Studies Press, Canberra, ACT, 1997) 202–3; Commonwealth Government, *Commonwealth: Yirrkala Bark Petitions 1963* (2000) Documenting a Democracy: Australia's Story http://www.foundingdocs.gov.au/places/cth/cth15.htm#significance at 26 November 2003.
    Mandawuy Yunupiṉu also offers a very personal account of his sorrow at having witnessed the desecration of his hereditary lands and waters through the development of this mine from childhood in Yothu Yindi, 'Gone is the Land' in *Garma* (Producers Andrew Farriss and Lamar Lowder, Mushroom, MUSH332822, 2000) track 12.

Territory from 1970–71[7] probed the complexities of Yolŋu law and its traditional provisions for managing property rights.[8] Galarrwuy, who had joined the newly established Yirrkala Town Council in 1969, acted as an interpreter for his elder kin throughout these proceedings and witnessed their eventual defeat in 1971 when Justice Blackburn ruled that Yolŋu proprietary interests in land could not be recognised under Australian law.[9]

Further insult to Yolŋu dignity came with Justice Blackburn's finding that he was also unconvinced of the plaintiffs' descent from the people who had owned the contested lands when Captain Arthur Phillip took possession of Australia in the name of the British Crown on 26 January 1788.[10] In 'Luku-Wäŋawuy Manikay (1788)', Galarrwuy scathingly satirises the absurdity of this ruling to Yolŋu sensibilities. He suggests that Captain Phillip and his First Fleet would have been hastily repelled had they not landed some 2500 kilometres away from the Yolŋu homelands of northeast Arnhem Land and had Yolŋu leaders at Yirrkala not waited more than 130 years to be informed of their arrival by latter-day missionaries and government representatives.[11]

The remaining seven couplets of 'Luku-Wäŋawuy Manikay (1788)' are a staunch affirmation of Yolŋu sovereignty over northeast Arnhem Land. In keeping with Yolŋu epistemology,[12] they trace proprietary interests in land back to the *waŋarr* (progenitorial ancestors) who initially shaped, named and populated the Yolŋu hereditary estates.[13] As Yothu Yindi would again declare in 'Treaty',[14] the ancestral bestowal of these perpetual interests on Yolŋu was in no way extinguished by the planting of the Union Jack at Sydney Cove in 1788 and was not directly contested by any alien power until construction of the Nabalco bauxite mine commenced in 1962.

---

[7] *Milirrpum and Others v Nabalco Pty Ltd and the Commonwealth of Australia* (1971) 17 FLR 141 ('*Milirrpum v Nabalco*').

[8] Nancy Williams, *The Yolŋu and Their Land: A System of Land Tenure and the Fight for its Recognition* (Australian Institute of Aboriginal Studies, Canberra, ACT, 1989) 109–203.

[9] *Milirrpum v Nabalco* (1971) 17 FLR 141–294 (Blackburn J).

[10] Ibid, 198.

[11] Indeed, the Commonwealth Government did not even count Yolŋu and other Indigenous peoples of Australia in the census as Australian citizens until after the referendum of 1967. For detailed discussion of this milestone event see Attwood and Markus, above n 7.

[12] See Williams, above n 9, 42–3; Ian Keen, *Knowledge and Secrecy in an Aboriginal Religion: Oxford Studies in Social and Cultural Anthropology* (Clarendon Press, Oxford, 1994) 103; Djiniyini Gondarra, 'Customary Law' (Speech delivered at the Garma Festival 2001: Ŋärra' Legal Forum, 2001) session 7, 15–20.

[13] For the purposes of this chapter, the authors define sovereignty as the right of the duly appointed and recognised leaders of any discrete human society to hold and exercise supreme authority and jurisdiction within their territories, and to be recognised by other sovereign states.

[14] Yothu Yindi, above n 5.

The foundation described

Yolŋu believe that they, as well as the geomorphic features and living ecologies of their hereditary estates, are the physical consubstantiations of metaphysical ancestral forces that exist eternally on a *waŋarr* plane of reality.[15] Yolŋu rights in their hereditary properties and the social authority of Yolŋu leaders are believed to flow from this ancestral plane of existence and through the *waŋarr* (progenitorial ancestors) who initially shaped, named and populated northeast Arnhem Land to their human descendants. There are more than sixty patrifilial Yolŋu *mala* (groups) who, by virtue of this ancestry, recognise each other's ownership and legal jurisdiction over hereditary tracts of land and sea in this area, and who commonly work together to observe the rightful execution of traditional legal processes through ceremonial performance.[16]

The very title of '<u>L</u>uku-Wäŋawuy Manikay (1788)' describes a fundamental tenet of Yolŋu ownership and proprietary interests in hereditary tracts of land and sea by virtue of ancestral bestowal. *<u>L</u>uku* can be translated from Yolŋu-Matha as 'foot', 'footprint' and 'step', as well as 'root', 'anchor' and 'foundation'.[17] This term and its synonym, *djalkiri*, circumscribe all signs of ancestral activity in the physical world including the names and geomorphic features of hereditary *wäŋa* (estates), the *gurruṯu* (kin) relations between people, *mala* (patrifilial groups) and *matha* (language).[18] As an expression of the 'foundation' of Yolŋu law and culture, *<u>l</u>uku* 'is simultaneously a way of moving through life, coming and going out of being, visiting the same camping places, sitting around a hearth which has been used by family members long gone, reproducing or re-performing everyday activities in the right way, and following the way taught and the footprints left by the ancestors'.[19]

---

[15] See Williams, above n 9, 23–4; Keen, above n 13, 105–6; John Rudder, *Yolŋu Cosmology: An Unchanging Cosmos Incorporating a Rapidly Changing World* (DPhil Thesis, Australian National University, 1993) 48–50; David H. Turner, *Afterlife Before Genesis, An Introduction: Accessing the Eternal Through Australian Aboriginal Music*, Toronto Studies in Religion, 22 (Lang, New York, NY, 1997) 26–30.

[16] David R. Zorc, *Yolŋu-Matha Dictionary* (Batchelor College, Batchelor, NT, 1996) passim; Geoffrey Bagshaw, 'Gapu Dhulway, Gapu Maramba: Conceptualisation and Ownership of Saltwater Among the Burarra and Yan-Nha u Peoples of Northeast Arnhem Land' in Nicolas Peterson and Bruce Rigsby (eds), *Customary Marine Tenure in Australia* (University of Sydney, NSW, 1998) 155–73.

[17] Franca Tamisari, 'Body, Vision and Movement in the Footprints of the Ancestors' (1998) 68 *Oceania* 250–1; Aaron Corn, *Dreamtime Wisdom, Modern Time Vision: Tradition and Innovation in the Popular Band Movement of Arnhem Land, Australia* (PhD Thesis, The University of Melbourne, Victoria, 2002) 83–4.

[18] Tamisari, above n 18, 250.

[19] Ibid, 251.

More specifically, however, the term *ḻuku-wäŋawuy* refers to the 'foundation sites' on *wäŋa* (estates) in northeast Arnhem Land where *waŋarr* (progenitorial ancestors) initially bestowed law and hereditary possessions on humans of their descent by embedding themselves deep into the earth. Galarrwuy's 'Ḻuku-Wäŋawuy Manikay (1788)' casts Captain Phillip's planting of the Union Jack at Sydney Cove two centuries earlier as a foundation myth on which the Commonwealth of Australia has relied to justify its claim to the continent, yet affirms that contemporary Yolŋu derive their own sovereignty over northeast Arnhem Land from the legal foundations bestowed upon them by their *waŋarr* (progenitorial ancestors).

This sardonic treatment of the raising of the Union Jack as legal claim to Australia that the bicentennial celebrations in 1988 marked, fittingly mirrors Justice Blackburn's findings in 1971 that hereditary Yolŋu proprietary interests in land were solely religious in their nature and, therefore, less than real.[20] Galarrwuy's parody of this foundation myth is further enhanced by the song's setting in the revivalist folk style that became popular among Australians of British–Irish descent in the 1950s, and in which so many canonical Australian folk songs about the rampant colonial expansionism of their ancestors were composed.[21]

Yolŋu conceptualisations of legal jurisdiction and process are encapsulated within those of *ḻuku*, *maḏayin* and *rom*.[22] *Maḏayin* is a term that connotes great beauty and pertains to the sacred properties in language, songs, dances and designs that are owned in perpetuity and deployed in ceremony by each Yolŋu *mala* (patrifilial group).[23] In a pragmatic sense, these sacra function as title deeds, and represent the ancestrally bestowed proprietary interests of each *mala* (patrifilial group) in the discrete tracts of land and sea that comprise their hereditary *wäŋa* (estates, homelands). Among the most important of these sacra are the sculpted and exquisitely adorned sacred objects known as *raŋga*. As direct representations of the *waŋarr* (progenitorial ancestors) who initially shaped, named and populated the Yolŋu hereditary estates, raŋga are revealed only in *ŋärra'* (restricted) ceremonial contexts and symbolise the ultimate authority of each *mala* (patrifilial group) over its hereditary properties by virtue of ancestral bestowal.

Rom is most commonly described as 'law' or 'culture' in English.[24] However, Keen suggests that it can also be translated from Yolŋu-Matha as

---

[20] *Milirrpum v Nabalco* (1971) 17 FLR 141–294 (Blackburn J).
[21] Graeme Smith, 'Folk Music' in Warren Bebbington (ed.), *The Oxford Companion to Australian Music* (Oxford University Press, Melbourne, Victoria, 1997) 222–3.
[22] Keen, above n 13, 137; Tamisari, above n 18; Goṉḏarra, above n 13, 19–20.
[23] Williams, above n 9, 29.
[24] Keen, above n 13, 137.

'right … or proper practice' or, to capture something of its religious conno-
tation, 'the way'.[25] *Rom* is formally expressed and upheld through ceremonial performances in which participating *mala* (patrifilial groups) deploy
their sacred properties in language, songs, dances and designs. Following
ancestral precedent, whether they be precedents for *rom* (proper practice)
established by *waŋarr* (progenitorial ancestors) or introduced by forebears
known in life, is a most profound Yolŋu virtue.[26]

Yolŋu conventionally demonstrate this virtue through their knowledge of *rom* (proper practice) for routine everyday practices and for the
deployment of their *maḏayin* (sacra) in ceremonies. Yolŋu believe that they
accumulate *märr* (inner strength, ancestral power, social harmony and spiritual well-being) by diligent following of *rom* (proper practice). Moreover,
it is necessary for mature Yolŋu, and men in particular, to have arduously
attained consummate knowledge of their hereditary canons of names,
songs, dances and designs before they can be recognised as *ḻiya-ŋärra'mirr(i)*
(wise, learned) elders with the authority to undertake social and ceremonial leadership roles.

It is by these fundamental precepts of *ḻuku* (foundation), *maḏayin*
(sacra) and *rom* (proper practice) that Yolŋu define themselves as people of
law, and in their totality the legal traditions bestowed upon Yolŋu by their
waŋarr (progenitorial ancestors) provide for:

- the protection of each patrifilial group's primary ownership rights and
  proprietary interests in its hereditary *wäŋa* (estates, homelands) and
  maḏayin (sacra)
- the regulation of matrifilial access and succession rights to the hereditary *wäŋa* (estates, homelands) and *maḏayin* (sacra) of other *mala*
  (patrifilial groups)
- the universalising regulation of inter-personal and inter-*mala* (patrifilial group) socio-economic relations through *gurruṯu* (kinship) and
  mälk (moiety subsections, skin names)
- the ceremonial co-operation of related *mala* (patrifilial groups) who
  share common *maḏayin* (sacra) at jointly owned *reŋgitj* grounds[27]
- the creation and renewal of diplomatic alliances between *mala* (patrifilial groups) through exchange ceremonies and marriage betrothals
- the negotiation of binding legal and political decisions by *ḻiya-
  ŋärra'mirr(i)* (wise, learned) men in *ŋärra'* (restricted) ceremonial

---

[25] Ibid.
[26] Ibid, 149.
[27] *Reŋgitj* are places located at the confluence of surrounding estates of the same patri-moiety
where Yolŋu *mala* (patrifilial groups) congregate to participate in public (*garma*) ceremonies:
Keen, above n 13, 312.

contexts, and of public assent to them in *dhuni'* (exo-restricted) and *garma* (public) ceremonial contexts[28]
- the division of domestic and ceremonial responsibilities and labour between males and females
- the authority of elders to instil in their young people the principles of *rum'rumthun* (discipline, decorum, social etiquette)
- the authority of elders to induct individuals to greater positions of social and ceremonial responsibility and eventual leadership
- the life-giving knowledge of ecology and natural resource management applied by *djambätj* (skilled) hunters
- the life-saving knowledge of illnesses and pharmacology applied by *marrŋgitj* (healers)
- warfare and the life-threatening knowledge of *galka* (assassins)
- extensive funeral and purification ceremonies
- the punishment and peaceful resolution of crimes through *makarrata* ceremonies.

The foundation negotiated

At present, these legal traditions are not recognised by Australian governments. The Commonwealth Government holds no formal treaty with any Indigenous people in Australia, and until 1993, maintained that the continent had been unowned (that is, *terra nullius*) when the British claimed possession in 1788.[29] Contemporary Yolŋu leaders nevertheless maintain that this was the system of law through which northeast Arnhem Land was governed unchallenged at the time of the British First Fleet's arrival in 1788, and decades beyond the establishment of the first Methodist mission at Miliŋimbi in 1923.[30]

Indeed, men of the Djapu' *mala* (patrifilial group) who killed five Japanese sailors guilty of serial rapes and an attempted murder in 1932 had acted under the legal authority of their leader, Woŋgu, to mete out these

[28] Gondarra, above n 13, 17.
[29] *Mabo v Queensland (No.2)* (1992) 175 CLR 1 FC. The doctrine of *terra nullius* in Australia was overruled when the High Court of Australia (1992) found that the Meriam people of the Torres Strait Islands held native title over Mer (Murray Island) that predates the landing of the British First Fleet at Sydney Cove in 1788. The key principles behind this ruling were soon after enshrined by the Commonwealth Government in the *Native Title Act 1993* (Cth).
[30] Yothu Yindi, above n 6; Yothu Yindi, above n 5; Gondarra, above n 13, 15; Galarrwuy Yunupiŋu, *'We Know These Things to Be True'*, *The Third Vincent Lingiari Memorial Lecture*, 1998, Australasian Legal Information Instititute: Reconciliation and Social Justice Library http://www.austlii.edu.au/au/special/rsjproject/rsjlibrary/car/lingiari/3yunupingu.html at 26 November 2003.

punishments. Police from Darwin were dispatched to investigate these kill-
ings in 1933. Their leader, Constable Albert McColl, sexually assaulted the
wife of the accused Dhäkiyarr Wirrpanda and was summarily executed.
At the behest of Methodist missionaries, Dhäkiyarr allowed himself to be
extradited to Darwin where, in 1934, he was tried in a *Balanda* court for
killing the Constable. He was found guilty of murder and sentenced to
death, but was later released on appeal.[31]

Dhäkiyarr disappeared under suspicious circumstances before returning
home[32] and, in 2003, his family performed a major ceremony outside the
Supreme Court building in Darwin to commemorate his death, to release his
spirit and to reconcile with attending members of McColl's family.[33] Despite
the largely unsympathetic attitudes of *Balanda* authorities in the early twentieth century towards Indigenous peoples, there should now be no question
that Dhäkiyarr and the other Yolŋu protagonists in these incidents were justified under Yolŋu legal jurisdiction in protecting themselves against such
violent and malicious acts and in punishing those who perpetrated them.

With pressure from Methodist missionaries mounting throughout the
mid-twentieth century and the gradual enfranchisement of Yolŋu leaders
to the local government councils that replaced mission authorities from the
mid-1960s, many of the traditional legal powers that Yolŋu leaders had exercised over matters of crime and punishment in *makarrata* (dispute resolution)
ceremonies came under the jurisdiction of *Balanda* police, courts and prisons.
In 1978, the newly established Northern Territory Government began to
recruit Indigenous police aides whose primary role still today is to mediate
disputes, and to facilitate the activities of police, courts and correctional services in their own communities. Yolŋu police aides are sometimes able to exert
considerable influence in mediating between elders and magistrates to find
mutually agreeable court solutions to matters of crime and punishment that
divert Yolŋu defendants from jails. However, as there remains no formal recognition of this effective legal plurality or the traditional legal authority of
Yolŋu elders by Australian governments, such considerations are left to the
discretion of each presiding magistrate on a case-by-case *basis*.[34]

---

[31] Mickey Dewar, *The 'Black War' in Arnhem Land: Missionaries and the Yolŋu 1908–40* (NARU,
Darwin, 1982); Richard Trudgen, *Why Warriors Lie Down and Die: Towards an Understanding
of Why the Aboriginal People of Arnhem Land Face the Greatest Crisis in Health and Education
Since European Contact* (Aboriginal Resources and Development Services, Darwin, NT, 2000)
35–8.

[32] Trudgen, above n 32.

[33] Northern Land Council, *Land Rights News: Remembering Dhäkiyarr* (2003), online at http://
www.nlc.org.au/html/wht_lrn_2003_jun01.html at 27 November 2003.

[34] These issues are addressed in great detail by the Australian Law Reform Commission, *The
Recognition of Aboriginal Customary Laws*, Report No 31 (1989).

The foundation championed

'Luku-Wäŋawuy Manikay (1788)' was not the only staunch affirmation of Yolŋu sovereignty to which Galarrwuy Yunupiŋu contributed in 1988. Amid the year-long bicentennial celebrations of British settlement in Australia, Indigenous leaders of the Northern and Central Land Councils chose Prime Minister Robert Hawke's visit to the Barunga Festival of Sport and Culture on 12 June to present him with a statement that called on the Commonwealth Government to recognise the pre-existing sovereignty of Indigenous Australians, their continuing ownership and proprietary interests in their hereditary estates, their rights to be educated in their own languages and cultures and their pre-existing legal traditions through the negotiation of a formal treaty or compact.

The defeat of the Yolŋu case against the Nabalco mine in the Northern Territory Supreme Court had precipitated a Federal inquiry into Indigenous land rights[35] that led to the establishment of the Northern and Central Land Councils under the *ALRA*. However, their powers and resources under this Act are limited in scope.[36] Galarrwuy Yunupiŋu became the second and longest-serving Chair of the Northern Land Council in 1977, and with his counterpart from the Central Land Council, Wenten Rubuntja, handed the Barunga Statement[37] to Prime Minister Hawke in person. Hawke's immediate response was to vow that his government would enter into a treaty with Indigenous Australians by 1990. His government's subsequent failure to honour this promise was the catalyst for Yothu Yindi's release of 'Treaty' in protest.

Formal calls for Australian Government recognition of pre-existing Indigenous legal traditions were again raised at the Ŋärra' Legal Forum, which was convened under the auspices of the Yothu Yindi Foundation on the reŋgitj ground at Gulkula from 23–24 August 2001.[38] We, the authors, both participated in a men's discussion group facilitated by Michael Dodson[39]

---

[35] John Woodward, *Aboriginal Land Rights Commission: Second Report* (Commonwealth of Australia, Canberra, ACT, 1974).

[36] The functions of a Land Council are set out in s 23 of the *Aboriginal Land Rights (Northern Territory) Act 1976* (Cth).

[37] Galarrwuy Yunupiŋu *et al.*, 'Barunga Statement 1988' in Morphy, above n 7, 258; Bain Attwood and Andrew Markus, *The Struggle for Aboriginal Rights: A Documentary History* (Allen & Unwin, Sydney, NSW, 1999) 316–17.

[38] Galarrwuy and Mandawuy Yunupiŋu are the respective Chair and Secretary of the Yothu Yindi Foundation.

[39] Michael Dodson is a member of the Yawuru people for the Kimberley region in northwest Australia. He is a barrister who specialises in Indigenous legal matters, a former Aboriginal and Torres Strait Islander Justice Commissioner, a Chair of the Australian Institute of Aboriginal and Torres Strait Islander Studies and Convenor of the Institute for Indigenous Australia at the Australian National University.

at this Forum on 23 August which determined that emergent government strategies to grant Indigenous communities piecemeal control over discrete portfolios such as land access, marine protection and diversionary programs for substance abusers fell well short of a comprehensive approach to the formal recognition of Indigenous legal traditions in a treaty or compact with the Commonwealth Government.[40] Under the provisions of the *ALRA*, the Commonwealth Government granted inalienable freehold title to the Arnhem Land Aboriginal Land Trust, on behalf of Aboriginal traditional owners of the land.[41] However, while this Act recognises to a limited extent the authority of Aboriginal custom and tradition within the Land Trust area, it gives no standing to the full body of Yolŋu laws pertaining to people–land relationships, and can in no way be a substitute for the comprehensive traditional legal provisions under Yolŋu law described earlier in this chapter.

Our group also considered whether the applicability of Indigenous laws to non-Indigenous people who break them should be renewed,[42] and on the following afternoon the forum found as one of its four key recommendations to Australian governments that, 'where legal pluralism enables justice and fairness, then the recognition of customary law should be legislated to ensure that all Australians obtain the benefit of a combined system of laws that works to the benefit of Indigenous and non-Indigenous Australians alike'.[43] The enshrinement of such legal pluralism in Australia would hold benefits that far exceed the current diversion of Indigenous people from the criminal justice system into community based justice programs, regardless of the legislative difficulties that may need to be overcome.

Elders such as the *liya-ŋärra'mirr(i)* (wise, learned) Yolŋu of northeast Arnhem Land whose leadership roles in their own communities are undermined in virtually all respects by the institutionalised absence of government recognition for their authority, would be better supported in their localised efforts to maintain socio-cultural stability and the rule of law. This strategy would also bring recognition for *liya-ŋärra'mirr(i)* Yolŋu whose arduous traditional career paths in leadership and law have been severely eroded by the increased roles of *Balanda* police, courts and correctional services in northeast Arnhem Land since the mid-twentieth century, and might even assist the current Yolŋu leaders in attracting their young to this calling.

As Yolŋu legal processes are formally expressed through ceremonies, the continuance of these legal traditions and of *liya-ŋärra'mirr(i)* leaders

---

[40] Yothu Yindi Foundation, *Ŋärra' Legal Forum: Report and Recommendations* (2001) http://www.garma.telstra.com/pdfs/ngarra.pdf at 2 December 2003.
[41] *Aboriginal Land Rights (Northern Territory) Act 1976*, Schedule 1.
[42] Yothu Yindi Foundation, above n 41.
[43] Ibid.

who know how to execute them is a further imperative to the survival of the hereditary canons of names, songs, dances and designs that constitute the cornerstone of the Yolŋu community's fledgling participation in the global market economy. For example, how can the growing international trade in highly-valued Yolŋu art works be sustained without the consummate knowledge of *liya-ŋärra'mirr(i)* elders who are trained in the traditional body of laws that inform and necessitate their production?[44]

The Northern Land Council's Mala Elders Program,[45] which calls on the authority and expertise of elders to assist with the rehabilitation and repatriation of long-term substance abusers from remote Indigenous communities who live in Darwin, has the support of both the traditional owners of Darwin in the form of the Larrakia Nation Aboriginal Corporation and the Northern Territory Government.[46] It demonstrates how the specialised knowledge and skills of elders might benefit us all should one day their status as the duly appointed and authorised leaders of sovereign Indigenous peoples and the reality of the legal plurality that their continuing presence in Australia currently engenders be recognised in a formal treaty or compact with the Commonwealth Government.

The foundation eternal

That *Balanda* say Yolŋu lost their land in 1788 is a preposterous proposition that denies Yolŋu rights as an ancient political entity and as people of law with comprehensive legal jurisdiction over their hereditary territories. Nevertheless, at each turn in their recent history, Yolŋu leaders have favoured negotiation and the cultivation of mutual respect as a means of seeking formal recognition from Australian governments for their people's fundamental human right to self-determination and freedom under the rule of law. In response, Australian governments have repeatedly dismissed Yolŋu calls for the comprehensive recognition of their political rights and legal jurisdiction over northeast Arnhem Land on grounds that these rights were somehow extinguished when British troops took possession of the entire continent in 1788 more than 130 years before Yolŋu leaders were

---

[44] Howard Morphy, *Ancestral Connections: Art and an Aboriginal System of Knowledge* (University of Chigago Press, Chicago, 1991); Howard Morphy, *above n 7.*

[45] Established in 2003.

[46] Northern Land Council, *Land Rights News: Mala Elders Tackle Itinerants Issue* (2003), online at http://www.nlc.org.au/html/wht_lrn_2003_jun02.html at 27 November 2003; Peter Toyne, 'Mala Elders Program Heralds New Approach' (2003), Press Release, Northern Territory Government, online at http://www.nt.gov.au/ocm/media_releases/20030515_mala.shtml at 27 November 2003; see also Langton and Palmer, this volume.

first informed of this event by missionaries and government representatives in the early twentieth century.

Nevertheless, the satirisation of this history offered by Galarrwuy Yunupiŋu in 'Luku-Wäŋawuy Manikay (1788)' and other songs by Yothu Yindi such as 'Treaty' continue to inform audiences in Australia and internationally about the plight of contemporary Yolŋu. Moreover, recent initiatives such as the Ŋärra' Legal Forum[47] and the Mala Leaders Program[48] demonstrate the dedication and constructivism with which contemporary Yolŋu leaders have sought to promote their profound ancestral bonds to their hereditary estates and legal traditions, and to find pragmatic solutions to complicated legal matters involving their people. Continued investment in such dialogues may one day be rewarded with formal recognition of their rights as peoples and an Australian nation re-shaped by greater recognition of the self-evident legal and political plurality and different cultural traditions.

---

[47] Yothu Yindi Foundation, above n 41.
[48] Northern Land Council, 'Mala Elders', above n 47.

PART 2

Recognition and Resolution in Treaty Making in Settler States

Introduction

Contested Territory: Divided Past, Common Future[1]

Maureen Tehan

The attempt to resolve first nations land claims is really a contest over the past. The issue is whether the injustices and actions of the past should lie under the gravestones of time, or whether society has an obligation to acknowledge past experiences and use them to determine modern policy... History resonates throughout the land claims debate, providing justification and support for all positions, clearly showing that the past is not a set of 'facts' but contested territory.[2]

Colonisation of the New World took many forms, but a constant was the dispossession of Indigenous inhabitants from land and water and their accompanying resources, whether as a result of purported agreement and consent through treaties or without consent. The contested territory of the past that resounds also in the present as contestation over sovereignty and dispossession, underpins claims for Aboriginal rights and title to land and water, reparation for past injustice and reconciliation based on recognition. In Canada, Borrows sees resolution of this contestation rooted in rethinking citizenship[3] and re-imagining the institutions that underpin it: federalism, democracy, rule of law and protection of minorities.[4] Finding an institutional place for Indigenous voices within the nation-state requires a re-thinking of the moral, legal and spatial territory of the nation-state's claims to dominion and authority.

---

[1] Ken Coates, 'Divided Past, Common Future: The History of the Land Rights Struggle in British Columbia' in Roslyn Kunin (ed.), *Prospering Together: The Impact of the Aboriginal Title Settlements in British Columbia* (The Laurier Institution, Vancouver, 1998) 1–43.

[2] Ibid, 31.

[3] John Borrows, *Recovering Canada: The Resurgence of Indigenous Law* (University of Toronto Press, Toronto, 2002) 138–158.

[4] Ibid, 111–137.

The tension between the competing claims of the original inhabitants and the coloniser remains a dominant element in the modern relationship between them, and it is these claims that form the basis of the contributions in this section. These contributions make it clear that this tension is played out in different ways in each jurisdiction, but that there are common themes which might inform the strategic and public debate in each, and the idea and reality of treaties in some form or other is central.

In Canada, treaties were the historical tool for managing competing claims, and the interpretation and implementation of these treaties remain a central element of the contemporary Indigenous–settler relationship. Negotiation of modern treaties or comprehensive agreements, backed by common-law recognition and constitutional protection of Aboriginal rights and title, are now the preferred tool. Uncertainty and institutional difficulties bedevil this modern process. Chartrand, de Costa and Tehan each bring a different, but strikingly coherent, critique to the modern treaty process. Resonating with Borrows's analysis, Chartrand identifies the failure to provide institutional support for a modern, inclusive treaty process as the major contemporary treaty issue. However, Chartrand remains committed to the notion of treaty, in its Canadian manifestation, as central to achieving a new relationship. In a micro-analysis, de Costa and Tehan identify other shortcomings of the Canadian treaty approach in British Columbia, not the least of which is the tendency to seek extinguishment of rights as a price for a treaty. It is evident that there is a missing ingredient; a treaty process backed by common law and constitutional recognition and imposing obligations on the Crown is not sufficient to produce resolution. Here, Borrows's themes of federalism and democracy—multiple governments that operate with respect for aboriginal autonomy—resonate as the key components of a resolution through treaty.

Williams's contribution provides insight into the role of treaty settlements that are not backed by direct legal force but which nonetheless underpin all aspects of New Zealand's constitutional and legal relationships. The emphasis on the distinctively New Zealand response reminds us of the cultural specificity of treaty making and enforcement. Here, too, the key elements of past dispossession and contemporary recognition and institutional support are identified as the basis for the continuing negotiation of a new relationship of recognition and respect.

In all of these contributions we see the force and power of negotiations between nations or entities of government. Land, but also moral, legal and spatial territory are central to the negotiations through which it is possible to observe negotiations encompassing recognition of an autonomous aboriginal citizenship and forms of aboriginal governance.

In achieving this outcome, as Borrows has said, 'each party needs to explore these issues more fully and to negotiate and reconcile their differences through joint effort'.[5]

---

[5] Ibid, 137.

Chapter 6

Towards Justice and Reconciliation: Treaty Recommendations of Canada's Royal Commission on Aboriginal Peoples (1996)

Paul L.A.H. Chartrand

Introduction

It's inconceivable, I think, that in a given society one section of the society have a treaty with the other section of society. We must all be equal under the laws and we must not sign treaties amongst ourselves.

Prime Minister Pierre Trudeau, 1969 [1]

Treaties need to become a central part of our national identity and mythology. Treaties ... were made between the Crown and nations of Aboriginal people, nations that continue to exist and are entitled to respect ... They are fundamental components of the constitution of Canada, analogous to the terms of union under which provinces joined Confederation ... The fulfilment of the spirit and intent of the treaties is a fundamental test of the honour of the Crown and of Canada ... Their non-fulfilment casts a shadow over Canada's place of respect in the family of nations.[2]

---

[1] Canada, Royal Commission on Aboriginal People, *Report of the Royal Commission on Aboriginal Peoples: Restructuring the Relationship*, vol. 2, part 1 (Supply and Services Canada, Ottawa, 1996) 14.

[2] Ibid, 18.

... Our essential conclusions about the historical treaties are equally applicable to treaties that will be made in the future.[3]

Royal Commission on Aboriginal Peoples, 1996

These quotations show the widely divergent views in the debate about treaties in Canada. They also prefigure the difficulties inherent in adopting the recommendation of the Royal Commission on Aboriginal Peoples (RCAP) to make treaties a continuing and vital part of Canadian life.[4]

In this chapter, the approach and recommendations of the RCAP which aimed to make treaties a continuing and vital part of Canadian life are reviewed and examined in light of contemporary treaty policy and practice.

The chapter is organised in the following way: first, the general approach of the RCAP to the subject matter of treaties is reviewed, followed by a description of three of the specific recommendations that are central to the RCAP vision. These recommendations are captured in the following three propositions:

1. Only nations may have treaty relations with the Crown.
2. The treaty process must be extended to all aboriginal peoples.
3. Neutral and independent institutions must be established in order to implement the process recommended by the RCAP.

The description of these recommendations is followed by brief commentaries on the Federal Government's official response to them, and on recent changes and developments.

The general approach of the RCAP

The RCAP adopted the view that the treaty parties must devise the appropriate processes for reviewing, implementing and renewing treaty relationships or making new treaties with the aboriginal peoples, but it offered some guidance on the possible content of treaty processes and their possible results.[5]

---

[3] Ibid, 60.

[4] The RCAP investigated (i) the legal status, implementation and future evolution of aboriginal treaties, including modern-day agreements; (ii) specific solutions, rooted in domestic and international experience; and (iii) mechanisms to ensure that all treaties are honoured in the future. The Commission was also given scope to investigate the historical practices of treaty making and to analyse treaty implementation and interpretation (RCAP, vol. 2, part 1, above n 1, 58).

[5] In Canada, the aboriginal peoples are the Indian, Inuit and Métis peoples, whose rights are recognised and affirmed in the *Constitution Act 1982*, being Schedule B to the *Canada Act 1982* (UK) c 11, s 35:

The RCAP's vision of treaty fulfilment is based upon three elements:

- the achievement of **justice** by implementing those provisions of the treaties that are set out clearly in legal documents
- **extension** of the treaty relationship to all aboriginal nations in Canada
- **reconciliation** between the spirit and intent of the treaties and the rights of Canadians as a whole, on the basis that the purpose of the treaties was to provide a *modus vivendi*—a working arrangement that would enable peoples who started out as strangers to live together as neighbours. The RCAP vision contemplates that the rights or interests of aboriginal peoples are to be reflected in treaties that protect the corporate interest of each treaty nation. The treaties will reconcile the national interest of each aboriginal treaty party with the interests of other Canadians.[6]

The RCAP proposed a realigning of the relationship between aboriginal peoples and Canadian governments as a new 'nation-to-nation' relationship governed by historic and new treaty agreements. The RCAP recommended a Canada-wide process of building or rebuilding aboriginal nations so that they can take their place as a third order of government within Canada, along with the Federal Government and the provincial governments. The new relationship would be brought about by a process comprising four basic elements:[7]

1. the promulgation by the Parliament of Canada of a royal proclamation and companion legislation to implement those aspects of the renewed relationship that fall within Federal authority[8]
2. activity to rebuild aboriginal nations and develop their constitutions and citizenship codes, leading to their recognition through a proposed new law, the Aboriginal Nations Recognition and Government Act
3. negotiations to establish a Canada-wide framework agreement to set the stage for the emergence of an aboriginal order of government in the Canadian federation
4. the negotiation of new or renewed treaties between aboriginal nations and other Canadian governments.

---

1. The existing aboriginal and treaty rights of the aboriginal peoples of Canada are hereby recognised and affirmed.
2. In this Act, 'aboriginal peoples of Canada' includes the Indian, Inuit and Métis peoples of Canada.
6 RCAP, vol. 2, part 1, above n 1, 21.
7 Ibid, 64ff, 311ff.
8 The objectives of the *Royal Proclamation* are listed at ibid, 65–66, and those of the companion legislation are listed at ibid, 67. See also recommendations 2.2.7 and 2.2.8, which are reproduced in Canada, Royal Commission on Aboriginal People, *Report of the Royal*

The RCAP explained that it was recommending a process to reconcile the different understandings of treaties and to engage in a constructive dialogue on issues on which agreement had been reached. It did not propose to renegotiate historic treaties, which are viewed as based upon a sacred relationship with the Crown, but rather, implementing the spirit and intent of the treaties, including completing them when appropriate or amending the treaty text in circumstances in which the parties acknowledge that it does not embody their true agreement. Entry into the process recommended by the RCAP must be voluntary, and a treaty nation is free to leave its treaty relationship as it is. The timing of the process had to be realistic. 'A generation may well have passed before both treaty parties feel that the true principles of their treaty have been restored.'[9] The magnitude of the task is illustrated by an examination of the three propositions described at the beginning of the chapter.

Only nations may have treaties with the Crown

This relates to the role and significance of the aboriginal nation. Treaties are for nations, and not all groups of aboriginal people are eligible for treaty-nation standing. Groups intending to enter into treaty relations with the Crown must meet objective criteria.

The Commission noted that the Crown had acknowledged the nation-hood of Indian nations at an early stage and made undertakings not to interfere with internal matters. In time, however, policy and practice shifted, and the government actively undermined the integrity of the aboriginal nations with which it had treaty relations. From 1876 on, the federal *Indian Act*[10] created 'bands' as the legal embodiment of Indian political structure, defined both a band and its membership, and gave authority to a government minister to recognise and create bands and to divide their membership and assets. 'The act not only provided a legislative basis for the denial of Indian nationhood, but also recast the relationship between Indian people and the Crown in administrative instead of political terms.'[11] Indian treaty nations were deliberately broken up as a step toward their members' assimilation into the larger society. 'After almost 120 years, the *Indian Act* has taken its toll—not only in the quality and the basis of the relationship between Indian nations and the Crown, but also with respect to the internal organisation of the Indian and treaty nations.'[12]

Commission on Aboriginal Peoples: Renewal—A Twenty-year Commitment, vol. 5 (Supply and Services Canada, Ottawa, 1996) 150–51.

[9] RCAP, vol. 2, part 1, above n 1, 71.
[10] *Indian Act*, RSC 1985, c 1–5.
[11] RCAP vol. 2, part 1, above n 1, 88.
[12] Ibid, 89.

The RCAP concluded that, as the right of self-determination was vested in 'peoples', so the domestic right of self-government is vested in larger aggregations of people, which it termed 'nations'. The right is not vested in local communities, such as small Indian bands, and aboriginal people must identify their own national units for purposes of exercising the right of self-government. An aboriginal nation entitled to exercise a domestic right of self-government has the following specific attributes:[13]

- It has a collective sense of national identity that is evinced in a common history, language, culture, traditions, political consciousness, laws, government structures, spirituality, ancestry, and homeland.
- It is of sufficient size and capacity to enable it to assume and exercise powers and responsibilities flowing from the right of self-determination in an effective manner.
- It constitutes a majority of the permanent population of a certain territory or collection of territories and, in the future, will operate from a defined territorial base.

This is a functional approach, tied to the notion that if treaty nations are to be self-governing, they must have the attributes of effective governments, including sufficient size to assume their powers and responsibilities.[14]

In the RCAP's view, opening up the treaty process:

> to Aboriginal groups that do not meet the criteria of a nation would detract from the fundamental nature of treaties and the integrity and status of the nations that make them. This does not preclude a variety of other initiatives to give effect to the rights and aspirations of groups that do not qualify as nations. It simply preserves the essential nation-to-nation nature of the treaties.[15]

The proposed Aboriginal Nation Recognition legislation mentioned above would set the guidelines for the application of the criteria to identify nations, and the Aboriginal Lands and Treaties Tribunal mentioned below would have an advisory role in making recommendations to the federal Cabinet on recognising nations entitled to negotiate self-government arrangements in the treaty process.

At the same time, the RCAP took pains to point out that aboriginal nations have group rights *qua* communities, and that their members are

---

[13] Ibid, 182.

[14] The discussion of the nation criteria is in ibid, 177–84. At ibid, 163–65, the Commission discusses the three attributes of effective governments: (i) legitimacy, or the enjoyment of the confidence and support of the governed; (ii) power, or the acknowledged legal capacity to act; and (iii) resources, or the physical capacity to act, including not only financial, economic and natural resources for security and growth, but also human resources in the form of skilled and healthy people.

[15] RCAP vol. 2, part 1, above n 1, 62–63.

entitled to enjoy those rights by virtue of their membership in the group, not by virtue of their personal antecedents or biological descent. It is important to make this point in Canada, where the idea of 'racial discrimination' has been popularised, and where the concept of special group status in law is confused with notions of individual equality. The conclusion of the RCAP was that aboriginal peoples who are entitled to negotiate self-government treaties are not groups of individuals united by racial characteristics; they are organic political and cultural entities.[16]

The treaty process must be extended to all the aboriginal peoples

Treaty relationships and access to treaty institutions should be extended to all nations of aboriginal people that want to have them, and not restricted as formerly to 'Indians' recognised by Federal legislation.[17] The parties to these extended-treaty processes may prefer to use other labels such as compacts, accords or other terms; the term 'treaty' has been used primarily in relation to first nations, (the name increasingly used instead of 'Indian bands' or 'Indian nations').[18]

New institutions to assist the treaty process

The RCAP concluded that 'by nature the law is an inconsistent and politically inappropriate vehicle for resolving the deepest issues of treaty fulfilment.'[19] Nevertheless, the Supreme Court of Canada has been consistent in assuming jurisdiction over the subject matter of treaties.[20]

> When the courts arrive at the limits of legal analysis and the law as legitimate tools for determining rights, they will be compelled to recommend a negotiated political settlement based on such rights as they have found to exist. Courts can describe rights. They cannot make a relationship based on those rights work. At some point we may have to stop looking to the courts for assistance.[21]

---

[16] Ibid, 176–7.

[17] Ibid, 62–4, where it is mentioned that Inuit people have participated in treaty making in the modern comprehensive land claims process since 1975, and that Métis people in the Northwest Territories have been involved in treaty negotiations with Federal officials since 1990.

[18] The Métis Nation of western Canada, represented by the Métis National Council, negotiated a *Métis Nation Accord* in the *Charlottetown Accord*, a national agreement in a proposal for Constitutional reform with the Federal and provincial governments that fell with its rejection in a national referendum in 1992. (See RCAP vol. 2, part 1, above, n 1, 55–56).

[19] Ibid, 31. See generally, Lorne M. Sossin, *Boundaries of Judicial Review: The Law of Justiciability in Canada* (Carswell, Toronto, 1999).

[20] RCAP vol. 2, part 1, above n 1, 35.

[21] Ibid, 36.

Another concern of the RCAP was that the court process does not contribute to its adopted goal of reconciling all the parties, but creates winners and losers and little opportunity for gaining legitimacy. Treaties offer a means of clarifying the relationship between the parties.

The RCAP concluded that restoring the treaty relationship by making new treaties and implementing and renewing existing treaties will require the establishment of at least two types of independent and neutral institutions: treaty commissions and a specialised Aboriginal Lands and Treaties Tribunal. Their functions would be quite distinct, but vital to the success of the proposed process.[22]

Treaty commissions

These should be 'permanent, independent and neutral forums where negotiations as part of treaty processes can take place'.[23] Commissions to facilitate treaty discussions and negotiations would be created by the government of Canada, the provinces or territories, and aboriginal or treaty nations. Corresponding laws or resolutions of aboriginal and treaty nations would be required, following full and open consultations with aboriginal or treaty nations before the Crown establishes them.

The commissions would assist the treaty parties to resolve political and other disputes arising in the treaty process. The commissions, at the same time, would respect the political and diplomatic nature of treaty processes, and remain neutral and independent of the parties. Commissions could not legitimately have any authority to resolve disputes unless such authority was conferred on them by the parties.[24] Commissions would serve as the guardians or keepers of treaty processes. In order to give them the best chance of achieving this status, there would have to be full and open consultations with aboriginal and treaty nations before the Crown brought the commissions into being.

An aboriginal lands and treaties tribunal

The RCAP recommended that the tribunal play a supporting role in treaty processes, with three main elements in its mandate:[25]

(i)   jurisdiction over process-related matters such as ensuring that the parties negotiate in good faith
(ii) the power to make orders for interim relief
(iii) jurisdiction to hear appeals on funding issues.

---

[22] Ibid, 90.

[23] Ibid.

[24] The features and functions of the commissions are outlined in ibid, 92.

[25] The RCAP introduced the recommendation for a tribunal in RCAP vol. 2, part 1, above n 1, 93–94; the tribunal is discussed in detail in ibid, ch 4.

Another important function relates to the recognition of nations for purposes of treaty negotiations. Panels would make recommendations to the Federal cabinet on the acceptance of applicant groups, on the basis of applying objective criteria to determine the existence of a contemporary nation able to effectively govern its members and participate in government-to-government relations.

The tribunal would be a forum of last resort in treaty processes, and every attempt should be made to provide for the negotiated, mediated or arbitrated resolution of treaty disputes with the assistance of treaty commissions, which would have primary responsibility for ensuring that treaty processes are kept moving and on track. The existence of the tribunal should not shape treaty processes. Its jurisdiction over treaty processes should be limited to deciding particular matters that might otherwise have been litigated in court and to acting as an appellate body in relation to certain functions of the treaty commissions. Most importantly, in the treaty processes the tribunal must be only one of an array of dispute-resolution mechanisms available to the treaty parties.

Commentary

The following subsections offer commentaries on the Federal Government's official response to the RCAP's recommendations, and on recent changes and developments.

The general approach of the RCAP

The late 1980s and early 1990s saw bitter conflicts and disappointments that gained international attention. The Federal Government of the day responded by appointing a royal commission with an unprecedented, comprehensive mandate to study and recommend policies on aboriginal issues. However, by the time the final report was published in 1996, a new government was in power, and it exhibited in the work of the RCAP the low level of interest typical of new governments in regard to their predecessors' initiatives. In January 1998, the Federal Government issued its official response to the RCAP report.[26] None of the 'fundamental' changes that the RCAP had said were required were included. While an official nod went in the direction of some features of the RCAP approach, in practice the government's 1995 policy, adopted before the RCAP report was published,

---

[26] Canada, *Gathering Strength: Canada's Aboriginal Action Plan* (Minister of Public Works and Government Services Canada, Ottawa, 1997).

continues to guide the Federal approach to contemporary treaty negotia-tions. Policy and practice among the provinces vary, but none has adopted the RCAP recommendations concerning provincial participation in the treaty process.

The four-stage national process envisaged by the RCAP as necessary to demonstrate the government's commitment to a visible, national process aimed at making treaties a viable and significant part of the national life of Canada has not been adopted. The current prime minister has not partici-pated in the government's reaction to the RCAP report. At times, aboriginal leaders have called for first ministers' meetings, but there has been no public response from the government to those calls.

A Canada-wide framework agreement to establish the treaty process as a national project involving the co-operation of the provinces as well as the Federal Government is vital to the RCAP vision. It would create national guidelines that would be supported by both government and aboriginal representatives to guide the local and regional nation-to-nation negotia-tions across Canada. These guidelines can be expected to identify the scope of the possible in these treaty negotiations, and thereby perform the salu-tary function of giving the Canadian public some measure of appreciation of the nature and scope of the negotiations. This can be expected to allay unreasonable fears, garner public support and confidence, and weaken the effect of the irrational rhetorical attacks that continue to plague the public dialogue about aboriginal rights and issues.

Today, if treaties are to assume the national significance envisaged by the RCAP, the general failure to understand the true basis for the treaties remains one of the biggest obstacles to be overcome. While some of the confusion seems related to the notions about racial and liberal equality in the *Charter of Rights and Freedoms*,[27] much also seems to be related to questions about his-tory based rights and the legitimacy of Canada's sovereign borders.[28]

The existence of different views about treaties is important because the views lead to different conclusions about what justice requires. This difference implies the need for a reconciliation of these conclusions. The RCAP thought that a public education program was important to explain the role and significance of the treaties, but left the details to be designed

---

[27] *Canadian Charter of Rights and Freedoms*, Part I of the *Constitution Act 1982*, being Schedule B to the *Canada Act 1982* (UK), c 11, esp. s 15.

[28] Paul L.A.H. Chartrand, 'Aboriginal Self-Government: The Two Sides of Legitimacy' in Susan D. Phillips (ed.), *How Ottawa Spends: A More Democratic Canada...? 1993–1994* (Carleton University Press, Ottawa, 1993) 234. See also, for a discussion of the differences between apartheid and the American civil rights goals, and the goals of aboriginal self-government in Canada: Will Kymlicka, *Liberalism, Community and Culture* (Oxford University Press, New York, 1989).

by governments to whom the recommendation was addressed.[29] The Treaty Commission in British Columbia[30] and the Office of the Treaty Commissioner in Saskatchewan have initiated public education projects, the latter including curriculum materials for use in public schools.[31]

The aboriginal 'nation'

The 1998 policy statement, entitled 'Gathering Strength', responds to the RCAP recommendation that self-government treaty negotiations be negotiated only with nations by offering a rather weak philosophical endorsement of the concept, and a statement that consultations would be held on 'appropriate instruments to recognise Aboriginal governments'.[32]

The RCAP explained that the idea of a nation for negotiating self-government treaties would not apply to most bands because of their small size, which would prevent them from governing effectively. What would be required to follow the RCAP model would be a policy of recognition that would result in negotiations only with larger aggregations of bands or other aboriginal communities that met the objective criteria of a nation. Larger nations are more able to govern effectively, including governing the administration of justice and protection of individual human and civil rights.[33] The incentive to aggregate would consist of the advantages of participating in an effective self-government with resources for self-sufficiency. This incentive is countered, in practice, by the weight of vested interests in the existing institutions. Current practice indicates that the government is investing in the status quo represented by band governments created by Federal legislation.[34]

---

[29] RCAP vol. 2, part 1, above n 1, 22, Recommendation 2.2.1.
[30] See the BCTC website http://www.bctreaty.net at 17 November 2003.
[31] See the OTCS website http://www.otc.ca at 17 November 2003.
[32] *Gathering Strength*, above, n 26, 15.
[33] The 1991 Aboriginal Justice Inquiry of Manitoba recommended that small communities aggregate into larger ones for the purpose of administering their own justice systems on an American regional model from the northwest of the United States. It is difficult to judge one's neighbour fairly. See Alvin Hamilton and Murray Sinclair, *Report of the Aboriginal Justice Inquiry of Manitoba: The Justice System and Aboriginal People* (Queen's Printer, Winnipeg, 1991).
[34] For example, see Bill C-6, an Act to establish the Canadian Centre for the Independent Resolution of First Nations Specific Claims to provide for the filing, negotiation and resolution of specific claims and to make related amendments to other Acts, 18 March 2003 (Canada), available online: http://www.parl.gc.ca/37/2/parlbus/chambus/house/bills/government/C-6/C-6_3/C-6 at 17 November 2003. Also see, Bill C-7, First Nations Governance Act, 2003 (Canada), available online at: http://www.parl.gc.ca/37/2/parlbus/chambus/house/bills/government/C-7/C-7_1/90192bE.html at 17 November 2003. And see, Bill C-49, an Act providing for the ratification and the bringing into effect of the Framework Agreement on First Nation Land Management, 1998 (Canada), available online at: http://www.parl.gc.ca/36/1/parlbus/chambus/house/bills/government/C-49/C-49_1/C-49_cover-E.html at 17 November 2003.

That practice may be illustrated by reference to the process in British Columbia, where treaties are being negotiated for the first time due to an historical anomaly which saw only a very few treaties entered into in the early days of settlement. The British Columbia process involves negotiations on 'self-government' agreements with single Indian bands or aggregations of Indian bands. Only bands recognised in the *Indian Act* and historically administered by Indian and Northern Affairs Canada (INAC) qualify, although the outcome of a treaty process is likely to result in removing the band status and replacing it with a corporate entity defined by the aboriginal party, as was done in the *Nisga'a Treaty*.[35]

In the British Columbia treaty process, advanced treaty negotiations that expressly identify governance as a subject matter are being conducted with bands that vary in population size from 136 to 7517 people, with an average of 1782 and a median of 800 people.[36] Even the largest of these will have a relatively small physical capacity to govern effectively on the RCAP standards. It is possible that the eventual results of the negotiations will recognise 'self-government' more in name than in substance. In any case, the process indicates that changes from the status quo and moves towards the creation of larger federal entities will be, at best, slow and incremental, and that effective self-governing entities are not a likely outcome in the short term.[37]

Extension to all aboriginal peoples

'Gathering Strength' states that the government is prepared to negotiate treaties with any aboriginal group, but only where the provinces agree.[38] In practice, the treaty negotiations have not been extended beyond the Indian and Inuit people who were previously recognised.[39] The RCAP model would require adopting recognition legislation containing objective criteria against which new applicant groups of 'non-status Indians',[40] and Métis people

---

[35] *Nisga'a Final Agreement Act* SBC 1999, c 2.

[36] The information about the treaty process is taken from the BCTC's website, above n 30, on 1 August 2003, and supplemented by inquiries made to government officials by Val Napoleon, whose able assistance is gratefully acknowledged.

[37] See de Costa, this volume; see Tehan, this volume.

[38] *Gathering Strength*, above n 26.

[39] Historical treaties have generally been entered into with 'Indian' groups, and modern treaties with Indian and Inuit groups. Outside the Northwest Territories, the Federal government has not negotiated with Métis groups, although that might change following a recent decision of the Supreme Court of Canada recognising the aboriginal rights of a Métis community: *R v Powley* [2003] SCJ No 43, QL SCC File No 28533, 19 September, 2003. See RCAP, vol. 2, part 1, above n 1; see also above n 17 and n 18.

[40] 'Non-status Indians' are Indians who do not meet the criteria for registration as an Indian under the federal *Indian Act*. They are consequently not members of federally recognised

would be assessed. Panels of the Aboriginal Lands and Treaties Tribunal would make recommendations on acceptance to the Federal Cabinet. Political conflicts between the Federal and provincial governments to avoid spending money on more aboriginal people appears to be one reason for resistance to an extension of the treaty process. But there is another fundamental issue:

> The practical reality is that Canadian governments will likely balk at the prospect of self-defining, sub-state, self-governing entities that claim the right to come into existence and to claim a particular population of Canadian citizens as being under their jurisdiction without regard to the other governments with whom they will be in a relationship. In particular, they will wish to retain for themselves the prerogative of having some say in whether or not they wish to deal with the new entities.[41]

Experience with recognition policy and practice in the United States of America suggests that objective criteria such as proposed by the RCAP are preferable to the alternative of allowing the courts and non-aboriginal governments to develop their own recognition criteria.[42]

As demonstrated by the evidence from the British Columbia Treaty Commission (BCTC) process, the present criteria for recognition continue the recognition policy of the nineteenth-century *Indian Act*, extended only in the cases of the Inuit of the north and the Métis in the Northwest Territories, where only Federal constitutional jurisdiction applies. A recent analysis concluded that, since the Constitution recognises three distinct groups of aboriginal peoples, 'the challenge is to design a principled and defensible recognition policy or statutory regime that extends to all three of the Aboriginal peoples of Canada: Indian, Inuit and Métis'.[43]

New institutions to facilitate the treaty process

At the time of writing, the House of Commons has passed a bill that would set up a commission and a tribunal to deal with a narrow range of issues

---

'bands' and are not entitled to live on Indian reserves. Status Indians are aboriginal people or non-aboriginal people who have married or been adopted by aboriginal people who meet the criteria and are registered. See generally Giokas and Groves, below n 43, 41–82.

[41] John Giokas, 'Domestic Recognition in the United States and Canada' in Paul L.A.H. Chartrand (ed.), *Who Are Canada's Aboriginal Peoples?: Recognition, Definition and Jurisdiction* (Purich Publishing Ltd., Saskatoon, 2002) 126–7.

[42] Ibid, especially Russel L. Barsh, 'Political Recognition: An Assessment of American Practice', in Chartrand (ed.), above n 41, 230–57.

[43] John Giokas and Robert Groves, 'Collective and Individual Recognition in Canada', in Chartrand, above n 41, 73.

called 'specific claims'.[44] The tribunal would not perform the range of functions outlined in the RCAP report.

There are two provincial bodies with functions related to those listed for commissions as proposed by the RCAP in the recommendations that were reviewed earlier in this chapter. The Office of the Treaty Commissioner of Saskatchewan (OTCS)[45] and the BCTC[46] both assist in processes of negotiations relating to treaties, the former in a province in which historic treaties have been signed and the latter in a province involved in negotiating new treaties.[47] It may be mentioned that each differs in some significant respects from the models proposed by the RCAP, but it is beyond the scope of this chapter to examine these bodies in detail.[48]

Towards justice and reconciliation

The RCAP idea of nation-to-nation relationships institutionalised in treaties between the Crown and aboriginal peoples has not been officially rejected by the Federal Government. Some ideas and models in the RCAP final report are being adopted, but in a slow, tentative and incremental fashion, typical of change in aboriginal policy in Canada. There have been no ringing endorsements or calls from governments for fundamental change of the kind envisaged by the RCAP, although aboriginal leaders continue, from time to time, to invoke the views of the RCAP. The report has also been endorsed by United Nations treaty bodies responsible for supervising Canada's obligations under the international human rights treaty regime.[49]

One of the enduring contributions of the final report is probably its analysis of the issues and demonstration that, where governments are committed to change, there are feasible and legitimate means to accomplish such change. The report is also a useful source of official support for aboriginal people and their aspirations, and goes some way in demonstrating that doing the right thing by aboriginal people is in fact in the national interest. Justice and reconciliation are elusive goals. The RCAP tried to make a difference in the way people conceived those goals in relation to the aboriginal peoples in Canada.

---

[44] Bill C-6, above n 34.

[45] OTCS, above n 31.

[46] BCTC, above n 30.

[47] Ibid.

[48] See de Costa, this volume.

[49] Two of the three reports are discussed in Ted Moses, 'The Right of Self-Determination and Its Significance to the Survival of Indigenous Peoples' in Pekka Aikio and Martin Scheinin (eds), *Operationalizing the Right of Indigenous Peoples to Self-Determination* (Institute for Human Rights, Abo Akademi University, Turku, 2000) ch 8.

Chapter 7

Treaties in British Columbia: Comprehensive Agreement Making in a Democratic Context

Ravi de Costa

Introduction

Agreement making in British Columbia arose out of a systematic campaign of contention and political development over several decades by native peoples[1] in the province.[2] A decade into negotiations, obstacles to reaching agreements remain, and reflect the large gaps between expectations held by the respective parties: while native peoples expect the recognition of their rights and justice for their historical and contemporary denial, governments appear more clearly focused on creating economic and legal certainty.

This chapter briefly describes the origins of treaty making in British Columbia. It sets out the major features of the process and examines those issues that have proved most complex in the search for comprehensive agreements between Indigenous peoples and government.

However, the advanced nature of discussions in British Columbia provides an opportunity to consider the growing scrutiny of agreements as representative and democratic acts. The chapter concludes with a short consideration of the difficulties in getting comprehensive agreements reached by political leaderships ratified and accepted by broader constituencies.

---

[1] I use the terms 'native/s' and 'native peoples' to refer to all Indigenous people in the province. The term 'first nation' denotes those native groups participating in the treaty process.

[2] Paul Tennant, *Aboriginal Peoples and Politics the Indian Land Question in British Columbia: 1849–1989* (University of British Columbia Press, Vancouver, 1991); Ravi de Costa, 'Treaty How?' (2003) 4 *The Drawing Board: An Australian Review of Public Affairs* 1–22.

Overview of treaty making

History

In Jean Barman's history of British Columbia, *The West Beyond the West*, she argues that 'provincial governments have been little concerned with a broader vision of what BC might become, were they to venture beyond the immediate demands of a resource-based economy'.[3]

Litigation and direct action

From the 1970s, natives in the province began demonstrating the limits and injustice of this vision by asserting a politics that had been developing through the twentieth century.[4] This was manifest both in a clear political philosophy and organisational sophistication. Combining litigation and direct action, natives were able to manage internal political differences and to present an increasingly united and effective challenge to the colonial state.[5]

Legal and physical challenge

By the 1980s, the range of legal and physical challenges was striking. Native communities disrupted a variety of resource industries, with a particular focus on logging, which in British Columbia is critical to the export economy and to employment. In the remote northeast, the Kaska-Dena people blocked access to logging roads; the Nuu-chah-nulth took similar action on Meares Island; on the Queen Charlotte Islands, Haida communities obstructed logging itself; the Kwakiutl protested on Deare Island; the Nisga'a in the Northwest, the Lillooet in the Cariboo or central interior and the Nlaka'pamux in the southern interior all obstructed railway constructions; Indians province-wide threatened not to participate in the census, which meant that British Columbia stood to lose up to $3000 per person in Federal transfer payments;[6] the Gitksan-Wetsuweten in the northwest took offensive action, hurling marshmallows at fisheries officers in a confrontation; McLeod Lake Band near the Alberta border not only obstructed a logging road but actually started taking logs themselves.[7] These and many other actions took place within a span of a few years in the mid-1980s.

---

[3]   Jean Barman, *The West Beyond the West: A History of British Columbia* (University of Toronto Press, Toronto, 1996) 356.

[4]   Tennant, above n 2, 174.

[5]   de Costa, above n 2, 1–22.

[6]   Larry Pynn, 'Indian Snub of Census Under Review', *The Vancouver Sun* (Vancouver, BC), 4 September 1986, A10.

[7]   Tennant, above n 2, 207.

Native people understood that their political development and success relied on the renewal of social identities based in the control over traditional lands and resources. By attacking the core of provincial legitimacy—resource development—natives were thereby energising their own political identity. The extent of their disruption both to provincial authority and to economic prosperity had figures in the Provincial Government extremely concerned. David Mitchell, a member of the Provincial Cabinet and Vice-President of the lumber company Westar, suggested that the provincial system for allocating resources had broken down completely: 'it is no longer certain who controls the forests in northwest BC'.[8]

Though Canada has a long history of agreement making, British Columbia saw very little of this.[9] In fact, the assumption of provincial authorities was, at least since the 1880s, that the territory was *terra nullius*.[10] This was overturned in *Calder et al v Attorney General of British Columbia*,[11] a ruling that gave further impetus to litigation and direct-action strategies, but which also forced the Federal government into a new policy of 'comprehensive claims'. Beginning with the Nisga'a, a number of British Columbian native communities entered into negotiations with the government of Canada.

However, the Province remained intransigent. Though constitutional authority over natives is held solely by the Federal Government, under s 91 (24) of the *Constitution Act 1867*,[12] provinces retained control over resources. Moreover, the bulk of Crown land is held in right of the Province. Consequently, it was only activism and litigation that forced the Province's reversal, which led to the tripartite process in place today. That contentious pre-history of treaty making clearly shaped the structure and expectations of the process that is now in place.

Structure of process

After that period of sustained conflict focused on natural resources, the initial phases of the treaty process were relatively consensual and optimistic. The Social Credit government began reform in the late 1980s and in 1990

---

[8] Terry Glavin, 'Westar Joins Northwest Timber Protest', *The Vancouver Sun* (Vancouver, BC), 23 February 1990, B3.

[9] The few exceptions include the Douglas treaties reached on Vancouver Island in the 1860s and Treaty 8 concluded in 1908, which straddled the Alberta–British Columbia border. The latter was the subject of an 'adhesion' by the McLeod Lake Band in 2000.

[10] In 1887, Premier William Smithe refused a petition from a delegation of Nisga'a chiefs, dismissing them as 'little better than the wild beasts of the field', quoted in Tennant, above n2, 58.

[11] [1973] SCR 313 ('*Calder*').

[12] *The Constitution Act 1982*, being Schedule B to the *Canada Act 1982* (UK) c 11, pt 1, s 1–34. The Constitution Act replaced the *British North America Act 1867*.

commissioned a task force to examine the issues. The 1991 *Report of the British Columbia Claims Task Force*[13] (*The Report*) was endorsed in full by the major stakeholders. Though the Provincial Government changed during this period, a formal agreement was signed by the so-called three 'principals' of treaty making: British Columbia, Canada and the First Nations Summit, a body which emerged quickly to represent first nations interested in negotiating.

The resulting *Tripartite Treaty Commission Agreement 1992* led to the *British Columbia Treaty Commission Act 1995*,[14] which created a body that would oversee the process and draw on public revenues. Specifically, the British Columbia Treaty Commission (BCTC) would chair meetings and keep records, but it would also determine 'readiness' and distribute Negotiation Support Funding to first nations (see below). By the end of 1993, the Commission was established and began to receive statements of intent from first nations.

Stage 1: Statement of intent

This is the first of six stages that comprise treaty making. Individual first nations initiate negotiations by submitting a formal Statement of Intent, comprising a rough indication of their traditional territories and a sense of who the relevant community is and how it is represented.

Stage 2: Demonstration of readiness and mandate

The second stage involves both first nations and the two governments, and requires them to demonstrate 'readiness' for negotiations; that is, the capacity of each party to undertake negotiations and to demonstrate that it has a 'mandate' from its constituents. Once this is done, the BCTC declares each 'table' ready to commence negotiations proper.

Stage 3: Framework Agreement

Stage three requires the parties to reach agreement about an agenda for negotiating, known as a 'Framework Agreement'. This includes detail on the structure of the negotiations—will side-tables on particular issues be required?—as well as a broad and inclusive indication of the issues that the parties wish to have discussed. Once a Framework Agreement is initialled at the table, it undergoes ratification processes set out at stage two. Some first nations have decided to take their agreements to their entire communities at each stage; others such as the Lheidli T'enneh have set up Community

---

[13] The British Columbia Claims Task Force, *The Report of the British Columbia Claims Task Force* (The Government of British Columbia: Treaty Negotiations Office, Victoria, BC, 28 June 1991).

[14] *British Columbia Treaty Commission Act* SC 1995, c 45.

Treaty Councils, on which a member of each family in the community deliberates on documents drafted at treaty tables.

Stage 4: Agreement in Principle

Stage four is the first substantive stage of negotiations: the parties work through the issues they have identified, the goal being to draft chapters of agreement on each topic, such as land and resources, fiscal relations or wildlife management. The collection of these drafts is an Agreement in Principle (AIP) and requires ratification once again; the Provincial Government ratifies an AIP via Cabinet approval.

Stage 5: Final Agreement

Stage five attempts to turn drafts into a complete text that would become the Final Agreement. At this point, a process of review is undertaken to ensure that nothing conflicts with the entitlements of all Canadians as set out in the Charter of Rights and Freedoms.[15] This stage requires ratification by all three parties, a community referendum in the case of first nations, as well as approval by both the British Columbia Legislature and the Parliament of Canada.

Stage 6: Treaty

On the 'effective date', the Final Agreement becomes a treaty in the terms of s 35 of the *Constitution Act*. Implementation, including transfer of resources and powers, comprises stage six of the process. At this point, the relevant community is no longer administered under the *Indian Act*,[16] but under terms of its own making.

A central imperative of *The Report* was that negotiations be 'comprehensive': simply, that discussion and agreements should include all matters that parties wish to deal with; unilateral refusals were not countenanced. This measure was an acknowledgment of the 'nation-to-nation' character of native claims through the 1980s.

Fairness and interest-based negotiation

However, the fact that small first-nation communities are in comprehensive negotiations with the Provincial and Federal governments means that a

---

[15] Canadian Charter of Rights and Freedoms being Part I of the *Constitution Act*. The *Constitution Act* also brought a number of protections for Indigenous peoples: s 35 defines the three aboriginal peoples of Canada (Indian, Inuit and Métis) and protects existing aboriginal and treaty rights, including those yet to be reached; s 35(1) obliges Canada to consult extensively with Indigenous peoples before amending these entitlements. However, the focus of the stage five review is primarily to ensure that draft agreements do not conflict with the entitlements of all Canadians set out in the Charter of Rights and Freedoms.

[16] *Indian Act*, RS 1985, c 32.

huge imbalance exists in both capacity and resources to negotiate, making the process of negotiating quite unequal. A remedy for this was Negotiation Support Funding: funding to first nations would be 80 per cent through loans, with 20 per cent in the form of grants. Loans are repayable seven years after each table reaches an Agreement in Principle or twelve years after the first loan if talks break down. As of September 2003, $255 million had been disbursed since the beginning of the process, $204 million as loans;[17] $38 million in total was available in 2002–2003.[18]

There are mixed views on the equity of this policy, but many first nations find it objectionable that they must go into debt in order to have their rights recognised. Debt also creates some practical problems, by obstructing first nations' access to commercial credit.[19]

Another measure to ensure fairness was a stated commitment to 'interest-based negotiation', which emerged from the work of the Harvard Negotiation Project.[20] Yet, this has been the subject of strong criticism amongst first nations.

An 'interest' for natives might be something like ensuring that zoning or resource-use decisions were highly sensitive to concerns for traditional burial grounds. This contrasts with the 'position' that native groups must control the zoning or resource-allocation processes themselves. One of the intentions of this alternative model of negotiation is to help create good will and trust among the parties.[21] It often seems not to have arisen. Although relations between individuals on tables are often good, it is the view of first nations that government negotiators do not come to the table to negotiate, but calculate their bottom-line away from treaty tables. Rick Krehbiel, analyst with the Lheidli T'enneh Band, summarised in 2000 the disappointment felt over interest-based negotiations on the crucial issue of the amounts of land and cash to be included in their settlement:

> [T]he first big lie! … if I ever get involved in litigating this process, the first issue I will raise on the bad faith issue is the myth of interest-based negotiations… One of the real problems with the process is that the land and cash stuff is never negotiated. It comes out of a cost-sharing formula, it's created by shadowy people who live in the basement in Victoria and Ottawa. It's not made by the

---

[17] British Columbia Treaty Commission, *British Columbia Treaty Commission Annual Report: Where Are We?* (BCTC, Vancouver, BC, 2003) 40.

[18] British Columbia Treaty Commission, *British Columbia Treaty Commission Annual Report: The Changing Landscape* (BCTC, Vancouver, BC, 2002) 29.

[19] Ravi de Costa, *New Relationships, Old Certainties: Australia's Reconciliation and the Treaty-Process in British Columbia* (PhD Thesis, Swinburne University of Technology, 2002) 213–6.

[20] Trudy Govier, 'Trust, Acknowledgment and the Ethics of Negotiation' (Paper presented at the Speaking Truth to Power: A Treaty Forum, Victoria, BC, 2–3 March 1999).

[21] Ibid.

treaty process, it's simply a financial tug-of-war between the lowest forms of bureaucrat … those 2 key things, the key to the whole process, are never negotiated.[22]

Central issues and major challenges at treaty tables

Such problems simply reflect the power imbalance between the parties. On the one hand, individual first nations are beholden in new ways to the state as well as to a range of outside experts in order to achieve the technical capacity simply to be able to negotiate with governments; on the other, key issues are not actually negotiated at the treaty table. Despite this, some tables have seen that on a range of issues common ground can be reached. Recently, a number of tables at stage four appear to have made progress with in-principle agreements on substantive issues such as the amount of lands and resources to be included in treaty settlements. These are considered later in the chapter.

However, other issues of importance to nearly every table have proved less amenable to resolution. Following is a discussion of two issues that go to the heart of the relationship between governments and first nation peoples: its past, in the form of compensation and its present, manifest in the issue of interim measures. Later, the chapter considers briefly the central issue for the future of the relationship between peoples, the question of native self-government.

Compensation

The Report clearly contemplated that compensation would be discussed, recommending discussions without 'unilateral restriction'. Moreover, it noted that negotiations may:

> include consideration of a financial component to recognize past use of land and resources and First Nation's ongoing interests … The task force encourages the parties to reach a negotiated solution by bargaining with good will and good faith in the determination of compensation.[23]

First nations maintain that compensation is one of the fundamental reasons they are involved in the comprehensive process. A resolution

---

[22] Interview with Rick Krehbiel, Treaty Analyst, Lheidli T'enneh First Nation (Prince George, BC, 26 August 2000).
[23] The British Columbia Claims Task Force, above n 13, part 2.

reached at the First Nations Summit in May 1998 by native leaders involved in the treaty process decided that no Final Agreements would be reached that did not clearly set out the wrongs committed against first nations and offer compensation for them.[24] The position reflects first nations' leaders like Sliammon Chief, Denise Smith:

> All the time the people have been in our territory, making money, building businesses, there's been no compensation for our people, and it will not be discussed in the treaty process.[25]

Canada maintains that 'history has been dealt with'[26] through its response to the Royal Commission on Aboriginal Peoples: Gathering Strength—Canada's Aboriginal Action Plan provided an official apology (particularly to the victims of the residential schools policy) and $350 million as a 'healing fund'.[27] Canada insists that the cash component of treaty settlements is therefore an exchange of 'value for value'; that is, the purchase of legal certainty.[28] British Columbia has allowed for a 'blend of approaches', recognising that while natives will probably see cash settlements as compensation, the Province sees them as providing the basis for future development.[29]

One could reflect on the kind of relationship that allows parties to openly differ on this matter: at one level it might appear to be an appropriate recognition of difference in community values. However, it could be argued that this ignores both the disparities of power between the parties, and the central historical rationale for comprehensive negotiations: natives' desire, steadfastly maintained since contact, for recognition and justice. The tacit agreement-to-disagree over compensation is disingenuous; such an attitude toward compensation for past injustice defeats its purpose. Compensation is fundamentally a positive recognition of the difference that originally justified native dispossession and abuse, and which now underpins their ongoing predicament of marginalisation.

---

[24] First Nations Summit, *The Road to Treaty Negotiations in British Columbia: A Chronology of Key Events* (First Nations Summit, Vancouver, BC, 2001).

[25] Denise Smith, 'Summary of Proceedings/Treaty Panel' (Speech delivered at the Island Coast Summit, 9 August 2000).

[26] Eric Denhoff, Negotiator for Canada (Speech delivered at the Gitanyow Main Table Meeting, Vancouver, BC, September 17, 1999).

[27] Government of Canada: Indian Affairs and Northern Development, *Gathering Strength—Canada's Aboriginal Action Plan* (Published under the authority of the Minister of Indian Affairs and Northern Development, Ontario, Ottawa, 1997).

[28] Tom Molloy, Chief Negotiator, Federal Treaty Negotiation Office, quoted in Burke Lewis, 'Into the Billions and Beyond' (1998) *British Columbia Report*, online at http://www.axionet.com/bcreport/web/980202f.html at 11 December 2000.

[29] Dale Lovick, 'Address to First Nations Summit' (Speech delivered at the First Nations Summit, Squamish, BC, 29 October 1999).

Interim measures

In Recommendation 16, *The Report* recognised that treaties would take time, explicitly calling for a process that would protect and share lands and resources before each treaty was concluded. A range of interim measure options was contemplated:

1. notification of potential impacts on issues that may be discussed at treaty tables, particularly unilateral action on lands and resources
2. consultation over that action
3. consent for such initiatives
4. joint management processes requiring consensus
5. restrictions or moratoria on land and resource use.

The Supreme Court ruling in *Delgamuukw v British Columbia*[30] clearly confirmed the wisdom of this policy and, as McNeil has argued, characterised resource activities as **requiring** native involvement.[31] Yet, first nations have been extremely dissatisfied with the interim measure policy. Again, the Province has been reluctant to contemplate interim arrangements until tables reach stage four. Chief Treaty Commissioner Miles Richardson pointed out the problem with such policy:

> First Nations are largely saying, and I think quite legitimately that, 'it's just not on that we continue sitting negotiating at treaty tables accumulating huge amounts of debt when the very assets, the very resources that we're talking about are rolling by our offices on logging trucks'.[32]

A raft of interim measures was reached through late 1999 and 2000, in part a response to the then-New Democratic Party (NDP) government's deep unpopularity and the perception that the treaty process was achieving nothing other than continued public expenditure and mounting first-nation indebtedness. Yet, upon examination, there is little substance to the agreements arising out of the interim-measure provisions and certainly not the native participation in the resource sector envisaged in *The Report*. Some of the measures provide basic infrastructure to native communities, such as the maintenance of access roads in winter.[33] In the late 1990s, an additional policy emerged under the name 'Treaty Related Measures': clearly designed

---

[30] [1997] 3 SCR ('*Delgamuukw*').

[31] Kent McNeil, 'Defining Aboriginal Title in the '90s: Has the Supreme Court Finally Got It Right?' (Paper presented at the Twelfth Annual Robarts Lecture, Robarts Centre for Canadian Studies, York University, Toronto, Ontario, 25 March 1998) 13.

[32] Interview with Miles Richardson, Chief Treaty Commissioner of British Columbia (Vancouver, BC, 12 October 1999).

[33] British Columbia Treaty Commission, *British Columbia Treaty Commission Annual Report: Update* (BCTC, Vancouver, BC, March, 2001).

to keep first nations in treaty discussions, it offered small amounts of funding to study economic ventures that may come to fruition after a treaty is concluded.[34] In its 2001 review of the process, *Looking Back, Looking Forward*, the Commission pointed out that, of sixty recently agreed measures, only one was a land-protection agreement.[35] The 'First Nations Economic Measures Fund' of $30 million, introduced by the incoming Liberal government in 2002, keeps entirely within these parameters.

Treaties in a democratic context

Fifty-three first nations are involved in the British Columbia treaty process. Several first nations sit at joint tables, meaning there are forty-two tables. Very few Indigenous groups have joined the process since the *Delgamuukw* judgment of late 1997. Others have deprioritised negotiations, while some have formally withdrawn. The bulk of first nations are entrenched in the first substantive phase of negotiations (stage four), working towards an AIP. One table—the Sechelt—reached stage five, though since 2000 they have been in litigation against the province. Another, the Lheidli T'enneh, concluded stage four in July 2003.

However, in 2003, a number of draft AIPs have been reached (that is, documents initialled at treaty tables but not yet ratified by first-nation communities). There is growing confidence that several more first nations may be ready to enter into stage five. Before considering these developments, it is necessary to consider the context of treaty or agreement making within a democratic setting such as contemporary British Columbia.

During the passage of the enabling provincial legislation in 1992, one event pointed to future complexity: though there was unanimity on the need for comprehensive negotiations, the then-NDP government arranged for a reception to celebrate the passage of the bill and the dawn of a new relationship between the peoples. It was planned in advance of the bill's presentation to the Legislature and clearly it was thought that Legislative approval was a mere formality; the real agreement had in actual fact taken place between government and the First Nations Summit. The Leader of the Opposition found this 'contemptuous' of the role of the Legislature, though this did not stop him and his party from supporting the bill.[36]

---

[34] Ibid.

[35] British Columbia Treaty Commission, *British Columbia Treaty Commission Annual Report: Looking Back, Looking Forward* (BCTC, Vancouver, BC, 2001) 11.

[36] British Columbia, *Official Report of Debates of The Legislative Assembly*, Legislative Assembly, 25 May 1993, 6482 (Gordon Wilson).

As negotiations began to deal with substance on issues like fiscal relations, land quantum and self-government, the merely formal role of the Legislature became untenable, and bipartisanship began quickly to dissolve. By the mid-1990s there was a chorus of disapproval about the lack of transparency and accountability in treaty making. It began within resource industry groups hostile to any transfer of control over resources to native peoples, but quickly found a political ally in the Provincial Liberal party.[37]

The ratification of the Nisga'a AIP in 1996 gave this campaign a great deal of momentum and set the ground for the referendum policy. When the Nisga'a Final Agreement came before the Legislature in 1999, the government rejected the myriad amendments proposed by the Liberal opposition. After the longest provincial debate ever on a single bill, the government used its numbers to close debate and force a vote; the Opposition voted against ratification but was defeated. Party unanimity on treaties was gone and a nasty period ensued, during which treaty making was smeared as undemocratic.[38]

Negotiations continued through the late 1990s but produced negligible results, with a number of first nations abandoning or downgrading their negotiations. In May 2001, a provincial election in British Columbia radically changed the political landscape: the NDP was tossed out of office, with the Liberals taking seventy-seven of seventy-nine seats in the Legislature. The new government began implementing its only stated policy on treaties: a referendum to determine what would be the Provincial Government's 'mandate' at treaty tables.

Consequently, eight referendum questions were put to provincial voters in 2002.[39] These set out principles on issues such as self-government, recreational access to resources and the protection of private (non-Indigenous) property, which, if approved, would become binding under provincial law on treaty negotiators. Much of this was too vague to be helpful: recreational access to which resources, under what circumstances? Other questions were transparently malicious in their presentation of issues that had not arisen at tables, such as the idea that private fee simple (freehold) land might be expropriated.

The entire referendum demonstrated how close the accumulated history of conflict was beneath the surface of an established process. Boycotts by native peoples and their supporters, including public ballot burning,

---

[37] de Costa, above n 19, 311–22.

[38] Craig McInnes, 'Nisga'a Closure Enrages Liberals', *The Vancouver Sun* (Vancouver, BC) 21 April 1999; Willcocks, 'BC Government Pulls Plug on Debate of Nisga'a Treaty', *The Globe and Mail* (Toronto, Ontario), 22 April 1999.

[39] For full details of the referendum questions and the results see Elections British Columbia, *Report of the Chief Returning Officer on the Treaty Negotiations Referendum* (2002) http://www.elections.bc.ca/referendum/refreportfinal.pdf at 19 October 2003.

raised the temperature around native issues, but also ensured that majority support for the measures would be overwhelming.[40] None of the eight questions was approved by less than 84 per cent of voters, with many receiving over 90 per cent approval.

The full effect of this referendum is not yet clear, though it may already be producing new approaches to the issue of self-government. The referendum had asked voters whether they thought that native self-government should be 'municipal'; that is, delegated from the province, as is the case for local government. This was resoundingly approved, though it flatly contradicts the Federal Government's 1995 policy of an **inherent** right to self-government.[41]

In the year since the referendum, several AIPs have come out of tables around the province, but no uniform approach to governance is visible: several drafts see the parties consent to a native government but agree that it will be a separate document, not part of the main treaty and not protected by the Constitution.

Moreover, the government will exist only for a fixed (unstated) term and will be subject to review by the parties at that time.[42] Others, such as that reached by the Tsawwassen First Nation, include a categorical statement that its self-government will be protected by the Constitution. The Lheidli T'enneh First Nation's AIP provides for some aspects to be protected with others reviewable, a situation that offers them flexibility provided the First Nation retains control over which aspects will be so protected.[43]

It is far from clear how this will articulate with the result of the referendum and what the effects on the government's legitimacy will be. Elsewhere in provincial politics, the populist and majoritarian vision of democracy is gathering steam, with a province-wide Citizen's Assembly on electoral reform well underway.[44]

[40] Damian Inwood, 'War Council to Battle Land-Claim Referendum', *The Province* (Victoria, BC), 20 July 2001; Aboriginal Rights Coalition, *Should I Vote No?* (2002) http://members.tripod.com/arcbc/index.htm at 2 April 2002.

[41] Government of Canada: Indian Affairs and Northern Development, *The Government of Canada's Approach to Implementation of the Inherent Right and the Negotiation of Aboriginal Self-Government: A Federal Policy Guide* (Published under the authority of the Minister of Indian Affairs and Northern Development, Ontario, Ottawa, 1995).

[42] See British Columbia Treaty Commission, *Sliammon Draft Agreement in Principle: Chapter 12* (2003) http://www.bctreaty.net/nations_2/agreements/SliammonAIP.pdf at 19 October 2003; British Columbia Treaty Commission, *Maa-nulth First Nation Treaty Negotiations: Chapter 12* (2003) http://www.bctreaty.net/nations_2/agreements/Maa-nulthAiP.pdf at 19 October 2003.

[43] Email from Rick Krehbiel, Treaty Analyst, Lheidli T'enneh First Nation to Ravi de Costa, 4 August 2003.

[44] See British Columbia, 'Citizens' Assembly on Electoral Reform' http://www.citizensassembly.bc.ca/citizensassembly.html at 19 October 2003.

Comprehensive negotiations are also subject to developments in other democratic processes. A recent judgment in the British Columbia Provincial Court, *R v Kapp et al*,[45] ruled as unconstitutional a federal licensing scheme to provide for native-only fisheries. Justice William Kitchen felt that, 'the most troubling aspect of this discrimination is that it is government sponsored. The government should be setting an example for the rest of society, but unfortunately, this has not been our history'.[46]

Begun in 1992 as a way to both acknowledge native rights and provide jobs and revenue for native communities, this licensing scheme was certainly part of the calculations of first nations working on agreements. Kim Baird, chief of the Tsawwassen First Nation—and one of the first nations most committed to treaty negotiations—is now calling for compensation for the loss of their commercial fishing rights: 'This is really going to affect our families ... We are very, very frustrated and upset, and this is definitely going to make the potential for conflict worse'.[47]

Such pressures will become acute as draft agreements go through community ratification procedures. The fact that throughout the history of the process, the bulk of substantive agreements made at treaty tables (that is, stage-four agreements) have been rejected by native communities, suggests that there may be discontinuities between the leadership negotiating the agreement and the community itself. Snuneymuxw First Nation was scheduled on 21 June 2003 to hold a ratification vote for the AIP initialled at their table. Jeff Thomas of the Snuneymuxw Treaty Office described why this did not happen:

> We had quite a number of our membership come forward that were not comfortable with the AIP. They did not understand enough to be comfortable in voting.[48]

Though Snuneymuxw are confident that patience and an education process will ensure ratification, part of the difficulties faced by native peoples in terms of ratification is the realisation that such agreements will increase the power of their own leaderships. During the ratification of the Nisga'a Final Agreement (conducted outside the British Columbia process but in a substantially similar manner), the final vote to ratify the agreement included a ballot on a future Nisga'a constitution that had at the time not been seen by the Nisga'a community.[49] The challenges to be faced by

---

[45] [2003] BCPC 0279.

[46] Ibid, 235.

[47] Rod Mickleburgh, 'Natives Vow to Catch and Sell BC Salmon Despite Ruling', *The Globe and Mail* (Toronto, Ontario) 2 August 2003, A7.

[48] Email from Jeff Thomas, Snuneymuxw Treaty Office to Ravi de Costa, 21 July 2000.

[49] Diane Rinehart, 'Close Vote on Nisga'a Deal 'Disappointment', *The Vancouver Sun* (Vancouver, BC), 12 November 1998; 'Nisga'a Head to Polls', *The Vancouver Sun* (Vancouver, BC), 6 November 1998.

Indigenous people in developing the capacity to realise the promise of these agreements and to trust in the new political and governing structures they create, are hardly insignificant.

Conclusion

There is much optimism surrounding the capacity for treaties to rebalance the colonial relationship. In Robert Williams' excellent history *Linking Arms Together*, he finds that, for American Indians, early colonial treaties were ways of demonstrating trust, of making personal connections and sharing stories. These highly symbolic 'acts of commitment', such as exchanges of gifts or smoking a common pipe, enabled shared processes of justice to begin.[50] In the words of Annette Beier, this is 'made settled by the fact that the first or early performers' example is followed, their confidence confirmed, general expectation of further conformity strengthened and so a general custom launched.'[51]

Shorn of their rhetorical boilerplate and corporate dressage, modern treaties look nothing like this. In British Columbia, discussion at treaty tables provide neither native or settler communities with models of exemplary behaviour, other than perhaps the common sense principle that it is good for people to talk to each other. In fact, treaty negotiations are highly technical expressions of future systems of rule; the codification of exemplary behaviour, rather than its performance.

It can be no other way. Compared to the early colonial examples, both 'sides' are far less homogenous than they were; connections between the two are innumerable and structures of legitimacy and authority significantly different. The hope that senior figures might together enact a performance (or text) that was wholly representative, widely supported and yet aspirational, appears lost amid the regulation and alienation of modern life.

Yet, two things about the British Columbia process suggest it is cast in anachronistic terms. One has been dealt with here: the issue of comprehensiveness; the second—'certainty' or finality—has been considered at length elsewhere.[52] A project that requires settler or native leaders, in the present moment, to comprehensively and conclusively set out the needs and desires of their communities, is ambitious to say the least. It places great faith in the forbearance of all others not to use democratic institutions and values in ways that alter or undermine treaties. The evidence from British Columbia encourages an incremental approach, even a permanent culture of negotiation.

---

[50] Robert Williams, *Linking Arms Together: American Indian Treaty Visions of Law and Peace 1600–1800* (Oxford University Press, New York, 1997) 125.

[51] Annette Beier, cited in Williams, above n 50, 125–6.

[52] de Costa, above n 19, 279–89.

Chapter 8

The Shadow of the Law and the British Columbia Treaty Process: '[Can] the unthinkable become common place'?[1]

Maureen Tehan

Introduction

Treaty making between Indigenous peoples and the Crown has been a part of the Canadian landscape since the early period of colonisation.[2] The latter part of the twentieth century has seen an explosion in agreement making, particularly through the modern comprehensive claims policy.[3] It is this political development, backed by some crucial developments in common law aboriginal rights and aboriginal title, that has made 'the unthinkable commonplace' throughout much of Canada. British Columbia remains the exception and, in spite of some major changes in the past ten years, such as the establishment of a treaty process, while agreement and treaty making is no longer 'unthinkable', it is far from 'common place'. This disjunction is the focus of this chapter.

---

[1] Bradford Morse, 'The Continuing Significance of Historic Treaties and Modern Treaty Making: A Canadian and United States Perspective' (Paper presented at the Negotiating Settlements: Indigenous peoples, settler states and the significance of treaties and agreements in the Beyond the Frontier Seminar Series, Institute of Postcolonial Studies, Melbourne, 22 July 2002).

[2] For more information on Treaties, see Indian and Northern Affairs Canada, *Bibliography By Treaty* http://www.ainc-inac.gc.ca/pr/trts/hti/bib/trea1_e.htm at 1 November 2003 and *Historic Treaties Information* http://www.ainc-inac.gc.ca/pr/trts/hti/site/maindex_e.html at 1 November 2003; see Morse, this volume.

[3] For example, the Inuvialuit Agreement and the Nunavut Agreement: see Indian and Northern Affairs Canada http://www.ainc-inac.gc.ca/pr/agr/index_e.html at 1 November 2003; see Morse, this volume.

Treaty and agreement making occur in the 'shadow of the law', but the law and the shadow's reach are not always congruent. Law defines the boundaries of the parties' rights and thus can both expand and limit the possible. It can transform social and political relations, making the unthinkable common place or the impossible possible. Yet, law may also limit possibilities by narrowly defining rights or creating uncertainty. This process is highlighted by the uneven impact of the legal regimes that frame agreement making across Canada and the slow pace of agreement making in British Columbia compared with the rest of Canada.

Drawing on de Costa's political analysis,[4] this chapter reflects on legal developments in British Columbia that both underpin and limit or hinder the treaty process. In exploring the law's impact on agreement making in British Columbia, I argue that the British Columbia experience suggests that agreement making is influenced by a range of factors. Significant among these is the British Columbia Government's position in relation to negotiations and litigation as one aspect of the political conflict over the control of territory and resources.

The legal context: Defining rights

Mandell has identified four aspects of the 'unique constitutional position of the aboriginal peoples'[5] and the ways in which this limits the powers of the Province of British Columbia: exclusive federal legislative authority for Indians and Indian lands;[6] unextinguished aboriginal title, which is a burden on the Crown's title; the fiduciary relationship between the Crown and aboriginal peoples, sometimes referred to as the honour of the Crown; and protection of aboriginal rights and title by section 35 of the *Constitution Act 1982*.[7] This protection is subject to the justificatory principle (explained later in this chapter).

---

[4] de Costa, this volume.

[5] Louise Mandell QC, 'Recommended Referendum Ballot: A Legal Analysis' (2002), 2 (unpublished, copy on file).

[6] *Constitution Act 1982*, being Schedule B to the *Canada Act 1982* (UK) c 11, s 91(24). British Columbia joined the Confederation in 1871.

[7] Mandell, above n 5. Section 35 of the *Constitution Act 1982* states: '(1) The existing aboriginal and treaty rights of the aboriginal peoples of Canada are hereby recognized and affirmed. (2) In this Act, "aboriginal peoples of Canada" includes the Indian, Inuit and Métis peoples of Canada. (3) For greater certainty, in subsection (1) "treaty rights" includes rights that now exist by way of land claims agreements or may be so acquired. (4) Notwithstanding any other provisions of this Act, the aboriginal and treaty rights referred to in subsection (1) are guaranteed equally to male and female persons.'

These factors have framed the treaty process and negotiation and settlement, although with varied impacts in British Columbia. The import of these limitations has been explored in a number of cases, and the practical impact exemplified in others. Notwithstanding that almost all of these cases have emanated from British Columbia, the cases failed to ignite treaty making in British Columbia.[8]

Commencing with *Calder v Attorney-General of British Columbia*[9] in 1973, the recognition of aboriginal rights and title and their jurisprudential development has underpinned the definition and content of aboriginal rights, including title, and the manner in which governments must deal with them. *Calder* prised open a whole new set of possibilities, providing the impetus for the development of the Federal Government's Comprehensive Claims Policy, which has subsequently driven the modern claims process and resulted in a number of agreements across Canada.[10] Federal Government activity has not been matched by British Columbia. Although the Federal Government commenced negotiations in 1973 with the Nisga'a,[11] the plaintiffs in *Calder*, it was not until 1990[12] that the British Columbia Government joined the Nisga'a negotiations and moved to establish the tripartite British Columbia Treaty Process.[13] Since that time, the Province has only falteringly involved itself in the Treaty Process. There have been serious impediments to treaty making and, in general terms, there has been little significant progress other than in relation to the Nisga'a Treaty.[14] Just as *Calder* and the developments in other parts of Canada failed to produce change in British Columbia, similarly there has been little discernible change since the Treaty Process was established, or in response to some of the major Supreme Court decisions on common law aboriginal rights and title, particularly the Supreme Court decision in *Delgamuukw v British Columbia*.[15] The Province

---

[8] See de Costa, this volume for a discussion of the progress of treaty making under the British Columbia Treaty Process.

[9] *Calder v Attorney-General of British Columbia* [1973] SCR 313 ('*Calder*'); see Morse, this volume, 61.

[10] For example, the Inuvialuit Agreement and the Nunavut Agreement, above n 3; see Morse, this volume, 62.

[11] Concluded in 1998: see *Nisga'a Final Agreement Act* 2000, c 7.

[12] For a discussion of the approach to treaty making in British Columbia prior to 1990 see Paul Tennant, *Aboriginal Peoples and Politics: Indian Land Question in British Columbia 1849–1989* (UBC Press, Vancouver, 1990); Frank Cassidy, *Reaching Just Settlements: Land Claims in British Columbia* (Oolichan Books, Lantzville BC, 1991); Christopher McKee, *Treaty Talks in British Columbia: Negotiating a Mutually Beneficial Future* (2nd edn, UBC Press, Vancouver, 2000) 26–31; and de Costa, this volume, 135.

[13] McKee, above n 12, 32–33.

[14] See de Costa, this volume, 143; McKee, above n 12, 92–101. The current status of negotiations is available at the BC Treaty Commission Website http://www.bctreaty.net/files_2/updates.html at 1 November 2003.

[15] *Delgamuukw v British Columbia* [1997] 3 SCR 1010 ('*Delgamuukw*').

continued to grant third party rights regardless of aboriginal rights or title; interim measures established under the Treaty Process were rarely used and the lower courts failed to protect aboriginal rights and title through general law remedies.[16]

What then are the aboriginal rights that have been delineated and how has the British Columbia Government responded to them in the Treaty Process?

Obligations of the Crown

Guerin v R[17] and *R v Sparrow*[18] enunciated and expanded understandings and limitations of the relationship between the Crown and first nations. In *Guerin* the Provincial Government took a surrender of reserve land from the Musqueam and then leased the land to a third party on conditions less favourable to the Musqueam than those contained in the surrender. The Musqueam argued that this action of the Crown breached the fiduciary obligation that the Crown had to them arising out of their aboriginal title rights. The Supreme Court agreed, both affirming the recognition of aboriginal title as articulated in *Calder* and identifying and expanding upon the nature of the Crown's fiduciary obligation to aboriginal peoples.[19] The relationship between the Crown and first nations was said to be sourced in the concept of aboriginal title, and the fiduciary obligation arose as a result of the discretion the Crown had in dealing with aboriginal title/land.[20]

Regulation and extinguishment

In *Sparrow* the Supreme Court of Canada dealt with the effect of the fiduciary obligation in relation to legislation. The issue arose when Sparrow was charged with breaching regulations under the *Federal Fisheries Act 1970*. The Court concluded that s 35 of the *Constitution Act 1982* affirmed and protected aboriginal rights that were in existence in 1982. The aboriginal right to fish, although regulated by the scheme that generally controlled the fishery and thus limited the right to fish, was not extinguished.[21] Such regulation was

---

[16] McKee, above n 12, 92–96; Hamar Foster, *'Getting There' Speaking Truth to Power: A Treaty Forum* (Vancouver Law Commission of Canada, British Columbia Treaty Commission 2001) 165–80.

[17] [1984] 2 SCR 335 (*'Guerin'*).

[18] [1990] 1 SCR 1075 (*'Sparrow'*).

[19] *Guerin* [1984] 2 SCR 335, 379–388; and see Richard Bartlett, 'The Fiduciary Obligation of the Crown to the Indians' (1989) 53 *Saskatchewan Law Review* 301; Brian Slattery, 'Understanding Aboriginal Rights' (1987) 66 *Canadian Bar Review* 727; Len Rotman, 'Provincial Fiduciary Obligations to First Nations: The Nexus Between Governmental Power and Responsibility' (1994) 32 *Osgoode Hall Law Journal* 735.

[20] *Guerin* [1984] 2 SCR 335, 388–389.

[21] Sparrow [1990] 1 SCP 1075.

permissible, although subject to the operation of s 35 and the justification principles.[22]

Infringement and justification

The justification principle gives force to s 35 and helps to define the outer limits of Crown power in relation to aboriginal rights and title. As a result, it is a crucial component in the interplay of rights within treaty negotiations.

If a law or Crown action satisfies the *justification principle*, then it is effective and operates to infringe aboriginal rights, but does not extinguish them. *Sparrow* explored this principle.[23] The *justification principle* has two elements, or limbs. The valid legislative objective must be sufficiently compelling and substantial to justify overriding the constitutional rights otherwise protected by s 35. The principle also requires that the Crown discharge its fiduciary duty to aboriginal peoples in particular ways. There should be 'as little infringement as possible in order to'[24] achieve the desired objective. The test was further considered in *R v Gladstone*[25] and seemingly liberalised[26] but was revisited by the court in *Delgamuukw*.

In *Delgamuukw* the Supreme Court affirmed the two-limb test.[27] The Court expanded on the detail required for justification. The standard for applying this test was higher when infringement of aboriginal *title* was contemplated.[28] The proposed infringing action by the Crown must be significant; that is, it must relate to issues such as 'the development of agriculture, forestry, mining and hydroelectric power'[29] as well as more general issues such as protection of endangered species and the general economic development of the Province.[30] The government action should involve aboriginal people in the proposed development and reduce barriers for participation.[31] Given the control over land that is the concomitant of aboriginal title, there should be involvement of aboriginal people in decisions taken about their land. This involvement should include consultation but, 'in most cases, it will be significantly deeper than mere consultation. Some cases may even require the full consent of an aboriginal nation'.[32]

---

[22] Ibid, 1113–1119.

[23] Ibid.

[24] Ibid, 1119.

[25] *R v Gladstone* [1996] 2 SCR 723.

[26] Kent McNeil, 'How Can Infringement of the Constitutional Rights of Aboriginal Peoples Be Justified?' in Kent McNeil (ed.), *Emerging Justice?: Essays on Indigenous Rights in Canada and Australia* (Native Law Centre, Saskatoon, 2001) 281.

[27] *Delgamuukw* [1997] 3 SCR 1010, 1107–8.

[28] Ibid, 1112.

[29] Ibid, 1111.

[30] Ibid.

[31] Ibid, 1112.

[32] Ibid, 1113.

Aboriginal rights and aboriginal title

Aboriginal rights are central to this map of obligations, responsibilities and limitations that impinge on treaty negotiations. After *Sparrow*, there was uncertainty about the distinction between aboriginal rights and aboriginal title, the extent of the rights encompassed by each, the requirements for bringing rights and title within the purview of s 35 protection and the justificatory principles to be applied under s 35 of the *Constitution Act 1982* and the Charter of Rights. The extent of aboriginal rights was considered in the *Van der Peet* trilogy,[33] and aboriginal title was ultimately recognised and partially defined in *Delgamuukw*.

The *Van der Peet* trilogy narrowed the definition of aboriginal rights.[34] The cases, emanating from British Columbia, involved prosecutions for taking fish in commercial quantities or selling fish without the requisite licences. The Supreme Court enunciated the test for determining whether a practice was protected under s 35 as requiring that a practice be 'integral to the distinctive culture of the aboriginal group claiming the right'.[35] The Court indicated that the modern forms of cultural practices were protected by s 35 of the *Constitution Act 1982*.[36] Such practices could evolve over time and unbroken continuity was not required.[37] In *Van der Peet* the Court found that the Musqueam had failed to establish that commercial fishing was integral to their distinctive culture.[38] However, in *Gladstone* selling herring spawn on kelp was held integral to the distinctive culture of the Heiltsuk, as their society was based on trade and therefore the right to sell was an aboriginal right attracting the protection of s 35.[39]

By the mid-1990s then, there were a number of legal propositions supporting the notion of enforceable, constitutionally protected aboriginal rights protected by the Crown's fiduciary duty to aboriginal peoples. On the other hand, the rights were not sufficiently clear or enforceable to produce any significant change in the British Columbia Government's approach in the Treaty Process. The rights were narrowly defined, and the test for the justification of infringement of rights appeared to have been blurred, perhaps allowing greater Crown activity in regulating aboriginal rights. The significant

---

[33] *R v Van der Peet* [1996] 2 SCR 507; *R v Gladstone* [1996] 2 SCR 723; *R v NTC Smokehouse Ltd* [1996] 2 SCR 672.

[34] John Borrows, 'Frozen Rights in Canada: Constitutional Interpretation and the Trickster' (1997) 22 *American Indian Law Review* 37.

[35] *R v Van der Peet* [1996] 2 SCR 507, 549.

[36] Ibid, 554.

[37] Ibid, 557.

[38] Ibid, 571. There was a similar failure in *R v NTC Smokehouse Ltd* [1996] 2 SCR 672.

[39] *R v Gladstone* [1996] 2 SCR 723, 747; see also Langton and Palmer, this volume, and their discussion of trade as an Aboriginal right in Australia.

question of whether there was a separate and more robust aboriginal title to land, what it might consist of, how it was protected and what obligations its constitutional protection imposed on the Crown, remained unclear.[40]

The Supreme Court, in *Delgamuukw*, removed any uncertainty about the existence of aboriginal title as a fulsome and constitutionally protected right, imposing obligations on the Crown in its dealings with aboriginal titleholders. Throughout the litigation, the British Columbia Government had argued that if there was a common-law aboriginal title, it had been extinguished prior to confederation. It argued this even though, since 1990, it had been engaged in negotiations both with the Nisga'a and others within the Treaty Process. This ambivalent and paradoxical position adopted by the British Columbia Government may in part explain the difficulties and lack of progress in negotiations during this period.[41] Even after the decision, the British Columbia Government was very slow to embrace the decision and to give it effect within the treaty negotiating framework and the interim measures process.[42]

Delgamuukw

The *Delgamuukw* case is instructive because of the time and cost of the litigation, the ambivalent response to it by governments and its failure to produce significant change in the treaty negotiations. The claim for aboriginal title was filed in 1987. The claim was largely unsuccessful at first instance, in 1991, and in the British Columbia Court of Appeal in 1993. The appeal litigation ran in tandem with the Treaty Process until the Supreme Court decision in December 1997. The Supreme Court ordered a new trial.

The plaintiffs, a number of Gitxsan and Wet'suwet'en hereditary chiefs, sought declarations that they had aboriginal title to 58,000 square kilometres of land in the central area of the Province of British Columbia and a right to self-government. At first instance, the case occupied 374 days, with the judgment of McEachern CJ covering almost 400 pages plus schedules.[43]

[40] Kent McNeil, 'Aboriginal Title and Aboriginal Rights: What's the Connection' (1997) 36 *Alberta Law Review* 117.

[41] See generally, Foster, above n 16.

[42] British Columbia Treaty Commission, *After Delgamuukw: The Legal and Political Landscape* (BCTC, Vancouver, 1999) http://www.bctreaty.net/files_2/pdf_documents/after_delgamuukw.pdf at 1 November 2003; McKee n 12, 88–109; see de Costa, this volume.

[43] *Delgamuukw v British Columbia* [1991] 3 WWR 97. For commentary on this decision see Michael Asch and Catherine Bell, 'Definition and Interpretation of Fact in Canadian Aboriginal Title Litigation: An Analysis of *Delgamuukw*' (1992) 19 *Queen's Law Journal* 50. For a detailed consideration of the evidence in relation to the Wet'suwet'en see Antonia Mills, *Eagle Down Is Our Law: Wet'suwet'en Law, Feasts and Land Claims* (UBC Press, Vancouver, 1994). See also Dara Culhane, *The Pleasure of the Crown* (Talon Books, Vancouver, 1998).

McEachern CJ rejected the notion of a title to land based on occupation, and found only that some subsistence activities based in pre-European
contact may amount to aboriginal rights.[44] However, colonial enactments
had extinguished these rights.[45] There was insufficient evidence of an established system of governance and thus no right to self-government.[46]

The British Columbia Court of Appeal[47] largely agreed with these conclusions and reasoning. However, they concluded that there was no extinguishment of aboriginal rights by general provincial legislation, and that
extinguishment depended upon specific Crown grants, which may allow for
co-existence of interests.[48] The Court of Appeal decision put to rest the idea
that all aboriginal rights and title had been extinguished in British Columbia,
but the narrow findings of fact, and the content of any aboriginal rights,
meant that the rights with which the Provincial Government was prepared
to deal in treaty negotiations were exceedingly limited. The decision, together
with the disregard by the Province of the interim measures provisions, meant
that negotiations within the Treaty Process following this decision were less
than productive. This remained the position until the Supreme Court of
Canada delivered its judgment in the appeal in December 1997.[49]

Supreme Court decision[50]

The Supreme Court allowed the appeal and ordered a new trial[51] because
of the trial judge's failure to give proper weight to the oral evidence.[52]
Although the dispute between the parties could not be finally determined

---

[44] *Delgamuukw v British Columbia* [1991] 3 WWR 97, 395.

[45] Ibid, 411.

[46] Ibid, 388.

[47] *Delgamuukw v R* (1993) 104 DLR (4th) 470. Macfarlane JA, with Taggart JA concurring.
Wallace J largely concurred. Hutcheon J dissented on the evidence issue. Lambert JA
dissented and in a lengthy judgment foreshadowed the approach ultimately taken by the
Supreme Court of Canada.

[48] Interestingly, MacFarlane JA suggested that even fee simple grants may not necessarily
exclude aboriginal uses (see *Delgamuukw v R* (1993) 104 DLR (4th) 470, 532 citing *R v
Bartleman* (1984) 12 DLR (4th) 73), a view confirmed in specific statutory circumstances by
the Supreme Court of Canada in *R v Badger* [1996] 1 SCR 771.

[49] McKee, above n 12 91–93; British Columbia Treaty Commission, *British Columbia Treaty
Commission Annual Report 1999* (BCTC, Vancouver, 1999) http://www.bctreaty.net/annuals
2/99_index.html at 1 November 2003.

[50] *Delgamuukw* [1997] 3 SCR 1010. The main judgment was that of Lamer CJ (with whom
Cory and Major JJ concurred). La Forest J (with whom L'Heureux-Dube J concurred)
delivered a separate but largely concurring judgment; see Pearson, this volume, for some
further discussion of the import of this decision.

[51] *Delgamuukw* [1997] 3 SCR 1010, 1079. Negotiations between the Province and the Gitxsan
and Wet'suwet'en were recommenced after the decision was handed down in order
to try to avoid a new trial. Both the Gitxsan and the Wet'suwet'en are in Stage 4 of the
Treaty Process. The Gitxsan reached some interim agreements governing forestry in June

by the Supreme Court, significant issues of law concerning the nature and protection of aboriginal title were given attention.[53]

The claim to a surviving right to self-government was not dealt with[54] and thus the question of whether self-government is a right recognised by the common law and constitutionally protected remains open and hanging in treaty negotiations.[55]

However, the rights of aboriginal parties in the Treaty Process were significantly expanded by two aspects of the decision: extinguishment and the existence and content of aboriginal title itself. In considering extinguishment issues, the court clarified that the Province did not have constitutional power to extinguish aboriginal title after 1871.[56] Laws of general application did not extinguish, even though they applied to aboriginal people as a result of the operation of s 88 of the *Indian Act 1985*. After 1871, then, laws or grants might be valid but would not extinguish aboriginal title. After 1982, their validity was subject to the justification test.

As for aboriginal title, the Court found that the title is sourced in 'the prior occupation of Canada by aboriginal peoples.'[57] It is 'a *sui generis* interest in land'[58] which provides the principle unifying the 'various dimensions of that title',[59] such as its inalienability and communal nature.[60] The *sui generis* aspect of aboriginal title is that the possession giving rise to the title is possession or occupation enjoyed before the assertion of British sovereignty. This is the key in the 'relationship between common law and pre-existing systems of aboriginal law'.[61]

2003: Gitxsan Chief's Office, *Gitxsan and BC Agree to Incremental Approach: Forestry Interim Agreement* http://tools.bcweb.net/gitxsan/news.shtml?x=2383&cmd[67]=x-66-2383 at 1 November 2003.

[52] *Delgamuukw* [1997] 3 SCR 1010, 1066. The Chief Justice concluded at 1079–1080 'that trial courts must approach the rules of evidence in light of the evidentiary difficulties inherent in adjudicating aboriginal claims and second, that trial courts must interpret that evidence in the same spirit.' This approach is in contrast to that taken by the Australian High Court in *Members of the Yorta Yorta Aboriginal Community v State of Victoria* (2002) 194 ALR 538; see Pearson, this volume.

[53] Ibid, 1079–80.

[54] Ibid, 1114–5.

[55] Whether there was a surviving right to self-government was considered in the challenge to the validity of the Nsiga'a Treaty: *Campbell v British Columbia (Attorney General)* (2000) 189 DLR (4th) 333. The British Columbia Supreme Court found that a right to self-government was such a right. The plaintiff in this case was the leader of the opposition in the British Columbia parliament when the case was brought. The appeal from this decision was abandoned when Campbell was elected Premier. The decision is currently good law.

[56] *Delgamuukw* [1997] 3 SCR 1010, 1120.

[57] Ibid, 1082.

[58] Ibid, 1081.

[59] Ibid, 1082.

[60] Ibid, 1082–3.

[61] Ibid.

The title 'encompasses the right to *exclusive use and occupation of land* held pursuant to that title for a variety of *purposes*'.[62] Once occupation or title is established, the rights that accompany it are not limited to those deriving from custom and thus might include rights to minerals for example.[63] In other words, the right to exclusive occupation must be related to aboriginal custom, but once the occupation is established, the only limitation on use is that it must be reconcilable with custom or the nature of the attachment to the land.[64]

Aboriginal title is a species of aboriginal rights[65] protected by s 35(1) of the *Constitution Act 1982*. Protection of aboriginal activities on aboriginal title land need not be individually protected because the title itself is protected, the activities undertaken being 'parasitic on the underlying (aboriginal) title'.[66]

The crucial element of proof of title is that occupation must have been exclusive at sovereignty; that is, there must have been the ability to exclude others from the land[67] or 'the intention and capacity to retain control'.[68] Evidence of both actual physical occupation and elements of the traditions and culture connecting a group with the land is required.[69] Unbroken continuity' is not required[70] but there must be 'substantial maintenance of the connection between the people and land'.[71] The nature of the occupation may have changed 'as long as a substantial connection between the people and land is maintained.'[72]

At the end of his judgment the Chief Justice exhorted the parties to settle the issues by negotiation, s 35(1) of the *Constitution Act 1982* providing 'a solid constitutional base upon which subsequent negotiations can take place'.[73] Given the characterisation of aboriginal title, the expanded understanding of the justification principle and the new trial order, such an exhortation from the Chief Justice might have fallen on fallow ground but, unfortunately, this was not so.

---

[62] Ibid, 1086–7.

[63] Ibid, 1084.

[64] Ibid, 1089, to permit actions that would threaten that special connection with land would be inconsistent with the protection afforded by the common law.

[65] Ibid, 1094.

[66] Ibid.

[67] Ibid, 1104.

[68] Ibid, quoting Kent McNeil, *Common Law Aboriginal Title* (Clarendon Press, Oxford, 1989) 204.

[69] Ibid, 1099–101.

[70] Ibid, 1103 quoting *Van der Peet* [1996] 2 SCR 507, 557.

[71] *Delgamuukw* [1997] 3 SCR 1010, 1103.

[72] Ibid, 1098.

[73] Ibid, 1123.

Post-Delgamuukw state of play

Now that the central element of the argument about the existence and nature of aboriginal title had been accepted by the Supreme Court, it was thought that a clear statement of aboriginal title would reinvigorate the Treaty Process. This was especially so since first nations now had a clearly defined and significantly broad title to land, the uncertainty generated by the *Delgamuukw* litigation was now settled and at least some of the key questions about aboriginal title answered.[74] There was optimism based upon a notion that the negotiating parties, namely the Federal and Provincial governments, would embrace the substance and import of the decision and adjust their approaches in the Treaty Process.[75]

The optimism was misplaced. The governments, particularly the Provincial Government, were slow to respond to the decision and developed no new approach for more than eighteen months.[76] This, together with a number of other issues, meant that little or no progress resulted from the decision. The other issues included the failure of the interim measures provisions established under the Treaty Process; the need for first nations to litigate the implementation of *Delgamuukw*; the ambivalent approach of provincial courts to providing relief to protect aboriginal title land from development; and the time required to obtain such relief either at first instance or on appeal. In addition, much provincial activity in relation to land and resource management approvals continued unabated.[77]

This experience underlines the nebulous nature of the role of law, especially the common law, as a trigger or instigator for negotiations. It suggests that the mere existence or statement of rights will not produce outcomes. There must be, at the least, a sharp definition of rights, the capacity to enforce those rights and some measure of acceptance of those rights by the relevant parties. In other words, as de Costa suggests,[78] the political dimension of these complex relationships cannot be underestimated and law is but one of a number of factors that may impact on the process of negotiation. The failure of the political process makes it necessary to engage in the time-consuming process of litigating the applicability of the broad principles through the 'time honoured methodology of the common law'[79]

---

[74] The issue of whether the right to self-government was among the rights that survived the acquisition of sovereignty was not decided. See above n 55.

[75] McKee, above n 12, 92–96.

[76] British Columbia Treaty Commission, *A Review of the BC Treaty Process* (BCTC, Vancouver, 1999).

[77] First Nations Summit, *Discussion Paper On: Interim Measures* November (1999) http://www.fnsbc.ca/ at 1 December 1999; Foster, above n 16, 175–80.

[78] See de Costa, this volume.

[79] *Wik v Queensland* (1996) 187 CLR 1, 184, Gummow J quoting McLachlin J, as she then was, in *R v Van der Peet*[1996] 2 SCR 507, 641.

—on a case-by-case basis. The vagaries of this process, as applications wend their way through first instance and appeal courts in the post-*Delgamuukw* era, the reliance on general remedies and the failure of the interim measures provisions exemplify this point.

Interim measures, justification and remedies

The interim measures provisions in the Treaty Process were said to accommodate development during the period in which Treaty negotiations were taking place. Inherent in the idea was that aboriginal rights and title, and the resources central to their enjoyment, would be preserved and the development in question should not disrupt the Treaty negotiations. However, the Provincial Government never really embraced the interim measures and very few agreements under these provisions were reached in the early period of the Treaty Process.[80] The interim measures provisions did not mandate negotiations or limit development approvals while treaty negotiations were in progress. The effectiveness of the provisions, therefore, depended upon the parties' willingness to embrace both the concept and the reality of the limitations imposed by the notion of interim or limited approvals for development on aboriginal title land and support by the courts.

In enforcing elements of the interim measures provisions, aboriginal negotiators were left with general legal remedies.[81] There appeared to be no doubt that the Crown had a general duty to negotiate in good faith.[82] However, it was uncertain what actions constituted good faith negotiations, the precise circumstances in which the obligation arose, whether the obligation extended to negotiations within the Treaty Process, and whether it was necessary that aboriginal title be established before relief, such as injunctions, would be granted.

The courts had shown an ambivalence about supporting aboriginal negotiators. They provided few remedies preventing the Province or third parties from undertaking projects inconsistent with aboriginal rights or title. For example, in *Haida Nation v British Columbia*[83] the British Columbia Court

---

[80] The current status of negotiations is available at British Columbia Treaty Commission Website http://www.bctreaty.net/files_2/updates.html at 1 November 2003. There were 80 interim measures agreements negotiated up to June 2003: British Columbia Treaty Commission, *British Columbia Treaty Commission Annual Report 2003: Where are We?* (BCTC, Vancouver, 2003) 5. There were few negotiated before 2000: see Foster, above n 16.

[81] General legal remedies in these circumstances will usually be injunctions or declarations. See Daniel Sweeney, 'Interlocutory Injunctions to Restrain Interference with Aboriginal Title—The Balance of Convenience' (1994) 17 *University of Queensland Law Journal* 141–168.

[82] *Halfway River First Nation v British Columbia (Minister of Forests)* [1997] 4 CNLR 45. This case involved treaty rights under Treaty 8.

[83] (1997) 153 DLR (4th) 1.

of Appeal found that aboriginal rights, **if established**, would give rights in forests and operate as an encumbrance on tree licences, but did not provide further remedy. As a result, the corpus of negotiations—rights to resources and title to land—was in danger of being exploited and even destroyed before the negotiations for a treaty could be completed, and was a source of major dissatisfaction.[84] This ambivalence resulted in unpredictable decisions at first instance and the possibility of decisions being overturned on appeal. Governments, particularly the Provincial Government, continued to negotiate while seeking to limit its obligations in various proceedings in courts.

Three cases exemplify this ambivalence: *Gitanyow First Nation v Canada*,[85] *Taku River Tlingit First Nation v Tulsequah Chief Mine Project*,[86] and *Haida Nation v British Columbia (Minister of Forests)*.[87]

Gitanyow raised two broad questions which, surprisingly, suggested that, eight years into the Treaty Process, the government participants in the tripartite negotiations may not have been negotiating in good faith: did the Crown's fiduciary obligation also bind the provincial Crown and were negotiations within the British Columbia Treaty Process subject to the requirement of good faith negotiations and amenable to judicial supervision?

Williamson J granted a declaration that the Crown in right of Canada and British Columbia were obliged to negotiate in good faith.[88] There was no obligation to negotiate, but once negotiations were entered into, including within the Treaty Process, both Canada and the Province were bound to negotiate in good faith.[89] The fiduciary duty of the Crown was intertwined with s 35 of the *Constitution Act 1982*, and the Treaty Process must be viewed 'in light of s 35(1) which imports the unique fiduciary relationship existing between the Crown [both Federal and Provincial] and the plaintiffs'.[90] The Process was essentially a political one, and 'while the courts should be chary of interfering in the process itself, it is appropriate for the courts to assist in determining the duties of the parties'.[91] Although not determining the detailed content of the duty to negotiate in good faith, the duty would include: 'the absence of any appearance of "sharp dealing"... disclosure of relevant factors ... and negotiation "without oblique motive"...'[92]

---

[84] For a more detailed discussion of the failure of interim measures in this regard see de Costa, this volume.

[85] [1999] 3 CNLR 89 ('*Gitanyow*').

[86] (2000) 77 BCLR (3rd) 310 ('*Taku River Tlingit*').

[87] [2001] 2 CNLR 83 ('*Haida Nation*').

[88] *Gitanyow* [1999] 3 CNLR 89, 105.

[89] Ibid, 101–102.

[90] Ibid, 98.

[91] Ibid, 103.

[92] Ibid, 105.

In *Taku River Tlingit* the Province argued that these obligations did not arise 'until such time as the Tlingits have established the aboriginal rights and title they say would be unjustifiably infringed by the project';[93] that is, until there has been a court determination of the right or title. The Court found that once the Crown had 'undertaken treaty negotiations with the Taku River Tlingit First Nation' 'under both the federal comprehensive claims process and the BC treaty process',[94] the Crown's constitutional and fiduciary obligations were engaged.[95] The Province knew that there was some acknowledgment of the existence of aboriginal rights based on prior occupation in the Province's framework agreement to negotiate under the Treaty Process. No determination of aboriginal title was required.[96] The British Columbia Court of Appeal upheld the view that it was not necessary to establish specific aboriginal rights or title as a precondition to the obligation to consult on proposals that would adversely affect those rights or title. To require such would be to defeat the purpose of the constitutional protection afforded by s 35 of the *Constitution Act 1982*.[97]

As with *Gitanyow*, this case indicated most starkly the approach of the Provincial Government to its relationship with aboriginal nations and their rights and title. That the Province was still arguing in 2002 that it had no obligation arising out its fiduciary duty to consult unless specific rights or title had been determined, indicated that the Province was not necessarily seriously engaged in the Treaty Process, nor did it reveal any commitment to the process of consultation and resolution. Coupled with its referendum questions, the Province's attitude indicated a lack of commitment to the Treaty Process.[98]

Surprisingly, the view that it was necessary to obtain a judgment that title existed and would be infringed, before a declaration or injunction would be granted requiring 'consultation', retained currency. In August 2000, in *Haida Nation*, the British Columbia Supreme Court at first instance took this view, also finding that the Crown's duty to consult in relation to tree-licence renewals was a moral rather than a legal or equitable duty.[99]

---

[93] *Taku River Tlingit* (2000) 77 BCLR (3rd) 310 para 125.
[94] Ibid, para 120.
[95] Ibid.
[96] Ibid, para 130.
[97] *Taku River Tlingit First Nation v Tulsequah Chief Mine Project* (2002) 211 DLR (4th) 89, 159–170. The decision has been appealed to the Supreme Court of Canada. The appeal, together with that in *Haida Nation v British Columbia and Weyerhaeuser Ltd* (see below n 100 and 102) has been heard. By March 2004 judgments had not been handed down.
[98] See de Costa, this volume.
[99] *Haida Nation* [2001] 2 CNLR 83, 104.

In February 2002, the British Columbia Court of Appeal in *Haida Nation v British Columbia and Weyerhaeuser Ltd*[100] overturned the first-instance decision and granted a declaration that a duty to consult in good faith and endeavour to reach an accommodation existed as a legal obligation and arose prior to any Court declaration that aboriginal title exists. In the circumstances of the case the Court did not grant an injunction but indicated that injunctions could properly be granted in these cases and that in applying the balance of convenience rule, the strength of the claim for aboriginal title would be an important consideration. This view was in line with that taken in the *Taku River Tlingit* appeal.[101]

More interestingly, the Court revisited its decision in August 2002 and found that the duty to consult also extended to the third party recipient of the licences.[102] Weyerhauser Ltd was aware of the aboriginal title claims of the Haida, and also had an obligation 'to consult with [the Haida] in good faith and to endeavour to seek workable accommodations between the aboriginal interests of the Haida people on the one hand and the short-term and long-term objectives of the Crown and Weyerhauser' [103] in relation to the licences. The source of this third-party obligation was threefold: the condition of consultation upon which the exclusive licence was granted, the strength of the Haida case, and the requirement of justification upon the Crown which flows through to Weyerhauser, obliging Weyerhauser to conduct itself in accordance with any justificatory requirements. Weyerhauser must satisfy itself that the Crown has discharged its obligation.[104]

Pending the outcome of the appeal, litigation continues. The Haida lodged a claim for aboriginal title and rights to Haida Gwai and surrounding waters in March 2002.[105] In its defence the Province does not 'admit the existence of the "Haida nation"'[106] and asserts that the claim is statute barred.[107] The Federal Government defence denies that the Haida 'ever constituted a "single unified aboriginal collectivity capable of holding aboriginal title"'.[108] As with *Delgamuukw*, the cycle of litigation and challenge continues.

---

[100] [2002] 2 CNLR 121.

[101] *Taku River Tlingit First Nation v Tulsequah Chief Mine Project* (2002) 211 DLR (4th) 89.

[102] *Haida Nation v British Columbia* (2002) 216 DLR (4th) 1.

[103] Ibid, 36–7.

[104] Ibid.

[105] Alison Lawlor, *Haida Lay Claim to Queen Charlottes* Globe and Mail http://www.globeandmail.com at 6 March 2002.

[106] Charlie Smith, 'Chief Attacks BC Response to Haida Lawsuit' *Georgia Straight*, 2–9 October 2003.

[107] Ibid.

[108] Ibid. This argument resonates with native title litigation in Australia, particularly the decision in *Members of the Yorta Yorta Aboriginal Community v State of Victoria* (2002) 194 *ALR* 538.

It remains to be seen whether and how these recent cases will impact on the approach of the Federal and Provincial governments in the continuing process of treaty negotiations.

Conclusion

An examination of the ebb and flow of aboriginal title and rights jurisprudence and its application in specific lower-court disputes reveals the rolling but uneven terrain over which the Treaty Process ranges. While there has been an expansion of aboriginal rights in appellate courts, the uncertain application of the principles has provided fallow ground for resistance or grudging engagement in the process by governments. The Treaty Process has been marked by the Provincial Government's failure to embrace the range of rights articulated by appellate courts or to otherwise accord respect to probable aboriginal rights and title. Nowhere has this been more evident than in its failure to utilise or to belatedly embrace the interim measures process in its resource dispositions. The Provincial Government's approach to treaty making has been, at best, ambivalent and at worst negative and disruptive. Its attitude to the Treaty Process is one aspect of the continuing interplay between law and politics in the battle for control over access to resources based on rights emanating from recognition of prior occupation. While law has gradually expanded and redefined the legal relationship between aboriginal peoples and the Crown in relation to these competing interests, the power of law to effect change is revealed as limited and often ineffectual. Ultimately, the determinant of any new relationship based upon recognition and respect for aboriginal rights sourced in prior occupation requires more than law: only then will 'the unthinkable become common place'.

Chapter 9

Treaty Making in New Zealand/
Te Hanga Tiriti ki Aotearoa

Joe Williams

The *Treaty of Waitangi* now has a central place in the political life of New Zealand and in the relationship between Maori and *pakeha*.[1] In this chapter I describe the experience of treaty making and implementation in the New Zealand context. I assess the advantages and disadvantages of the approach adopted in New Zealand and then consider how that approach may develop into the future.

A brief overview

The *Treaty of Waitangi* is generally accepted as the founding document of New Zealand. However, that is a statement of political fact rather than legal precision. Technically, New Zealand was annexed by Proclamation of Governor Gipps in New South Wales on 14 January 1840 (three weeks before the *Treaty* was signed).

In any event, the *Treaty* was signed on and after 6 February 1840 by Captain Hobson, on behalf of the British Crown, and around 540 Maori chiefs representing many of the tribal communities then extant in New Zealand. It is important to note, however, that not all tribes signed the *Treaty*—a number of the most important chiefs then living refused.

The *Treaty of Waitangi* was not a land transfer deed of the kind familiar to nineteenth-century North America.[2] It was a fairly simple framework document, designed to address the basic issues important to the parties at that time. It was drafted in two languages. All but around 30 of the Maori

---

[1] A New Zealander of European descent.
[2] See Morse, this volume.

signatories signed the Maori text. The two texts are not translations one of the other.[3] They say significantly different things. The ideas inherent in each are reconcilable, though not without difficulty. Put in its most simple terms, Maori agreed to hand over to the Crown some form of central law-making authority of a kind which did not then exist in those islands. In Article One of the English version, Maori gave up 'sovereignty'. It was in that text a treaty of cession. In the Maori version, Maori gave up *kawanatanga*, a transliteration of the English term 'government'. They also gave to the Crown a monopoly on the purchase of Maori land. In return, the British Crown promised to protect Maori tribal authority, lands and resource rights, and to provide what today would be called 'equal protection'. The guarantee of tribal authority was contained in the Maori text of Article Two—the phrase used was *tino rangatiratanga*. The term familiar to Canadians today would be 'first-nations' self-government'. The tension between British and later New Zealand Crown sovereignty, on the one hand, and tribal authority, on the other, is obvious. It is the key tension in the *Treaty*. It has always been a key tension in race relations in New Zealand, and it remains so today.[4]

It is worth reiterating that the *Treaty* was an **exchange** of promises, not a mere declaration of rights. The moral legitimacy of the New Zealand Government's law-making power is to be found in the *Treaty* even if its political legitimacy is located in the orthodoxy of majoritarian rule. The *Treaty* sanctioned both central government and settlement. Thus, the right of non-Maori to be in New Zealand can, at least as a moral proposition, also be found in the *Treaty*.

While it is clear that the law does not yet accept that the *Treaty* was the legal means by which sovereignty was acquired by the British, or that the *Treaty of Waitangi* is New Zealand's 'Constitution', there is no question as to its political importance. The Waitangi Tribunal has said that the *Treaty* must be seen as a 'basic constitutional document'.[5] The Privy Council has described the *Treaty* as 'of the greatest constitutional importance to New Zealand'.[6] Sir Robin Cooke (as he then was), speaking extra judicially, in 1990 described the *Treaty* as 'simply the most important document in New Zealand's history'.[7]

---

[3]   New Zealand Government Website, *Find Out About the Treaty of Waitangi* http://www.govt.nz/en/search/topic-service-single-record/?urn=urn:nzgls-sn:000008:1000009 at 15 October 2003; New Zealand Government Website, *The Treaty of Waitangi* http://www.govt.nz/en/aboutnz/?id=77737fd3275e394a8ed9d416a72591d0 at 15 October 2003.

[4]   See generally McHugh P., 'Proving Aboriginal Title' (2001) August *New Zealand Law Journal* 303; Aotearoa Website, *A Quick Guide and Brief History of the Treaty of Waitangi* http://aotearoa.wellington.net.nz/back/quick.htm at 15 October 2003.

[5]   Waitangi Tribunal, *Ngai Tahu Report* (1991) at 224, Waitangi Tribunal Website http://www.waitangi-tribunal.govt.nz/reports/sichat/wai27/wai027l.asp at 15 October 2003.

[6]   *New Zealand Maori Council v Attorney General* [1994] 1 NZLR 513 at 516.

[7]   Sir Robin Cooke, 'Introduction [To Waitangi Issue]' (1990) 14 *New Zealand University Law Review* 1 at 1.

Despite its obvious importance, the *Treaty* remains essentially unenforceable as a matter of law. In the famous 1877 decision of Chief Justice Prendergast in *Wi Parata v The Bishop of Wellington*[8] the *Treaty* was declared to be 'a simple nullity'.[9] The Privy Council in 1941 ruled that:

> It is well settled that any rights purported to be conferred by such a Treaty of Cession cannot be enforced by the Courts, except insofar as they have been incorporated in Municipal Law.[10]

The *Treaty* is certainly not a constraint on the legislative supremacy of the New Zealand parliament.[11]

That is not to say that the legal status of the *Treaty* is nil. In *Huakina Development Trust v Waikato Valley Authority*[12] Chillwell J held:

> the Treaty has a status perceivable, whether or not enforceable, in law ... there can be no doubt that the Treaty is part of the fabric of New Zealand society. It follows that it is part of the context in which legislation which impinges upon its principles wish to be interpreted when it is proper, in accordance with the principles of statutory interpretation, to have resort to extrinsic material.[13]

A number of cases have followed this administrative law 'relevant consideration' approach. In *Barton Prescott v Director General of Social Welfare*,[14] the full Court of the High Court held:

> We are of the view that since the *Treaty of Waitangi* was designed to have general application, that general application must colour all matters to which it has relevance, whether public or private, and that for the purposes of interpretation of statutes, it will have a direct bearing whether or not there is a reference to the *Treaty* in the statute.[15]

How we got there

It is necessary to traverse briefly the development of these ideas in law and policy before turning to the question of whether the *Treaty of Waitangi* provides a sound basis for either nation building or indigenous protection in New Zealand.

As in other parts of the British Commonwealth, the rise in indigenous consciousness and assertiveness began in the 1960s and '70s. New Zealand's

---

8   [1877] 3 NZ Jur (NS) 72.
9   Ibid, 78.
10   *Te Heuheu Tukino v Aotea District Maori Land Board* [1941] NZLR 590 at 596 (PC).
11   See generally *New Zealand Maori Council v Attorney General* [1987] 1NZLR 641 (CA).
12   [1987] 2 NZLR 188 (HC).
13   Ibid, 210.
14   [1997] 3 NZLR 179 (HC).
15   Ibid, 184.

perspective on that phenomenon was that it was the children of those who had moved from the villages to the cities in search of work in the 1950s and '60s who provided the vanguard for this movement. The level of Maori protest and anger quickly produced a small number of important policy and legislative changes. A country the size of New Zealand, with a relatively large indigenous minority[16] living in close proximity to the majority race could not have sustained the level of dissent then developing for long. The most important change was the creation in 1975 of the Waitangi Tribunal—a standing commission of inquiry whose job it would be to investigate indigenous grievances and report on them to government.[17] Most of these grievances could not be the subject of ordinary suit because either the Crown action complained of was lawful or because suit was barred by statute. In the early 1980s, the Waitangi Tribunal investigated and reported on a number of high-profile indigenous claims. The reports of the Tribunal articulated to the wider non-Maori audience the principled basis for Maori grievances.[18] This had never been done before.

The response of the reformist fourth Labour government was to enact various measures that contained '*Treaty* clauses'. In most cases the politicians had no idea what the *Treaty* clauses meant. The advice from officials was that they were not significant, and the prevailing mood was that some gesture would be necessary in order to settle Maori unease at the wide-ranging structural and economic reforms being pursued. The most famous *Treaty* clause was Section 9 of the *State Owned Enterprises Act 1986* (NZ). This Act provided for the divestment of Crown commercial and quasi-commercial activities. Maori opposed the legislation on the ground that it provided for the sale of the very assets they claimed in compensation for their unresolved grievances. Section 9 provided:

---

[16] In 1971, Maori made up approximately 8 per cent of New Zealand's population (Statistics New Zealand Website, *Population Facts* http://www.stats.govt.nz/domino/external/web/prod serv.nsf/htmldocs/Population+Facts at 15 October 2003).

[17] See generally the *Treaty of Waitangi Act 1975* (NZ), especially sections 6 and 8; and The Waitangi Tribunal Website http://www.waitangi-tribunal.govt.nz at 15 October 2003.

[18] For example, the Te Atiawa people of Taranaki made a claim in 1981 to the Waitangi Tribunal in relation to the pollution of fishing reefs. They claimed the pollution was not in line with the principles of the *Treaty of Waitangi*, which allowed their tribe full, exclusive and undisturbed possession of their fisheries (Waitangi Tribunal Website http://www.waitangi-tribunal.govt.nz/forschools/motunui/mw3.asp at 15 October 2003). See also, the Waiheke Island claim, which was brought on behalf of the Ng ti Paoa on 8 March 1985. The claim concerned the disposal of land by the Board of Maori Affairs. The claimants alleged that, by overlooking them when the board disposed of the lands, the policies of the Crown failed to support the tribal groups that were parties to the *Treaty of Waitangi* and, in particular, those tribes like Ng ti Paoa now rendered almost landless (Waitangi Tribunal Website http://www.waitangi-tribunal.govt.nz/reports/northislandnorth/wai010/default.asp at 15 October 2003).

Nothing in this Act shall permit the Crown to act in a manner that is inconsistent with the principles of the *Treaty of Waitangi*.

When the Crown began to transfer assets pursuant to the Act, Maori sought injunctive relief, arguing that without a regime to protect the integrity of Maori claims, the transfers were in breach of Section 9. In what has come to be called the *Lands* case[19] the New Zealand Court of Appeal upheld the Maori argument. This chapter is not the place to traverse the reasoning in that case, though it is interesting to note that the Court based its findings on the new concept of a *Treaty* partnership. That is a study in itself. What is important to note, though, is that the decision produced a cascade of legislative, policy and operational responses from government. Some had admittedly been in the pipeline—the long title to the *Environment Act 1986* (NZ);[20] s 4 of the *Conservation Act 1987* (NZ);[21] sections 6, 7 and 8 of the *Resource Management Act 1991* (NZ)[22]—but the *Lands* case lent an air of respectability to these legislative developments. Many other measures would follow with specific *Treaty* clauses: s 4 of the *Crown Minerals Act 1991* (NZ); s 181(b) of the *Education Act 1989* (NZ); s 3 *Foreshore and Seabed Endowment Revesting Act 1991* (NZ); s 3 of the *Harbour Boards Dry Land Endowment Revesting Act 1991* (NZ); s 10 of the *Crown Research Institutes Act 1992* (NZ); s 8 of the *Hazardous Substances and New Organisms Act 1996* (NZ); s 6 of the *Hauraki Gulf Marine Park Act 2000* (NZ); s 6(d) of the *Energy Efficiency and Conservation Act 2000* (NZ); and the highly controversial s 4 of the *New Zealand Public Health and Disability Act* of the same year.

At the same time, the Cabinet Manual, the authoritative guide to central government decision making in New Zealand, was amended. Ministers were, for the first time, directed to draw the attention of Cabinet to any aspect of any Bill which 'may have implications for, or may be affected by … the *Treaty of Waitangi*'.[23] The *Treaty* had become a bona fide legal and policy risk to be managed within the entire machinery of the bureaucracy.

Thus, in addition to specific provisions dealing with Maori claims or directly with Maori subject matter, *Treaty* and Maori clauses may be found

---

[19] *NZ Maori Council v AG* [1987] 2 NZLR 641.

[20] Clause (c)(iii) states that it is 'an Act to ensure that, in the management of natural and physical resources, full and balanced account is taken of the principles of the *Treaty of Waitangi*'.

[21] Section 4 states that '[t]his Act shall be so interpreted and administered as to give effect to the principles of the *Treaty of Waitangi*'.

[22] Section 8 states that '[i]n achieving the purpose of this Act, all persons exercising functions and powers under it, in relation to managing the use, development, and protection of natural and physical resources, shall take into account the principles of the *Treaty of Waitangi (Te Tiriti o Waitangi)*'.

[23] *Cabinet Manual* pp. 68–69, Department of Prime Minister and Cabinet *Cabinet Manual* http://www.dpmc.govt.nz/cabinet/manual/ at 15 October 2003.

in a raft of generally applicable legislative measures. I have mentioned environmental legislation, a controversial arena in which Maori spiritual concerns and resource claims clash with the regulatory regime. Section 8 of the *Resource Management Act 1991* (NZ)[24] requires regulators to 'take account of the principles of the *Treaty*'. A stronger provision is found in s 4 of the *Conservation Act 1987* (NZ)[25] regarding the management of the Crown's prodigious conservation estate. Clauses of varying strength can be found now in health, education, broadcasting and, as can be seen, many areas of local government. These provisions do not try to resolve the content of the *Treaty* rights or interests being protected. They do not attempt to undertake the incredibly difficult balancing exercise between Maori and non-Maori interests usually required within the statutory regime in question. That, as I argue below, would be too problematic an exercise for the political system. Instead, these clauses hand on the 'hard issues' to the judiciary to resolve on a case-by-case basis.

Perhaps more importantly, *Treaty* issues have become 'vertically integrated' into the systems of government. That is, in most of the areas in which New Zealand's large bureaucracy is active, some form of *Treaty* responsiveness process or program is in place. Some of it is token, poorly thought out, or undirected. I suspect a good deal of it is undertaken in a grudging fashion. That will not change until core attitudes change, and it is fair to say that the signs in that regard are not always promising. But the requirements are there and must be grappled with in a transparent manner.

Political acceptance of these provisions and of the bureaucratic infrastructure which underpins them has faltered in recent times as issues of relations between Maori and non-Maori increase in electoral importance, as experience of the potential potency of the clauses deepens, and as a decade of implementation produces the inevitable examples of abuse or alleged abuse. The latter phenomenon is often a convenient basis for strident calls to throw the Maori baby out with the bath water. New Zealand's entire history has demonstrated a deep non-Maori ambivalence to both, but not always outright antagonism. But the three important points are that *Treaty* and Maori protection mechanisms are now in place across a wide range of legislative categories; bureaucratic process must address these issues in all new legislative proposals; and the entire machinery of government must at least attempt to be responsive to the rights and interests of Maori under the *Treaty*. As a result, though they remain highly (and sometimes cripplingly) controversial, *Treaty* matters are far less susceptible to political mood swings than in the past.

---

[24] Section 8 *Resource Management Act 1991(NZ)*, above n 22.
[25] Section 4 *Conservation Act 1987 (NZ)*, above n 21.

Some lessons

The legal status of the *Treaty of Waitangi* has remained ambiguous, even elusive ever since 1840. At best, the law currently says that the *Treaty* is **relevant** to statutory interpretation when it is not specifically provided for in the statute. Hardly a revolutionary idea. No Court has yet said that the *Treaty* is enforceable in its own right. Though there is some acceptance that the core idea of the *Treaty* was the exchange of law-making power for the protection of tribal authority and resource rights, there is no real consensus between Maori and non-Maori about what that might mean in any concrete way today. There is certainly no mood in favour of entrenching the *Treaty* in a constitutional instrument as the Canadians have done in s 35 of the *Canadian Constitution Act 1982*. There are few on either side of the debate who wish to hand the power, to determine what the *Treaty* may mean at that high level, to the judiciary. Nor is there any inclination to attempt to give greater clarity to the framework promises in the *Treaty* by introducing some sort of Maori Bill of Rights based on the *Treaty* into the legislative process. It would be political suicide for the proponent of such a measure. At least for now.

Put simply, New Zealand is nowhere near closure on these issues. By 'closure' I mean broad-based agreement on a system for *Treaty* recognition or implementation. Instead, in New Zealand's characteristically prosaic way, the *Treaty* is considered for application to the circumstances of the problem, case by case, program by program, issue by issue sometimes by the judges, sometimes by the bureaucrats and sometimes by the politicians, both local and central government. The truly difficult cases are sent to the judges because the politicians do not wish to deal with them and, in any event, the legislative mechanism lacks the finesse to deal with them well. The bureaucrats probably deal with ninety per cent of them. The process is relatively unspectacular, except for those directly affected. There is little fanfare. We almost never get to enjoy or celebrate this daily problem solving as a nation. Non-Maori New Zealanders probably think of it more like medicine that tastes bad: they know it is necessary, and they just want to swallow it and move on as quickly as possible. That hope is probably unrealistic.

What is abundantly clear is that the *Treaty* will not go away. In a country of four million souls, over 500,000 of them Maori,[26] *Treaty* issues will remain on the 'A' agenda for the foreseeable future. With the number of Maori politicians steadily increasing in a Mixed Member Proportional (MMP) system of government, they are likely to become more pressing rather than less. I suspect that for these reasons the ad hoc, but workable,

---

[26] In 2001, Maori made up almost 15 per cent of New Zealand's total population (Ministry of Maori development *2001 Census Results* http://www.tpk.govt.nz/Maori/population/default.asp at 15 October 2003).

approach to *Treaty* issues which has applied for the past decade will soon outlive its usefulness. We are likely to see a strong push for structural change in the next few years. It is unlikely to be in the form of *Treaty* entrenchment or codification as discussed above, for the reasons I have given. It is more likely to be process- rather than outcome-based. It may, for example, be in the form of a proposal to delegate certain specific powers and functions to a special parliamentary committee of Maori MPs—the beginnings of a separate, but still fully integrated, Maori law-making body **within** the Parliamentary system. I say the 'beginnings' because such an idea would probably take a generation to work through to its final form. There would, however, be a certain elegance in that kind of closure. In a curiously New Zealand way, the articulation of Maori autonomy as promised in the *Treaty*, within the very law-making power supposedly transferred to the settlers, seems to fit our experience as a nation.

There is a well-known and apposite Maori proverb with which to conclude this chapter:

> *Ko te pae tawhiti whaia kia tata*
> *Ko te pae tata whakamaua kia tina*

> Strive to make it to the distant horizon.
> And you will get to the closer one.

No reira e nga mana, e nga reo, e nga karangatanga maha, tena koutou katoa.[27]

---

[27] Therefore I acknowledge the prestige, the variety of languages and the diversity of cultures of all. Greetings to you.

PART 3

Negotiating Beyond Native Title

Introduction

Negotiating Co-existence

Maureen Tehan

Settling native title issues by agreement rather than litigation is almost universally supported. We are no strangers to the spectacle of the chiefs of great corporations and the leaders of state governments encouraging and even participating in an agreement making process with the people who are identified by their Aboriginal inheritance and their continuing bonds of law and culture.[1]

The broad canvas contestation that is the subject of Part 2 in this volume is most often played out between the original inhabitants and coloniser in disputes, negotiations and agreements over land or particular resources. Part 3 focuses on some examples of this contestation in Australia and provides a backdrop for examining the variety of ways in which agreement making engages with Aboriginal and Torres Strait Islander jurisdiction.

The point of conflict and contestation is often over specific development proposals or resource use. These proposals may require access to Aboriginal or Torres Strait Islander land held under a variety of settler titles, including but not limited to native title. They may impinge upon areas of cultural significance, may have social and environmental impacts, may result in depletion of resources, or may attract possibilities for economic engagement. In any of these circumstances, the rights of the parties vary. However, regardless of the specific legal environment in which negotiations occur, what we call Aboriginal and Torres Strait Islander polities are recognised as the site of decision making and negotiation. This process occurs regardless of the legal framework governing particular negotiations. It is also evident that within these negotiations all parties may go beyond their strict legal rights that pertain to particular negotiations.

---

[1] Fred Chaney, 'Eddie Mabo Memorial Lecture' in John Rickard and Vince Ross (eds) *Unfinished Business: Text and Addresses From the Unfinished Business Conference* (Desbooks, Thornbury, 2002) 19–26, 22.

The examples of these negotiations in this Part highlight the creativity that can accompany negotiations which ultimately have meanings and create relationships that operate beyond the context of each specific negotiation. Strelein and Agius *et al.*, in particular, provide insights into the paradox of governments negotiating agreements, on the one hand, while challenging the very basis upon which the rights to negotiate are based. Even in this situation it is impossible for governments and third parties not to afford a measure of recognition to Aboriginal and Torres Strait Islander polities as parties to negotiations. The inexorable conclusion is that whenever there is engagement in negotiations there is either implicit or explicit recognition of the legitimacy of Aboriginal and Torres Strait Islander institutions, identity and laws. This is the recognition that Chaney references.

Neate provides a brief insight into the operation of the native title scheme, which has had a profound impact on negotiation and agreement making since 1994. His contribution emphasises that whether negotiating about the existence of a title to land and resources or about the terms on which access and use may be enjoyed by governments and third parties, the elements of each native claimant group is central. However, it is also clear that negotiations are not confined to the precise or narrow legal rights that might flow from the native title scheme—thus non-native title outcomes might be negotiated. The narrowness of this legal framework has been emphasised by Pearson elsewhere in this volume. However, moving beyond the constraint of the legal framework allows for a broader, more culturally relevant expression of Aboriginal and Torres Strait Islander jurisdiction.

This point is reinforced in the remarkable tale Harvey tells of Rio Tinto's move to embrace the moral claims of Aboriginal and Torres Strait Islander peoples and the consequential agreement with the communities in western Cape York. This process of negotiation over an extended period with Aboriginal peoples in the region, resulting in an overarching agreement, is in marked contrast to the number and diversity of agreements which Jackson details—agreements reached over a long period of time, with a variety of parties and under different legal regimes. The counterpoint provided by these papers illustrates the possibilities of coexistence at both the macro and micro levels.

It is the micro nature of the contributions that enables a picture of diverse modes of engagement, recognition and co-existence to emerge and to suggest that the jigsaw of agreements across Australia might ultimately amount to a total greater than the sum of its parts.

In the Introduction to this volume we said:

> ... in settler nation states that coincide with a number of aboriginal polities having their own customary law regimes, agreement making has evolved

among these diverse entities as a means of engaging rationally in dealings in land access and use, and resource distribution and governance.

It is clear that successful negotiations require non-Indigenous parties to engage rationally in dealings with Aboriginal and Torres Strait Islander entities and to afford respect and recognition of their particular modes of organisation and governance. The contributions in this section show the myriad of ways in which this might be done. In turn, they raise the prospect of a more formal recognition of Aboriginal and Torres Strait Islander laws and institutions.

Chapter 10

Agreement Making and the *Native Title Act*

Graeme Neate

Introduction

The recognition of native title by the High Court of Australia in its 1992 decision in *Mabo v Queensland (No 2)*[1] fundamentally changed the way in which Aboriginal and Torres Strait Islander peoples' interest in land was recognised by the general law of Australia. This was later given legislative recognition by the *Native Title Act 1993* (Cth) (*NTA*).

The background to the *NTA* predates the High Court's 1992 decision in *Mabo*. In this chapter I briefly examine the background to the *NTA*, and discuss one of the underlying principles of that Act, being its emphasis on agreement making as the preferred method of dealing with native title issues.

Background to the *Native Title Act*

When the British Crown assumed sovereignty over different parts of Australia, there was no recognition, under the introduced British law, of Aboriginal and Torres Strait Islander rights and interests in the land. The first act of possession on behalf of the Crown was by Lieutenant (later Captain) James Cook in 1770. Cook had instructions to 'take possession' of the land, 'with the consent of the natives'. He was instructed, if there were Indigenous people there, to 'cultivate a friendship and alliance with them ... shewing them every kind of civility and regard' and to promote the Crown's interest in the area. If he found the land 'uninhabited', he was

---

[1] (1992) 175 CLR 1 (*'Mabo'*).

to take possession for the Crown.[2] Cook did not find the land uninhabited, but he took possession for the Crown nonetheless, without the consent of the natives. The Crown progressively assumed sovereignty over different parts of Australia, from 1788 in Port Jackson through to 1825, then 1829 in Western Australia and in 1879 in the Torres Strait.[3]

The notion of *terra nullius* (land belonging to no one) which prevailed in relation to Australia did not necessarily assume that there were no people present in Australia, but that the people who were present were considered to be 'so low in the scale of social organisation that their usages and conceptions of rights and duties are not to be reconciled with the institutions or the legal ideas of a civilized society'.[4]

The Gove land rights case

This fiction of *terra nullius* proceeded, in a formal legal sense, unchallenged until the late 1960s, when the Commonwealth wanted to grant mineral leases on the Gove Peninsula area of the Northern Territory. The local Yolngu people of north-eastern Arnhem Land asserted that, among other things, the common law incorporated a doctrine of communal native title and that their pre-existing traditional rights to land persisted until they were validly terminated.

Justice Blackburn, while recognising that the clans on the Gove Peninsula had a recognisable system of law,[5] held that the doctrine of communal native title did not form, and had never formed, part of the law of any part of Australia. He also decided that, given that the plaintiffs' relationship to land was spiritual or religious in nature and had little resemblance to 'property' as the law understood it, the plaintiffs' claims were 'not in the nature of proprietary interests'.[6]

Land rights legislation

In the absence of judicial recognition of native title rights and interests, the debate moved to the parliaments and thus became a political issue. A range of Acts of Parliament, including the *Aboriginal Land Rights (Northern*

---

[2] 'British Admiralty, Secret Instruction Book' (Public Record Office, London) cited in John Michael Bennett and Alex Cuthbert Castles (eds), *A Source Book of Australian Legal History* (Law Book Company, Sydney, 1979) 253–254.

[3] See M.H. McLelland, 'Colonial and State Boundaries in Australia' (1971) 45 *Australian Law Journal* 671; G. Neate, 'Proof of Native Title' in Bryan Horrigan and Simon Young (eds), *Commercial Implications of Native Title* (Federation Press, Leichhardt, NSW, 1997) 240, 254–8.

[4] See *In re Southern Rhodesia* [1919] AC 211, 233.

[5] *Milirrpum v Nabalco Pty Ltd* (1971) 17 FLR 141, 267–268.

[6] *Milirrpum v Nabalco Pty Ltd* (1971) 17 FLR 141, 273.

Territory) Act 1976 (Cth), subsequently followed in different states and territories around the country.[7] A principle underpinning the land rights legislation is that, in the absence of judicially recognised rights to the traditional lands and waters of particular groups, it was essential for parliament to make laws if Aboriginal people and Torres Strait Islanders were to obtain legally enforceable rights to parts of their traditional country.[8]

The *Mabo* litigation

The development of the legal recognition of native title in Australia commenced with the decision of the High Court of Australia in *Mabo*, when, by a majority of 6 to 1, the Court held that:

> the common law of this country recognises a form of native title which, in the cases where it has not been extinguished, reflects the entitlement of the indigenous inhabitants, in accordance with **their laws or customs**, to their traditional lands (emphasis added).[9]

The decision in *Mabo* made a fundamental change in the way in which Aboriginal and Torres Strait Islander peoples' interests in land were to be dealt with by the general law of Australia. The common law now recognised that, in some parts of Australia, Indigenous Australians had legally recognisable and enforceable rights of a type which their ancestors held when the British Crown assumed sovereignty over the land and waters and the people, and which have passed from generation to generation to the present. This was the first time that an Australian court had recognised the entitlements of Indigenous Australian people to their traditional lands under their traditional laws. The Crown could not grant those rights. The people already had, and have, them.

The *Native Title Act*

The High Court, having declared that native title was recognised under Australian law except in those areas in which it had been extinguished, created a new framework within which the legal system was able to operate. However, the *Mabo* decision was a decision on the issues before the Court. It did not purport to answer every question that necessarily flowed from it. Numerous questions remained to be answered, including:

---

[7] See, for example, *Pitjantjatjara Land Rights Act 1981* (SA); *Maralinga Tjarutja Land Rights Act 1984* (SA); *Aboriginal Land Rights Act 1984* (NSW); *Aboriginal Land Act 1991* (Qld); and *Torres Strait Islander Land Act 1991* (Qld).

[8] See, for example, the preamble to the *Aboriginal Land Act 1991* (Qld).

[9] *Mabo* (1992) 175 CLR 1, 15.

- Where does native title exist? Is it confined to the Torres Strait or does it apply on the mainland? If it applies to the mainland, where does it apply? Which parts of the country are susceptible to native title?
- Who holds the native title?
- What native title rights and interests are capable of legal recognition and protection?
- How can future activity (such as exploration and mining) take place in areas in which native title has been recognised as existing or possibly existing?
- What are the best ways in which to resolve native title issues as they arise?

One of the early concerns that was expressed, and is still expressed years later, was the need for certainty: who had native title rights; what those rights were; where they existed; and whether other people would be able to explore, mine, build roads, construct pipelines, conduct tourism and other activities. Certainty about potentially invalid Acts was also an important issue.

The Federal Government of the day moved fairly quickly to legislate and, on 1 January 1994, Australia awoke to the *NTA* in operation and the National Native Title Tribunal (NNTT) as the body to administer that Act.[10]

The main objects of the *NTA* are:

1. to provide for the recognition and protection of native title
2. to establish ways in which future dealings affecting native title may proceed, and to set standards for those dealings
3. to establish a mechanism for determining claims to native title
4. to provide for, or permit, the validation of past acts and intermediate period acts now invalidated because of the existence of native title.[11]

Agreement making: a principle of the *Native Title Act*

One of the underlying principles of the *NTA*, which has become much more evident (at least in terms of legislative language) since its amendment in 1998, is the emphasis on agreement making as the preferred method of dealing with native title issues, and on mediation as a means of encouraging agreements.[12]

---

[10] For one discussion of the political context, see Don Watson, *Recollections of a Bleeding Heart: A Portrait of Paul Keating PM* (Random House, Australia, 2002).

[11] *Native Title Act 1993* (Cth) s 3, as ammended in 1998.

[12] For example, there are references to:
 – a procedure for ascertaining native title rights and interests by conciliation: preamble;

The *Mabo* case took ten years to work through the system, from commencement to judgment.[13] Although subsequent litigation would not necessarily take ten years, it was thought that litigating every aspect of native title was probably not the best way to proceed. A scheme was created to encourage negotiated or mediated outcomes to many native title issues, and hence avoid having to resort to the courts.

As Justice Kirby explained:

> the stated emphasis of the Act [is] on the facilitation of agreement through negotiation rather than through instant recourse to judicial decision.[14]

There are other statements by judges to a similar effect.[15]

The emphasis on agreement making is clear from the specific sections of the *NTA* as well as from the preamble to the Act, which sets out the policy considerations which the Federal Parliament took into account in enacting the *NTA*. One Federal Court judge observed that the Government had taken an unusual step in providing an extensive preamble to the *NTA* so that the purpose of the Act could be clearly revealed.[16] The preamble recites, among other things that:

– the mediation of matters relating to native title (ss 4(7)(b)(ii), 108(1B), 123(1)(b), 131A, 131B, 136H, 183, 203BB, 203BD, 203BF, 207A), including native title applications such as claimant applications (ss 79A, 86A–86G, 108(1A), 136A–136G) and certain land access agreements: ss 44F, 44G;

– the mediation of future act matters: ss 31(3), 43(2)(c), 43A(d), 181(4);

– parties making agreements about such matters as part or all of native title application proceedings in the Federal Court (ss 86A, 86B, 86D(2), 86F, 87, 136C(b), 136D(1), 136G(4)), proposed future acts (ss 24MD, 25, 26D(2), 28(1)(f), 31(1)(b), 36(4), 37, 38(1A), 39(4), 40, 41(1)(b), 41A(1), see also ss 34, 35(1)(b), 36A(1)(b)), access rights to certain non-exclusive agricultural and pastoral leases (s 44B), and other matters (s 24EC) or native title matters generally: ss 183, 203B(1)(e), 203BD(b)(iii), 203BE(3)(a), (5), (6), 203BF(1)(a), 203BH, 203BK(3), 108(1B)(b);

– agreements taking the form of Indigenous land-use agreements, negotiated and registered under the Act: ss 24BA – 24EBA, 69(1), 77A, 139(d), 141(4), 151(2), 169(2), 183, 199A-199F, 251A.

13 See Bryan Keon-Cohen, 'The Mabo Litigation: A Personal and Procedural Account' (2000) 24 *Melbourne University Law Review* 893–951.

14 *Fejo v Northern Territory* (1998) 195 CLR 96, 139.

15 Madgwick J has described the objects of the Act as including 'arriving at agreement if possible as to who are the appropriate native title claimants, or at least minimising the scope for such disputes' (*Eora People-Brown v NSW Minister for Land & Water Conservation* [2000] FCA 1238 (Unreported, Madgwick J, 17 August 2000) [27]). Emmett J has stated 'One important object and purpose to be found in the Act is resolution of issues and disputes concerning native title by mediation and agreement, rather than by Court determination. Detailed procedures are set out in the Act to achieve those objects'. (*Munn for and on behalf of the Gunggari People v Queensland* (2001) 115 FCR 109, 115). Branson J has noted that the Act 'discloses an intention of encouraging and facilitating the resolution of native title claims by agreement' (*Kelly on behalf of the Byron Bay Bundjalung People v NSW Aboriginal Land Council* [2001] FCA 1479 (Unreported, Branson J, 23 October 2001) [23]).

16 *Brownley v Western Australia (No 1)* (1999) 95 FCR 152, 160 [16] (Lee J).

A special procedure needs to be available for the just and proper ascertainment of native title rights and interests which will ensure that, if possible, this is done by conciliation and, if not, in a manner that has due regard to their unique character.

It continues:

Governments should, where appropriate, facilitate negotiation on a regional basis between the parties concerned in relation to:

(a) claims to land, or aspirations in relation to land, by Aboriginal peoples or Torres Strait Islanders; and

(b) proposals for the use of such land for economic purposes.

Having decided that agreement making is a core theme or policy basis for the *NTA*, Parliament took the next step and created bodies to facilitate the agreement-making process. The NNTT[17] is an administrative body[18] established[19] in accordance with the main objects of the *NTA*,[20] with power to make determinations about whether certain future acts may be done and whether certain agreements concerning native title are to be covered by the Act, and to provide assistance or undertake mediation in other matters relating to native title.[21] The NNTT also deals with matters such as applications for compensation, and assists people to negotiate Indigenous Land Use Agreements (ILUAs) on a wide range of topics.

The NNTT was not the only body with agreement-making functions created or recognised under the *NTA*.[22] Indigenous groups need to be represented in asserting their interests, and the Act provides for the recognition of native title representative bodies around the country. In many cases these are bodies which existed before the Act was enacted.

The *NTA* spells out in some detail the functions of these bodies.[23] They include:

---

[17] *Native Title Act 1993* (Cth) s 253: definitions of 'National Native Title Tribunal' or 'NNTT', 'Tribunal'.

[18] See, for example, *North Ganalanja Aboriginal Corporation v Queensland* (1996) 185 CLR 595, 621–623 (Brennan CJ, Dawson, Toohey, Gaudron and Gummow JJ), 636–637, 641 (McHugh J), 655 (Kirby J); *Fourmile v Selpam Pty Ltd* (1998) 81 FCR 151.

[19] *Native Title Act 1993* (Cth) s 107.

[20] *Native Title Act 1993* (Cth) s 3.

[21] *Native Title Act 1993* (Cth) ss 4(2), 4(7).

[22] *Native Title Act 1993* (Cth) ss 24BF, 24CF, 24DG, 44B, 44F (also ss 207A, 253) on the agreement making role of a 'recognised State/Territory body', and s 207B on 'equivalent State/Territory bodies'.

[23] *Native Title Act 1993* (Cth) ss 203B– 203BK.

1.   assisting people to research, prepare and make native title applications
2.   acting for or arranging representation for people in mediation and negotiations about claimant applications and a whole range of matters, including future acts
3.   mediating between the constituents in their areas about matters arising in the course of lodging claimant applications (for example, in relation to overlapping applications).

The Act also expressly empowers the Commonwealth Attorney-General to provide legal aid funding to various other parties where those parties want assistance; for example, to negotiate ILUAs and other types of agreements.[24]

The Federal Court also has a role in supervising mediation when an application for a determination of native title has been made, and to set time frames within which a mediated outcome should be achieved.[25] If parties can agree in the course of mediation that native title exists over a particular area, and that a particular group has native title, that agreement can be given formal effect under the *NTA* by way of a determination of native title made by the Federal Court.[26]

Judicial support for agreement making

There have been some very strong statements from superior courts about the importance of agreement making in relation to native title matters. In 1996 the High Court stated:

> If it be practicable to resolve an application for the determination of native title by negotiation and agreement rather than by the judicial determination of complex issues, the Court and the likely parties to the litigation are saved a great deal in time and resources.
>
> Perhaps more importantly, if the persons interested in the determination of those issues negotiate and reach an agreement, they are enabled thereby to establish an amicable relationship between future neighbouring occupiers. To submit a claim for determination of native title to judicial determination before the stage of negotiation is reached is to invert the statutory order of disposing of such claims.[27]

---

[24]   *Native Title Act 1993* (Cth) s 183.
[25]   See, eg, *Frazer v Western Australia* (2003) 198 ALR 303.
[26]   *Native Title Act 1993* (Cth) s 87. The Court must be satisfied that it is within the Court's power to make an order in, or consistent with, the terms of the agreement and that it is appropriate to do so.
[27]   *North Ganalanja Aboriginal Corporation v Queensland* (1996) 185 CLR 595, 617 (Brennan CJ, Dawson, Toohey, Gaudron and Gummow JJ).

This statement by the High Court repeats, in essence, what judges have often said in urging parties to settle cases. Some judges have quoted this passage in subsequent decisions.[28]

Although test cases are necessary to resolve outstanding legal questions (to create a clearer legal landscape in which to negotiate), there are practical reasons for usually preferring agreed outcomes. A litigated outcome is likely to be more costly (in financial, personal and temporal terms) than a mediated outcome, and the issues that are resolved are likely to be narrower. In some instances, a litigated (and imposed) outcome will be less satisfactory to one or more of the parties.

Experience has demonstrated the costs and other features involved in native title litigation. The *Yorta Yorta* case, for example, ran for 114 hearing days between 8 October 1996 and 4 November 1998. At the end of the trial, the Yorta Yorta people were unsuccessful in proving that they had native title.[29] In his judgement, Justice Olney highlighted the difficulties in litigating native title issues and illustrated that litigation may not be the best option to take. His Honour stated:

> Many of the difficulties inherent in litigating a complex native title determination application have been highlighted by what has occurred in this proceeding. A substantial portion of the enormous mass of evidence presented to the Court, prepared at considerable expense to the parties, deals with matters relating to the extinguishment of native title rights and interests, an issue which only arises in the event that the observance and acknowledgement of traditional laws and customs in relation to land are shown to have survived. As it happened, in light of the conclusion expressed above, it is unnecessary to embark upon a consideration of whether and to what extent, native title rights and interests have been subjected to extinguishing events, nor does the question of the coexistence of native title and other rights arise. The time and expense expended in the preparation and presentation of a large part of the evidence has proved to be unproductive, a circumstance which calls into question the suitability of the processes of adversary litigation for the purpose of determining matters relating to native title.[30]

---

[28] See *Byron Environment Centre Incorporated v Arakwal People* (1997) 78 FCR 1, 24 (Merkel J); *Fejo v Northern Territory* (1998) 195 CLR 96, 134 (Kirby J); *Mitakoodi/Juhnjlar People v Queensland* [2000] FCA 156 (Unreported, Spender J, 18 February 2000) [11]; *Anderson on behalf of the Spinifex People v Western Australia* [2000] FCA 1717 (Unreported, Black CJ, 28 November 2000) [8].

[29] *Members of the Yorta Yorta Aboriginal Community v State of Victoria* [1998] FCA 1606 (Unreported, Olney J, 18 December 1998). Appeals to the Full Federal Court and the High Court were unsuccessful.

[30] *Members of the Yorta Yorta Aboriginal Community v State of Victoria* [1998] FCA 1606 (Unreported, Olney J, 18 December 1998) [130]. The Judge found native title did not exist because of the lack of a continuing traditional Aboriginal community. The result was confirmed on appeal by the Full Federal Court, *Members of the Yorta Yorta Aboriginal*

More recently, in *De Rose v South Australia* (where the native title claim was unsuccessful), Justice O'Loughlin pointed to examples of 'how the adversarial process can be deficient' when dealing with native title.[31]

By comparison, the Miriuwung Gajerrong trial in Western Australia ran for 83 days between 17 February 1997 and 23 October 1998. The Federal Court recognised that native title existed, and that other people such as pastoralists and miners also had rights that had to be recognised. The Court stated that 'how concurrent rights are to be exercised in a practical way in respect of the determination area must be resolved by negotiation between the parties concerned. It may be desirable that the parties be assisted in that endeavour by mediation'.[32]

Other hearings have not taken as long as those cases but, by conventional litigation standards, at around 30–40 sitting days, native title hearings are protracted. The cost and delays for these sorts of actions are usually compounded by the desire of the Indigenous parties to hold at least some of the hearing 'on country'. The very rewarding experience of having hearings on country, which can enhance the quality of evidence and add dimensions of understanding to the evidence given by native title claimants, is to some extent offset by the amount of work involved in preparing that aspect of the trial as well as in hearing it.

At the end of the process (including appeals), the parties have to negotiate what their respective rights mean (or at least how those rights are to be exercised) on the ground.[33] By contrast, as more matters are resolved by agreement, the Federal Court has congratulated the parties for reaching quite specific agreements about issues that need to be dealt with on a case-by-case basis.[34]

Agreement making and determinations of native title

The principal formal outcome in some cases is an agreement that native title exists, expressed in a determination of native title. The process for reaching such agreement involves the following steps:

Community v State of Victoria (2001) 110 FCR 244, and the High Court, *Members of the Yorta Yorta Aboriginal Community v Victoria* (2002) 194 ALR 538.

[31] *De Rose v State of South Australia* [2002] FCA 1342 (Unreported, O'Loughlin J, 1 November 2002) [89], [144].

[32] *Ward v Western Australia* (1998) 159 ALR 483, 639.

[33] See also *Smith v Western Australia* (2000) 104 FCR 494, 500 [27].

[34] *Anderson on behalf of the Spinifex People v Western Australia* [2000] FCA 1717 (Unreported, Black CJ, 28 November 2000) [7]. See also *Passi on behalf of the Meriam People v Queensland* [2001] FCA 697 (Unreported, Black CJ, 14 June 2001) [9]; *Congo v State of Queensland* [2001] FCA 868 (Unreported, Hely J, 28 June 2001) [17]; *Ngalpil v Western Australia* [2001] FCA 1140 (Unreported, Carr J, 20 August 2001) [33].

1. An application for a determination of native title is filed in the Federal Court.[35]
2. The application is sent to the Registrar of the NNTT, who undertakes various administrative procedures (including applying the registration test to each application and notifying the relevant persons and bodies and the public about each application).[36] If the application satisfies conditions in the Act, it is admitted into the Register of Native Title Claims. While their applications are proceeding to resolution, Aboriginal and Torres Strait Islanders acquire certain procedural rights as though they were native title holders.
3. Applications for party status are assessed and determined by the Federal Court.[37]
4. As a general rule, each native title application is referred to the NNTT for mediation.[38]

The parties involved in the mediation process are often reluctantly drawn into the process. They are responding to an application that includes an assertion of native title rights and interests. Sometimes there are hundreds of parties to a particular application.

Many of the parties have no understanding of native title or the native title process. For mediation to be successful, the participants need to understand:

- what the process is about
- the nature of native title
- the respective roles of parties and institutions (including the Federal Court, the NNTT, and native title representative bodies)
- how their interests can be accommodated
- the possible outcomes
- the best result the parties might achieve out of this process.

The NNTT often provides pre-mediation assistance, after an application has been referred to it, so that parties have a sufficient level of understanding and capacity to actively and positively participate in the agreement-making process.

A series of mediation conferences, sometimes with all the parties, or with those who have a particular interest in common, are then scheduled.[39]

---

[35] *Native Title Act 1993* (Cth) ss 61, 61A, 62.
[36] *Native Title Act 1993* (Cth) ss 63, 190A–190C, 66(3).
[37] *Native Title Act 1993* (Cth) ss 84, 84A.
[38] *Native Title Act 1993* (Cth) s 86B.
[39] *Native Title Act 1993* (Cth) ss 136A-136F.

Graziers, miners, explorers, prospectors, fishers, state or territory governments and local authorities converse with the native title applicants in
order to ascertain what the native title applicants hope to achieve from the
process, and how any native title rights or other parties' interests might be
recognised, respected and exercised.

The *NTA* states that the purpose of native title claimant mediation is
to assist the parties to reach agreement on some or all of the specified matters,[40] including:

- whether native title exists
- if it does exist, who holds the native title
- the nature, effect and manner of exercise of the native title rights and
  interests
- the interests of other people (graziers, miners etc.) in relation to the area
- the relationship between the various rights and interests.

If agreement can be reached, the parties return to the Federal Court and
request a determination of native title in terms of the agreement. The Act
sets out what a determination must contain.[41] It must identify whether
native title exists or not, and if it does exist, determine:

- who the persons, or each group of persons, are who hold the common
  or group rights comprising the native title
- the nature and extent of the native title rights and interests in relation
  to the determination area
- the nature and extent of any other interests in relation to the determination area
- the relationship between the various rights and interests
- whether the native title rights and interests confer exclusive possession, occupation, use and enjoyment of any of the land or waters on
  the native title holders.

There are difficult cases that cannot be resolved by agreement, particularly
in cases in which there are disputes as to facts or outstanding legal issues.
For example, where two or more claimant groups are in dispute about who
has native title rights and interests over a particular area, experience has
shown that state governments and many other parties (even if they are
inclined to settle native title matters by agreement) will not decide between
disputing claimant groups.

Increasingly the trend is towards resolving native title determination
applications by agreement. The majority of claimant applications finalised

---

[40] *Native Title Act 1993* (Cth) s 86A(1).
[41] *Native Title Act 1993* (Cth) s 225.

to date have been resolved by agreement, many of them without the need for a trial. In others, agreements have been reached after commencement of trial.[42] This results in not only a saving in time and resources but, through the process of mediation, new relationships are formed.

While the matter is with the NNTT, the Federal Court supervises the mediation. The Court obtains information by requesting the NNTT to provide mediation progress reports,[43] or by receiving mediation progress reports initiated by the NNTT to assist the Court in progressing the proceeding.[44] If progress is not being made, the Court can set down the matter for trial.

Agreements associated with determinations of native title

Consent native title determinations are but one form of agreement for settling native title claimant applications. There are associated agreements. If, for example, the parties agree that native title exists over an area of land that includes pastoral leases, the parties may need to agree on how the various rights will be exercised. For example, how many people may come on to the land to exercise their native title rights? How much notice must be given to the pastoral lessee? May dogs, guns and vehicles be brought onto the land? Is shooting or hunting permitted on the property? Are these sorts of activities permissible all year round? Are gates to be left open or closed? Who is responsible for them? What about public liability insurance? Who carries the insurance cover? Who pays the premium? These are practical issues that must be addressed, and are best resolved by a land-use and access agreement.

Sometimes, these agreements take the form of ILUAs. They might be negotiated then registered before the determination of native title takes effect. At other times, the native title determination may be effective, provided that each party signs off on the agreements that have already been made in principle.[45]

Other agreements that may result in a settlement of a native title application can involve non-native title outcomes, such as statements of formal recognition of traditional ownership of lands in which native title had been or might have been extinguished, consultation or joint management

---

[42] For up-to-date information about determinations of native title, see the National Native Title Tribunal's website http://www.nntt.gov.au/ at 7 November 2003.

[43] *Native Title Act 1993* (Cth) ss 86E, 136G(2).

[44] *Native Title Act 1993* (Cth) s 136G(3).

[45] See, for example, National Native Title Tribunal, *The Kaurareg People's Native Title Determinations: Questions and Answers* (May 2001) http://www.nntt.gov.au/metacard/files/kaurareg/Kaurareg Q A final.pdf at 7 November 2003.

agreements in relation to the use of traditional lands, and grants of interests in those lands under state land rights legislation or otherwise.[46] Agreements of that type can result in a claimant application being settled by being withdrawn without any determination of native title, or with a determination that native title does not exist. The applicants in these situations may not have enough evidence to prove (in accordance with the current legal requirements) that they have native title, but other parties are willing to recognise that they are the traditional people for the area.

In exploring the way in which native title claimant applications can be resolved, it is possible to be fairly creative about a whole range of other agreements that can enable various interests to be accommodated. This chapter has highlighted the agreement-making process and options in relation to native title claimant applications. There are other processes and options under the *NTA* (including ILUAs) for dealing with future acts (such as exploration and mining) in areas in which native title has been proved to exist or to possibly exist, and matters such as compensation for loss or impairment of native title.[47]

Conclusion

The *NTA* did not emerge from a vacuum. It was shaped by more than 200 years of historical factors. It came at a particular time when an historic High Court judgment posed a number of very practical challenges to the Australian community. How those challenges were to be met and the procedures for meeting them were set out in the *NTA*. That Act prefers agreement making to litigation, if at all possible, and sets out processes and institutions to facilitate the agreement-making process. Accordingly, the vision of the NNTT is an Australia in which native title is recognised, respected and protected through just and agreed outcomes. The NNTT works with people to develop an understanding of native title and to reach enduring native title and related outcomes.[48]

We now exist in an environment of agreement making which was not apparent in the years immediately after the *Mabo* decision. As a nation we are increasingly accepting that native title is here to stay. It is part of the legal and social landscape, and the best way to sort out these issues is by agreement. As a result, there has been a considerable increase in the number and types of agreed outcomes.

---

[46] See *Frazer v Western Australia* (2003) 198 ALR 303, 310.

[47] For examples of these and other agreements, see the NNTT's *Annual Reports* at http://www. nntt.gov.au/publications/annual2001.html; and the ATNS Project database http://www. atns.net.au at 7 November 2003.

[48] See National Native Title Tribunal's *Strategic Plan 2003–2005*.

Chapter 11

Symbolism and Function: From Native Title to Aboriginal and Torres Strait Islander self-government

Lisa Strelein

Introduction

Chief Justice Gleeson, when delivering the judgement in *Western Australia v Ward,* suggested that no-one had been entirely successful in the case.[1] But what does this mean in relation to the recognition and protection of native title? For Aboriginal and Torres Strait Islander claimants, it has generally meant that their rights have been inadequately protected by the law, and for non-Indigenous interests it has meant that Aboriginal and Torres Strait Islander peoples' rights are not limited as they might have hoped. Neither the courts nor the legislature has done anything to build upon the recognition and protection of Aboriginal and Torres Strait people's rights as determined by the decision in *Mabo v Queensland [No 2].*[2]

Certainly, the disappointment over decisions in *Ward* and *Members of the Yorta Yorta Aboriginal Community v State of Victoria* must give pause for thought.[3] The limits of the legal concept of native title raises the question of whether the development of the common law has left an empty vessel for most Aboriginal and Torres Strait Islander peoples. In the eleven years since the decision of the High Court in *Mabo,* there has been sharp criticism of the lack of outcomes from the native title process despite the substantial

---

[1]   (2002) 191 ALR 1 ('*Ward*').
[2]   (1993) 175 CLR 1 ('*Mabo*').
[3]   (2002) 194 ALR 538 ('*Yorta Yorta*').

resources expended, not least by Aboriginal and Torres Strait Islander communities themselves.

However, before we can assess the outcomes against the cost, we must first consider what we count among the outcomes of native title and how much we value them. It is important, when we try to understand the effort that has been put into the native title process, that we look at both the legal conclusions of native title as well as its place in the recognition of Aboriginal and Torres Strait Islander self-government. The changes in the political and legal environment occasioned by the recognition of native title should also be considered amongst the outcomes of native title.

Despite being one of the most potent critics of the native title process, Noel Pearson recently was adamant that native title is not a 'dead issue'.[4] Native title is important in Australia's legal and political structures because it is a measure of our ability to accommodate the rights of Aboriginal and Torres Strait Islander peoples. The arms of the state cannot ignore the intensely symbolic nature of native title in their engagement with Indigenous peoples. For Aboriginal and Torres Strait Islander peoples in Australia, it is not merely a form of title: it is a fundamental recognition of the distinct identity and special place of the first peoples. The rights of Aboriginal and Torres Strait Islander peoples that (however inadequately) are reflected in native title are recognised by virtue of their existence as distinct peoples and as a constitutional entity, and not merely as a cultural minority within an otherwise homogenous Australian polity.[5] As a concept, native title is an acknowledgment of the continuation of Aboriginal and Torres Strait Islander society as a source of authority. For these reasons, the *Mabo* case is considered to be a high watermark in the relationship between Aboriginal and Torres Strait Islander peoples and the state.

In this chapter I consider how the potential of native title may have been curtailed by the courts as a result of impossible standards of proof, intricate inquiries and problematic jurisprudence. Yet, the idea of native title, or what native title symbolises, may have formed the basis for greater recognition of the rights of Aboriginal and Torres Strait Islander peoples to negotiate directly with government from a position of sovereign authority.

---

[4]   Noel Pearson, 'Where We've Come From and Where We're At with the Opportunity that is Koiki Mabo's Legacy to Australia' (Paper presented at the Native Title Conference 2003: Native Title on the Ground, Alice Springs, 2–5 June 2003) 2; see Pearson, this volume.
[5]   Patrick Macklem, 'Distributing Sovereignty: Indian Nations and Equality of Peoples' (1993) 45 *Stanford Law Review* 1311, 1325.

The limits of native title

In *Ward* and *Yorta Yorta* the High Court has confirmed its view that native title rights and interests must be construed as deriving from traditional law and custom. The common law recognises those rights and interests through the concept of native title. The Court held that native title is defined by the *Native Title Act 1993* (Cth) (*NTA*) in s 223(1), not by the common law.[6] The Court interpreted the statutory definition as needing two inquiries.[7] The first is to determine whether the claimants have established that they hold rights and interests under traditional laws and customs. This requires the identification of laws and customs themselves and then the articulation of the rights and interest conferred by those laws. The second inquiry is into the connection of the group to the land or waters. This does not require proof of physical occupation or continued use, but a connection through law and custom. That is, the Court has said that it is not how Aboriginal peoples use or occupy the land, but what the laws and customs say about their connection.[8]

Nevertheless, there still appears to be a level of confusion in the reasoning of the courts as to whether they require claimants to demonstrate a system of law and custom that binds them as a society, through which internal ordering of rights and interests in land is determined, or whether the courts are setting themselves as arbiters of traditional law, by requiring a detailed articulation of the laws and customs relating to entitlement to the land claimed. The High Court, in particular, has demonstrated its inability to articulate Aboriginal and Torres Strait Islander systems of law and custom. The majority in *Ward* clumsily excused themselves by lamenting the inherent difficulty of translating what they describe as the 'essentially spiritual' relationship with the land.[9] In *Ward*, the Court accepted that the 'right to speak for country' encapsulated a relationship to land that was as complete as any under common law, thus would be reflected in a right of exclusive possession.[10] Yet, the Court was quick to exploit the relationship of dependence and the irresistibility of sovereign power that had been established in the *Mabo* case in order to undermine Aboriginal and Torres Strait Islander authority by readily imputing extinguishment of any native title right to make decisions with respect to access and use.

---

[6] *Ward* (2002) 191 ALR 1, 17.
[7] Ibid.
[8] Implicit in this construction is an acknowledgment by the court that the observance of laws and customs is separate from the existence of those laws. A failure to exercise a right does not result in the loss of the right. Ibid, 32–33.
[9] Ibid, 15.
[10] Ibid, 38–39.

The Court in recent cases has displayed a disappointing readiness to find that the 'exclusive' character of native title was extinguished by almost any act, resulting in the loss of rights to control access or future development. The ever-expanding doctrine of extinguishment is recognised by the courts as operating in the common law sphere to withdraw recognition of rights that might otherwise continue under Aboriginal and Torres Strait Islander law. In *Ward*, however, extinguishment and the impact of non-Aboriginal and Torres Strait Islander interests was conflated with questions of proof, so that the onus was shifted to Aboriginal claimants to establish how their laws and customs could be explained in greater detail in order to build the concept of 'non-exclusive' native title from a bundle of distinct rights and interests.

Similarly, in *Yorta Yorta*, while the High Court recognised that native title protects rights and interests that emerge from a different body of law, the extent of recognition is determined by the colonising regime on its own terms. The Court requires proof that the society and the system of law and custom that give rise to rights to land have remained intact. Yet, it denies any continuing authority in that society. By operation of legal fiction, the system of legal authority is treated as a matter of fact but somehow not an exercise of sovereign jurisdiction.

The doctrine of native title has replaced *terra nullius* with a basis for dispossession no less reliant on a conception of Aboriginal and Torres Strait Islander society as a relic of prior sovereignty. The illogicality of such an impoverished judicial theory has led some commentators to reject, wholeheartedly, any role for traditional law and custom in the proof of native title, preferring an occupation-based analysis.[11] Noel Pearson's argument for an occupation-based doctrine of native title has a great deal of attraction for a legal theory that has become constrained by impossible internal contradictions, extraordinary levels of proof and unmanageable inquiries into competing interests and tenure histories.

Whatever the doctrine of proof applied in the courts, and whatever the limits that are placed on the 'legal conclusion' of native title, the 'idea' of native title reflects a deeper recognition of Aboriginal and Torres Strait Islander identity. This recognition has led to fundamental changes in the status of Aboriginal and Torres Strait Islander peoples in negotiations with the state. While the courts may be in a position to isolate the functional

---

[11] See Noel Pearson, 'Communal Native Title' (2000) 5 *Native Title Newsletter* 3. In this view, rights arise because of the fact of prior occupation of land by Aboriginal and Torres Strait Islander people rather than because of the detail of law and custom of the occupying group. Pearson points to Kent McNeil, 'Aboriginal Title and Aboriginal Rights: What's the Connection?' (1997) 36 *Alberta Law Review* 117. This view was explicitly rejected by the High Court in *Ward* (2002) 191 ALR 1, 39–40.

doctrine of native title from the symbolic recognition of Aboriginal or Torres Strait Islander authority on which it is based, the separation cannot be so easily drawn in negotiations between Aboriginal or Torres Strait Islander peoples and the state.

Agreements under the *Native Title Act*

From the outset, the recognition of Indigenous peoples in the *Mabo* case invigorated agitation for negotiations with the state and gave a new-found legitimacy to Aboriginal and Torres Strait Islander peoples' claims in the eyes of governments. In the original *NTA*, s 21 was included to allow native title holders to enter into an agreement with a state, territory or Commonwealth government to surrender their title, or to authorise future developments. Subsection (4) contained a negative reference to the fact that this section did not prevent agreement being made on a regional or local basis. Hence, a number of large-scale agreements began to be negotiated. Movements for regional autonomy in Cape York and the Kimberley, for example, had a new framework within which to negotiate.[12]

As part of the 1998 amendments to the *NTA*, the Indigenous Land Use Agreement (ILUA) provisions sought to encapsulate the needs of smaller ventures for greater security for agreements entered into with Aboriginal and Torres Strait Islander communities.[13] Despite the aggressiveness of the government's amendment plan, most parties to the native title process accepted a more detailed legislative regime to support these kinds of agreements. The ILUA provisions also recognised the desire on the part of commercial and Aboriginal and Torres Strait Islander interests to be able to deal directly with each other in relation to particular projects, removing government parties from some negotiations. The resulting ILUA regime provides a strict framework within which these agreements may be developed and continue to operate with some level of certainty for the non-Indigenous parties.

---

[12] A Cape York Heads of Agreement was signed in 1996 by Aboriginal and Torres Strait Islander organisations and peak industry and environmental groups. The Agreement was heralded as an historic land-use protocol that would set a precedent for negotiated settlements of land-use issues across the country. Original signatories were the Cape York Land Council and the Peninsula Regional Council of the Aboriginal and Torres Strait Islander Commission, the Cattlemen's Union, the Australian Conservation Foundation, and the Wilderness Society. In 2001, the Cape York Agreement was revisited and the State of Queensland became a party. The Balkanu Cape York Development Corporation, and the Cairns and Far North Environment Centre also signed. For the Agreement and commentary see the ATNS Project database at http://www.atns.net.au/biogs/A000107b.htm at 2 December 2003.

[13] See *Native Title Amendment Act 1998* (Cth) subdiv B.

South Australia statewide ILUA

With their genesis in providing contractual security for small commercial interests, the ILUA provisions do not recognise any status for native title-holding groups beyond one of many private users of land. Nevertheless, this has not stopped Aboriginal and Torres Strait Islander peoples from pushing the limits of the ILUA process.

Native title claimants in South Australia, for example, have entered into direct negotiations with the South Australian Government and peak industry bodies under the ILUA process to negotiate a 'state wide comprehensive settlement' of native title issues, with a view toward progressive legislative, administrative, constitutional and procedural reforms.[14] The process has been a collaborative one, with government providing substantial resources and a dedicated team of negotiators and the Aboriginal Legal Rights Movement of South Australia, as the native title representative body, facilitating Aboriginal peoples' direction of and engagement in the process. The process has also been supported by considerable research and procedural advice.[15]

For the claimants in South Australia, the idea of negotiating within the ILUA regime was initially met with some scepticism, particularly at the prospect of having to negotiate on the basis of extinguishment of native title. However, the negotiating strength and direct community empower-ment that could be gained through working together at the state level was seen as an opportunity worth pursuing. The focus of efforts has been in the development of appropriate processes and capacities within the claimant groups to participate effectively in negotiations of this scale.[16]

The South Australian partners have invoked criticism over perceived lack of outcomes and for the amount of funding required to establish this kind of 'bottom-up' negotiating structure. The process of engagement and the building of Aboriginal governance structures are clearly seen by the negotiating partners as 'outcomes' from native title.[17] Nevertheless,

---

[14] Parry Agius, Jocelyn Davies, Ritchie Howitt and Lesley Johns, 'Negotiating Comprehensive Settlement of Native Title Issues: Building a New Scale of Justice in South Australia' (2002) 2(20) *Land Rights Laws: Issues of Native Title* 4; see Agius et al, this volume. See also the ATNS Project database at http://www.atns.net.au/biogs/A001072b.htm at 2 December 2003; http://www.iluasa.com at 13 November 2003.

[15] See Parry Agius and Richie Howitt, 'Different Visions, Different Ways: Lessons and Challenges from the Native Title Negotiations in South Australia' (Paper presented to the Native Title Conference 2003: Native Title on the Ground, Alice Springs, 2–5 June 2003).

[16] The large-scale, statewide negotiations are supported by local authority structure across the State. Native title claimants have organised Native Title Management Committees (NTMCs) for each of their claims that meet statewide as the South Australian 'Congress' of NTMCs to negotiate over common issues. The Congress has also agreed on priorities and pilot negotiations to progress toward substantive incremental outcomes.

[17] Agius *et al.* 'Negotiating Comprehensive Settlement of Native Title Issues', above n 14, 2.

the ILUA regime operates within the constraints of native title—thus the subject matter of the resulting negotiations in South Australia is currently focused primarily on land use and resource exploitation. Understandably, claimants perceive the native title process as being part of a broader political context.[18] As a result, however, the processes for engagement that have strengthened the decision-making structures of the native title claimants may well extend beyond the current process.

Statewide famework agreements and comprehensive processes

The emergence of statewide framework agreements recognised that providing a mechanism for future act agreements does not remove the need for negotiations between Aboriginal and Torres Strait Islander peoples and the state over outstanding issues, including historical loss, government service delivery and autonomy options. These agreements have taken a number of forms, and while they have been primarily directed to native title, some also seek to incorporate other issues. Even at this level, however, the limits of the framework agreements are clearly based on the constraints of the current national legal framework. The first such agreement was signed in Victoria in November 2000. The Victorian protocol committed the State Government to negotiating native title outcomes in Victoria, recognising that litigation would pose difficult obstacles for native title claimants in Victoria, and to a further process of negotiation on a statewide basis.[19]

Western Australian comprehensive agreements

In October 2001, the Western Australian Government signed a *Statement of Commitment* for 'a new and just relationship' with Aboriginal peoples in that state, in order to achieve, among other things:

- recognition of the continuing rights and responsibilities of Aboriginal peoples of Western Australia, including traditional ownership and connection to land and waters
- legislative protection of Aboriginal rights

---

[18] See discussion in Agius and Howitt, above n 15, 8.

[19] In August 1999, a statewide consultation protocol, *Building Reconciliation,* was entered into between the Queensland Government and the Queensland Aboriginal and Torres Strait Islander Working Group, the latter representing the native title representative bodies in the State. The Queensland government and Aboriginal and Torres Strait Islander representative bodies chose to focus on a consultation protocol. See http://www.nrm.qld.gov.au/nativetitle/pdf/manual/protocol.pdf at 2 December 2003.

▪ regional and local approaches to address issues that have an impact on Aboriginal communities, families and individuals.

A 'Partnership Framework', which forms part of the *Statement* commits to reform formalised through 'agreements'.[20] The scope of this *Statement* is clearly much broader than others of its kind, and is unique in combining land and other issues across the broad spectrum of Aboriginal peoples' relationship with the state.

Pursuant to the *Statement of Commitment*, the Western Australian Government established the Aboriginal and Torres Strait Islander Affairs Advisory Committee to oversee its implementation and set priorities under the *Statement*. This commitment was underpinned in the 2003–04 budget papers, in which the Western Australian Government committed to negotiating three comprehensive agreements under the *Statement of Commitment*—the first with the Tjurabalan community, who secured one of the first native title determinations in the State,[21] the second with the South West Aboriginal Land and Sea Council (SWALSC) and the Noongar People, and a third with the Shire of Ngaanyatjarraku.[22] The other relevant major initiative concerns a proposal for negotiations over Martu local government, who were also the subject of a substantial positive determination of native title.[23]

Tjurabalan scoping study and Martu local government

The Tjurabalan people of the East Kimberley and the Martu people of the Western Desert in the Pilbara region were chosen as the focus of two of the original priority projects under the *Statement of Commitment*, in anticipation of large-scale determinations of native title. For the Tjurabalan people, the native title matters, so far as recognition is concerned, are resolved by the positive determination of native title. The Federal Court determined that the native title holders had the right to possess, occupy, use and enjoy the land and waters of the Determination Area to the exclusion of all others.[24]

---

[20] The parties to the *Statement of Commitment* are the Government of Western Australia, represented by the Premier and the Minister for Aboriginal and Torres Strait Islander Affairs, Aboriginal and Torres Strait Islander Commission, the Western Australian Native Title Working Group, the Western Australian Aboriginal Community Controlled Health Organisation and the Aboriginal Legal Service of Western Australia http://www.aad.wa.gov.au/policies/statestrategy/files/statemmentof commitment.pdf at 1 December 2003. See also the ATNS Project database at http://www.atns.net.au/biogs/A000921b.htm at 1 December 2003.

[21] *Ngalpil v Western Australia* [2001] FCA 1140.

[22] Parliament of Western Australia, *Budget Papers 2003–04*, vol 2, 992.

[23] *James v State of Western Australia* [2002] FCA 1208.

[24] *Ngalpil v Western Australia* [2001] FCA 1140, [33].

That right includes the right to live on the land, to make decisions about its use and enjoyment, and to control access and use by others; the right to hunt and gather, to take water and other traditionally accessed resources for personal and communal needs; the right to maintain and protect sites of significance; and the right to be acknowledged as the traditional Aboriginal owners of the area. The rights and interests are also exercisable in accordance with traditional laws and customs. Implementation and future native title negotiations will remain a significant part of the community's continuing engagement with the State and other interests.

The project has been adopted by the Council of Australian Governments (COAG) whole-of-government process, which co-ordinates government agencies in the provision of services to Aboriginal and Torres Strait Islander communities in a number of trial sites. Tjurabalan is one of up to ten sites around the country that will be the focus of this new approach between Commonwealth and state governments.[25] The scoping study that will form the basis for a comprehensive agreement will likely examine land use as well as service delivery, infrastructure and local government options. The COAG trials have avoided confronting outstanding claims to land either by choosing sites where land needs have been met through native title or land rights, or by excluding land issues from the scope of the project.

Like the Tjurabalan determination before it, the Martu determination of native title recognises exclusive possession and the distribution of rights and interests over the land in accordance with the laws and customs of the Martu. While the determination of native title says nothing about municipal government, the determination has prompted the State Government to examine options for self-government for the community within the local government regime. The Shire of Ngaanyatjarraku is an example of the application of local government models to remote regions in which populations are predominantly Aboriginal. The recognition of Martu self-government is an important step that many native title claim groups envisage as among their ultimate aims.

Noongar nation

The impact of recent court decisions on issues of proof and extinguishment make litigated outcomes undesirable in the settlement of native title for Indigenous peoples in the south-west region of Western Australia. If for no

---

[25] See Di Hawgood, 'Imagine What Could Happen If We Worked Together: Shared Responsibility and a Whole of Government Approach' (Paper presented to the Native Title Conference 2003: Native Title On The Ground, Alice Springs, 2–5 June 2003). See also the ATNS Project database at http://www.atns.net.au/biogs/A001242b.htm at 1 December 2003.

other reason, the land-tenure history will ensure that the process of determining the impact of extinguishing acts in the south-west is significantly more complex, even, than the process engaged in by the High Court in the *Ward* decision.[26]

Noongar people and SWALSC have initiated a single-claim policy that will see a single, united claim covering all Noongar country. The cultural, social and political reality of Noongar people has made this approach the most feasible basis for negotiating outcomes in the south-west. The internal process of negotiating agreements for representation and decision making among the Noongar people has proved to be a vehicle for social relationship building out of processes that may otherwise be a source of social atomisation.[27] The positive work done to achieve support for the single claim may also provide a strong base, with continuing structural reinforcement, for the cohesive identity of the Noongar community.

This renewed self-confidence has engaged the Government, and it has responded with a commitment to negotiate a comprehensive agreement. While the proposed comprehensive agreement process for the Noongar nation may result in a settlement of the native title claim, it is not likely to be focused on land-use agreements and protocols. Led by the Western Australian Department of Indigenous Affairs, the resulting process is likely to range over service delivery, financial arrangements and autonomy structures for Noongar people, rather than purely land outcomes.[28] The contrast for Noongar people is that their fight for self-government and autonomy must occur outside existing land-based models of ownership and jurisdiction. This has forced a detailed assessment of all the tools currently available to them to achieve their goals. Native title, and the single claim, however, remain central.

Using existing tools

Native title has not replaced the myriad avenues for recognition of Aboriginal and Torres Strait Islander involvement in land management and jurisdiction over Indigenous governmental functions. Developing a comprehensive

---

[26] National Native Title Tribunal, *Where Might Native Title Exist in Australia?* (National Native Title Tribunal, Canberra, 2003) http://www.nntt.gov.au/publications/1035767344 2152. html at 2 December 2003.

[27] Murray Jones, Roger Cook and Darryl Pearce, 'One Claim or Many? From Native Title to Nation Building' (Paper presented to the Native Title Conference 2003: Native Title on the Ground, Alice Springs, 2–5 June 2003) (unpublished).

[28] Section 86F of the *NTA* provides that some or all parties to a native title application may negotiate to settle the application through an agreement that involves matters other then native title.

approach toward self-government and regional autonomy within existing structures can achieve a significant amount. There are existing mechanisms for substantive native title determinations, procedural rights attaching to extant applications, heritage protection under state and Federal legislation, Indigenous Land Corporation purchases, joint management of national parks, state land rights legislation, existing Aboriginal and Torres Strait Islander service delivery and grassroots organisations in health, legal assistance, and schooling, Aboriginal and Torres Strait Islander Commission (ATSIC) regional authority options and, more recently, COAG whole-of-government commitments to service delivery.

However, Noel Pearson commented some years ago on the need to understand such tools for what they can and cannot provide:

> We are in a political guerrilla war, in a colonial circumstance which is powerful and against which we infrequently prevail. People in situations like ours must make do with the tools which are on hand … They are limited tools and to optimise results we must use them wisely and skillfully.[29]

Aboriginal and Torres Strait Islander peoples often make use of the tools available to them without necessarily accepting the legitimacy or authority of the various institutions. As such, Pearson has argued that both radical and moderate strategies must be implemented in order to secure results.[30] But the existing tools have severe limitations, some of which are practical, while others go much deeper, to the heart of the colonial relationship. These limitations prove even more of an obstacle when responses across levels of government and between departments are inconsistent. Recent initiatives in whole-of-government projects have begun to recognise the difficulties that Aboriginal and Torres Strait Islander peoples face in confronting bureaucratic intransigence and the constraints of current structures.

Tackling bigger issues

The value of emerging comprehensive self-assessments by Aboriginal and Torres Strait Islander peoples is that they are expressions of Aboriginal and Torres Strait Islander sovereignty in action. However, incremental approaches do not require governments to commit to negotiation over broader issues on terms determined by Aboriginal and Torres Strait Islander peoples. The use of existing structures avoids the politically sensitive and potentially divisive public debates on the merits of a treaty and Indigenous

---

[29] Noel Pearson, 'Aboriginal Law and Colonial Law Since Mabo' in Christine Fletcher (ed.), *Aboriginal Self Determination in Australia* (Aboriginal Studies Press, Canberra, 1994) 157.
[30] Ibid, 157.

self-government. But the outcomes from a piecemeal approach will remain incomplete and will be reliant on the existing statutory and bureaucratic arrangements. The outcomes will not be those that emerge from a reflective consideration of what it is that Aboriginal and Torres Strait Islander peoples want to control. The question is whether there is truly an exercise of self-determination in this process. It means that the Australian nation and the Australian people have still not come to terms with the fundamental rights of Aboriginal and Torres Strait Islander peoples to self-determination and self-government where that is their expressed desire.

The decisions of the minority judges in *Ward* called for significant reform. McHugh J expressed concern that the native title system had been stacked against native title holders,[31] and called for an arbitral system that would determine claims based on their merits, and not bound by historical tenures and the common law superiority of non-native title rights.[32] Callinan J went a step further, calling for a 'true and unqualified' settlement of lands or money.[33] In articulating the immense detail required to compare the rights and interests conferred by successive tenures, the High Court in *Ward* appears to have made a strong argument for an alternative process based negotiated settlement.

The reconciling of Crown sovereignty with Indigenous peoples' rights and status must acknowledge the diversity of Aboriginal and Torres Strait Islander peoples, and thereby must accommodate the needs, demands and potential of each community. It must be recognised that the kinds of issues where Aboriginal and Torres Strait Islander people may want to take control will be shaped by their experience of colonisation. The vision of self-determination of the Noongar nation will differ markedly from that of the Martu. However, the response from the state must be co-ordinated and comprehensive.

Where the legitimacy of Indigenous autonomy, authority and jurisdiction is accepted by governments at all levels, much greater attention can be paid to how this authority will operate in the different circumstances of Aboriginal and Torres Strait Islander peoples. A national commitment to comprehensive settlement of Aboriginal and Torres Strait Islander claims would be able to set a framework that allows broad ranging and creative negotiations based on recognition of rights, and negotiated options and limitations, whereby Aboriginal and Torres Strait Islander people can address issues not as a corporate interest but as a collective, self-governing and sovereign interest.

---

[31] *Ward* (2002) 191 ALR 1, 158.
[32] Ibid, 156.
[33] Ibid, 261.

The role of native title: symbolism and function

While acknowledging the limitations of the courts, Aboriginal and Torres Strait Islander peoples will continue to utilise the available tools to pursue their objectives. Governments must choose whether they will facilitate these initiatives or frustrate them. While the courts have made the first move to recognise Aboriginal and Torres Strait Islander systems of authority, other institutions of the state must now take the further step of developing alternative processes for negotiation of Aboriginal and Torres Strait Islander governance structures.

Jeremy Webber has argued that lawyers tend to think of rights in terms of the legal mechanisms that protect them (such as a written constitution or an Act of Parliament), but ignore their 'symbolic charge'.[34] However, Webber argues that it is impossible to escape the symbolism. Legal discourse is not insulated from popular discussion of issues of law and justice, because that general discussion and the 'connotations, implications and points of resonance' impact upon interpretation and shape the evolution of law.[35]

The judges in *Mabo* were aware of the symbolic nature of their decision.[36] The significance of the *Mabo* decision is carried in 'legal' native title, which is its practical or functional outcome. Native title became the symbol for, and therefore the measure of, non-Indigenous relations with Aboriginal and Torres Strait Islander peoples. Native title recognised not just an interest in land, but also the legitimacy of Aboriginal and Torres Strait Islander peoples' claims to be law-makers, and to be recognised as a legitimate source of rights and obligations.

The symbolic and functional aspects of native title can diverge and, indeed, operate in tension with one another. Nevertheless, the failure of governments to understand the connection between the recognition of native title and agreement making on a sovereign-to-sovereign scale can be a source of immense frustration for Aboriginal and Torres Strait Islander peoples. Each of the comprehensive negotiations between native title claimants and the state that have been highlighted here has been shadowed by vehement opposition to particular claims in the courts. For South Australia, while promoting negotiations under the statewide ILUA, the State was arguing that native title had been extinguished and that the Yunkuntjatjara people of De Rose Hill station were not native title holders

---

[34] Jeremy Webber, 'Constitutional Poetry: The Tension Between Symbolic and Functional Aims in Constitutional Reform' (1999) 21 *Sydney Law Review* 260, 265.

[35] Ibid, 262, 267.

[36] See for example *Mabo* (1993) 175 CLR 1, 109 (Deane and Gaudron JJ), who described the decision as 'a retreat from injustice'.

of their traditional country.[37] For the Noongar nation, negotiations over a framework agreement will take place against the backdrop of litigation of the Perth metropolitan claim. Agreements in relation to the Martu and Tjurabalan must deal with the fallout from *Ward*. The COAG trials more generally operate alongside the opposition to native title outcomes from the Commonwealth.

The state's opposition to native title in the courts is difficult to correlate with the rhetoric of framework agreements and whole-of-government commitments to improving the lives and opportunities of Aboriginal and Torres Strait Islander peoples. These 'joined-up' approaches by governments appear to exclude the offices of native title within the government who remain dedicated to opposing the recognition of native title as a legal outcome. As Noel Pearson has expressed, it is like playing a game: 'they pretend they are not resolutely opposing native title. We pretend the same thing in return'.[38]

Both functionally and symbolically, native title will continue to play a central role in any political settlement because, for better or worse, it now provides the framework within which non-Aboriginal and Torres Strait Islander people conceive of Aboriginal and Torres Strait Islander rights, and it provides the bulwark against which Aboriginal and Torres Strait Islander peoples can build their claims for greater recognition. Native title provides Aboriginal and Torres Strait Islander peoples with one of the only processes in which the state is required to engage. For Aboriginal and Torres Strait Islander peoples, too, native title is not merely a form of title. It is a fundamental recognition by the colonising state of the distinct identity and special place of Aboriginal and Torres Strait Islander peoples as the first peoples.

Symbolism reflects as well as defines what is important to us as a society. By suggesting what is important, symbols influence people's sense of involvement in the society in which they live. Native title is such a symbol. At its foundation, native title reflects the relationship between Indigenous and non-Indigenous peoples in Australia. It matters what we do and what we achieve with native title.

---

[37] *De Rose v State of South Australia* [2002] FCA 1342. At the date of writing the full Federal Court has heard the appeal in this case. The Court unanimously held that there were errors in the trial judge's reasoning but it could not decide the matter without further submissions. *De Rose Hill v State of South Australia* [2003] FCAFC 286 (Wilcox, Sackville and Merkel JJ, 16 December 2003, Unreported).

[38] Pearson, 'Where We've Come From', above n 4, 2.

Chapter 12

Comprehensive Native Title Negotiations in South Australia

Parry Agius, Jocelyn Davies, Richard Howitt, Sandra Jarvis and Rhiân Williams

Introduction

In South Australia, the evolving recognition of native title has nurtured a distinctive approach to agreement making. New sorts of relationships, co-operative exploration of a wide range of issues, and emphasis on **process** as a vehicle for exercising Aboriginal self-determination have emerged from an innovative, statewide negotiation process.[1]

The South Australian Government initiated serious discussion of a comprehensive settlement of native title issues in the state in the late 1990s. Since then, both government and non-government parties have come to accept that a negotiated response to native title issues, one that was capable of addressing Aboriginal needs, would have to encompass structural, administrative, legislative and constitutional reforms. In tackling such an ambitious agenda for change, the South Australian process targets outcomes that are broader than negotiations conducted locally, claim by claim. This scope has led some to talk about the South Australian process in terms of 'treaty making'. Yet, the process was not conceived as a 'treaty making' opportunity, nor is it aimed at signing a treaty—if by a 'treaty' one means a single settlement or agreement that reconciles the conflicting authorities and perceptions of rights and interests among native title claimants and government. Rather, the process has been envisioned as one that would reconfigure governance institutions of the state 'with native title built in' in ways that are properly authorised by Aboriginal people and which secure

---

[1]   See the ATNS Project database at http://atns.net.au/biogs/A001072b.htm.

recognition, participation and empowerment of native title groups and an appropriate range of other continuing benefits for the State's Aboriginal citizens. This is a process that has clearly set its vision wide and high.

This chapter:

- discusses the principles and characteristics of the South Australian process
- outlines background to the development of the negotiating process
- evaluates outcomes achieved to date
- reviews the prospects and barriers to concluding a comprehensive settlement agreement in South Australia
- considers the extent to which the South Australian experience might provide a model to other regions in Australia.

The chapter concentrates on process issues rather than the substantive issues under negotiation, for two reasons. First, confidentiality requirements limit what can be discussed about substantive issues. Second, process is inherently important, and it is particularly important in any evaluation of the broader lessons of the South Australian experience. Without good process, any agreements that are reached will not be 'owned' by native title claimants or by other parties. There may be agreement reached on paper, but relationships on the ground—and the structures and processes of governance—will remain reflective of historical injustice. Good process is an integral part of continuing relationships, and also keeps parties attentive to achieving a proper and lasting settlement on the ground, rather than a settlement merely on paper.

Underlying principles

The Aboriginal Legal Rights Movement of South Australia (ALRM), whose perspective on the South Australian process is presented in this chapter, is recognised as the Native Title Representative Body for South Australia, under the *Native Title Act 1993* (Cth) (*NTA*). ALRM bases its approach to the negotiations on the premise that decisions about the balance between litigation, legislation and negotiation in pursuing settlement of native title issues and about how native title groups exercise their rights now and into the future are the responsibility of native title groups themselves, not of ALRM, nor of technical or legal advisers. So, too, are political judgements about how Aboriginal societies are represented to the wider world through claims, negotiations and other activities. In managing its own role in the negotiations, ALRM has also pursued accountability to ten core (non-negotiable) principles:

1. **Native title is about people, not legal technicalities**: agreement-building must build relationships between people.
2. **Aboriginal claimants have standing as principals in the negotiations**: they are the people who hold native title rights and these are real property rights, as real as any other property rights.
3. **Non-extinguishment**: agreement-building does not **require** extinguishment of native title.
4. **Self-determination**: agreement-building involves the exercise of self-determination, rather than leading to self-determination.
5. **Fairness**: agreement-building should be fair. All participating groups should be better off, and none should be worse off because of an agreement, including not only native title groups, but also other Aboriginal groups and non-Aboriginal interests.
6. **Inter-generational equity**: agreements should recognise the principle of inter-generational equity because they are likely to set important aspects of the conditions facing Aboriginal people for several generations. They should not be short-term deals.
7. **Sustainability**: negotiated outcomes should be sustainable for the Aboriginal principals, for other interests and for natural and cultural resources.
8. **Meaningful benefits**: negotiated outcomes should be meaningful to the Aboriginal principals. Agreement-building is only worthwhile if the Aboriginal principals judge that it will produce outcomes they want.
9. **Benchmarks**: in order to be worthwhile, outcomes should not only be better than exist now, but should also be better than can be achieved through other means (for example, litigation or legislation) and reasonable against appropriate benchmarks (for example, in comparable international settings). Appropriate benchmarks should be reviewed over time and opportunities to improve benchmarks should be taken from time to time.
10. **An act of choice, not the only choice**: agreement-building should not lock Aboriginal people into an 'all-or-nothing' situation, in which they rely on complete settlement to achieve any gains at all—Aboriginal people should continue to negotiate only if they judge it to be producing worthwhile outcomes.

These principles were embedded in ALRM's vision from the start of its participation in establishing the negotiations process. As the process has developed, ALRM has continuously been challenged in its interactions with native title groups and other parties in order to ensure that the principles are made explicit.

Establishing the negotiations process

A significant factor in the emergence of an ambitious scope for native title negotiations in South Australia was a commitment by the then-Liberal government in 1999 that 'everything is on the table'.[2] This encouraged ALRM's involvement, given its view about the need for fundamental change in the governance institutions of South Australia. The development of these institutions, from the early days of the colony, has been largely predicated on the absence of Aboriginal rights, with Aboriginal people structurally excluded from a whole range of key institutions that affect their lives. Questions about wide-ranging reforms to legislation and to the South Australian Constitution, therefore, inevitably arose early in ALRM's and native title claimants' discussions about the potential scope of the negotiations.

The issue of the South Australian Pastoral Board was raised by ALRM in early discussions with the government, and is an illustration of where its concern for reform lies. The Pastoral Board is a statutory body that manages pastoral lease tenures and associated issues in the South Australian rangelands. Its members are appointed for their expertise in land management, the pastoral industry and conservation on the nomination of government, industry and conservation sectors. The Board has never included Aboriginal representatives. If native title is to be recognised as co-existing with pastoral leases, then native title interests would need to be represented on the Pastoral Board. However, if native title interests are included, then the Pastoral Board would no longer properly be a 'Pastoral' Board, because native title interests are not fundamentally about pastoral use of land. Similar points can be made about many other institutions. Once one recognises and includes native title, it is clear that many existing institutions of government unravel. They are simply not structured in a way that can effectively recognise native title.

Ground work for the South Australian negotiation process was laid by the 1998 amendments to the *NTA*.[3] Although aspects of these amendments have been widely criticised as racist,[4] other aspects provided some important

---

2   South Australian Solicitor-General Brad Selway, cited in Judith Morrison, *Uniting the Voices: Decision-making to Negotiate for Native Title in South Australia: Independent Review of Aboriginal Legal Rights Movement Native Title Unit's Facilitation of Decision Making by South Australian Native Title Management Committees July–October 2000* (Native Title Unit, Aboriginal Legal Rights Movement, Adelaide, 2001) 10.

3   *Native Title Amendment Act 1998*, amending the *Native Title Act 1993* (Cth).

4   See, for example, Aboriginal and Torres Strait Islander Social Justice Commission, *Native Title Report 2000: Report of the Aboriginal and Torres Strait Islander Social Justice Commissioner to the Attorney General as required by section 46C(1)(a) Human Rights and Equal Opportunity Commission Act 1986* (Aboriginal and Torres Strait Islander Social Justice Commission, HREOC, Sydney, 2000).

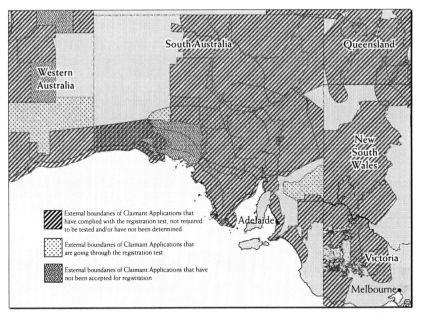

Figure 12.1: South Australia, showing Native Title Claims as at 30 September 2003. Source: Geospatial Analysis & Mapping, NNTT, 2003. © Commonwealth of Australia, reproduced by permission

triggers to ALRM's effort to building native title groups' capacity for self-governance. In particular, the amendments to the *NTA* introducing Indigenous Land Use Agreements (ILUAs) provided clearer mechanisms for effecting legally binding agreements concerning native title.[5] These amendments encouraged the South Australian Government and industry groups to consider negotiation as more effective than litigation or legislative extinguishment of Aboriginal rights in producing sustainable and workable outcomes.

The cost of litigation was a factor which led to statewide negotiations emerging as the South Australian Government's preferred option for resolution of native title claims. When statewide negotiation and conclusion of ILUAs was first mooted as an option in 1999, it was primarily fiscal cost that was foremost in the government's mind given the expensive preparations for the Federal Court hearing of the native title claim over De Rose Hill station,[6] in the far north of the State. However, litigation can also cost dearly in terms of social capital.[7] Leadership was also important in the decision to negotiate.

---

5   *Native Title Act 1993* (Cth) Division 3.
6   *De Rose v South Australia* [2002] FCA 1342 (Unreported, O'Loughlin J, 1 November 2002).
7   In *De Rose v South Australia* [2002] FCA 1342, the pastoralist and the Crown opposed the De Rose Hill Native Title claim of those Yankunytjatjara people who have connection to the property. The finding of the Federal Court in the first instance judgment was that Native

In 1999, the Attorney-General in the South Australian Government was The Honourable Trevor Griffin MLC, who was well disposed personally to negotiation. He had commenced his political career with carriage of the *Pitjantjatjara Land Rights Act*[8] in 1981, and wanted a similar positive outcome for Aboriginal people to mark the end of his career. He influenced the government to consider negotiation as an alternative to adversarial litigation or legislative extinguishment for resolving native title issues.

A further factor was that the 1998 amendments to the *NTA* had required the re-registration of all existing native title claims, and this had provided a mechanism for ALRM to work with native title groups on claim governance. As part of the re-registration process, ALRM was required to certify that all those with a claim to native title in a particular area had properly authorised the claim over that area. This process of re-registration and certification sorted out and resolved many instances of overlapping native title claims. In some other instances of overlapping claims, dispute resolution through mediation is still occurring, concurrently with the state-wide negotiation process.

At the same time as ALRM was meeting with native title groups about claim certification, it was also working with those groups to assist each of them to set up a Native Title Management Committee (NTMC). The *NTA* does not require such committees to be established, but their establishment is important for ALRM, and for the native title groups themselves, as they provide an appropriate and accountable avenue for claim governance that is reflective of the group's kinship and traditional decision-making processes. Each NTMC is authorised by the whole claimant community for that claim area to manage the progress of the native title claim. These NTMCs typically include the named applicants for the claim. They usually also include other claimants put forward by the community to represent various family interests, or because they have recognised skills. Twenty-three NTMCs have

---

Title was not automatically extinguished on pastoral leases in South Australia (at [541]), but that native title had not survived on De Rose Hill because the claimants had not maintained the necessary connections with their country during recent years (at [914]). The court processes leading to this finding were, inevitably, adversarial, lengthy and selective in the matters they took into account, notwithstanding efforts of the Court in this case to create an atmosphere that was conducive to claimants feeling comfortable giving their evidence. This finding has contributed to a spreading disillusion among Aboriginal people about whether the recognition of native title in *Mabo v Queensland (No 2)* (1992) 175 CLR 1 ('*Mabo*') will translate to any outcomes that are meaningful to them. At the date of writing the full Federal Court has heard the appeal in *De Rose v South Australia*. The Court unanimously held that there were errors in the trial judge's reasoning but it could not decide the matter without further submissions. *De Rose Hill v State of South Australia* [2003] FCAFC (286 (Wilcox, Sackville and Merkel JJ. 16 December 2003 Unreported).

8   *Pitjantjatjara Land Rights Act 1981* (SA).

been established and are involved in the statewide negotiations process. Most of these have registered claims; some have claims that are still proceeding through the registration process and others are still preparing claims for registration.

One outcome for ALRM from this engagement with claim registration, certification and establishment of NTMCs was a growing confidence that, in large areas of the State, agreements negotiated by native title groups would not be vulnerable to being challenged or undermined by other Aboriginal people. This means that negotiation with native title groups has the real prospect of delivering 'certainty' that government and industry seek in relation to native title issues.

Thus, in May 1999, when the government hosted a meeting with representatives from the South Australian Chamber of Mines and Energy (SACOME), the South Australian Farmers' Federation (SAFF) and ALRM, the stage was well-prepared for considering a peculiarly South-Australian approach to settling native title issues. At that meeting each of the participating groups identified its key concerns and issues. While some significant differences were obvious, there was also reasonable support for negotiation of a range of statewide and local-level agreements. ALRM made it clear that native title claimants themselves would need to be involved in these negotiations directly, in the 'driver's seat', and that any decision about signing-off on proposals would be a matter for the claimants. That was the beginning of a long process whereby all parties came to appreciate that negotiations would not proceed quickly to an agreement. Along the way, parties other than the ALRM have recognised that they also have to obtain authority from their constituents and bring their constituents with them through the negotiations, rather than simply presenting them with a signed agreement.

For ALRM there were particular challenges in establishing the negotiations because, unlike government and industry groups, native title claimants had no decision-making structure beyond the scale of their local group. How to facilitate consideration of the proposal to negotiate by a large number of native title claimant groups whose diverse members were scattered across the State and far beyond, and in some cases who had never previously met? How to present the 'bigger picture'—to excite claimants about the potential outcomes from negotiations—but also to encourage an appreciation of the practical realities involved in achieving such outcomes? How to build the required negotiating skills and how to facilitate informed decision making?

ALRM secured state government funding for a number of large NTMC meetings throughout 1999–2000. These aimed to provide information, debate options, set policies and make decisions about whether to negotiate on native title issues.[9] ALRM's experience in those meetings affirmed the importance of process. Process was crucial in generating mutual recognition, respect and understanding among diverse claimant groups. The key question was not about the substantive content of negotiations; it was 'how will your NTMCs work together?'

At a series of meetings in 2000, NTMCs debated diverse issues and struggled to construct a 'united voice' with which to speak to the government and industry groups. They put in place a structure, in the form of the Statewide South Australian Congress of Native Title Management Committees (Congress), which embodies this 'united voice' while providing for each individual NTMC to retain autonomy in its own decision making. Rather than the Congress having any overriding decision-making authority, ALRM encouraged an opt-in process by NTMCs for Congress decision making. This has involved proposals, formulated from presentations and discussions, being put forward in the plenary Congress forums, but with each NTMC debating and reaching its own decision as a small group, operating within its own decision-making framework. Each NTMC then reports back to the whole Congress on its decision. This process, together with language translation of most presentations and discussions, slows down the pace of these large Congress meetings. This can be frustrating for some people involved, but it does allow everyone present more time to engage with important issues. We think it has resulted in well-grounded decisions by Congress that belong to, and are understood by, all those involved. As such, it is a process that has demonstrated effective self-governance by traditional owner groups, while at the same time building their capacity for self-governance at the statewide scale.

The governance capacity of native title groups is critically important in ensuring that their priorities and protocols are respected in the process of negotiating and in the issues that are negotiated. In reflecting on their experience in complex negotiations, Canadian First Nation leaders have said that they felt like they were negotiating the constitution of a new country.[10] In order to generate the required capacity for Indigenous self-governance in such negotiations, it is necessary to develop new competencies within the native title system, within the claimant community, and between Indigenous and non-Indigenous stakeholders. This has raised serious resourcing issues for ALRM, given the costs involved in bringing native title claimants together,

---

9   In an effort to maintain a level of transparency and accountability to the NTMCs, the ALRM Native Title Unit commissioned an independent review of the process (Morrison, above n 2). The Report is available online at http://www.iluasa.com/alrm.asp#Publications at 1 December 2003.

10   Billy Diamond, 'Villages of the Dammed' (1990) 1(3) *Arctic Circle* 24.

informing them, facilitating their communication and decision making, and supporting their role as principals in the negotiations.

Structure of the negotiation process

The basic structure for the statewide negotiations was established in late 1999. The peak forum, known as the 'Main Table', initially involved representatives from the South Australian Government, led by the Attorney-General's Department, and SAFF, SACOME and ALRM. From 2003, the South Australian Local Government Association, Seafood Council (SA) Inc. and the South Australian Fishing Industry Council also began actively to participate in the Main Table, indicating the importance of local government, fisheries and sea rights in developing approaches to the settlement of native title issues,[11] (see Figure 12.2).

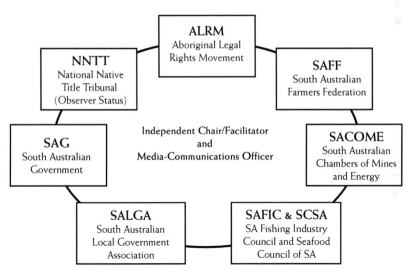

Figure 12.2: Participants in the 'Main Table' structure of the South Australian statewide native title negotiations process at mid-2003

The Main Table is a meeting of leaders from each of these groups, and it carries the leadership and management responsibility of the overall negotiations process. It has an independent chair, and representatives of the National Native Title Tribunal attend with observer status. The parties have an agreed protocol about what issues the Main Table will address and

---

[11] On the negotiations website, each peak body outlines its interests in the negotiation process. See *Native Title Negotiations* http://www.iluasa.com at 28 November 2003.

how they will address them. They jointly engage a media/communications officer who ensures that there is a constructive media and public interface.

Substantive issues affecting native title are not negotiated at the Main Table. That is not, and cannot be, its role, since native title groups are not directly represented. Rather, the Main Table is a planning and review forum—it carries the responsibility for overseeing the entire process, provides a voice for any party that has key issues to raise about the process, and reviews and endorses work programs and outputs from components of the process. Among the substantive planning and management issues that the Main Table allows parties to consider is support for each other to secure the resources necessary for effective participation in the negotiations process.

Workhorses of the negotiations process at the statewide scale are called 'Side Tables'. Six Side Tables have now been constituted to deal with substantive issues (see Figure 12.3). Each involves participants from ALRM, the state government and at least one of the other Main Table parties. Side Tables are mainly forums for exploration of technical issues, and involve technical and legal experts as well as leaders or designated representatives from various peak bodies.

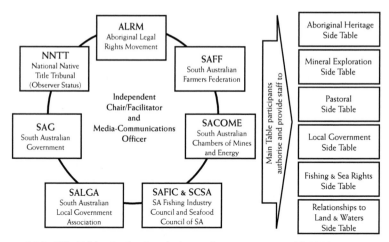

Figure 12.3: Side Tables in the South Australian process at mid-2003

It is indicative of the concern with institutional reform that the first public output from the negotiations process was a discussion paper in relation to Aboriginal heritage law reform developed through the Heritage Side Table and authorised through the Main Table.[12] When it was launched in

---

[12] Aboriginal Legal Rights Movement, South Australian Chamber of Mines and Energy, South Australian Farmers Federation, South Australian Government Indigenous Land Use Agreement Negotiation Team, *A Proposal to Change South Australia's Aboriginal Heritage Protection Scheme* (2002) http://www.iluasa.com/heritage_prot_scheme.asp at 21 November 2003.

May 2002, the discussion paper was badged with the logos of each of the Main Table parties. The discussion paper is aimed at improving Aboriginal heritage management, taking into account changes that came into force with the introduction of the *Aboriginal Heritage Act 1988* (SA), and the need to comply with laws concerning native title.

The Relationships to Land & Waters Side Table, at which **all** peak bodies at the Main Table are represented, was established at the end of 2001. Its operations reflect ALRM's concern with process. Unlike the other Side Tables, it does not focus on the concerns of any particular industry sector. Its objective is to develop tools to help negotiating parties address matters such as their feelings in relation to attachment to land, prior dispossession and injustice, and the notion of authority to speak for, and make decisions about, land and waters. For claimants, such matters underpin all their concerns about native title. These matters also arouse strong feelings in other parties, such as pastoralists.

The Relationships to Land & Waters Side Table has actively encouraged people of the various parties to the pilot negotiations to build relationships among themselves before negotiating on substantive issues, such as by conducting facilitated workshops that encourage participants to respect differing points of view, understand each other's personal motivations and identify common values. These set the basis for agreement-making to be an active process, building agreement on the basis of genuine understandings, consistent with the first of ALRM's ten core principles, that 'native title is about people, not legal technicalities'.

One of this Side Table's projects concerns terminology, specifically building understanding of what some key terms mean to different people. This project picks up on issues raised by ALRM in early discussions with the government about approaches to negotiation. Terminology is important, because no-one will feel bound by an agreement that they don't understand or that includes terms that are misunderstood between the parties. Thus, if lawyers define the terms in an agreement which are either not understood or agreed to by one or more of the negotiating parties, there may well be dispute after the agreement has been signed. And if an Aboriginal person says 'I want my native title recognised', other parties to the negotiation need to understand what **that person** means by 'native title', not what a lawyer or a court says that native title means.

Side Table deliberations have led to considerable advances in the understanding of all parties over the actual issues for negotiation, over which issues can be readily negotiated through local native title group processes, and which require consideration of policy change or legislative reform at the level of Congress. However, Side Tables are not, themselves, forums for negotiations about agreements or outcomes that will have impacts on native title rights. This reflects ALRM's commitment not to intrude on native title claimants' own responsibilities and their prerogative to negotiate about native title. Because native title claimants are not directly represented at the Main Table or Side Tables, these forums are not able to negotiate directly about native title. The Congress of NTMCs is the forum which has authority, based on principles from Aboriginal customary law, to authorise how native title groups should be involved in the negotiations at the statewide level, including the Main Table and Side Table deliberations. However, resource limitations have precluded Congress from fully considering the issues associated with direct participation in these forums. Questions that need to be carefully engaged with include who would represent Congress and its constituent NTMCs, in what capacity, and how those individuals would maintain accountability to all the NTMCs for whom a particular issue is relevant. Resource limitations have also meant that a formal relationship between ALRM and the Congress of NTMCs has not yet been finalised. However, the relationship that operates in practice is not unclear to those involved, as it is derived from principles of Aboriginal customary law. In this relationship, each NTMC 'speaks for country' within its claim area and contributes through the Congress meetings to articulating statewide and regional policy positions that are consistent with these local-scale views and to authorising policies that guide ALRM's role in the Main Table and Side Table forums.

At a local scale, selected native title groups have been directly engaged in pilot negotiations with various industry sectors since 2001. They have been developing local ILUAs and testing how well draft template agreements and other policy options developed by Side Tables address local issues. The people involved are representatives of the native title groups for selected local areas, authorised by the whole group, ALRM staff and other parties directly representing government or industry interests. The overall management of these pilot negotiation processes—involving timetabling, allocating resources and reviewing progress—is part of the Main Table's responsibilities, and the negotiations may be informed by the work done by the Side Tables on scoping and researching issues. However, these local negotiations themselves are confidential to the parties involved.

Outcomes and achievements to date

Since 1999, the South Australian process has provided a forum and a process whereby discussions have moved well beyond the confines of technical legal issues and opportunistic deal-making about specific future acts. ALRM has drawn on both legal insights and those from the human services arena in developing its approach to native title issues. It has worked hard to ensure that 'experts' have not driven the process and that the process itself is an exercise in self-determination, rather than a precursor to some future achievement of self-determination. While an agreed conclusion to statewide negotiations remains a long way off, the process has been delivering meaningful outcomes along the way, rather than locking claimants into waiting for an all-or-nothing settlement. To date, it has delivered significant procedural, emotional and substantive outcomes, including:

- high levels of community and stakeholder participation in relationship building and cross-cultural recognition
- establishment of the Congress recognised as an Aboriginal governance institution based on traditional ownership and authorised by NTMCs as their peak body
- development of NTMCs' capacity to make decisions for themselves and to participate directly in decision making and deliberations about native title and indigenous rights
- significant increases in the capacity of NTMCs and the Congress to drive and manage complex negotiations
- reduced anger, frustration and time delays for native title interests and other parties in native title processes
- withdrawal of government backing for the argument that native title was historically extinguished across the State in 1836[13]
- substantial amendment of the Native Title (South Australia) (Validation and Confirmation) Amendment Bill 1999 (SA)[14] before it was presented to the South Australian Parliament in December 2000, that reduced its impact on native title rights
- Aboriginal representation on the state government's Ministerial Advisory Board
- authorisation of several pilot projects involving a range of sectoral issues—pastoralism, protected areas, local government, minerals exploration and fishing and sea rights—leading to negotiations between NTMCs and development interests to produce draft Memoranda of Understanding and ILUAs with support from the Congress
- multi-stakeholder working parties actively reviewing a range of issues via the Side Tables and developing directions for institutional reform at regional and statewide levels
- political support for the negotiation process from both State Liberal and Labor parties

---

[13] See Lisa Strelein, 'Feature: *De Rose v South Australia* [2002] FCA 1342 (1 November 2002)' (2002) 5 *Native Title Newsletter* 2, 6.

[14] This resulted in the *Native Title (South Australia) (Validation and Confirmation) Amendment Act 2000* (SA), amending the *Native Title (South Australia) Act 1994* (SA).

▪ Better cross-cultural understanding and greatly improved personal relationships and communication channels among key leaders and officers of industry peak bodies, ALRM and the government.

These outcomes are significant, and have facilitated a degree of Aboriginal, industry and government confidence in a process that targets a transformative approach to the politics of native title. In light of the hostility at the federal level, the continuing commitment of the South Australian parties to this process is a significant achievement in its own right. There has been no legal imperative driving these engagements in South Australia. The continued commitment of Aboriginal, industry and government stakeholders to discussing a comprehensive settlement package suggests that they see the process as delivering outcomes that are more valuable, certain and robust than the alternatives. In ALRM's view, supporting negotiations that secure strong foundations for Aboriginal self-determination and Aboriginal peoples' participation in and contributions to nation-building—both Aboriginal and national processes—should be the urgent priority of both public and Aboriginal policy.

Prospects for concluding a comprehensive settlement in South Australia

As noted earlier in this chapter, ALRM has been working on building understanding among other parties of the need for structural reform. Early in this process, ALRM began talking about the outcomes from the native title negotiation process as rebuilding South Australia 'with native title built-in'. This vision puts all the institutional accoutrements of governments concerning how Aboriginal people participate in, or are excluded from, decision-making on the table for discussion and reform.

The importance of the principle of direct participation by native title claimants in the negotiations has been consistent in ALRM's vision. Those people whose rights are at stake should be the principals and the decision makers in negotiations, with capacity to hold the representative body and expert advisers accountable. As far as possible, the native title groups should be the ones making decisions about outcomes, rather than having to accept outcomes negotiated by others.

ALRM has nurtured a process in which native title groups do not get locked into conclusion of a final agreement as the only outcome. ALRM and its technical advisers have wanted a process that native title groups could walk away from if that was their decision, but where they would still have gained some real and sustainable beneficial outcomes in terms of empowerment and strengthened governance, at the very least through participation in the negotiation process. Finally, ALRM has anticipated that this kind of process would produce some sort of power shift in support of effective Aboriginal governance.

The *NTA* does not allow for any formal recognition of Aboriginal self-government, and it does not anticipate the resources that are required for effective Aboriginal governance associated with native title. Although regional representative structures for Aboriginal decision making exist, notably Aboriginal and Torres Strait Islander Commission (ATSIC) regional councils, these are not representative of or accountable to Aboriginal customary law. Their authority is, instead, founded in the principles of representative democracy that underlie the contemporary Australian nation-state. Prescribed Bodies Corporate established under the *NTA* are, similarly, constructions of non-Aboriginal governance rather than an outcome of Aboriginal self-determination, explicitly required to conform to the terms of the legislation rather than drawing their authority from customary law. In South Australia, native title claimant communities have been developing and consolidating their local governance structures—the NTMCs. The prospect of statewide negotiation gave impetus to developing a structure—the Congress—that native title groups can work within on a statewide basis on issues that extend beyond the local scale, up to and including such issues as legislative and constitutional reform. ALRM has, however, struggled to achieve the resources needed for native title groups to build strong capacity for self-governance, both at the statewide level, through the Congress of NTMCs, and at a local level.

Prospects for successful conclusion of comprehensive negotiations in South Australia will, of course, depend on the process itself. While many observers have commended the scope and ambition of the process, there have been critics who have assessed ALRM's agenda as being too ambitious and politically unrealistic. Yet, the South Australian Government and industry stakeholders have remained with and grown into the relationships on which a negotiated settlement will rely. Pilot projects and formal evaluation of the feasibility of the proposal for truly comprehensive settlement have been funded and have received political, industry and community support. Some critics have suggested that any comprehensive settlement will be dependent upon Commonwealth Government co-operation, and that the hostility of the current Commonwealth Government to the principle of Indigenous self-determination means that there are no prospects for 'success'. Others have argued that, even within the arena of state politics, the prospects for such a radical engagement with Aboriginal self-determination risks electoral repercussions that make it unthinkable as a policy option for the major parties.

We beg to differ from those critics who feel that ambition, consultation, grassroots support, accountable expertise and an honest engagement with the developmental demands of comprehensive agreement making is too much to expect in the current discussion of native title issues in Australia. Indeed, we would challenge the appropriateness of any vision for agreement making that marginalises the Aboriginal principles (and principals, in the form of the claimants themselves) and re-imposes some form of 'deep colonisation'[15] to which Aboriginal parties are expected to consent as the culmination of the 'judicial revolution'[16] started by the *Mabo*[17] decision.

Is South Australia a model for agreement making?

The constructive approach to native title that has emerged in South Australia has articulated a vision for agreement building and the pursuit of Aboriginal self-determination in ways that have not been experienced previously in Australia. The participatory approach developed in South Australia has ensured a level of control of the process by the Aboriginal principals. This approach has generally been unavailable in other parts of the evolving native title system, which has been dominated by legal, judicial and anthropological experts, and legislatively defined institutions and procedures, rather than Indigenous governance structures. There are many factors influencing the process that reflect the particular geography and history of South Australia and, since every state is unique in this regard, we do not claim that the structures for negotiations that have been developed in South Australia should be copied elsewhere. Nevertheless, there are some wider lessons to be drawn from this example.

First, any comprehensive settlement of Indigenous issues requires consideration of an agenda that is shaped by the Indigenous people who are affected, rather than technical experts who decide what is or is not permissible. Second, negotiation should be an exercise of grassroots self-determination and Indigenous governance. Third, process must be given much more attention than it has had to date. In particular, further consideration needs to be given to the emotional and procedural needs of Indigenous principals and other people in native title negotiations, rather than continued

[15] Deborah Rose, 'Indigenous Ecologies and an Ethic of Connection' in Nicholas Low (ed.), *Global Ethics and Environment* (Routledge, London, 1999) 175.

[16] Margaret Stephenson and Suri Ratnapala (eds), *Mabo, A Judicial Revolution: The Aboriginal Land Rights Decision and Its Impact on Australian Law* (University of Queensland Press, St Lucia, 1993).

[17] *Mabo* (1992) 175 CLR 1.

attention to expert views on substantive issues. Finally, there needs to be recognition that the evolving native title system has failed and continues to fail to deliver a means of achieving just, equitable and sustainable self-determination or practical improvements in most Indigenous domains in Australia. Indigenous Australians whose lives are affected negatively by this fact cannot be expected to participate in or accept the results of deal-making negotiations that reinforce this situation. The South Australian process is not negotiating a 'treaty'. Yet, as an exercise in agreement making, it has moved towards implementation of some fundamental principles that would underpin any treaty. It offers some significant challenges to proposals that would pursue a comprehensive treaty at national or statewide scales without first securing the institutional means for grassroots Indigenous participation in and control over negotiations that purport to exercise cultural, political, social and environmental responsibilities within Indigenous polities, and to deal with Indigenous rights and Indigenous futures.

Chapter 13

Maritime Agreements and the Recognition of Customary Marine Tenure in the Northern Territory

Sue Jackson[*]

Introduction

Australian Indigenous people argue that recognition of the saltwater component of their estates is crucial to the integrity of their relationships with country. Traditional sea estates can extend many kilometres offshore and are inseparable from clan estates on land. Customary marine tenure is described by Sharp:

> sea property includes foreshore, reefs and sandbanks, sites of spiritual potency and seabed. It also includes the saltwater itself, stretching to the horizon or even beyond it. These sea territories belong to clans and other groups and these marine areas are not always extensions of clan land boundaries into the sea but may form a patchwork of 'plots' of sea belonging to different groups.[1]

Coastal Indigenous communities are seeking a primary role in the use, ownership and management of marine and coastal environments and resources. These efforts are not confined to areas designated for conservation, such as marine parks. Indigenous people also express a desire to benefit from the commercial use of marine resources, including research and development activities, and to pursue employment opportunities within the fishing, aquaculture and natural-resource management sectors.

In the Northern Territory, the adequacy of existing legislative provisions

[*] The assistance of Peter Pender, John Harrison, John Hicks, Ron Levy, Paul Josif and Catherine Elderton is appreciated. I am grateful to Lisa Palmer for the use of material collected during the course of her ARC post-doctoral research.
[1] Noni Sharp, *Saltwater People: The Waves of Memory* (Allen & Unwin, Sydney, 2002) 31.

for the protection of customary marine tenure remains contested. Claims by Aboriginal people for exclusive possession of marine environments have encountered opposition from governments and fishing groups, who assert that the common law public right to access the seas should be upheld. Divergent views on who owns, and therefore can control and exploit, the fish and other resources within the intertidal zone (the area between the high- and low-water marks) on Aboriginal land, and the seas adjoining Aboriginal land, continue to dominate marine policy debates.

National environmental policy making in oceans and fisheries management, marine protected areas, and coastal zone management has been challenged to address native title rights and interests held by Aboriginal and

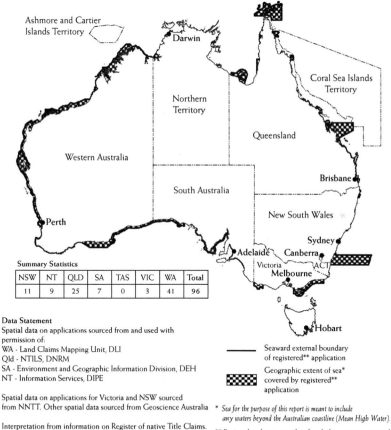

Summary Statistics							
NSW	NT	QLD	SA	TAS	VIC	WA	Total
11	9	25	7	0	3	41	96

Data Statement
Spatial data on applications sourced from and used with
permission of:
WA - Land Claims Mapping Unit, DLI
Qld - NTILS, DNRM
SA - Environment and Geographic Information Division, DEH
NT - Information Services, DIPE

Spatial data on applications for Victoria and NSW sourced
from NNTT. Other spatial data sourced from Geoscience Australia

Interpretation from information on Register of native Title Claims.
(c) The State of Queensland (Department of Natural Resources
and Mines) 2003 for that portion where their data has been used

——— Seaward external boundary
of registered** application

▦ Geographic extent of sea*
covered by registered**
application

* *Sea for the purpose of this report is meant to include*
any waters beyond the Australian coastline (Mean High Water).

** *Registered applications are those for which an entry appears on the*
Register of native Title Claims

Figure 13.1: Areas of sea subject to claim as per Native Title Claimant Applications on the Register of Native Title Claims as at 30 June 2003. Source: Geospatial Analysis & Mapping, NNTT, 2003. © Commonwealth of Australia, reproduced by permission

Torres Strait Islander peoples.[2] Within Indigenous Australian communities, the *Mabo*[3] decision, and the subsequent *Native Title Act 1993* (Cth) *(NTA)*, raised expectations of greater recognition of customary marine tenure and enhanced involvement in marine management. This is evident by the high number of native title sea claims lodged around the country. By July 2003, ninety-six native title claim applications that include sea within the area claimed have been registered with the National Native Title Tribunal; nine of those are from the Northern Territory (see Figure 13.1).[4]

Government efforts to address competing claims in the Northern Territory's coastal zone have been hesitant, *ad hoc* and generally inadequate. In response to a first wave of sea-rights legal action (sea closure applications under Northern Territory law) the Government established seven Aboriginal fisheries consultative committees in the mid-1990s. The committees have been criticised for being merely advisory and for being limited in their scope,[5] although some coastal Aboriginal communities have continued to participate and appear to value the opportunity this process affords.[6] For twenty years the Northern Territory Government's moribund coastal policy failed to recognise and engage with the diverse nature of Aboriginal interests in the coastal and marine zone. The policy, intended to be implemented through regional plans that were never prepared, did not prioritise integrated coastal zone management, nor did it identify conflict between competing uses as a key issue requiring attention. No mention was made of Aboriginal customary rights, or cultural values in the sea and coast, such as sacred sites. When the policy was eventually redrafted in 2001, it was released without public comment, representing a missed opportunity to address the desire, expressed on numerous occasions, for greater Aboriginal participation in coastal zone management.[7] Since that time, a

---

[2] See, for example, Dermot Smyth, 'Management of Sea Country: Indigenous People's Use and Management of Marine Environments', in Richard Baker, Jocelyn Davies and Elspeth Young (eds), *Working On Country: Contemporary Indigenous Management of Australia's Lands and Coastal Regions* (Oxford University Press, Melbourne, 2001) 60; Cathy Robinson and David Mercer, 'Reconciliation in Troubled Waters? Australian Oceans Policy and Offshore Native Title Rights' (2000) 24 *Marine Policy* 349.

[3] *Mabo v Queensland (No.2)* (1992) 175 CLR 1 ('*Mabo*').

[4] National Native Title Tribunal, *Areas of Sea Subject to Claim as per Native Title Claimant Applications on the Register of Native Title Claims as at June 2003* (2003) http://www.nntt.gov.au/publications/data/files/sea_RNTC_A4.pdf at 6 November 2003.

[5] Ron Lamilami and Mary Yarmirr, 'Building Partnerships for the Coastal Environment' (Paper Presented at the Wise Use of Wetlands in Northern Australia: Indigenous Use Workshop, Batchelor, 29–30 September and 1 October 1998) 13.

[6] For example, Tiwi Island communities.

[7] The Northern Land Council, Tiwi and Anindilyakwa Land Councils released a set of principles around which a new approach to seas management should be built. They were endorsed by the Full Council of the Northern Land Council in November 2002. The principles are as follows: Meaningful recognition of Aboriginal interests in the sea; the need for an integrated

new government has commenced a more transparent review of the policy by a multi-stakeholder advisory committee.

This long-standing policy vacuum has compelled Aboriginal people and their representative bodies to pursue a number of strategies: vigorous legal intervention to clarify the extent of Indigenous sea rights; regional land and sea management strategies (including sea ranger programs) in which people exercise inherited rights and responsibilities to sea country; public education about customary marine tenure; and the negotiation of agreements with parties interested in utilising or accessing marine and coastal areas and/or resources.

This chapter outlines the complex legal context in which Aboriginal people and coastal and marine user groups operate. It describes the various types of agreements reached. These are classified into four categories: conservation, commercial, recreational and research.

Legal context

The existence since 1976 of statutory Aboriginal land rights in the Northern Territory has been a fundamental basis for the degree of Aboriginal control asserted over terrestrial resources and marine activities requiring a land base. Approximately 87 per cent of the Northern Territory coastline is Aboriginal owned, under the *Aboriginal Land Rights (Northern Territory) Act 1976* (Cth) (*ALRA*). In all agreements relating to marine resources, the need for the consent of the traditional owners for the use of an essential land base has been critical in securing a negotiated outcome. The land rights regime established during the 1970s, however, failed to give sufficient protection to the maritime rights and interests of Aboriginal people.[8]

In submissions to the Woodward Commission of Inquiry (1973),[9] the

---

management approach by government; Aboriginal people must be able to access economic benefits; Marine and coastal use and management must be environmentally and culturally sustainable; Commitment to adjust management and institutional arrangements where needed. See also, 'Saltwater Land Councils Speak With One Voice' (2002) 4 *Land Rights News* 15.

8 David Allen 'Some Shadow of the Rights Known to Our Law' (Paper presented at the Turning the Tide Conference, Northern Territory University, Darwin, 14–16 July 1993) 53. Recent socio-cultural research in anthropology and geography has sought to explain the cultural bias towards land as a source of meaning and economic value in Western societies and the consequent impact of this bias on colonised coastal or island communities. See Sue Jackson, 'The Water Is Not Empty: Cross-Cultural Issues in Conceptualising Sea Space' (1995) 26 *Australian Geographer* 87; Sharp, above n 1.

9 In 1973 the Whitlam Government established the Aboriginal Land Rights Commission under Justice A.E. Woodward. The Commission's terms of reference were to examine how Aboriginal land rights should be recognised.

Northern Land Council (NLC)[10] proposed that an area stretching 12 miles out to sea be treated as part of Aboriginal land. Woodward, conscious of potential economic impacts on resource sectors, recommended a buffer zone of 2 kilometres to protect traditional fishing rights and privacy of adjacent Aboriginal land.[11] It was envisaged that commercial fishermen and tourists would not be able to legally enter this zone, except in an emergency. Eventually, the sea-closure provisions of the *Aboriginal Land Act 1978* (NT) (*ALA*) were instituted.[12] A sea closure provides a non-exclusive right of access and use of marine resources within a 2-kilometre zone.[13] It does not confer title, nor does it provide for a recognised place for Aboriginal people in fisheries or marine management. Existing commercial licence holders may continue to fish the area, but recreational fishers must seek permission, as must new commercial fishers, who are required to negotiate with the traditional owners for fishing rights. Described by Allen as a 'ponderous device' with a lengthy claims process and weak in enforcement conditions, it is not surprising that few sea-closure applications have been pursued.[14]

During the past decade, a large number of claims under the *ALRA* has been lodged over different maritime elements or zones,[15] raising many complex legal questions about the definition of land under that Act; the extent of government jurisdiction offshore; the definition of 'low-water'; and the nature of property in the marine environment.

Land titles granted under the *ALRA* currently extend to the low-water mark and therefore include the inter-tidal zone, but the Act does not contain an explicit definition of 'land' or 'sea'. The inter-tidal zone comprises the area of seashore and tidal flats between the levels of high and low tide. Valuable aquatic resources, such as barramundi and crab, constituting approximately

---

[10] The NLC is a statutory authority established under the *ALRA* to represent the Aboriginal people in the north of the Northern Territory. The NLC prepares claims to land and sea on behalf of traditional owners and protects the interests of traditional Aboriginal owners of, and other Aborigines interested in, land. The NLC has the statutory responsibility to consult with traditional owners over any proposal concerning the use of Land Trust land. With consent, a licence agreement or lease, outlining the terms and conditions upon which the business is to be conducted, is prepared and entered into by the proponent and Land Trust. The NLC is also a Native Title Representative Body under the *NTA*.

[11] John Reeves, *Building on Land Rights for the Next Generation: Report of the Review of the Aboriginal Land Rights (Northern Territory) Act 1976*, (Aboriginal and Torres Strait Islander Commission, Canberra, 1998) 224.

[12] See *Aboriginal Land Act 1978* (NT) pt III.

[13] See generally Anthony Bergin, 'Aboriginal Sea Claims in the Northern Territory of Australia', (1991) 15 *Ocean and Shoreline Management* 171.

[14] Allen, above n 8, 57.

[15] Reeves, above n 11, 219. In 1998 there were twenty-two outstanding claims to banks and beds of rivers, ten to the inter-tidal zone, and seventeen to the seas and sea beds. Few have been heard in the intervening period.

70 per cent of the commercial fish take, are fished within the zone.[16] Legal action under the *ALRA* was initiated by the NLC in 1997, in order to clarify the nature of traditional owners' interests[17] and to control access to the waters in the inter-tidal zone and in inter-tidal rivers.[18] At first instance, the Federal Court held that traditional owners controlled fishing in tidal rivers but not in the inter-tidal zone, due to the operation of the public right to fish.[19] On appeal the Court declined to resolve the legal issues for technical reasons relating to the case having proceeded without a comprehensive hearing of evidence.[20] The issues were due to be considered in a case concerning Blue Mud Bay in 2004.[21] This claim is to be heard under the *NTA*.

Claimant groups have also sought to extend the seaward boundary of Aboriginal land tenure. Their legal argument is distilled by Reeves:

> it is argued that the mudflats and other areas on the seaward side of the low water-mark are also (Aboriginal) land and since they have not been alienated from the Crown, they are therefore available for claim under the Land Rights Act, at least to the boundary of the Northern Territory's territorial waters.[22]

In his review of the *ALRA*, Reeves recommended it be amended to provide that future land claims only be made to the high-water mark and that a joint management structure be established with Aboriginal and fishing representatives to manage the inter-tidal zone.[23] A test case regarding the seabed in bays and gulfs reached the High Court in 2002, when it was found that land rights under the *ALRA* did not extend over the seabed below the low-water mark.[24]

Native title claims (under the *NTA*) to the sea were also lodged during this period of legal activity. The first native title sea claim determined in Australia was to 2000 square kilometres of the Croker Island seas and sea-bed (see Figure 13.2).[25] The character of the rights claimed, particularly whether they were of an exclusive and commercial nature, was argued. Although the claim of exclusive possession by the Croker Island clan groups

---

[16] Ibid.

[17] Ron Levy, 'Who Can Fish Tidal Waters On Aboriginal Land?' (2001) 5 *Indigenous Law Bulletin* 17.

[18] *Director of Fisheries (Northern Territory) v Arnhem Land Aboriginal Land Trust* (2001) 185 ALR 649.

[19] *Arnhemland Aboriginal Land Trust v Director of Fisheries (Northern Territory)* (2000) 170 ALR 1.

[20] *Director of Fisheries (Northern Territory) v Arnhem Land Aboriginal Land Trust* (2001) 185 ALR 649.

[21] Personal communication with Ron Levy, Principal Legal Officer, Northern Land Council (Darwin, 9 September 2003).

[22] Reeves, above n 11, 232.

[23] Reeves, above n 11, 247.

[24] *Risk v The Northern Territory of Australia* (2002) 210 CLR 392.

[25] *Commonwealth of Australia v Yarmirr* (2001) 208 CLR 1.

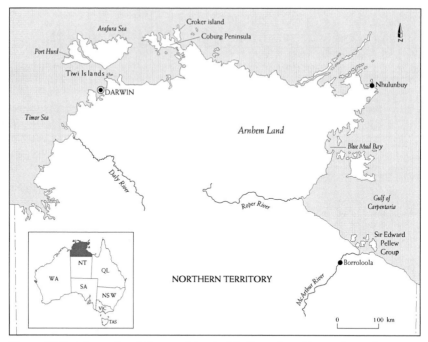

Figure 13.2: Arhnem Land. Source: School of Anthropology Geography and Environmental Studies (SAGES), University of Melbourne, reproduced by permission

was denied, it is significant that the first agreement with Aboriginal people over the commercial use of sea applies to that determination area. This was achieved despite the 1998 amendments to the *NTA* which limited the rights arising from native title to the sea, especially the right to negotiate over activities or developments affecting marine waters. Indigenous Land Use Agreements under the *NTA* have not yet been employed to settle Northern Territory native title sea claims.

The legal status of Indigenous rights to water resources and their use, including marine, estuarine and inter-tidal resources, remains unclear.[26] As Langton and Palmer note, the inadequate legal recognition is being, in part, off-set by an array of agreements which

> are setting up a practical precedent regarding the need for non-indigenous interests to consider the jurisdiction of Aboriginal groups in the seas. It is an incremental process of relationship building and agreement making that could have long-term policy implications for the management of seas and other waterways in the Northern Territory and elsewhere in Australia.[27]

---

[26] Marcia Langton and Lisa Palmer, 'Modern Agreement Making and Indigenous People in Australia: Issues and Trends' (2003) 8, *Australian Indigenous Law Reporter* 1.

[27] Ibid, 17.

Negotiated agreements relating to marine space or resources

Conservation agreements

There are three agreements relating to marine conservation and environmental management in the Northern Territory. These relate to Garig Gunak Barlu National Park (1996), the dugong sanctuary at Borroloola (1996) and the Dhimurru Indigenous Protected Area (2002), covering land and sea in north-east Arnhem Land. The latter agreement has been described elsewhere and, for reasons of brevity, will not be addressed in this chapter.[28]

Garig Gunak Barlu National Park

Australia's first integrated terrestrial and marine park jointly managed by Aboriginal owners and a conservation agency was established by agreement between the NLC and the Northern Territory Government.[29] The Aboriginal-owned Garig Gunuk Barlu National Park on the Cobourg Peninsula was established in stages as a result of the negotiated settlement of a land claim (see Figure 13.2). The National Park, formerly known as Gurig, was formalised by the passage of the *Cobourg Peninsula Aboriginal Land and Sanctuary Act 1981* (NT). Inalienable title to the land is vested in a Land Trust on behalf of the traditional owners, who receive an annual fee. Subject to the Act, traditional owners are entitled to use and occupy the sanctuary.[30]

Establishing Aboriginal control of the waters surrounding the National Park has involved protracted negotiations. The original agreement with the Northern Territory Government for joint management of the National Park included the adjacent 2 kilometres of sea. The government had undertaken to legislate to include the waters when it took control of offshore areas under the *Offshore Constitutional Settlement*.[31] The Cobourg Marine Park, the largest in the Northern Territory, was declared in 1983, with control

---

[28] See, Dhimurru Land Management Aboriginal Corporation Website http://www.dhimurru.com.au at 6 November 2003; ATNS Project database, *Dhimurru Indigenous Protected Area* http://www.atns.net.au/biogs/A000453b.htm at 6 November 2003.

[29] The Park covers 4,500 square kilometres and includes the entire Cobourg Peninsula, the surrounding waters of the Arafura Sea and Van Diemen Gulf and some of the neighbouring islands.

[30] S. Woenne-Green, R. Johnston, R. Sultan and A. Wallis, *Competing Interests: Aboriginal Participation in National Parks and Conservation Reserves in Australia: A Review*, (Australian Conservation Foundation, Melbourne, 1994).

[31] See M.C. Holm, *An Overview of Legal Issues Relevant to Coastal Zone Management in Australia* (Consultancy Report Commissioned by the Resources Assessment Commission Coastal Zone Inquiry, Canberra, 1992). During the 1980s the Commonwealth and States/Northern Territory negotiated this agreement in relation to jurisdiction over the three nautical miles from land and the resources contained within that zone.

remaining with the Northern Territory's Parks agency under the *Territory Parks and Wildlife Conservation Act 1976.*[32]

The marine park was not subject to the joint management provisions of the *Cobourg Peninsula Aboriginal Land and Sanctuary Act 1981* (NT) until 1996, when the Act was amended to extend the powers of the Cobourg Peninsula Sanctuary Board, which comprises an equal number of traditional owners and government representatives.[33] The Chair, selected from among the traditional owners, holds the casting vote. Smyth notes that a significant shortcoming of this arrangement is the Board's lack of jurisdiction over fisheries management within the marine park.[34] Following an NLC submission to government for the transfer of the Fisheries Divisions' powers in relation to aquatic resource management to the Board, a concerted effort is now being made to incorporate fisheries management into the Board's management planning responsibilities.[35]

With regard to the Cobourg Peninsula, a negotiated agreement was considered to be preferable to a land claim process that, if successful, would not have granted Aboriginal people primary responsibility for their marine estates. Following twenty years of consistent negotiation, traditional owners are very close to realising their goal of an integrated management regime that accommodates co-existing uses and interests. Issues that have generated conflict, such as privacy, or buffer zones around outstations which allow amateur and commercial fishers to traverse but not fish or anchor, are being negotiated within the Board structure and show positive signs of being satisfactorily resolved.[36]

Dugong Sanctuary at Borroloola

Repeated drownings of dugongs in fish nets motivated the Aboriginal communities of the Borroloola region to reach an agreement with the commercial fishing sector over wildlife protection in 1996 (see Figure 13.2). Dugong sanctuary closures in the southern Gulf of Carpentaria are now formally included in the Northern Territory Barramundi Fishery

---

[32] Woenne-Green *et al.*, above n 30. The Gurig National Park Plan of Management (Cobourg Peninsula Sanctuary Board, Winnellie, 1987) acknowledged that management of the two parks was 'inextricably linked' and recommended that management of the marine park come under Cobourg Peninsula Sanctuary Board control.

[33] *Cobourg Peninsula Aboriginal Land Sanctuary and Marine Park Act* (1996) (NT).

[34] Smyth, above n 2, 71.

[35] Personal communication with David Lawson, Conservation Policy Officer, Northern Territory Parks and Wildlife Commission (Darwin, 28 July 2003).

[36] Interview with Peter Pender, Marine Agreements Officer, Northern Land Council (Darwin, 8 August 2003); interview with John Harrison, Executive Officer, Amateur Fisherman's Association (Darwin, 30 July 2003).

Management Plan.[37] Under this agreement, areas in which dugong feed are protected, while commercial operators retain access to key fishing grounds. Fish-net sizes have been altered to reduce by-catch and death if captured. This agreement was only partially successful because it afforded little protection to inshore waters.[38]

Commercial agreements

Pearling agreements are the most common maritime agreement in the Northern Territory, perhaps reflecting a need for certainty and long-term security of land tenure within that industry. Agreements have also been reached with commercial fishing interests.

All agreements have been secured because of the proponent's need for Aboriginal land from which to launch marine activities or house equipment and staff, rather than an acknowledgement on the part of a commercial aquatic resource user that Aboriginal people have a property right in fish. The industry is of the view that fish are the common property of the Crown and that Aboriginal people do not have a commercial interest in their exploitation.[39]

Following the *Croker Island* case[40] proponents are now more willing to reach agreement over use of the sea.[41] As legal argument over the inter-tidal zone continues to draw out, fishers utilising that zone, such as barramundi licensees, may choose to negotiate directly with the NLC on behalf of traditional owners, in anticipation of legal findings favourable to Aboriginal interests. A commercial advantage might be obtained in this way. Similarly, some sports-fishing tour operators perceive an agreement with Aboriginal land owners as a means of ensuring exclusivity in a market which values highly a remote and isolated fishing experience, one that may include a cultural component.[42] Opinion within the recreational sector also points to a sense of inevitability and pragmatism about further legal recognition of sea rights.[43]

Agreements offer Aboriginal people opportunities to share in the benefits derived from marine resource utilisation and to control the effects of

---

[37] The Barramundi Fishery Management Plan, in force under the *Fisheries Act 1988* (NT), comprises the Regulations 1998, No 4, and came into operation on 1 February 1998.

[38] Pender, above n 36. Pressure from the recreational sector has since resulted in the closure of the MacArthur River to commercial barramundi fishing.

[39] 'A Framework for the Future of NT Fisheries', *Fishing Industry News* (Darwin), June–July 1994, 4.

[40] *Commonwealth of Australia v Yarmirr* (2001) 208 CLR 1.

[41] Pender, above n 36.

[42] Interview with Bernard Higgins, Senior Project Officer Tourism, Northern Land Council, (Darwin, 25 August 2003).

[43] Harrison, above n 36.

an external party's activities within customary estates. Some Aboriginal communities have expressed interest in acquiring licences to harvest or fish aquatic resources commercially, such as trepang, mud crab and barramundi. However, lack of finance, suitable vessels and processing facilities has precluded them from purchasing a licence on the open market.[44]

In 1998, native title holders in the Croker Island area signed the first native title agreement over the sea.[45] The agreement related to a pearl culture lease over land and sea which would return $2 million in royalties over a twenty-year period.[46] Lamilami and Yarmirr regard this and other marine agreements as:

> strong indicators that native title is working and that we are working closely with private enterprise for mutually beneficial outcomes. We are now interested in entering into agreements with other fishermen, particularly the amateur sector ... [47]

The range of commercial agreements negotiated by the NLC is presented in Figure 13.3. For commercial reasons, the location and name of the commercial partner may not be listed, and financial details are not provided.

Figure 13.3: Maritime agreements negotiated by the Northern Land Council[48]

Agreement type	Date negotiated	Features
Pearl	mid-1980s	■ three land bases, additional leases now wanted ■ forty-year term ■ financial package did not include use of the sea ■ agreement with company provides rental monies, fuel, some assistance with service delivery to communities and other standard elements ■ Northern Territory-based pearling company
Pearl	1998	■ one land base ■ two sea leases—first of its kind ■ ten-year term with option for extension ■ use of 2 square kilometres of sea ■ area lies within Croker Island native title determination area ■ company is negotiating a second agreement within the claimed area

---

[44] The exception has been in the Borroloola region, where Aboriginal people have held two licences in the commercial barramundi fishery.

[45] Lamilami and Yarmirr, above n 5.

[46] Robinson and Mercer, above n 2.

[47] Lamilami and Yarmirr, above n 5, 31.

[48] The information contained in this table was sourced from interviews or personal communications with Northern Land Council officers: Levy, above n 21, Pender, above

Agreement type	Date negotiated	Features
Pearl	1999	▪ three land bases and several sea leases ▪ twenty-year term with options for extension of ten years ▪ two Western Australian companies are involved
Pearl	2003	▪ three sea leases, no land base ▪ financial package includes provision of fuel
Mud crab	late 1990s	▪ two agreements in the northern Blue Mud Bay region of Arnhem Land ▪ agreements with leaseholders who act on behalf of the licence owners
Mud crab	2003	▪ two agreements in southern Blue Mud Bay ▪ consultations in progress with two remaining leaseholders with land bases in Blue Mud Bay area
Trepang	late 1990s	▪ harvest of trepang required land base in eastern and western Arnhem Land ▪ agreements now expired
Sport fishing*	1992	▪ camp site is held under a lease to Bawinanga Aboriginal Corporation (BAC) at Maningrida for ranger activities, including sports fishing ▪ BAC holds a licence over the Liverpool and Tomkinson River systems in central Arnhem Land ▪ BAC has a management agreement with a sport-fishing tour operator who has returned in excess of $100,000 to traditional owners
Sport fishing	1998	▪ licence applied to Ilamaryi River system, Cobourg Peninsula ▪ lapsed
Sport fishing	1999	▪ licence applies to Cape Don area, Cobourg Peninsula ▪ negotiated with traditional owners and ratified by Cobourg Sanctuary Board of Management ▪ extension currently under consideration
Sport fishing	2001	▪ licence applied to Endyalgout Island, Cobourg Peninsula ▪ no longer current, proposal has been received for consideration
Sport fishing	2001	▪ licence applies to Minjalang area, Croker Island ▪ licence is being transferred to another operator with the permission of traditional owners
Sport fishing	2002	▪ licence applies to Port Essington, Cobourg Peninsula ▪ negotiated with traditional owners and ratified by Cobourg Sanctuary Board of Management

n 36, Higgins, above n 36; the Northern Land Council Annual Reports for 2001– 2002 (Northern Land Council, Darwin, 2002); also* from ATNS Project database http://www. atns.net.au/biogs/A000676b.htm at 6 November 2003.

There are a number of consistent features in all pearling agreements. All protect the right of traditional owners to enter and travel through the lease. Sacred sites, whether on land or sea, are defined and delimited, and traditional owners retain the right to control areas for ceremonial purposes. Environmental protection measures are outlined, as are employment opportunities. The agreements do not prejudice the native title rights of affected communities.

According to the NLC, the conditions relating to employment are now being tightened to include more prescriptive clauses which set employment targets.[49] Previously, companies were expected to pursue their 'best endeavours', which did not result in any significant employment. In one case, a Pearl Management Committee with NLC representation has been established to address the non-financial aspects of the agreement, particularly employment and training programs. There is interest in establishing such a structure for another pearling enterprise.

The mud crab fishery is the most valuable wild harvest fishery managed by the Northern Territory Government, representing approximately 40 per cent of the total value of Northern Territory landings (excluding aquaculture). Crabbing effort is concentrated in the Borroloola region, the Roper River, Darwin and Arnhem Land (see Figure 13.2). Land tenure is critical to agreement making over mud crabbing, hence the only crabbing agreements with Aboriginal people apply to Aboriginal land at Blue Mud Bay, Arnhem Land. Fishers crabbing in or close to areas that are not held under Aboriginal title tend to be less interested in negotiating agreements with Aboriginal land holders.[50] The two agreements in northern Blue Mud Bay have been in place for four or five years, and have recently been through their third renewal phase. A further two agreements applying to the southern portion of the Bay have recently been settled. The NLC continues to urge police to prosecute illegal fishers, although informal agreements between traditional owners and crabbers frustrate police efforts.[51]

As Figure 13.3 illustrates, several companies have agreements in place with traditional owners to allow sport fishing on Aboriginal land. All sports-fishing agreements are made in accordance with land-use consent requirements of the *ALRA* and managed under a licence. They specify a fee, identify 'open' and 'closed' areas, and protection of sacred sites. Employment opportunities tend to be limited.[52]

---

[49] Pender, above n 36.

[50] Ibid.

[51] Interview with Paul Josif, Caring for Sea Country Coordinator, Northern Land Council (Darwin, 20 August 2003).

[52] Lisa Palmer, *Indigenous Interests in Fishing and Safari Hunting Tourism in the Northern Territory*, Wildlife Tourism Report No. 8, Status Assessment of Wildlife Tourism in Australia Series, (CRC for Sustainable Tourism, Gold Coast, 2001).

The Tiwi Land Council (TLC) has an agreement with a barramundi aquaculture company which produces fish in sea cages at Port Hurd (see Figure 13.2). In that case, a requirement for a land base necessitated negotiation of an agreement under the *ALRA*.

Recreational fishing

Recreational fishing assumes considerable significance in Northern Territory marine policy debates. For many years the government has promoted the sector as a vital feature of the Territory's outdoor lifestyle.[53] A 1995 survey found that 35 per cent of the Northern Territory's non-Indigenous population fished annually for recreation, while the sector generated more than $30 million annually. Fishing-related tourism is considered to be an important and growing stimulus to regional economies.[54]

The peak recreational fishing body, the Amateur Fishermen's Association of the Northern Territory (AFANT), considers access to fishing places as its single most important issue. John Harrison, AFANT's Executive Officer, says:

> When you have eighty-five per cent of the coastline inaccessible by terrestrial means then you have a challenge to overcome overcrowding and pressure on resources.[55]

The fishing in places such as the Tiwi Islands, Nhulunbuy and Daly River regions of the Northern Territory (see Figure 13.2) is considered to be outstanding. Harrison argues that the pattern of Aboriginal land holdings restricts amateur fishing access to areas concentrated in the Darwin region. Fishing organisations view the transaction costs involved in seeking permits and negotiating access as substantial.[56] AFANT sees value in devoting considerable effort to creating 'access opportunities'[57] via agreement with the Land Councils, such as the TLC, to provide for access to its members.

Unauthorised access by recreational fishers to the Tiwi Islands and surrounding waters has long been a source of concern to the Aboriginal landowners. In the mid-1980s, illegal fishing and unregulated boating prompted the TLC to apply to close the waters surrounding the islands under the *ALA*.

---

[53] Lisa Palmer, 'Fishing Lifestyles: "Territorians", Traditional Owners and the Management of Recreational Fishing in Kakadu National Park' (2004) 42(1) *Australian Geographical Studies* 60-7.

[54] Department of Business, Industry and Resource Development, *Primary Industries in the Northern Territory* http://www.nt.gov.au/dbird/dpif/general/industry/industry.shtml at 6 November 2003.

[55] Harrison, above n 36.

[56] Ibid.

[57] Amateur Fisherman's Association of the Northern Territory Inc., *Fishing the Tiwi's* http://www.afant.com.au/tiwis.htm at 6 November 2003.

After reconsideration of the legal costs and likely limited impact of a sea closure, their application was withdrawn. It was decided that direct contact with fisheries authorities and amateur fishers might be more productive of a better outcome.[58]

From the mid-1990s, regular meetings between the Tiwi land owners and fishing interests were held to discuss resource sharing and illegal access to land, rivers and creeks, particularly by fishers using 'mother-ships' from which six or seven dinghies could be launched. The Director of the TLC, John Hicks, outlined Tiwi aspirations in one such meeting:

> To rectify some of these problems (Tiwi) wish to work with government in a joint marine resource management regime. They would like to participate in patrolling their coastline and to close certain areas to commercial fishing in favour of subsistence fishing. In addition, the Tiwi would like to see research being carried out on the fish stocks around the Islands. They also intend to develop their own industries, which would include fisheries and they want government support in this.[59]

Following discussions between the Fisheries Division, AFANT and the TLC, an agreement was reached in 1998 whereby six beaches on Bathurst and Melville Islands were made available for camping. Fishers are issued with a permit for a fee administered by AFANT. Tiwi people receive approximately 80 per cent of the fee. Fishers are made aware of major sacred sites, are required to remove rubbish and asked to report any undesirable conduct.

The agreement was intended to engender a co-operative relationship between the organisations in which their respective needs can be addressed. The TLC has been flexible in reviewing the cost of permits for fishing clubs and has relocated camping sites to more appealing areas.[60] Compliance and enforcement is an outstanding problem because of the history of unregulated access by fishers resident in nearby Darwin.

The original intention of a negotiated agreement was to regulate entry of adjoining seas and parts of the islands, yet the current agreement regulates land access only. Tiwi people are concerned about unauthorised use of all their waters, yet they currently have insufficient power to control use of the 'water column'.[61] Their strategy has been to provide opportunities for use under regimes they manage, in the hope that they can displace the demand for access via 'mother-ships' and other means such as helicopters.

---

[58] Interview with John Hicks, Director, Tiwi Land Council (Darwin, 1 September 2003).
[59] Tiwi Coastal Waters Consultative Committee Minutes, Meeting No. 9 (22 June 1998).
[60] Harrison, above n 36.
[61] 'Water column' is defined as 'the vertical column of water in a sea or lake extending from the surface to the bottom' (R. Lincoln, G. Boxshall, P. Clark, *A Dictionary of Ecology, Evolution and Systematics* (2nd edn, Cambridge University Press, Cambridge, 1998)).

It remains to be seen whether through re-negotiation of the agreement, or through other mechanisms, Tiwi people can negotiate successfully to have the coastal waters incorporated into regional management structures. John Hicks says that face-to-face discussions with resource managers and users has created a forum for resolution of problems, assisted in the provision of resources to protect marine resources around the Islands,[62] and served as an 'interesting lever for the future'.[63]

AFANT sees the Tiwi agreement as a model for the Territory's waters. Negotiations with the NLC over this issue have slowed due to difficulties in financing Aboriginal participation in Territory-wide discussions, and the absence of a management framework to support traditional owners' wider management aspirations. According to the NLC:

> if there was a solid management forum, which has got ... strong traditional owner input, to manage the seas and waterways in a particular area, traditional owners would feel more confident, we believe, of increasing amateur access knowing that that management agency would adequately monitor, enforce, or help enforcement of such an agreement ...[64]

Research agreements

The Arafura-Timor Sea Research Facility, to be established jointly by the Australian National University and the Australian Institute of Marine Science, intends to conduct research in the region over coming years. In establishing the facility, the research organisations and the NLC have discussed an agreement as a means of addressing Aboriginal interests. To that end, a draft Memorandum of Understanding between the NLC and the Australian Institute of Marine Science is being developed, covering issues such as permission protocols to access areas, involvement of traditional owners in research activities, collaboration with sea ranger management groups, investigation of commercially viable species for aquaculture development, and protection of cultural and intellectual property.[65]

---

[62] Two sea rangers have been employed to implement the agreement and carry out other sea monitoring activities.

[63] Hicks, above n 59.

[64] Lisa Palmer, interview with Peter Pender, Fisheries Officer, Northern Land Council (Darwin, 21 August 2002).

[65] Josif, above n 51.

Conclusion

Significant and continuing legal uncertainties in the area of Indigenous sea rights are likely to stimulate further negotiated settlements.[66] Agreements engender co-operative relationships between parties in which a range of issues, beyond the financial, may be resolved. There is evidence from the Northern Territory experience that negotiation of collaborative management structures, with pearling companies, amateur fishing groups, or government conservation and fisheries agencies, offers a 'formula'[67] by which to address Aboriginal and other co-existing interests. In the case of Garig Gunak Barlu National Park, a management structure, in the form of a Board, provided a forum in which amateur fishers and traditional owners could be confident that increased recreational fishing access could be achieved without compromising the privacy of outstation residents. The buffer zone concept might be seen to represent an exclusive right to an area, albeit one that is asserted within a context that recognises the interests of other parties. Negotiated outcomes offer the opportunity to develop management models premised on concepts which, when presented in precedent-making court cases, can polarise competing groups. What is required, according to the Amateur Fishermen's Association, is a 'paradigm shift' that allows 'Aboriginal people to have a say in their estates'.[68]

Creative and impartial policy, sensitive to the substantial cultural differences in environmental perceptions and ways of governing marine areas, is required if long periods of unresolved conflict and frustrated aspirations are to be avoided. Progress could be greatly assisted by innovative research into property concepts and resource management regimes cognisant of differing traditions of resource use and tenures. In the meantime, incremental advances made through agreements will continue to contribute to the recognition of Indigenous sea rights.

---

[66] See Gillian Triggs, this volume.
[67] Pender, above n 36.
[68] Harrison, above n 36.

Chapter 14

Rio Tinto's Agreement Making in Australia in a Context of Globalisation

Bruce Harvey[*]

The common law and statutory recognition of Aboriginal land rights and native title in Australia has had a profound impact on the minerals industry. In particular, the High Court's recognition of native title in *Mabo v Queensland (No 2)*,[1] despite its subsequent corruption through statutory codification and amendments, has changed the social landscape for mining company–Indigenous agreement making in Australia. At the same time, Rio Tinto has been engaged in a program of internal cultural change, exemplified in its agreement making with Indigenous communities. The Western Cape Communities Co-existence Agreement (WCCCA) between Rio Tinto's subsidiary, Comalco, Indigenous peoples of Cape York (in far north Queensland) and the Queensland Government, illustrates this change.

This chapter is in two parts. The first focuses on the WCCCA, while the second part extends the discussion of the issues set out in the first part of the chapter beyond Australia and interprets Rio Tinto's agreement making in the context of globalisation. This analysis is retrospective and has not informed Rio Tinto's activities over the past decade.

---

[*] The views expressed in this paper are my own and do not necessarily reflect those of Rio Tinto.
[1] (1992) 175 CLR 1 ('*Mabo*').

Rio Tinto and Indigenous community agreement making

History

Rio Tinto was formed in 1995 by the merging, under a dual-listed companies structure, of the Australian-based CRA Limited and the United Kingdom-based The RTZ Corporation plc. The Group's headquarters is in London, and there is a corporate office in Melbourne. Rio Tinto has operations in some twenty different countries, with approximately 47 per cent of its assets in Australia and New Zealand. It is predominantly engaged in the mining and smelting of minerals and metals, and is a major producer of iron ore, coal, copper, diamonds, borax and aluminium. It also produces substantial volumes of gold, nickel, zinc, titanium oxide, uranium and industrial salt.[2]

For ten years following the passing of the *Aboriginal Land Rights (Northern Territory) Act 1976* (Cth), the mining industry failed to come to terms with Aboriginal land rights. It stonewalled, completely refusing to recognise any form of customary or Indigenous rights, concentrating instead on litigation and arguments advocating legislative review.

Why did this happen? The 1970s and 1980s was a period of self-conscious nation-building, during which activities of Australia's resource explorers and miners were coming to fruition. There was an export boom based on an expanding international demand for mineral commodities, and the people who worked in the resources industry sensed that they were part of a project of immense national significance. As a young exploration geologist, I remember thinking that I was working at the frontier—the so-called 'uninhabited frontier'[3]—on a project of national economic importance. The job was well paid, but I was driven by a sense of national endeavour, and I believe many geologists and engineers shared similar feelings at the time.

It was, therefore, a great shock to the mining industry to discover that the nation was no longer enthralled by what they were doing. In the 1960s and 1970s, the mining industry had been encouraged by governments to expand the frontier of resource development. In the 1980s, coincident with the rise in environmental awareness, there suddenly arose a ground swell of opposition to mining and, particularly in the southern parts of Australia, there was increasingly popular support for the struggle for Aboriginal land rights. For the following ten years the industry was in denial and mounted

---

[2] See generally, Rio Tinto, http://www.riotinto.com/ at 14 November 2003.
[3] At the time I, along with others, had no sense or idea that it was only recently uninhabited due to many Aboriginal people having migrated or otherwise having been relocated out of their home country to missions or government settlements.

arguments based on national interest and the need for expediency, frequently without reference to political and socio-economic analyses.

Paradigm shift

In the early 1990s there was a paradigm shift. After ten years of long and contentious legal debate, the *Mabo* decision was handed down by the High Court and the *Native Title Act 1993* (Cth) (*NTA*) was passed. However, the *NTA* served to confuse the situation as much as to clarify it. At about the same time the position that some in the resources industry had been advocating for some time began to be taken seriously. That is, that there would be no solutions borne out of adversarial approaches and litigation: instead, mining access to Aboriginal land needed to be based on soundly built relationships.

In 1995, Rio Tinto's predecessor, CRA Limited, appointed a new Chief Executive Officer, Leon Davis. With strong words of encouragement from some prominent Australians such as Ron Casten[4] and Lowitja O'Donoghue,[5] Davis publicly declared his recognition of Aboriginal land rights. This recognition was of huge significance, reflecting his aspiration for a total cultural change within CRA: until then CRA had been viewed as the staunchest member of the mining hard-liners.

In a major speech to the Australian Securities Institute in March 1995, Davis said, 'In CRA, we believe there are major opportunities for growth in outback Australia which will only be realised with the full cooperation of all interested parties'. He went on to say that the *NTA* 'laid the basis for better exploration access and thus increased the probability that the next

---

[4] Ron Castan AM QC (1939–1999) was appointed a Queen's Counsel in 1980 and was one of the leading barristers at the Melbourne Bar. He had a distinguished career in the law and appeared in a number of major cases. He was part of the Commonwealth's legal team in the landmark Gordon below Franklin Dam case in 1983; represented Eddie Mabo in the High Court; and was a significant player in the development of the *NTA* in 1993. He subsequently appeared for claimants in major native title cases. Mr Castan also served for several years as a part-time Hearing Commissioner for the Human Rights and Equal Opportunity Commission. In 1993, he was appointed a Member of the Order of Australia for service to the law, especially in relation to civil liberties and constitutional reform.

[5] Dr Lowitja O'Donoghue, AC CBE, is a Yankunytjatjara woman from South Australia's far north. Her contribution to the advancement of Aboriginal people is great and widely recognised. Her positions have included inaugural Chairperson of the Aboriginal and Torres Strait Islander Commission; Deputy Chairperson of the Aboriginal and Torres Strait Islander Development Corporation; a member of the Council for Aboriginal Reconciliation, the Indigenous Land Corporation, the National Australia Day Council and the Board of Trustees of the United Nations Voluntary Fund for Indigenous Populations (Geneva); and Director of Aboriginal Hostels Limited.

decade will see a series of CRA operations developed in active partnership with Aboriginal people'.[6]

A month later, at the annual company conference, Davis told the managing directors of CRA:

> It is my desire to move away from a litigious framework, I wish to open channels to those who are not favourably disposed to CRA. I want to establish innovative ways of sharing with and/or compensating Indigenous people. I believe that a negative attitude will produce negative results, I have an open mind on how we should approach the question.[7]

Policy

Davis then initiated a program of cultural change within CRA, and deliberately set out to establish a relationship with prominent Australian Aboriginal leaders. These leaders were, understandably, initially suspicious of him. It was eighteen months before the company earned enough trust with those leaders for them to accept the task of helping Rio Tinto write its Aboriginal and Torres Strait Islander policy. This policy states that:

> In all exploration and development in Australia, Rio Tinto will always consider Aboriginal and Torres Strait Islander issues. Where there are traditional or historical connections to particular land and waters, Rio Tinto will engage with Aboriginal and Torres Strait Islander stakeholders and their representatives to find mutually advantageous outcomes. Outcomes for Aboriginal and Torres Strait Islander people will result from listening to them. Economic independence through direct employment, business development and training are among the advantages that Rio Tinto will offer. Strong support will be given to activities that are sustainable after Rio Tinto has left the area.
>
> This policy is based upon recognition and respect. Rio Tinto recognises that Aboriginal and Torres Strait Islander people in Australia have been disadvantaged and dispossessed; have a special connection to land and waters; have native title rights recognised by law. Rio Tinto respects Aboriginal and Torres Strait Islander peoples' cultural diversity; aspirations for self sufficiency; interest in land management.[8]

Rio Tinto's objective is to transform this policy into action. Since 1995, wherever Rio Tinto explores for or develops a mine in Australia, it has sought to formally acknowledge and consult with Aboriginal and Torres

[6]   Leon Davis, 'New Directions for CRA' (Speech delivered to the Securities Institute Australia, Sydney, March 1995).
[7]   Leon Davis, 'New Competencies in CRA' (Speech delivered to the CRA Annual Company Conference, Townsville, April 1995).
[8]   Rio Tinto, *Aboriginal and Torres Strait Islander Policy* (January 1999).

Strait Islander people. It does this through a formal negotiation and agreement process that, where appropriate, is tri-partite, involving Indigenous
people, Rio Tinto and government. Rio Tinto has now signed five major
mine development agreements and more than fifty exploration access
agreements across Australia.[9]

Western Cape Communities Co-existence Agreement

The Western Cape Communities Co-existence Agreement (WCCCA) is a
recent example of this new era of agreement making. The agreement concerns
Rio Tinto's subsidiary, Comalco, which has a mining operation at Weipa on
western Cape York Peninsula. Comalco has developed and mined bauxite
at Weipa since 1960, until recently without any consultative involvement
or formal agreement with the Aboriginal traditional owners for the mining
area. In 1996, Comalco sought to modernise its relationship with Aboriginal
people and commenced negotiations aimed at reaching a comprehensive
regional agreement with the Cape York Land Council (CYLC)[10] representing
traditional owners. Agreement was reached in early 2001.[11]

The WCCCA is multi-lateral; its signatories include eleven traditional
owner groups (Alngith, Anathangayth, Ankamuthi, Peppan, Taepadhighi,
Thanikwithi, Tjungundji, Warranggu, Wathayn, Wik and Wik-Way, and
Yupungathi), four Aboriginal community councils (Aurukun, Napranum,
Mapoon and New Mapoon), Comalco, the CYLC and the Queensland
Government. The latter provided financial benefits, additional to Comalco's,
when the agreement was registered as an Indigenous Land Use Agreement
(ILUA) under the provisions of the *NTA*.[12]

Significant aspects of the agreement include:

- recognition for traditional owner groups and their claims for native
  title
- registration of the agreement as an ILUA under the *NTA*

---

9   See generally, ATNS Project database http://www.atns.net.au at 17 November 2003.
10 Cape York Land Council is the Representative Body for Cape York under the *Native Title Act*.
    See generally, Cape York Land Council Website http://www.cylc.org.au/ at 17 November
    2003.
11 See the ATNS Project database, *Western Cape Communities Co-existence Agreement* http://www.
    atns.net.au/biogs/A000088b.htm at 17 November 2003.
12 National Native Title Tribunal, *Registered ILUA Summary* http://www.nntt.gov.au/ilua/30.
    html at 17 November 2003.

- progressive relinquishment of parts of the Comalco mining lease, no longer needed for mining, to the State Government for return to Aboriginal ownership
- $2.5 million each year (minimum) to a Western Cape Communities Trust for projects benefiting traditional owner groups and the Western Cape communities. This amount grows with increases in Weipa production and with higher aluminium prices
- $500,000 annual Comalco expenditure on employment, training and youth educational programs, endorsed by the Western Cape Communities
- a State Government contribution of about $1.5 million a year to the Western Cape Communities Trust for allocation to local community development projects and traditional owner proposals once the Agreement was registered as an ILUA
- cultural heritage surveys and site protection plans, and cultural awareness training for all Comalco staff and principal contractors
- support for community development, Aboriginal business enterprises and establishment of outstations on suitable areas of the mining lease.

There was particular recognition for the traditional owners of land on which the Weipa Township is established and which remains under continuing use and development. Provision was also made for transfer to the traditional owners of Sudley, a Comalco-owned, 1,325 square kilometre pastoral property located about 70 kilometres east of Weipa.

Under the agreement, financial contributions are distributed to the Western Cape Community Trust, which comprises a majority of traditional owner representatives. The trustees have stipulated that the majority of funds be placed in secure long-term investments to provide a sustaining economic base for all its beneficiaries, and particularly to provide for future generations.

A co-ordinating committee, comprised of two representatives from each traditional owner group across the lease area, a representative from each of the four community councils, and a representative from each of Comalco, the State Government and the CYLC, was established to deal with the day-to-day matters arising from the agreement. The co-ordinating committee is consulted by Comalco on policies and programs involving:

- Aboriginal employment and training
- business development
- cultural awareness
- cultural site protection.

The committee also consults with relevant traditional owners on issues such as land management, regeneration plans, environmental applications, and any review of the land access permit system.

What has been said above does not adequately convey all that transpired during the negotiation process and what has evolved since. The scope of the agreement is truly regional; an ambitious undertaking that seeks to encompass all affected Indigenous people in the region, not only those with customary connections, but people with historic connections through re-location and contemporary connections through marriage. Under such circumstances, **process** is all important, and it must be founded and maintained on trust and mutual goodwill beyond any definitions in the WCCCA.

For instance, early in the negotiations, the High Court found in the case of *Wik* that the Comalco mining leases were valid under Queensland and Commonwealth law and had extinguished native title.[13] This decision in effect relieved Comalco of any legal obligation to negotiate with the local Aboriginal community. In addition, the 1998 amendments to the *NTA* further reduced any legal imperative for Comalco.

However, Comalco's lease at Weipa extends to 2062, and the company recognised that a sustainable long-term relationship with traditional owners and neighbouring communities was essential. Furthermore, under the ILUA provisions of the *Native Title Amendment Act 1998*,[14] there now existed a process through which this long-term relationship could be formalised. The ILUA provisions allow parties to negotiate flexible and pragmatic agreements to suit individual circumstance. This includes agreement on the relationship between native title rights and interests, and other rights and interests in relation to an agreement area. Once registered, ILUAs bind all the parties and all persons holding native title in an agreement area to the terms of the agreement.

In this case, the intent of the desired agreement was that the Aboriginal parties to the WCCCA would support Comalco's future mining operations in return for support, benefits, employment, business development and educational opportunities, and the full recognition of their status as traditional owners on their own lands. The spirit, intent and richness of the WCCCA relationship is not necessarily reflected in the written content of the Agreement. For example, the principal of mutual obligation looms large in the Agreement. If the trajectory of local Aboriginal employment fails to remain on track for a target of 35 per cent by 2010, Comalco is obliged to increase the level of pre-employment spending on education and training. However, if the level of Indigenous Year–10 graduation in the region drops

---

[13] *Wik Peoples v State of Queensland* (1996) 187 CLR 1.
[14] Now s 24C of the Consolidated *Native Title Act 1993* (Cth).

below the same trajectory, the company is relieved from this obligation. In other words, the schools, the students and their families have account-abilities equal to that of Comalco's. In addition, however, Comalco's Chief Executive Officer has made a further commitment, outside the terms of the Agreement; he has said that **every** Year–10 Aboriginal graduate from western Cape York will be offered training and a job on the mine.[15]

The signing ceremony on Wednesday 14 March 2001 was itself a highly significant event. In the speeches of senior Comalco staff, the com-pany apologised for taking forty years to formally recognise Aboriginal land connections. The Minister for Transport, Steve Bredhauer, representing the Premier, spoke on behalf of the Queensland Government and apologised for the coerced removal of Aboriginal people from the area in 1963. In many respects the acknowledgment, the apologies and the ceremony were worth as much as the agreement and the benefits. They represented a recognition of history that had formerly been denied.

A context of globalisation

The WCCCA is the result of the vision of one company and a number of communities to formally re-define their relationship; it reflects a determi-nation to achieve a formal relationship appropriate to local circumstances. But how does the WCCCA fit with an international context? I believe it can be seen as part of a much broader process of globalisation.

Globalisation is many things; in particular it is, arguably, a transfor-mation of social geography with far-reaching implications for governance. Public affairs are no longer managed solely, if they ever were, through the framework of sovereign statehood. The case can be made that it is the large-scale diminution of geographic sovereignty that really makes contemporary globalisation new and different to the incipient globalisation we saw at the end of the nineteenth century, rooted as it was in nation states. The govern-ance challenge of the twenty-first century is to find ways of creating social contracts reflective of this new age of globalisation, beyond the boundaries of state sovereignty.

That is not to say that nationalistic social geography is no longer rel-evant. On the contrary, nations, states and territorial identities continue to exert very significant influences over local governance. However, globali-sation co-exists with nationalism and they inter-relate in complex ways. Globalisation, by confining itself to matters of economic reach, has the

---

[15] Sam Walsh, Chief Executive Officer, Comalco (2001).

potential to contribute to a new form of governance that leaves aside the perceived need for coercive cultural aggregation of sub-national identities. The old nation-builders wanted economic aggregation, but they mistakenly believed that to achieve this they also had to engage in spiritual, cultural and religious aggregation.

The rules for social order under nationalism emanate largely from federal authorities or national governments. The epitome, of course, is sovereign statehood in which a government body has exclusive control over its designated territories and its inhabitants. However, in the globalised world, sovereign states are quite unable themselves to control phenomena such as mass media, satellite remote sensing, global ecological issues and financial markets. Many people have acquired loyalties that supplement and, in some cases even override, their feelings of national solidarity. Moreover, many people in the globalising world have become increasingly ready to give values such as economic growth, human rights and ecological integrity a much higher priority than state sovereignty with its associated nationalist interpretation.

Globalisation does not necessarily lead to the demise of the sovereign state. Most states, particularly strong states, are surviving very well. What is happening is that state sovereignty, as traditionally understood, is changing, just as the terms sovereignty, crown ownership and royalty payments no longer carry their original literal meaning. Nation states can no longer aspire to be the supreme, unqualified rulers of discrete jurisdictions based on territorial control. In the challenge of government, states are increasingly turning away from unilateral control based on geography, and instead are adopting multi-lateral approaches.

Whereas the optimising scale of government in the 'Industrial Age', dictated by railways, steam ships and the telegraph, was the geographically defined nation-state; in the 'Information Age' of jetliners, Cable News Network (CNN) and the Internet, the optimising scale is global. Thus, strong central control over information and authority is no longer possible in the 'Information Age' and, in order to cope, governance needs to be many-faceted and diffuse.

To date, this trend towards global governance, aside from a few exceptions such as international hotels and airports, has not, as people feared, produced an homogeneous global culture. In fact, quite the opposite has occurred. People all over the world are actually choosing to accentuate their local identities. In places, there is a celebration of this diversity; elsewhere it is the basis, sadly, of political fragmentation and conflict.[16] The apparent

---

[16] This is the situation in areas such as Bouganville, Lebanon, Congo, Cyprus, and the Balkans.

246 Honour Among Nations?

paradox of globalisation and local diversity, I think, finds explanation in the innate countervailing nature of people. One phenomenon drives the other. As people perceive themselves as losing control over their daily economic lives, they react by taking and expressing greater control over their cultural, social and spiritual lives. For instance, Indigenous peoples in many parts of the world, but particularly in common law countries, are finding a voice and rejuvenating in a very robust way. Not only are Indigenous peoples experiencing escalating interest in their cultural, social, spiritual and economic pursuits, their unique cultural presence is being recognised and protected by sovereign law. Examples of this are the legal recognition of customary land connection through native title in Australia, the recognition and inclusion of traditional environmental knowledge in environmental impact assessment in Canada[17] and Maori consultation enshrined in development processes in New Zealand.[18] Whether through compliance or negotiated contract, many corporations are also choosing to afford formal recognition to diverse Indigenous interests in the regions in which they operate, the WCCCA being a prime example.

The apparent paradox of growth of the global economy and rejuvenating social diversity and formal recognition at a local level has resulted in the emergence of a 'tri-polar' world. Business and community (the latter frequently supported by non-government organisations (NGOs) now increasingly transact directly with each other, rather than through the pole of government. Global companies now deal with provincial, state and federal authorities, and local institutions as much as, or even more than, central government. Sub-state authorities have created networks of their own that largely bypass nation-states. For instance, most of the world's financial infrastructure and its transactions emanate from little more than a dozen or so virtual city states.[19]

Concurrently, there has also been a great increase in the number of supra-state institutions, some with regional and others with global scope. Governance in a globalising world involves, for instance, the European Union (EU), the International Monetary Fund (IMF), North Atlantic Treaty Organisation (NATO), Organisation for Economic Co-operation and Development (OECD), the World Trade Organisation (WTO), the World Bank, the International Labour Organisation (ILO) and many other bodies that were non-existent or insignificant fifty years ago. Many individual com-

---

[17] See, for example, Diavik Diamond Mines Inc, *Diavik Diamond Project Environmental Agreement* (8 March 2000) http://www.diavik.ca/pdf/DiavikEnvironmentalAgreement.PDF at 17 November 2003.

[18] Section 8 *Resource Management Act 1991* (NZ); see Williams, this volume.

[19] These include, amongst others, New York, London, Singapore and Tokyo.

panies, business organisations and sub-state institutions have developed direct links with these multi-lateral bodies. Along with the dispersion of authority upwards and downwards from the sovereign state, there have also been lateral shifts in governance from the public to non-government sectors.

In this context, local governance bodies whose scope of authority is limited may nevertheless have considerable power in that they can transact directly with global corporations. Comalco and the Western Cape communities' negotiation of the WCCCA is tangible proof of this phenomenon.

Conclusion

The most far-reaching implication of globalisation concerns the question of governance. I suggest that globalisation has enabled a shift away from dominating national sovereignties to a situation of multi-faceted and diffuse identity and regulation. Local agreement making, corporate citizenship and global financial scrutiny offer counterweights to potential sovereign governance deficits in the globalising world, particularly in countries in which public-sector arrangements are not adequate for human security, social justice and democracy. This may seem very difficult to conceive, but then who in the sixteenth century, when sovereign states were defined by allegiance to divine majesty, would have imagined that within 200 years the norm would be nation-states with comprehensive public sectors as the unifying governance framework.

In the twenty-first century, far from being the sole domain of sovereign states, it will be free market institutions, international agencies, civil society, corporations, religious institutions, local communities and NGOs in a myriad of multi-lateral networks that will provide the necessary power balance and transparent governance. To a large extent the driver for this governance shift is the communication and transmission of common ideals, made possible by new technology.

The emerging underlying societal trend away from rigid government intermediation to multi-lateral relationships is what inspires both global citizenship and local agreement making. As described early in this chapter, no statutory or legal imperative required Comalco to negotiate a formal community agreement on western Cape York. Instead, the driving factors were Rio Tinto and Comalco's pragmatic desire for rights-based recognition of customary land connections, on-going mining approval, transparent governance and a sustainable relationship.

Whatever the local drivers for the WCCCA (and they were real and their realisation long overdue) the enabling factor was the advancing tide of globalisation.

PART 4

The Opportunities and Constraints of Agreement Making

Introduction

Agreement Making, Outcomes, Constraints and Possibilities

Lisa Palmer

Land and water subject to Indigenous ownership and governance constitute a significant and substantial proportion of the Australian continent, particularly in northern and central Australia.[1] However, in order to overcome the legacy of colonial history and the crisis of underdevelopment, emerging because of increasing population growth and the failure of service delivery to meet the needs of Aboriginal and Torres Strait Islander peoples in Australia, urgent economic reform in the area of policy and program delivery is required.[2] As Aboriginal and Torres Strait Islander people engage in agreement making in Australia, the parties with whom they engage, particularly governments, are constructing by default the terms and conditions of a 'new deal' for the Indigenous sector.[3] Because negotiated agreements involve Indigenous peoples as consensual parties, rather than as 'stakeholders', the terms and conditions of their agreements are the building blocks of arrangements that are inherently more just than the imposed administrative solutions to which Aboriginal and Torres Strait Islander people have been subjected since colonisation. Moreover, as many of the chapters in this section demonstrate, these arrangements hold the potential to supersede the formal denial of Aboriginal and Torres Strait Islander group rights by Australian settler legal and political culture, and recognise Aboriginal polities as an integral part of the continuing nation-building dialectic.

---

[1] Aboriginal and Torres Strait Islander people are 2.4 per cent of the Australian population and currently own and manage an estimated 18 per cent of the land mass, or what might be termed the 'Indigenous estate'.

[2] Marcia Langton, 'A New Deal? Indigenous Development and the Politics of Recovery' (Speech delivered at the Dr Charles Perkins Memorial Oration, University of Sydney, 4 October 2002) 18.

[3] Ibid.

Good governance, and the importance of cultural autonomy and legitimacy in establishing capable governing institutions, is emerging as the key factor necessary for successful Indigenous economic development. On the basis of their research into sovereignty and nation-building among Indian tribal governments in the United States of America, Cornell and Kalt write that a nation's ability to deliver effective governance and economic development is the outcome of 'de facto' sovereignty: sovereignty in fact and practice.[4] 'Sovereignty', they conclude, 'is one of the primary development resources any tribe can have' and, in this sense, economic development on Indian reservations 'is first and foremost a political problem'.[5] Similarly in Australia, agreement-making processes which increase the effective exercise of sovereignty or jurisdiction by Aboriginal and Torres Strait Islander groups have the potential to both safeguard social and cultural rights and interests and deliver economic development, in many cases revitalising the rural and remote areas in which Aboriginal populations constitute significant majorities.

There is a wide range of agreements, covering an immense breadth and scope, between Indigenous groups and others in Australia today.[6] These include agreements relating to mineral resources, education and health service delivery, native title determinations, local government, arts and tourism, national parks and environmental management. However, as many of the chapters in this section demonstrate, while it is important to recognise and investigate this emerging trend toward agreement making, the mere fact of an agreement does not of itself guarantee equitable outcomes for Indigenous parties. Agreement making is a process, a relationship between two or more parties that rarely begins or ends with the signing of an actual agreement. Rather, the relationship between parties is subject to a broad spectrum of material, social, cultural and historical influences that impact upon, as much as they are limited by, the content of the agreement itself.

The chapters in this concluding section of *Honour Among Nations?* critically examine the emerging culture of agreement making in the areas of health, race relations, publishing and mining in Australia, and developments in oil and gas resource treaties along Australia's northern continental shelf.

---

[4]   Stephen Cornell and Joseph P. Kalt, 'Sovereignty and Nation Building: The Development Challenge in Indian Country Today' (PRS 98–25 Harvard Project on American Indian Economic Development, John F. Kennedy School of Government, Harvard University, 1988), 1, online at http://www.ksg.harvard.edu/hpaied/docs/PRS98-25.pdf at 20 July 2002.

[5]   Ibid, 30, 32.

[6]   Marcia Langton and Lisa Palmer, 'Modern Agreement Making and Indigenous People in Australia: Issues and Trends' (2003) 8 (1) *Australian Indigenous Law Reporter* 1–31.

By examining the historical trajectory of certain agreement-making trends and the recent outcomes of these processes for Aboriginal and Torres Strait Islander parties,the first four chapters of this section highlight some of the limits and possibilities of treaty and agreement making in Australia. While Anderson (Chapter 15) examines the relative success of strategic, process-oriented Health Framework Agreements for Aboriginal and Torres Strait Islander people, McGlade and Grossman (Chapters 16 and 17 respectively) conclude that agreement making has had faltering success with respect to the elimination of racial discrimination and protection of copyright, respectively. This, they find, is due largely to the cultural biases and entrenched racism that continue to permeate settler societies' responses to the recognition and protection of Indigenous rights and interests.

While many of the outcomes of agreement making are difficult or impossible to quantify, O'Faircheallaigh (Chapter 18) explores key research questions and ways of developing a methodology to evaluate agreement outcomes in the mining industry. O'Faircheallaigh argues that the now fashionable 'ideology of agreement making' in Australia needs to be tempered by an interrogation of the substantive outcomes of actual agreements, especially as this relates to issues of equity and sustainability.

Examining one particular instance of agreement making, in the final chapter Triggs (Chapter 19) stresses the potential of agreements to enable 'creative conflict resolution' over seemingly intractable issues. Triggs focuses on disputes over ownership of offshore oil and gas resources in the Timor Sea and the negotiation of the new Timor Sea Treaty between Australia and East Timor, and argues that the outcome of agreement making in this instance has been to the strategic advantage of both parties.

Modern agreement making between Indigenous peoples and others in Australia offers powerful possibilities for the recognition and protection of Indigenous rights and interests, and for the expansion of the Indigenous domain in social, political and economic terms. Colonial histories, continuing inequalities of power and the legacy of underdevelopment make this task both urgent and problematic.

Chapter 15

The Framework Agreements: Intergovernmental Agreements and Aboriginal and Torres Strait Islander Health

*Ian Anderson**

The health disadvantage experienced by Aboriginal and Torres Strait Islander peoples is well documented. It is perhaps most striking with respect to the relative differences in life expectancy. In 2001, the life expectancy for Aboriginal and Torres Strait Islander Australians was about twenty years less than for the total Australian population. The life expectancy of Aboriginal and Torres Strait Islander men was fifty-six years, compared with seventy-seven years for their non-Indigenous counterparts, and for Aboriginal and Torres Strait Islander women it was sixty-three years, compared with eighty-two years for all Australian women.[1] Relative to other Australians, Aboriginal and Torres Strait Islander people experience higher rates of mortality across all age groups.[2] In addition, Indigenous Australians encounter a significantly greater burden of illness.[3]

---

* The author would like to acknowledge the number of people who contributed to the developmeent of this chapter. Ms Haydie Gooder assisted by undertaking searches of the literature. Mr Robert Griew (Northern Territory Department of Health and Community Services), Ms Yael Cass and Mr Alan Thorpe (both Office for Aboriginal and Torres Strait Islander Health, Commonwealth Department of Health and Ageing) provided advice and critical insights that were invaluable to the development of this chapter. Core funds for the VicHealth Koori Health Research and Community Development Unit are provided by the Victorian Health Promotion Foundation and the Commonwealth Department of Health and Ageing.

[1] Australian Bureau of Statistics, *Deaths Australia 2001* (Australian Bureau of Statistics, Canberra, 2002) 7.

[2] Ibid, 21.

[3] See, for example, Australian Bureau of Statistics, *The Health and Welfare of Australia's*

Currently, national strategies to improve outcomes for Indigenous Australians have a dual focus on health-system reform and strategies that address the determinants of poor health through other sectors, such as housing, education and employment.[4] Recent health-sector reforms aim to improve Indigenous health outcomes through a mix of strategies that include reform of health financing and workforce development, building the capacity of the primary health care services, and improving the quality of research and health data systems.[5] In 1995, the Commonwealth health portfolio was given the mandate to take a lead role in the development of national strategy in Aboriginal health. Since that time, institutional mechanisms have been established to facilitate national collaborative processes in policy and planning.

In this chapter it is my intention to examine one recent health-sector initiative: the development of intergovernmental agreements, the Framework Agreements in Aboriginal and Torres Strait Islander health (Framework Agreements). The first round of Framework Agreements was signed between 1996 and 1999. They were, in fact, multi-sectoral agreements. As such, the signatories to these agreements include the Commonwealth Government, state and territory governments, the Aboriginal and Torres Strait Islander Commission (ATSIC) and the Aboriginal community controlled health sector. The exception to this was the Torres Strait Agreement (the last to be signed in the first round) whose signatories included Queensland and the Torres Strait Regional Authority (instead of ATSIC). With the exception of the Torres Strait Agreement, the initial round of Framework Agreements expired on 30 June 2000.[6]

The Framework Agreements commit signatories to four areas of co-operative action in Aboriginal and Torres Strait Islander health:

Aboriginal and Torres Strait Islander Peoples (Australian Bureau of Statistics, Canberra, 2003); Australian Institute of Health and Welfare (AIHW), *Health Expenditure Australia 2001–02: Expenditure Series No 17* (Australian Institute of Health and Welfare, Canberra, 2003).

4 See, for example, National Aboriginal and Torres Strait Islander Health Council (NATSIHC), *National Strategic Framework for Aboriginal and Torres Strait Islander Health: Framework for Action by Governments* (National Aboriginal and Torres Strait Islander Health Council, Canberra, 2003); National Aboriginal and Torres Strait Islander Health Council (NATSIHC), *National Strategic Framework for Aboriginal and Torres Strait Islander Health: Context* (National Aboriginal and Torres Strait Islander Health Council, Canberra, 2003).

5 Ian Anderson, 'Critical Issues in National Aboriginal Health Strategy: A Framework for Health Gain?' (Discussion Paper No 6, VicHealth Koori Health Research and Community Development Unit, University of Melbourne, 2002); Ian Anderson, Harriet Young, Milica Markivic and Lenore Manderson, 'Aboriginal Primary Health Care in Victoria: Issues for Policy and Regional Planning' (VicHealth Koori Health Research and Community Development Unit, Discussion paper no 1, February 2001); NATSIHC, above n 4.

6 Commonwealth Department of Health and Ageing (CDHA), EPU 'Health Strategy' (unpublished briefing, 2003).

- increasing the allocation of resources to reflect need
- joint planning processes—including regional planning and joint identi-fication of priorities to improve health services
- improving access to both mainstream and Aboriginal and Torres Strait Islander-specific health and health-related services
- improving data collection and evaluation.

At the August 1999 meeting of the Australian Health Ministers' Conference (AHMC), it was decided in principle to 'extend the Framework Agreements at the completion of the current three year term for a further period with the details of the new arrangements to be worked out and ratified.'[7] A second round of Framework Agreements has been signed in each juris-diction, the majority of which will continue to operate until at least June 2004. Of the nine second-round Framework Agreements, in four jurisdic-tions they will remain in operation until the parties terminate or vary the Framework Agreements, three expire in June 2004 and two expired in June 2003. Development of a third round of Framework Agreements has commenced.[8] It is likely, on this basis, that the Framework Agreements will continue to be key structural elements of the Aboriginal health landscape for the next few years.

In a federally structured health system such as Australia's, strate-gies to reform the health system require, at a minimum, the agreement of those stakeholders with responsibility for service development and delivery. Intergovernmental agreements, such as the Australian Health Care Agreements (AHCAs) or the Public Health Outcome Funding Agreements (PHOFAs) have been used as funding mechanisms and more strategically to guide reform. The purpose of this paper is to locate the Framework Agreements historically within the context of national strategies in Aboriginal health, and to characterise them relative to other intergovern-mental agreements in the health sector.

The Australian health system

The federal structure of the Australian health system is fundamental to its financing, program administration and service delivery. Financing of health

---

7   Aboriginal and Torres Strait Islander Commission, 'Health Memorandum of Understanding and Framework Agreement', in *Submission to the House of Representatives Standing Committee into the needs of Urban Dwelling Aboriginal and Torres Strait Islander Peoples*, Attachment F (Aboriginal and Torres Strait Islander Commission, 2000); http://www.atsic.gov.au/issues/inquiries/inquiry_urban_dwelling/urban_dwelling_submission/Sub_Urban_Dwelling_attachF.asp at 3 December 2003.
8   Personal communication with Yael Cass, September 2003.

care is a responsibility shared by Commonwealth, state and local governments and the private sector. For the 2001–02 financial year, total Australian health expenditure was $66.6 billion. Of this total, the Commonwealth Government provided $30.7 billion, states and local government $14.8 billion and the non-government sector (including the private sector and personal contributions) $21.0 billion.[9] While the Commonwealth has played a dominant role in health financing since the 1970s, its direct role in health program administration is quite marginal.[10] State and territory governments administer the majority of health programs, including hospital and public health programs. However, given the fact that the Commonwealth raises significantly more revenue than is required for its outlays, the Commonwealth funds the shortfall (including for health programs) to state and territory governments through two mechanisms: untied funding revenue raised by the Goods and Services Tax[11] and Specific Purpose Payments (in which expenditure is tied to agreed objectives or outcomes).[12]

Specific Purpose Payments, and their related intergovernmental agreements, have been a feature on the landscape of health financing in Australia since the late 1940s.[13] However, it was not until the introduction, in 1975, of the hospital funding agreements component of Medibank, Australia's

---

[9] AIHW, above n 3, 23.

[10] This dominant position had been established relatively slowly through the history of federation. At Federation the role of the Commonwealth was restricted to quarantine in the Australian *Constitution* while the states retained public responsibility for health services. Commonwealth legislation was passed in 1908 in line with the exclusive health power given to the Commonwealth for quarantine of diseases such as smallpox, plague, cholera, yellow fever, typhus and leprosy. A Constitutional amendment in 1946 gave the Commonwealth a new head of power in the area of 'pharmaceutical sickness and hospital benefits, medical and dental services', s 51(23A). This and s 96 of the *Constitution* enabled Commonwealth governments from the Chifley Labor government onwards to develop a greater role in health care. See Ian Anderson and Will Sanders, 'Aboriginal Health and Institutional Reform within Australian Federalism' (Discussion Paper No 117, Centre for Aboriginal Economic Policy Research, Australian National University, 1996); see also Jim Butler, 'Health Care' in Brian Galligan, Owen Hughes and Cliff Walsh (eds) *Intergovernmental Relations and Public Policy* (Allen & Unwin, North Sydney, 1991) 163–87. Until the 1970s, the growth of Commonwealth funding of health care was largely provided through subsidy schemes for medical services and pharmaceuticals. It did not result in significant intergovernmental activity, see Butler, 168.

[11] The funding provided by Goods and Services Tax (GST) revenue replaced an older, untied funding arrangement called Federal Assistance Grants to the States (FAGS) from 1 July 2001. Although growth in GST funding is expected, it is currently less than that previously provided through the FAGS. This shortfall is currently made up through Budget Balancing Assistance Grants; see Hal Swerrissen and Stephen Duckett, 'Health Policy and Financing' in Heather Gardner and Simon Barraclough (eds) *Health Policy in Australia* (Oxford University Press, South Melbourne, 2nd edn, 2002) 13–48.

[12] Ibid.

[13] Butler, above n 10, 163–87.

first national health insurance scheme, that intergovernmental agreements first came to play such a significant role in Australia's health financing.[14] Even though the relative contribution of Specific Purpose Payments to health-sector financing has fluctuated since this time, intergovernmental agreements continue to be a significant conduit for the funding of the hospital and public health sector.[15] As significantly, they have also been used as instruments through which Commonwealth and state/territory governments make agreements on health-policy objectives. They play an important role, in this respect, in providing for a national framework in the Australian health system.

Two significant examples of Specific Purpose Payments and intergovernmental agreements in health financing are the hospital funding agreements, previously known as the 'Medicare Agreements', and now known as the AHCAs and the PHOFAs. These are described in more detail below.

The AHCAs are the legal framework through which the Commonwealth has provided to state and territory governments approximately 50 per cent of public hospital expenditure since 1984.[16] Over the life of the 2003–08 AHCAs, the Commonwealth will provide $42 billion.[17] Signatories to the 1998–2003 AHCAs also agreed to key principles including the provision of public hospital services free of charge to public patients, access to public hospital services on the basis of clinical need and within a clinically appropriate period, and equity of access to public hospital services regardless of the geographical location of patients. These AHCA principles have a legislative basis in the *Health Care (Appropriation) Act 1998* (Cth).[18] The 1998–2003 AHCAs also provided specific funding (through the National Health Development Fund) to reform the public hospital system, and provided an additional $600 million over five years to support quality improvement and enhancement practices in public hospitals.[19] As an accountability measure, the Commonwealth and the states and territories were required under the

---

[14] Ibid, 168–9.

[15] Under the Fraser Coalition Government, funding provided for the hospital sector through these specific-purpose payments was shifted between 1981–82 to the untied funding stream, although it retained the label of identified health grants. This move was unwound with the development of the Medicare national health insurance scheme in 1984, see Butler, above n 10, 170–1.

[16] John Deeble 'Funding the Essentials: The Australian Health Care Agreements, 2003–2008' (2002) 25.6 *Australian Health Review* 1, 2.

[17] CDHA, *Australian Health Care Agreements 2003–2008* (Commonwealth Department of Health and Ageing, Canberra, 2003) http://www.health.gov.au/budget2003/fact/hfact2.htm at 3 December 2003.

[18] CDHA, Health Access and Financing Division, *Australian Health Care Agreements* (Commonwealth Department of Health and Ageing, Canberra, 2002) http://www.health.gov.au/haf/docs/hca/index.htm at 5 December 2003.

[19] Ibid.

1998–2003 AHCA to publish outcomes against agreed performance indicators in order to:

- stimulate improvement in service performance and health outcomes
- inform national and state and territory acute health policy development and, where possible, consumer decisions
- facilitate best practice service delivery.[20]

The PHOFAs were first established for the years 1997–98 to 1998–99. These agreements pooled specific-purpose funding previously provided through eight discrete public health programs (including the National Drug Strategy, National HIV/AIDS Strategy, National Immunisation Program, BreastScreen Australia, National Cervical Screening Program, National Women's Health Program, National Education Program on Female Genital Mutilation and Alternative Birthing Program).[21] Following the initial set of PHOFAs, a second round of agreements was established for the five years covering 1999–2000 to 2003–04. In 1999–2000 the Commonwealth provided approximately $177 million to the states/territories under the PHOFAs.[22] The key components of these pooled funding agreements include:

- agreement on the level and distribution of Commonwealth assistance provided through the broadbanded funding mechanism
- agreement on key principles, values and general processes to be pursued throughout the operation of the agreements
- agreement on performance indicators including outcome, impact and process measures for each of the programs for which Commonwealth funding has been provided
- the removal of nationally agreed input and process controls so that states and territories have the flexibility to use pooled Commonwealth/ state funds according to local needs and priorities in order to achieve the agreed targets and outcomes
- delineation of roles and responsibilities for each level of government in working towards the achievement of these national objectives.[23]

Both the AHCAs and the PHOFAs provide a structural framework that links the financing of health care to its program administration by state and territory governments. In both instances, program parameters and principles

[20] CDHA, Health Access and Financing Division, *The Australian Health Care Agreements Annual Performance Report 1998–1999* (Commonwealth Department of Health and Ageing, Canberra, 2002) http://www.health.gov.au/haf/docs/hca/ahcarpt98.htm at 5 December 2003.
[21] CDHA, Population Health Division, *Public Health Funding Agreements* (Commonwealth Department of Health and Ageing, Canberra, 2002) http://www.health.gov.au/pubhlth/about/phofa/phofa.htm at 5 December 2003.
[22] Ibid.
[23] Ibid.

and outcome measures were agreed in order to establish an institutional framework for health-sector reform. Later in this chapter, I consider the Framework Agreements in greater detail in order to characterise them relative to health agreements such as the AHCAs and the PHOFAs. Before doing so, I explore further the historical context of their development.

Developing a Commonwealth program for Aboriginal health

Australia did not begin to develop a national program for Aboriginal health until the 1967 national referendum resulted in the removal of the constitutional barriers to Commonwealth involvement in Aboriginal affairs. Until this time, the Commonwealth had been constrained from developing national programs for Indigenous Australians by specific race clauses in the Australian *Constitution*.[24] Following the 1967 referendum, the Commonwealth established an Office for Aboriginal Affairs. Health was identified as a priority by this new Office, which subsequently provided Specific Purpose Grants to the states for the development of Aboriginal health programs.[25]

Around the same time, Aboriginal communities began to mobilise politically on health issues, and to establish community controlled health services, initially in urban communities such as Redfern in Sydney and Fitzroy in Melbourne. While the original community controlled services had been established on a voluntary basis, the Commonwealth began to fund them to provide health services from 1970–71.[26] In the decades that followed, the number of Aboriginal Community Controlled Health Services (ACCHS) across Australia grew significantly, as did their scope and the sophistication of their service provision. By the financial year 1998–99 the Commonwealth funded 113 ACCHS across Australia.[27] Typically, ACCHS have an Aboriginal board of directors elected from the local Aboriginal community, and provide a range of primary health care services (depending

---

[24] The original Australian *Constitution* contained two specific references to Aboriginal people. Section 51(xxvi) stated 'the Parliament shall subject to this Constitution, have power to make laws for the peace, order, and good government of the Commonwealth with respect to the people of any race, other than the Aboriginal race in any State, for whom it is deemed necessary to make special laws.' In s127 the following clause was included 'in reckoning the number of people of the Commonwealth, or of a State or other part the Commonwealth, aboriginal natives shall not be counted.' The 1967 referendum resulted in the amendment of s51(xxvi) to allow the Commonwealth to make laws for Aboriginal people, and the repeal of s127.

[25] Australian Indigenous Health InfoNet, *Major Developments in National Indigenous Health Policy, 1967–1999* http://www.healthinfonet.ecu.edu.au at 5 December 2003.

[26] Anderson and Sanders, above n 10.

[27] CDHA, *Service Activity Reporting 1998–99* (Commonwealth Department of Health and Ageing, Canberra, 2001).

on needs and available resources) which include general practice care, and programs in maternal and child health, emotional and social well-being, health promotion, dental care and welfare support.[28]

Even though the initial Commonwealth investment in Aboriginal health was made through Specific Purpose Payments to state and territory governments, over the subsequent decades the ACCHS progressively received a higher proportion of funding, while direct Commonwealth support for state programs declined.[29]

Today, the ACCHS are a very significant provider of primary health care to Aboriginal Australians, and Aboriginal communities have established a stake in the health-care debate both as recipients of health care and as service providers. Significantly, the ACCHS represent one of the few instances in which the Commonwealth plays a direct role in health program administration. However, Aboriginal and Torres Strait Islander Australians also access health care from other primary health care providers such as general practitioners in private practice, community health centres and state or territory funded primary care clinics. Aboriginal and Torres Strait Islander people also access non-primary care 'mainstream' health services such as acute hospital care and related hospital outpatients' services. Funding of the health services used by Aboriginal and Torres Strait Islander people includes a mix of Indigenous-specific and mainstream funding mechanisms.

Strategies to reform the provision of health care need to take account of the fact that Australian governments have a shared responsibility for the provision and funding of Aboriginal health care services, even though they may play different roles. Additionally, it needs to be recognised that the Aboriginal community controlled health sector is also a significant stakeholder in the provision of services. Accordingly, national strategies that aim to reform the effectiveness or appropriateness of the Australian health system will require co-ordination and agreement between the different levels of government and the Aboriginal community sector. The first attempt to develop such a national approach came with the release of the National Aboriginal Health Strategy in 1989.

Developing national strategies in Aboriginal health

The final report of the National Aboriginal Health Strategy Working Party, *A National Aboriginal Health Strategy* (NAHS), was presented to a Joint Ministerial

---

[28] See, for example, Sophia Couzos and Richard Murray, *Aboriginal Primary Health Care: An Evidenced Based Approach* (Oxford University Press, Melbourne, 1999).

[29] In 1970–71, states received $0.64 million in grants while ACCHS received $0.04 million (3 per cent of total). However, by 1994–95, states grants were $1.11 million, while ACCHS received $68.06 million (98 per cent of total), see Anderson and Sanders, above n 10.

Forum of Commonwealth and state/territory ministers in Aboriginal Affairs and Health in 1989.[30] It was the first national health strategy that had been developed with the input of the Aboriginal community controlled sector and endorsed by Commonwealth and state and territory levels of government.[31] The NAHS provided a comprehensive approach to Aboriginal health gain, giving priority to reforms such as developing Aboriginal community control of health services, increasing Aboriginal and Torres Strait Islander participation in the health workforce, reforming mainstream health services and increasing funding to Aboriginal and Torres Strait Islander health services.

The Joint Ministerial Forum subsequently established the Aboriginal Health Development Group (AHDG), a group of Commonwealth, state and territory government representatives to develop an implementation plan for the NAHS.[32] The AHDG in turn recommended a number of institutional reforms, including the establishment of state/territory tripartite forums that represented the Aboriginal community controlled health sector, the Commonwealth Government and the relevant state or territory government. A national policy mechanism structured along similar tripartite lines, the Council of Aboriginal Health, was also recommended. The AHDG also recommended the creation of a specialised health branch, the Office of Aboriginal Health, within ATSIC, and the provision of funding for a national Aboriginal community controlled health organisation.[33] The Commonwealth Ministers within the Joint Ministerial Forum subsequently submitted the NAHS to Cabinet for a formal Commonwealth response.[34]

The Commonwealth Cabinet responded by appropriating $232.25 million (over five years) to support the implementation of the NAHS. Of this total, $171.1 million was allocated for housing and infrastructure, $46.95 million for health services, $6.30 million to ATSIC for running costs,

---

[30] Ian Anderson 'The National Aboriginal Health Strategy' in Heather Gardner (ed.), *Health Policy in Australia* (Oxford University Press, Melbourne, 1997) 119–35.

[31] One of the first actions of the Aboriginal Health Branch established in 1973 in the Commonwealth Department of Health, was to propose a Ten Year Plan for Aboriginal Health; see Australian Indigenous Health InfoNet, above n 25; see also John Gardiner-Garden, 'Innovation Without Change? Commonwealth Involvement in Aboriginal Health Policy' (Current Issues Brief No 12, Parliamentary Research Service, Canberra, 1994). This plan was, however, in essence a Commonwealth plan, rather than a national strategy that had been negotiated with state or territory governments and other relevant stakeholders.

[32] National Aboriginal Health Strategy Evaluation Committee (NAHSEC), *National Aboriginal Health Strategy: An Evaluation* (Aboriginal and Torres Strait Islander Commission, Canberra, 1994); Anderson, 'The National Aboriginal Health Strategy', above n 30; Gardiner-Garden, above n 31. Community representation on this forum was included later, with one member, Ms Naomi Mayers from Redfern AMS in Sydney, appointed to chair the AHDG.

[33] Mike Codd, *Developing a Partnership: A Review of the Council for Aboriginal Health* (Council for Aboriginal Health Review Team, Canberra, 1993).

[34] Anderson, 'The National Aboriginal Health Strategy', above n 30.

$7.3 million to the National Campaign Against Drug Abuse and $0.6 million to the Australian Institute of Health.[35] It was intended that these funds would also be used to lever, through intergovernmental agreements, additional resources from state and territory governments to support the implementation of the NAHS. The newly established ATSIC was the Commonwealth agency leading these negotiations. However, the first round of intergovernmental agreements was never completed, with only interim funding agreements being agreed for the 1991–92 financial year. The Commonwealth NAHS program investment was subsequently allocated to ACCHS through ATSIC regional councils.[36]

When the implementation of the NAHS strategy was evaluated after five years, it was bluntly reported that the 'National Aboriginal Health Strategy was never effectively implemented'.[37] Following this review, the responsibility for administration of the national Aboriginal health program was shifted from ATSIC to the Commonwealth health portfolio. With the Commonwealth health portfolio taking a lead role, the negotiations that led to the establishment of the Framework Agreements were commenced not long after this transfer took effect. However, before I consider this next phase in the development of intergovernmental agreements in Aboriginal health, I want to take a brief detour to consider in greater detail the historical development of planning mechanisms in health that included Aboriginal and Torres Straits Islander peoples.

Aboriginal participation in health planning and policy development

The first national advisory structure in Aboriginal health, the Council of Aboriginal Health, was established in 1992. Prior to this, a number of state governments had already established processes to enable Aboriginal people and representatives of ACCHS to have input into health policy development.[38] One of the earliest of these forums, for example, was the Victorian Aboriginal Health Resources Consultative Group, which had been established in 1981 with representation from those Aboriginal organisations delivering health

---

[35] An additional Commonwealth appropriation was made in the context of the 1994–95 budget for additional funding through to the 1998–99 financial year of $499.3 million in total which included $161.8 million for health and $337.5 million for community housing and infrastructure; see NAHSEC, *National Aboriginal Health Strategy: An Evaluation*, above n 32, 19; see also Australian Indigenous Health Infonet, above n 25.

[36] NAHSEC, above n 32, 28.

[37] Ibid, 3.

[38] Ian Anderson, 'Aboriginal Australians, Governments and Participation in Health Systems' in Pranee Liamputtong and Heather Gardner (eds), *Health, Social Change and Communities* (Oxford University Press, South Melbourne, 2003), 224, 235.

programs in their community, the Department of Aboriginal Affairs and the Victorian Health Department.[39] Commonwealth governments had previously established national consultative mechanisms in Aboriginal affairs, such as the National Aboriginal Consultative Committee and its successor, the National Aboriginal Conference.[40] With the creation of ATSIC in 1989, Indigenous policy advice was integrated with program management. This new statutory authority bundled together existing Commonwealth programs in Aboriginal affairs with a participatory structure that included Regional Councils, elected by Aboriginal and Torres Strait Islander people and a Board of Commissioners, elected by ATSIC Regional Councillors.[41] Yet, despite the willingness of the Commonwealth to establish more generic advisory structures in Aboriginal affairs, and the recommendations of the AHDG, the development of participatory policy mechanisms that were specific to health were neglected until 1992, when the Council of Aboriginal Health was created. However, the Council of Aboriginal Health only met four times until October 1993, when the decision was taken to review it.

Following the transfer of administrative responsibility for the Commonwealth Aboriginal health program in 1995, the Commonwealth Department of Health and Human Services, through its Office of Aboriginal and Torres Strait Islander Health Services, established the National Aboriginal and Torres Strait Islander Health Council (NATSIHC) in June 1996. Its membership consisted of eight National Aboriginal Community Controlled Health Organisation (NACCHO) representatives, three ATSIC representatives and representatives of the Torres Strait Regional Authority, the Australian Medical Association and the National Health and Medical Research Council.[42] Despite a brief hiatus that resulted from a political dispute between NACCHO and the Commonwealth Department of Health, and some changes in the structure of representation at Council, NATSIHC continues to function as a participatory policy process.[43]

There had been more success under the NAHS in establishing the recommended tripartite forums at a state and territory level. These jurisdictional

---

[39] Ian Anderson, *Koorie Health in Koorie Hands: An Orientation Manual in Aboriginal Health for Health Care Providers* (Health Department of Victoria, Melbourne, 1988) 123.

[40] With members elected by Aboriginal people in all states and territories, the brief of this committee was to provide advice to the Commonwealth on both issues to do with access to goods and services and 'territory' and 'autonomy'; see Barry Smith, 'Commonwealth/ State Relations: Some Historical Background' (Occasional Paper No 6, Australian Institute of Aboriginal and Torres Strait Islander Studies, Canberra, 1996) 16.

[41] Ibid, 22.

[42] Anderson and Sanders, above n 10, 16.

[43] Robert Griew, B. Sibthorpe, Ian Anderson, Sandra Eades and T. Wilkes, '"On Our Terms": The Politics of Aboriginal Health in Australia' in Judith Healy and Martin McKee (eds) *Accessing Health Care—Responding to Diversity* (Oxford University Press, Oxford, in-press).

forums were established to oversee the implementation of the NAHS representing the Commonwealth, state/territory governments and the Aboriginal community sector. While these jurisdictional tripartite forums had substantially greater longevity than the Council of Aboriginal Health, their role was, to some extent, undermined by the unanticipated creation of ATSIC.[44] As the Commonwealth resources for the implementation of the NAHS became absorbed through the resource allocation processes established under ATSIC, the already tenuous link between the tripartite forums and resource allocation was in effect severed. This significantly limited the role of the forums and created a context in which the tripartite processes were in effect partially duplicating the ATSIC Regional Council and Commission processes.[45]

The Framework Agreements

The negotiations that led to the development of the initial round of Framework Agreements were aligned with the National Commitment to Improved Outcomes in the Delivery of Programs and Services for Aboriginal peoples and Torres Strait Islanders (National Commitment), which had been endorsed by the Council of Australian Governments in December 1992.[46] The National Commitment outlined a multilateral, co-operative framework for Aboriginal service development that recognises that 'the planning and provision of government programs and services to Aboriginal peoples and Torres Strait Islanders is a shared responsibility and a legitimate policy interest of all spheres of government.'[47] The National Commitment also recognised that, with respect to service delivery, there was 'a preferred role of Aboriginal and Torres Strait Islander organisations in the delivery of programs and services.'[48] Consequently, the National Commitment also established, as a principle:

> the need to negotiate with and maximise participation by Aboriginal peoples and Torres Strait Islanders through their representative bodies, including the Aboriginal and Torres Strait Islander Commission, Regional Councils, state and Territory advisory bodies and community-based organisations in the formulation of policies and programs that affect them.[49]

---

[44] Anderson, 'The National Aboriginal Health Strategy', above n 30.

[45] Ibid.

[46] Anderson and Sanders, above n 10; Council of Australian Governments (COAG), *National Commitment to Improved Outcomes in the Delivery of Programs and Services for Aboriginal Peoples and Torres Strait Islanders* (Australian Local Government Association, Canberra, 1992) http://www.alga.asn.au/policy/indigenous/nationalCommitment.php at 5 December 2003; Smith, above n 40, 23.

[47] COAG, above n 46, para 2.1b.

[48] Ibid, para 6.15.

[49] Ibid, 4.3.

The content of the Framework Agreements varied a little between jurisdictions and between the first and second round of agreements. However,
these variations were relatively minor and the agreements have, on balance,
remained quite consistent and so are represented here by reference to the
South Australia Framework Agreement, signed 1 August 2001. The content
of this agreement is divided into six main sections: statement of intent;
aims and outcomes; roles and responsibilities; intersectoral collaboration;
reporting and monitoring arrangments; and duration of agreement.

In the South Australia Agreement, the 'Statement of Intent' situ-
ated the Framework Agreement in its broader policy context, linking it to
important underpinning strategies, such as the revised NAHS (see below),
the Royal Commission into Aboriginal Deaths in Custody and Regional
Plans developed by the Joint Planning Forums (established under the first
round of the Framework Agreements). The aims of the South Australian
Framework Agreement include:

- Improving access to both mainstream and Aboriginal and Torres Strait
  Islander specific health and health-related programs which reflect the
  level of need.
- Increasing the level of resources allocated to reflect the higher level of
  need of Aboriginal and Torres Strait Islander peoples, including within
  mainstream services, and transparent and regular reporting for all services and programs.
- Joint planning processes, which will inform the allocation of resources
  and allow for:
    - full and formal Aboriginal and Torres Strait Islander participation in
      decision making and determination of priorities
    - improved co-operation and co-ordination of current service delivery,
      both Aboriginal and Torres Strait Islander-specific services and main-
      stream services, by all spheres of government
    - increased clarity with respect to the roles and responsibilities of the
      key stakeholders.
- Promoting greater accountability in relation to outcomes in Aboriginal
  health and well-being across all Commonwealth and state govern-
  ment-funded organisations.
- The development of a co-ordinated approach to the collection and use
  of data.[50]

---

[50] State of South Australia, Commonwealth of Australia, Aboriginal and Torres Strait Islander
Commission and Aboriginal Health Council of South Australia, *Agreement on Aboriginal and
Torres Strait Islander Health* (Commonwealth Department of Health and Ageing, Canberra,
2001).

The accountability requirements and processes required under the Framework Agreements are broadly similar to those of other current inter-governmental agreements in the health sector. State and Commonwealth signatories are required to report on progress in implementing commitments under the Framework Agreement and action plan at each Australian Health Ministers' Conference. The 2001 South Australian agreement specifies, for instance, that such reporting should include, at a minimum:

- funding for community controlled health services
- improved outcomes for mainstream services
- linkages between community controlled and mainstream services, including innovation in co-ordinated care.[51]

The agreement to report against national performance indicators for Aboriginal and Torres Strait Islander health aligns the accountability processes associated with the Framework Agreement with the reporting requirements of the AHCAs and the PHOFAs, which require reporting against a set of agreed output and outcome measures.

When the South Australian Framework Agreement was signed, NATSIHC had commenced a process to revise the NAHS. This process stalled when the NACCHO Annual General Meeting of December 2000 resolved that the NACCHO representatives on the NATSIHC would pull out of the Council in protest over the approach taken in the review.[52] Following further negotiations, it was agreed that the NAHS would not be revised per se, but a National Strategic Framework for Aboriginal and Torres Strait Islander Health would be produced that was aligned with the original NAHS. The National Strategic Framework was developed with the Framework Agreement parties, but was framed as a plan for action by governments. It received whole-of-government endorsement at the Commonwealth and state/territory level over early 2003, and was signed by all health ministers in July 2003. The National Strategic Framework provides a more detailed set of strategies that flesh out the actions agreed to within the Framework Agreements.[53] It provides for an annual reporting process (specific to

---

[51] Ibid.

[52] National Aboriginal Community Controlled Health Organisation, 'Peak Aboriginal Health Body Pulls Out of Government Advisory Group in Protest' (Press Release, 8 December 2000).

[53] The overarching goal for the National Strategic Framework is to ensure that Aboriginal and Torres Strait Islander peoples enjoy a healthy life equal to that of the general population that is enriched by a strong living culture, dignity and justice. Its aims (in summary) are to:
  – increase life expectancy to a level comparable with non-Indigenous Australians
  – decrease mortality rates in the first year of life and decrease infant morbidity by reducing relative deprivation and improving well-being and quality of life

health portfolio activity), biennial reporting (encompassing whole-of-government activity) and an independent evaluation process overseen by the NATSIHC.

In addition to the development of the National Strategic Framework, there have been a number of other significant developments in Aboriginal and Torres Strait Islander health strategy that have occurred during the life of the first and second round of Framework Agreements. Significantly, these developments are consistent with, and elaborate, the priorities of these agreements. These include:

- The development of national performance indicators in Aboriginal and Torres Strait Islander health. In August 1997, the AHMC endorsed, subject to further refinement, a set of national indicators and targets against which governments were required to report in order to monitor performance in Aboriginal and Torres Strait Islander health. Following further work, the Australian Health Ministers' Advisory Council (AHMAC) agreed to a refined set of performance indicators in October 2000 to be used for reporting from 2001 onwards.[54]
- The development of a new Commonwealth funding program, the Primary Health Care Access Program (PHCAP), that aims to improve access to, and provision of, appropriate primary health care services for Aboriginal and Torres Strait Islander peoples, and to establish a framework for the expansion of comprehensive primary health care services. Funding for this program has been preferentially allocated to priorities identified through the regional planning processes established under the Framework Agreements.[55]
- The agreement by AHMAC in October 1997 to the National Indigenous Health Information Plan. The National Health and Medical Research Council also initiated the development of the NHMRC Road Map: A Strategic Framework for Improving Aboriginal and Torres Strait Islander

---

- decrease all-causes mortality rates across all ages
- strengthen the service infrastructure essential to improving access by Aboriginal and Torres Strait Islander peoples to health services and responding to:
  - chronic disease
  - communicable disease
  - substance misuse, mental disorder, stress, trauma and suicide
  - injury and poisoning
  - family violence, including child abuse and sexual assault
  - child and maternal health and male health.

[54] National Health Information Management Group (NHIMG) *National Summary of the 2000 Jurisdictional Reports Against the Aboriginal and Torres Strait Islander Health Performance Indicators*, AIHW cat. No. IHW 10 (Australian Institute of Health and Welfare, Canberra, 2003).

[55] Anderson, 'Critical Issues in National Aboriginal Health Strategy', above n 5.

Health Through Research.[56] Both these initiatives aimed to refocus research and data systems in order to enhance the evidence available to policy makers and practitioners in the field of Aboriginal health.

■ The agreement by AHMAC to an Aboriginal and Torres Strait Islander Health Workforce National Strategic Framework in 2002.[57]

This list does not exhaust the institutional reform strategies that are relevant to the Framework Agreements, but it illustrates the range of processes and outcomes for which the Framework Agreements provide a context. Further to this, the Framework Agreements articulate with broader health strategy through their links with other intergovernmental agreements. For example, in the 2003–08 AHCAs the implementation of the Framework Agreements was supported through principles articulated in the AHCAs. For example, in the New South Wales AHCA it was agreed that:

> The Commonwealth and New South Wales will implement this Agreement consistent with the principles outlined in: (a) the agreement on Aboriginal and Torres Strait Islander Health (Framework Agreement); (b) the National Aboriginal and Torres Strait Islander Health Information Plan; and (c) the National Strategic Framework for Aboriginal and Torres Strait Islander Health as endorsed by state governments.[58]

The PHOFAs likewise refer to the Framework Agreements and the National Performance Indicators in Aboriginal and Torres Strait Islander Health; for example:

---

[56] Aboriginal and Torres Strait Islander Research Agenda Working Group, *The NHMRC Road Map: A Strategic Framework for Improving Aboriginal and Torres Strait Islander Health Through Research* (National Health and Medical Research Council, Canberra, 2002).

[57] This national strategic framework proposes five key objectives:
1. increase the number of Aboriginal and Torres Strait Islander people working across all the health professions
2. improve the clarity of roles, regulation and recognition of Aboriginal and Torres Strait Islander health workers as a key component of the health workforce, and improve vocational education and training sector support for Aboriginal and Torres Strait Islander health workers
3. address the role and development needs of other health workforce groups contributing to Aboriginal and Torres Strait Islander health
4. improve the effectiveness of training, recruitment and retention measures targeting both non-Indigenous Australian and Indigenous Australian health staff working within Aboriginal primary health services
5. include clear accountability for government programs to quantify and achieve these objectives, and support for Aboriginal and Torres Strait Islander organisations and people to drive the process. See House of Representatives Standing Committee on Aboriginal and Torres Strait Islander Health, Commonwealth of Australia, *Aboriginal and Torres Strait Islander Health Workforce National Strategic Framework* (2002).

[58] Commonwealth of Australia and State of New South Wales, *Australian Health Care Agreement 2003-08* (Commonwealth Department of Health and Ageing, Canberra, 2003), para 15, at http://www.health.gov.au/oatsih/pubs/pdf/health_eval/health_eval_execsum.pdf.

The specific performance indicators in Schedule 5 are drawn from the National Performance Indicators and Targets and were developed in order to actively support other commitments of the Commonwealth and States and Territories in relation to the needs of Aboriginal and Torres Strait Islander peoples.[59]

The key purpose of the Framework Agreements is to provide an institutional framework that draws together governmental and Aboriginal community sector stakeholders by establishing the key priorities for reform within the health sector and providing agreed mechanisms and process (the joint planning forums) through which agreed strategies can be collaboratively planned, implemented and monitored. They outline key reform strategies—but do not provide detail on how these strategies are to be implemented. Consequently, the link between the Framework Agreements and those related strategies (such as the National Strategic Framework, the National Health Information Plan, the National Performance Indicators in Aboriginal and Torres Strait Islander Health etc.) are critical. Furthermore, the horizontal linkage between the Framework Agreements and other intergovernmental agreements in the health sector has the potential to reinforce the implementation of these agreements particularly with the 'mainstream' components of the health sector.

The Framework Agreements in this context are strategic agreements. However, they are limited by the extent to which they are focused on health-sector reform. They do not provide a structural mechanism that could draw together agreement-making processes with other sectors. Given the dual focus in national strategy on improving Indigenous health outcomes through action both within the health sector, and through other sectors such as housing, education and economic development, it is important that consideration be given to the development of mechanisms and processes to strengthen whole-of-government decision making.

One of the key differences between the Framework Agreements and other intergovernmental agreements in the health sector is the extent to which they are tied to health-financing mechanisms. The Framework Agreements began as essentially strategic agreements with no funding tied to them. Without direct funding the Framework Agreements also lack the necessary legislative framework required for money appropriations. The specific legislation that framed the 1998–2002 AHCAs was, as mentioned above, the *Health Care (Appropriation) Act 1998* (Cth). Without being tied to a particular appropriation of money, the Framework Agreements *per se*

---

[59] Commonwealth of Australia and State of Victoria, *Victorian Public Health Outcome Funding Agreement 1990/00–2003/2004* (Commonwealth Department of Health and Ageing, Canberra), 142, at http://www.health.gov.au/pubhlth/about/phofa/agreements/0004/vic.pdf.

do not attract the degree of central agency (Prime Minister and Cabinet, Treasury and Department of Finance) oversight that occurs with the large intergovernmental funding agreements such as the AHCAs. As another consequence of fiscal size, the AHCAs are included in the Commonwealth Grants Commission's formulae for calculating the relative distribution of Commonwealth funds to state and territory governments. As essentially an un-funded agreement, this is not necessary for the Framework Agreements. Notwithstanding, the Framework Agreements articulate and integrate with a number of national policy processes that have been developed by the AHMC, such as the development of the national performance indicators for Aboriginal and Torres Strait Islander health (from 1998) and the development of the National Health Information Plan (from 1997).

While it is true that the Framework Agreements are not directly attached to a particular funding program, Commonwealth funding provided through the PHCAP was distributed on the condition of completed regional plans, against priorities identified in those plans. Although the PHCAP funding program addresses some, but not all, of the priorities laid out in the Framework Agreements, it has been used in a way to leverage or stimulate action between the different sectoral interests engaged with these Agreements. It is this emphasis on joint planning processes that is another distinguishing feature of these agreements.

One significant difference between the Framework Agreements and other health-sector agreements is in the social and political context in which they are implemented. The AHCAs and the PHOFAs are primarily focused on intergovernmental relations. They do, of course, sit in a social context which has a range of provider and consumer interests. The medical profession, and medical professional bodies, are engaged in the debate on public hospital funding and routinely provide commentary that reflect their interests in the AHCAs. The PHOFAs also attract a range of professional and community stakeholders who are engaged in policy debates about funding process and reform priorities. The PHOFAs include funding for state-based HIV/AIDs programs, and there is a vibrant and engaged community sector in this field. Only the Framework Agreements, however, attempt to directly engage Aboriginal community stakeholders in the agreement-making process. This reflects the priority in national strategy on establishing partnerships with the Aboriginal community sector. It possibly also reflects the degree to which Aboriginal interests have been marginalised from health-policy structures and processes.

Ultimately, one of the fundamental achievements of the Framework Agreements is that they have set the foundation for structured and formal partnership arrangements, at the national and state/territory levels. Co-ordination of planning, priority setting for resource allocation, program development and monitoring is essential in Aboriginal and Torres Strait Islander health. The Framework Agreements have formalised these partnership arrangements so that co-ordination of effort is less vulnerable to changing political agendas and the personal commitment of key stakeholders. At the national level the NATSIHC meets quarterly and all the stakeholders must 'eye ball' each other and account for their collective efforts and roles and responsibilities to improve Aboriginal and Torres Strait Islander health.

At the state and territory level, the Health Forums also meet quarterly. They are accountable to AHMAC for action taken to implement the Framework Agreements. In some states these forums have been resourced with independent secretariats to take on joint policy development and planning, and have set a precedent for Commonwealth, state and community sector collaboration.

The key issue is to keep these partnership arrangements vibrant and productive. If they become token arrangements, then the Framework Agreements are not worth the paper they are written on. The Framework Agreements, in this sense, are an innovation in Aboriginal health strategy that attempt to engage the challenges of health reform in a federal system in addition to the challenges of developing working collaborations between the government sector in health and Aboriginal community structures and processes. Like other agreements in the health sector, they have a clearly developed strategic role. The link between the Framework Agreements and health funding mechanisms is, however, less direct than is the case for other intergovernmental agreements such as the AHCAs and the PHOFAs. While it is not possible, at this stage, to predetermine their impact on institutional reform, it is clear that they represent a significant advance on the unco-ordinated approaches to Aboriginal health reform that have characterised past approaches to this significant health challenge.

The most significant structural difference between the Framework Agreements and other intergovernmental agreements in this sector is their multi-party basis. The inclusion of the Aboriginal and Torres Strait Islander Commission and the peak bodies representing Aboriginal community controlled sectors marks them apart from the other, bilateral, intergovernmental agreements in health.

Chapter 16

Race Discrimination in Australia: A Challenge for Treaty Settlement?

Hannah McGlade

Introduction

The call for a treaty by Indigenous Australians, highlighted by the work of the Aboriginal and Torres Strait Islander Commission (ATSIC) and the Council for Aboriginal Reconciliation (CAR), is driven by the wrongful dispossession by British colonialists in 1788 of the lands of the many nations of Aboriginal and Torres Strait Islanders. This wrongful dispossession was upheld by the Australian legal system for over 200 years on the basis of the legal doctrine of terra nullius. Lands that were truly empty and unoccupied could properly, under international law,[1] be acquired by colonising powers on the basis of *terra nullius*, but the lands of Indigenous peoples could not properly be claimed in such a manner.[2] Although this doctrine was expanded to justify the theft of the lands of Indigenous Australian peoples, it was firmly rejected by the International Court of Justice in the 1975 *Western Sahara* case.[3] *Terra nullius* was subsequently rejected by the High Court of Australia in the 1992 case of *Mabo v Queensland [No 2] ('Mabo')*.[4]

Despite this rejection of *terra nullius* by the judicial orders in *Mabo*, this chapter shows, and my experience as a Nyungar person confirms, that the discrimination underpinning Aboriginal and Torres Strait Islander peoples' dispossession remains. Even the recognition of native title by Australian common law allows for the 'extinguishment' of our title, requires onerous

---

[1] *Mabo v Queensland [No 2]* (1992) 175 CLR 1, 32 (Brennan J) (*'Mabo'*).
[2] Ibid, 40, 42.
[3] *Western Sahara* [1975] ICJ Rep 3.
[4] *Mabo* (1992) 175 CLR 1, 42 (Brennan J).

proof of connection to our own lands and fails to recognise our traditional laws and customs in their own right. It is not an equitable response to the 1788 wrongful dispossession. Many Indigenous and non-Indigenous Australians believe that true justice will occur only with the negotiation of a treaty founded on the consent of Aboriginal and Torres Strait Islander peoples.

Historical background

The prohibition of race discrimination under Australian law must be central to treaty negotiations. *Terra nullius* is an extreme example of racial discrimination which has wrought devastating trauma upon generations of colonised Indigenous Australian peoples. It was the act of colonisation based on racial discrimination that allowed for continuing legalised forms of discrimination that dramatically impacted upon the lives of all Aboriginal people. The operation of the *Aborigines Act 1905* of Western Australia permitted the removal of Aboriginal children from their families and the cruelty of their lives in so-called 'humanitarian' institutions.[5] It was this same legislation which legalised the indenturing (or forced slavery) of men, women and children to white farmers, pastoralists and pearlers, and which established the apartheid-like reserve system, encouraging police surveillance over the lives of hard-working, decent people. Of course, Aboriginal people in Western Australia, like in most other states, did not have basic citizenship rights accorded to them. They could apply for such rights if they could prove that they had adopted the ways of 'the civilised race'.[6] This is not ancient history—it is the story of my grandfather and great-grandmother.

1967 Constitutional reform

There is some misconception that Aboriginal and Torres Strait Islander peoples gained citizenship as a result of the 1967 constitutional referendum. What the referendum actually did was to alter the 'races power' of s 51 (xxvi) of the *Australian Constitution (Constitution)*[7] to give the Commonwealth the power to make laws for people of any race including the 'Aboriginal

---

[5] Exemplified dramatically in the recent film *Rabbit Proof Fence*, directed by Phillip Noyce, Miramax Films (2002).

[6] See also Evans, this volume.

[7] s 51(xxvi) of the *Constitution* originally read: 'The Parliament shall, subject to this Constitution, have power to make laws for the peace, order and good government of the Commonwealth with respect to the people of any race, other than aboriginal people, for whom it is necessary to make special laws.' The words 'other than aboriginal people' were removed.

people'.[8] It also removed a constitutional provision which provided that the 'Aboriginal people' were not to be counted in the national census.[9] The referendum did not remove s 25 of the *Constitution*, which allows for persons to be disqualified from voting on the basis of race.[10] The 1967 referendum stands as the most successful Australian referendum and can be seen as an overwhelming rejection of discrimination against Indigenous Australian people. Interestingly, the referendum was held shortly after the signing of the *International Convention on the Elimination of All Forms of Racial Discrimination (ICERD)*[11] by the Australian Government in 1966—an event which may have influenced voters.

Interpreting the effect of the change to s 51 (xxvi) in the *Hindmarsh Island Bridge Case*,[12] Kirby J was the only High Court Justice prepared to give effect to the intention of the voters of the 1967 referendum, and to ascribe the 'races power' with what was obviously a beneficial intention.[13] At this moment in Australian legal history, it is entirely unclear whether or not the *Constitution* allows for laws against a race of people that may be adverse or discriminatory in their impact or intent. According to international human rights expert Professor Hilary Charlesworth, this decision means that 'the text of the *Constitution* apparently reveals no "overarching reason" to prevent a government from legislating to establish a system of racial discrimination, or indeed from systematically violating any human right.'[14]

Bill of rights

Australia now stands alone among settler common law countries in its failure to introduce a Bill of Rights that would entrench the prohibition of

---

[8] Discussed in Bain Attwood and Andrew Marcus, *The 1967 Referendum, or When Aborigines Didn't Get the Vote* (Aboriginal Studies Press, Canberra, 1997).

[9] *Constitution* s127, which originally read: 'In reckoning the number of people of the Commonwealth, or of a State or other part of the Commonwealth, aboriginal natives should not be counted'.

[10] Discussed in Council for Aboriginal Reconciliation (CAR), *Reconciliation: Australia's Challenge. Final Report of the Council for Aboriginal Reconciliation to the Prime Minister and the Commonwealth Parliament* (Council for Aboriginal Reconciliation, Canberra, 2000) 105 (*Reconciliation: Australia's Challenge*); and in Geoff Clarke, 'Constitutional Change: Australian Experience and Future Prospects for a Treaty' in Glenn Patmore (ed.) *The Big Makeover: A New Australian Constitution: Labour Essays 2002* (Pluto Press, Annadale, 2002) 151, 157–8.

[11] Opened for signature 7 March 1966, 660 UTS 195 (entered into force 4 January 1969).

[12] *Kartinyeri v Commonwealth of Australia* (1998) 195 CLR 337 ('*Hindmarsh Island Bridge Case*').

[13] Ibid, 407–8.

[14] Hilary Charlesworth, *Writing in Rights: Australia and the Protection of Human Rights* (University of New South Wales Press, Sydney, 2002) 33.

race discrimination under Australian law.[15] Australia's commitment to the prohibition, as evidenced by the signing of the *ICERD*, is a legislative one under the *Racial Discrimination Act 1975* (Cth) *(RDA)*. However, the difficulty with a legislative prohibition against racial discrimination is that it may be repealed, amended or possibly 'suspended' by a government that lacks a commitment to human rights.

This serious problem was made clear to all Australians, particularly Aboriginal and Torres Strait Islander peoples, during the passage of the 1998 amendments to the *Native Title Act 1993* (Cth) *(NTA)*. Concern that the amendments would be a breach of the *RDA* and therefore invalid, gave rise to parliamentary discussions concerning the possible 'suspension' of the *RDA*. However, s 7 of the amended *NTA* provides that it be construed subject to the *RDA*, except that the *RDA* applies only to the 'performance of functions and the exercise of powers' conferred by the amended *NTA*. Section 7 provides that the *RDA* does not affect the validation of 'past acts' or 'intermediate period acts'; that is, acts that discriminatorily extinguish or impair Aboriginal and Torres Strait Islander peoples' native title interests.[16]

The United Nations Committee on the Elimination of Racial Discrimination (CERD), responsible for overseeing *ICERD*, considered the 1998 *NTA* amendments to be discriminatory, creating 'legal certainty for governments and third parties' at the expense of native title holders.[17] Such was CERD's concern that it placed Australia under an 'early warning/urgent action' procedure, invoked in circumstances in which there is serious cause for concern over a country's obligations under *ICERD*.[18]

The validity of the *NTA* amendments, and the status of the *RDA* in relation to the amended *NTA*, has not been subject to litigation in the domestic courts. The ambivalence to the prohibition of race discrimination evidenced by the High Court in the *Hindmarsh Island Bridge Case* can be contrasted with opinion of the same court in *Mabo*. Here, Justice Brennan declared that although 'the common law does not necessarily conform with international law ... international law is a legitimate and important influence on the development of the common law, especially where international law declares the existence of universal human rights'.[19]

---

[15] See, for example, *Bill of Rights Act 1990* (NZ); *Canadian Bill of Rights* 44 C 1960; *United States Constitution*.

[16] Gillian Triggs, 'Australia's Indigenous People and International Law: Validity of the *Native Title Amendment Act 1998* (Cth)' (1999) 23 *Melbourne University Law Review* 372, 378.

[17] Committee on the Elimination of Racial Discrimination, A/54/18, 54th sess, 1331st mtg, [6] (1999).

[18] Ibid [12].

[19] *Mabo* (1992) 175 CLR 1, 42, (Brennan J). In the *Hindmarsh Island Bridge Case*, Kirby J upheld this statement, arguing that 'where there is ambiguity in the common law or a statute, it is legitimate to have regard to international law' (1998) 195 CLR 337, 418.

It is not clear what weight the presently constituted High Court would give to the views of CERD that the *NTA* as it stands is a racially discriminatory statute in breach of international human rights law. The views of the government responsible for the amended *NTA*, however, are very clear. They have entirely rejected the CERD findings, claiming they are 'unbalanced' and 'an insult to all Australians'.[20]

The uncertainty surrounding the status of the *RDA*, exemplified by the 1998 amendments to the *NTA*, highlights the need for prohibition of racial discrimination to be entrenched either through a Bill of Rights or a specific constitutional amendment. This was clearly the view of CAR, which recommended in its 2000 report to government,[21] that Parliament prepare legislation for a referendum that seeks to 'remove s 25 of the *Constitution* and introduce a new section making it unlawful to adversely discriminate against any people on the grounds of race'.[22]

CAR also recommended legislative endorsement of 'a process which will unite all Australians by way of an agreement or treaty'[23] through which unresolved issues of reconciliation could be resolved. These recommendations have largely gone unheeded by the present government. CAR's recommendations were considered in 2003 by the Senate Legal and Constitutional References Committee[24] as part of its inquiry 'Reconciliation: Off Track'. While the Government stated that it had agreed to resolve issues of reconciliation, it thought this should be achieved outside of the legislative framework. The Government was 'generally supportive of the proposal to remove section 25 [of the Constitution] and stated that it would put the matter to a referendum "at an appropriate time"'.[25] However, neither the Government nor the inquiry appears to have considered CAR's recommendation in full, which also called for the Constitutional prohibition of racial discrimination. The issue of a Bill of Rights was canvassed briefly, with the Government's opposition noted. However, it was considered to be outside the scope of the inquiry.[26] This is a serious matter, especially since CAR was a statutory body established for a ten-year term for the purpose of enhancing reconciliation between Indigenous and non-Indigenous Australian peoples.

---

[20] Attorney-General's Department (Commonwealth), 'United Nations Committee Misunderstands and Misrepresents Australia' (Press Release, 19 March 1999).

[21] CAR, *Reconciliation: Australia's Challenge*, above n 10, 105.

[22] Ibid.

[23] Ibid, 106.

[24] On 27 August 2002, the Senate referred the CAR report to the Senate Legal and Constitutional References Committee, whose report was tabled on 9 October 2003, http://www.aph.gov.au/senate/committee/legcon_ctte/reconciliation/report/report.pdf at 4 March 2004.

[25] Ibid, ¶5.50.

[26] Ibid, ¶5.65.

United Nations Special Rapporteur

The lack of government commitment to human rights and the prohibition of racial discrimination was again evidenced by its response to the recent findings of a United Nations Special Rapporteur on Contemporary Forms of Racism, Racial Discrimination and Xenophobia. The Special Rapporteur was invited to Australia and hosted by the Government.[27] His report of February 2002[28] considered matters such as discrimination in the administration of justice, over-representation of Aboriginal people in the criminal justice system, the discriminatory nature of mandatory sentencing laws, difficulties in the reconciliation process, the lack of response to the important recommendation concerning the need for treaty negotiations and amendment of the *NTA*.

In response to the Special Rapporteur's report, the offices of Ministers Downer and Ruddock[29] issued a media release claiming that the 'United Nations Report has no credibility'.[30] These Ministers believed that the report 'added little to public debate or international understanding of Australia's approach to eradicating racism or xenophobia, to which the government remained strongly committed'.[31]

The alleged 'poor quality'[32] of the Special Rapporteur's report was used to justify an earlier Government argument following the CERD findings (concerning the *NTA* amendments) about an apparent need for 'reform to strengthen the effectiveness and credibility of the United Nations human rights mechanisms'.[33] However, as foremost Australian international jurist Elizabeth Evatt has pointed out, the consensual nature of international

---

[27] Australia has had a standing invitation to the Special Rapporteur since 1998. His visit was preceded by comments from the Minister for Immigration, Multiculturalism and Indigenous Affairs that the visit 'underlied the government's commitment to engaging constructively with the Special Rapporteur and the United Nations more generally, on our approach to addressing racism and intolerance.' Minister for Immigration and Multicultural and Indigenous Affairs, 'Visit by United Nations Special Rapporteur on Contemporary Forms of Racism, Racial Discrimination and Xenophobia' (Press Release, 12 April 2001) MPS 043/2001. This welcoming approach differed from the response of the Government following the conclusion of the Special Rapporteur's report, at below n 30.

[28] Special Rapporteur on Contemporary Forms of Racism, Racial Discrimination and Xenophobia, *Mission to Australia*, UN ESCOR, 58th sess, Agenda Item 6, UN DOC E/CN.4/2002/24/Add.1 (2002).

[29] At the time, Phillip Ruddock was Minister for Immigration and Multiculturalism and Indigenous Affairs, and Alexander Downer was Minister for Foreign Affairs.

[30] Minister for Immigration and Multiculturalism and Indigenous Affairs, and Minister for Foreign Affairs, 'UN Report Has No Credibility' (Press Release, 22 March 2002) MPS 17/2002.

[31] Ibid.

[32] Ibid.

[33] Ibid.

human rights law means that it is weakened by governments which show little hesitation in attacking and disputing outright the findings of the independent expert committees responsible for the upholding of the obligations under the human rights conventions.[34] Undoubtedly, Australia's international human rights reputation and credibility is harmed by such a disrespectful attitude towards human rights law. As Evatt politely pointed out, Australia's behaviour, its 'unwillingness to be accountable for its human rights performance, or to respect the views of the monitoring bodies, means that it has lost its claim to be described as a good international citizen in the human rights area'.[35]

The Special Rapporteur's report, which was attacked so openly by the Government, is actually a very straightforward assessment of Australian human rights mechanisms, and broadly reflects the information presented to the Special Rapporteur by those government and non-government bodies that met with him during his Australian visit. It generously 'hails the significant progress made in action to combat racism and racial discrimination against Aboriginals'.[36]

The report gives an overview of the legislative and administrative framework for action to combat racism and discrimination, Human Rights and Equal Opportunity Commission (HREOC) (the legislative body with responsibility for the domestic implementation of ICERD under the *RDA*), and the various state Commissions empowered to uphold human rights and the prohibition of race discrimination. These laws and institutions are established in fulfilment of Article 6 of *ICERD*, which provides that:

> States parties shall assure to everyone within their jurisdiction effective protection and remedies, through the competent national tribunals and other State institutions, against any acts of racial discrimination which violate his [sic] human rights and fundamental freedoms contrary to this Convention, as well as the right to seek from such tribunals just and adequate reparation or satisfaction for any damage suffered as a result of such discrimination.

Domestic remedies for race discrimination

My academic research and practical experiences with Commonwealth and state laws and institutions have caused me to seriously doubt whether 'effective protection and remedies' are in fact assured in Australia.

---

[34] Elizabeth Evatt, 'Australia's Performance in Human Rights' (2001) 26(1) *Alternative Law Journal* 11.
[35] Ibid, 15.
[36] Special Rapporteur, *Mission to Australia*, above n 28, 52.

In 1995, HREOC initiated a twenty-year review of the *RDA*. My assessment of this review was that it highlighted the following:

- race discrimination is very difficult to prove and harder to establish than sex discrimination
- very low damages are awarded for successful complaints of race discrimination
- the only clear act of racism identified by the Commission is the refusal of service in hotels.[37]

The United Nations Special Rapporteur, in his report in reference to the *RDA*, stated: 'one of the specific characteristics of Australian law is that it does not require proof of discriminatory intent or motive for an act to be characterised as unlawful'.[38] This is certainly true as a matter of law, but seemingly not as a matter of practice. It is consistent with the findings of the High Court in a 1989 case concerning sex discrimination, *Australian Iron & Steel v Banovic*.[39] However, in the practice of race discrimination law, complaints are routinely rejected or dismissed on the basis of reasoning that implies there was no discrimination because there was no motive or intent.

The following cases are clearly illustrative of this. In *Steven Mead v Southern Districts Football League*,[40] the Aboriginal complainant was suspended from the team for a season because of an assault on another player. This was considered an overly serious penalty when compared to that applied to non-Aboriginal persons and an appealed was lodged. Further explanation was given that the assault was in response to serious racial abuse. The League, however, determined that the incident was 'unprovoked' and increased the penalty for an additional six months.[41] The then-President of HREOC, Sir Ronald Wilson, found that Steven Mead 'was not accorded equal treatment' and that it was 'unusual and ... extraordinary' for the League to increase a penalty on re-hearing. Nonetheless, he did not believe that the so-called 'honourable' members of the League had been affected 'either consciously or unconsciously by a racist bias'.[42] The unusual and extraordinary treatment did not appear to be explained in any manner by the League, and it does not seem that it was called upon to do so by the Hearing Commissioner.

---

[37] Hannah McGlade, 'Reviewing Racism: HREOC and the *Race Discrimination Act* Review' (1997) 4(4) *Indigenous Law Bulletin* 12.

[38] Special Rapporteur, *Mission to Australia*, above n 28, 11.

[39] (1989) 168 CLR 165.

[40] [1991] HREOC 12.

[41] Ibid.

[42] Ibid.

In a case concerning the race hatred provisions under the *RDA, Albert Corunna and others v West Australian Newspaper Ltd*,[43] HREOC was to reject a complaint of Nyungar elders despite finding that the cartoon complained of had:

- presented a demeaning portrayal of Yagan, a Nyungar warrior whose head had been cut off and displayed in various fairs, sideshows and museums in England[44]
- contained derogatory and demeaning references to the Waugal, the Nyungar ancestral creation spirit
- treated the issue of death in a manner offensive to Aboriginal people
- referred to the mixed ancestry of elders and also suggested a lack of Aboriginality because of that racial mix (this was particularly offensive, considering that one of those elders gave evidence of his mother's rape)
- reinforced a misinformed and stereotypical view of Aboriginal people misusing government funding.

Nonetheless, the Hearing Commissioner still found that the cartoon was exempted under s 18D of the *RDA* on the basis that the respondent acted 'reasonably and in good faith' and he relied upon an apparent lack of 'dishonesty or fraud' or 'malice'.[45] Obviously, the adverse findings made by the Commission could have been relied upon to defeat the respondent's claim to have acted reasonably and in good faith. It appears that the complainants were placed under an impossible burden of proving explicit motive and intent. This case illustrates well my argument that proper remedies are being denied by the responsible bodies.[46]

Cases that most explicitly reveal racist motives may have some chance of success, but these cases are the more infrequent examples of racism and discrimination, which by its nature nowadays is often less overt. One example in which intent was clearly evidenced is a New South Wales Equal Opportunity Tribunal decision concerning police behaviour towards a young Aboriginal actor. The police actions were captured on an ABC television documentary, and the evidence showed that on apprehending the

---

[43] [2001] HREOC, 98/27 (Unreported, Commissioner Innes, 12 April 2001).

[44] For further information about the circumstances of the repatriation see Hannah McGlade, 'The Repatriation of Yagan; A Story of Manufacturing Dissent' (1998) 4(1) *Law Text Culture* 245.

[45] *Albert Corunna and others v Western Australian Ltd* [2001] HREOC, 98/27 (Unreported, Commissioner Innes, 12 April 2001).

[46] Another example is *Joan Martin v State Housing Commission* [1997] EOC (Unreported, Commissioner Hasluck, 25 July 1997). Joan Martin successfully appealed to the Supreme Court of Western Australia, but this was overturned by the Full Court, *State Housing Commission v Martin* (1999) ¶92–975.

complainant, Wesley Patten, the police officers treated him in a demeaning manner, explicitly questioning in front of the television crew, whether he was 'a coon or what?' The Tribunal found the officers had treated the complainant unfavourably, completely disregarding his right to be treated with respect and without harassment. Significant damages were awarded.[47]

One of the few successful cases under s 18C, the race hatred provisions of the *RDA*, was *Wanjurri v Southern Cross Broadcasting (Australia) Ltd (Wanjurri)*.[48] In this case, a controversial radio announcer was found to have racially vilified Nyungar people by encouraging the most extreme and disrespectful references to their religion and culture. Even the radio station (which is part of a broadcasting chain) was held vicariously liable for failing to train staff in the provisions of the *RDA*. Although a significant damages award was made to the complainant, at that time damages awards made by HREOC were technically unenforceable[49] and the station subsequently engaged in similar provocative conduct.

Sharing jurisdiction

In my view, the ineffective domestic response to race discrimination is due both to the exclusion of Aboriginal and Torres Strait Islander peoples from the development of legislative response and from the institutions established to effect such a response and to opportunities for change, such as the 1995 HREOC review of the *RDA*,[50] not properly being taken up.[51]

A further review by the Western Australian Anti-Discrimination Commissioner[52] found that, despite Aboriginal people's serious 'lack of confidence in the process and the likelihood of positive outcomes',[53] a significant proportion of them continued to use the law. I can certainly agree with this finding based on my own experiences of race discrimination law.

---

[47] *Patten v New South Wales* [1997] NSWEOT 91, 92.
[48] (2001) EOC ¶93–147 ('*Wanjurri*').
[49] *Brandy v Human Rights and Equal Opportunity Commission* (1995) 183 CLR 245, 259.
[50] Race Discrimination Commissioner, *Racial Discrimination Act 1975: A Review* (Australian Government Publishing Service, Canberra, 1995).
[51] Ibid, viii. The most substantial result of the review was the publication of seminar papers, none of which was given by Indigenous Australian peoples or which specifically raised Indigenous Australian issues in relation to the *RDA*. The review was supposed to result in policy and legislative amendments but this did not eventuate.
[52] Western Australian Anti-Discrimination Commissioner, *Aboriginal Participation Within the Complaints Process*, Occasional Paper No 2 (2001).
[53] Ibid, 14.

Personal experience

In my experience, I have found the laws and institutions to be formal and costly, legalistic and alienating, burdensome and overly time consuming. I have even detected a presumption that Aboriginal and Torres Strait Islander people (including myself) who dare to pursue such complaints are not *bona fide*, or are vexatious litigants. I have not witnessed any respect for Aboriginal and Torrres Strait Islander self-determination, participatory or cultural rights—rights that are now clearly being recognised under international human rights law.

Primarily, my concern lies with the power of Australian courts, the members of which are almost entirely non-Indigenous people and who lack an adequate understanding of, and commitment to, the international and domestic prohibition of race discrimination. As Patricia Monture, a first nations Canadian lawyer once wrote, 'combating racism in law is, and can only be, a partial solution until the parameters of law are redefined in a way that is inclusive of our experiences'.[54]

In 1997 I made a complaint against a West Australian Senator who publicly opposed the teaching of Aboriginal studies in schools by claiming that Aboriginal people 'are the most primitive people on earth'.[55] He also claimed that our culture was an abhorrent one full of terrible killing and sexual practices. Although I had learnt of this kind of racism as a child, I was genuinely shocked and offended by these remarks and I made a complaint to HREOC under the race hatred provisions of s 18C of the *RDA*.[56] Despite the fact that the statements were published in the state's only daily newspaper, HREOC placed considerable pressure on me to prove that the statements had been made. Ultimately, HREOC dismissed the complaint under a legislative provision that allowed it to do so if it considered a complaint 'frivolous, vexatious, misconceived or lacking in substance'.[57] I believe that many complaints have been wrongly dismissed under this provision.[58]

That decision was overturned in the Federal Court of Australia.[59] My case was referred back to HREOC for a determination according to law, and

---

[54] Patricia Monture, 'Reflecting on Flint Woman' in Richard Devlin (ed.) *Canadian Perspectives on Legal Theory* (Emand Montgomery Publications, Toronto, 1991) 351, 360.

[55] Anne Burns, 'Lightfoot, Court, Clash on Aborigines', *The West Australian* (Perth) 13 May 1997, 6.

[56] *McGlade v Lightfoot* (1999) EOC ¶93–003.

[57] *Racial Discrimination Act 1975* (Cth) s 25x; see below n 58.

[58] This provision was later repealed by the *Human Rights Legislation Amendment Act 1999* (Cth) sch 76.

[59] *McGlade v Human Rights and Equal Opportunity Commission* (2000) 104 FCR 205.

argued again before the Commission. Subsequently, the case was referred to the Federal Court for a determinative hearing.[60]

Although Justice Carr of the Federal Court found in my favour (and against a serving Federal Senator),[61] the decision shows once again the unwillingness of the non-Indigenous judiciary to uphold the legally binding domestic and international prohibition of racial discrimination and vilification.

In declining to award damages, Justice Carr also found that:

> reasonable members of the Aboriginal community would be aware that the respondent's intolerant comments were not only out-of-line with mainstream Australian attitudes but probably unlawful. While the respondent's act was offensive and insulting to them I think that they would be more likely than not to take a fairly robust view of where that conduct stood in the general scheme of things.[62]

These comments were made despite evidence from a number of Nyungar witnesses as to the serious impact of the comments. I was made aware of widespread support from local Nyungar people, all of whom would be described as 'reasonable members' of my community. It is unclear to me how an objective test of race relations was relevant to the legal test at hand.

Hagan's case

I believe that the exclusion of Aboriginal and Torres Strait Islander peoples and our experiences under race discrimination law has recently come to the high-water mark in a Federal Court case.[63] This case, initiated by an Aboriginal and Torres Strait Islander Councillor from Toowoomba, Stephen Hagan, concerned a large public sign at a local football stadium referring to an area as the 'Nigger Brown' stand. Apparently, the sign was in reference to a 1920 club member who was given this name because he had used shoe polish then known as 'nigger brown'. Hagan's attempts to have the sign removed were unsuccessful, as were his complaints before HREOC and the Federal Court. His application to the High Court for special leave to appeal against the finding of the Full Federal Court was sharply rejected by Justices Gaudron and Hayne.[64]

---

[60] This is in contrast with *Wanjurri* where a non-binding determination was delivered (2001) EOC ¶93–147.

[61] *McGlade v Lightfoot* [2002] FCA 1457.

[62] Ibid, [88].

[63] *Hagan v Trustees of Toowoomba Sports Ground Trust* (2000) 105 FCR 56 ('*Hagan*').

[64] Transcript of Proceedings, *Hagan v Toowoomba Sports Ground Trust* (High Court, Gaudron, Hayne JJ, 19 March 2002) (Gaudron J).

The case gave the High Court its first opportunity to consider s 18C of the *RDA*, the domestic implementation of art 4(a) of *ICERD* that requires states to 'declare an offence punishable by law all dissemination of ideas based on racial superiority or hatred'.[65] However, the abrupt dismissal of the special leave application is illustrative of the lack of understanding and respect even our highest judicial body has for the prohibition of racial discrimination and vilification.

Justice Gaudron, in her brief consideration of the complaint, considered it analogous to signs referring to 'pink trucks' which she thought could reasonably offend 'pink persons' such as herself.[66] If her Honour had given due regard to the word complained of she would have understood that 'nigger' is a derogatory reference to dark-skinned people.[67] More understanding and respect was shown by a West Australian newspaper columnist, who commented on Justice Gaudron's 'curious suggestion that "nigger" is no more offensive to a black person than "pinky" to a white one, [which] betray[s] appalling racial insensitivity and a serious underestimation of the power of words'.[68]

Legal interpretations of the causation requirement for proving racial discrimination seemed to have also been relied upon by Justice Gaudron, who implied that there was no connection between the act done and the race of the offended person. Apparently, 'to maintain a course of attitude because of the attitude or the tacit approval of people of a particular race is not to do something because of the race or colour of those people'.[69] Apparently, the maintenance of a course of attitude, the upholding of offensive racial stereotypes in other words, is not an act for the purpose of the legislation!

Justice Gaudron's attitude to Stephen Hagan's complaint can be contrasted with her understanding of racism expressed in *Mabo*, in which she declared that the doctrine of *terra nullius*:

---

[65] ICERD, opened for signature 7 March 1966, 660 UTS 195, art 4(a) (entered into force 4 January 1969).

[66] Transcript of Proceedings, *Hagan v Toowoomba Sports Ground Trust* (High Court, Gaudron, Hayne JJ, 19 March 2002) (Gaudron J).

[67] A number of dictionaries and encyclopaedias support this contention. Nigger is 'now a term of racist abuse', Tony Thorne, *Dictionary of Contemporary Slang* (Bloomsbury Reference, London 3rd edn, 1997) 272; 'probably the most offensive, hateful, hurtful term in the language today', Robert Hendrickson, *Encyclopaedia of Word and Phrase Origins* (Facts on File, New York, 1997) 278; 'used as a disparaging term for a Black person', *The American Heritage Dictionary of the English Language* (Houghton Mifflin, Boston, 3rd edn, 1992) 1224; 'now virtually restricted to contexts of deliberate and contemptuous ethnic abuse', *Oxford English Dictionary* (Clarendon Press, Oxford, 1989) vol x, 402.

[68] André Malan, 'Offensive N-Word Has Had Its Day', *The West Australian* (Perth), 21 March 2002, 20.

[69] Transcript of Proceedings, *Hagan v Toowoomba Sports Ground Trust* (High Court, Gaudron, Hayne JJ, 19 March 2002) (Gaudron J).

provided the legal basis for the dispossession of the Aboriginal people of most of their traditional lands. The acts and events by which that dispossession in legal theory was carried into practical effect constitute the darkest aspect of the history of this nation. The nation as a whole must remain diminished, unless and until there is an acknowledgment and retreat from, those past injustices.[70]

And, yet, the doctrine of *terra nullius* as enlarged and applied to Australia was clearly based on the prevalent beliefs of the period that Indigenous Australian peoples were 'mere savages' or 'niggers' in the racist language and world view of the colonists.

The *Hagan* case stands as a real reminder that a proper acknowledgement and retreat from the injustices of *terra nullius* is still far from realisation. Hagen appealed the decision to CERD,[71] which found the:

> use and maintenance of the offending term ... offensive and insulting, even if for an extended period it may not have necessarily been so regarded ... The Committee recommends that the State party take the necessary measures to secure the removal of the offending term from the sign in question, and to inform the Committee of such action it takes in this respect.[72]

In response, a spokesperson for the Commonwealth *Attorney*-General commented:

> the government notes (that CERD)...is not a court and its views are not binding. In particular, it does not adopt the rigorous judicial standards employed by our own domestic courts. The government's serious concerns regarding the quality and standards applied by United Nations complaint bodies are a matter of public record. In the absence of real reform of the United Nations treaty body system, those concerns remain.[73]

Conclusion

In the past three decades, Australia has declared its intention to respect international prohibitions of racial discrimination. It has enacted laws and established domestic bodies to give effect to that fundamental principle of human rights law, and has rejected the racially offensive legal doctrine that underpinned its colonial foundation.

---

[70] *Mabo* (1992) 175 CLR 1, 109 (Deane J, Gaudron J).
[71] CERD, *Stephen Hagan v Australia*, Communication No 26/2002, UN Doc CERD/C/62/D/26/2002 (2002).
[72] Ibid, [7.3], [8].
[73] Stephen Hagan, 'Only in Australia', *Koori Mail* (Lismore), 7 May 2003, 14.

However, according to the HREOC Race Discrimination Commissioner Bill Jonas, Australia-wide consultations have shown that 'racism is still alive and well in Australian society'.[74] The need for constitutional protection of human rights, and the strengthening of inadequate anti-discrimination laws was especially emphasised to HREOC.[75] They are certainly matters of national importance that must be addressed in the event of future treaty negotiations.

In the words of one Aboriginal woman, 'we just live with racism every day. It's like getting up, washing your face and having a cup of tea'.[76] Could a stronger claim ever be made for the need to negotiate a strengthened prohibition of race discrimination under Australian law?

---

[74] Mark Mallabone, 'Racists, Report Finds "Unfair Go"', *The West Australian* (Perth) 4 December 2001, 1.

[75] Aboriginal and Torres Strait Islander Social Justice Commission, *Social Justice Report* 2001, Report to the Attorney-General as required by section 46C(i)(a) of the *Human Rights and Equal Opportunity Commission Act 1986* (Aboriginal and Torres Strait Islander Social Justice Commission, HREOC, Sydney, 2002) 194.

[76] Mallabone, 'Racists, Report', above n 74.

Chapter 17

A Sovereign Text? Copyright, Publishing Agreements and Intellectual Property Issues for Aboriginal and Torres Strait Islander Authors

Michele Grossman[*]

This discussion of some contemporary copyright and intellectual property issues for Aboriginal and Torres Strait Islander authors suggests that this area of law and agreement making is ultimately underpinned by struggles over forms of Indigenous power, control and self-determination that have their parallel in efforts to gain and advance Indigenous rights in relation to law, land and sovereignty. These struggles are bound up with the dilemmas that arise for Australian Indigenous cultural producers who seek to balance customary law, cultural integrity and social control over both Indigenous heritage **and** Indigenous innovation with the economic imperative to transform cultural production into commercially and ethically sustainable enterprises that value, recognise and protect Aboriginal and Torres Strait Islander entitlements as cultural creators and custodians.

What is 'copyright'? Who is an 'author'?

In modern terms, 'copyright', or the rights to 'copy', may be described as a set of laws which belongs to a larger group of laws governing intellectual

---

[*] My thanks to Stephen Gray, Marcia Langton, Lisa Palmer and Kathryn Shain for comments on an earlier version of this chapter.

property.[1] In addition to copyright, intellectual property law includes laws governing patents, designs, trademarks, trade secrets, and other confidential information.[2] Copyright law in Australia is based on the *Copyright Act 1968* (Cth) (*Copyright Act*) and its subsequent interpretation and application in various court decisions and legislative amendments. Modern Australian copyright law is also governed by Australia's status, along with more than 150 other countries,[3] as a signatory to the *Berne Convention for the Protection of Literary and Artistic Works 1886*[4] (last amended in 1979). The *Berne Convention* provides a regulatory 'uniform international system', successively modified and elaborated between 1908 and 1979, that standardises and extends an author's domestically enshrined rights, including moral rights, over his or her copy to the context of publication in international markets.[5] The *Berne Convention* continues to be a crucial instrument for the protection of authors' and publishers' rights in the contemporary period, as globalisation and the digital age create new opportunities for nefarious trade practices, including textual piracy and black-market reproduction and distribution.

It is critical to note that the 'copy' in 'copyright' does not refer exclusively to the term's primary or everyday meaning of reproduction or imitation. The term originates in English from the Medieval Latin term *copia*, meaning 'abundance' or 'plenty', and is later extended to the idea of the plenitude associated with the transcription of oral utterance into writing. The *Oxford English Dictionary* cites the first usage as early as 1375,[6] some 100 years before the emergence of the English printer William Caxton's first printed book at Westminster in 1477.[7] By Caxton's time, however, another meaning attaches to the term 'copy'; this sense denotes 'copy' as meaning either 'an individual example of a manuscript or print', or, in an explicitly literary sense that foreshadows the emergence of the individualised 'author' in Western culture, 'the original work of art, writing, etc. **from which a copy is made**' (emphasis added).[8]

---

[1] Australian Copyright Council, *Indigenous Arts and Copyright: A Practical Guide* (Australian Copyright Council, Redfern, NSW, 1st edn, August 1999) 3.

[2] Ibid.

[3] As at 15 July 2003.

[4] *Berne Convention for the Protection of Literary and Artistic Works 1886*, opened for signature on 4 May 1886, ATS 1972 No. 13 (entered into force 5 December 1887) (*Berne Convention*). This Convention entered into force in Australia on 1 March 1978.

[5] Sir Frank McKinnon, 'Notes on the History of English Copyright' in Margaret Drabble (ed.), *Oxford Companion to English Literature* (Oxford University Press, Oxford, 1985) 1113, 1117.

[6] *The Compact Edition of the Oxford English Dictionary* (Oxford University Press, Oxford, 1971) 1 [978] 555, 'Copy' I.1.

[7] McKinnon, above n 5, 1113.

[8] *The Compact Edition of the Oxford English Dictionary*, above n 6, 'Copy' IV.8.

The phrase 'copyright' thus historically encodes a sense of rights over both the actual content of a work—in the sense that the work is an original creation—**and** over the reproduction and distribution of copies of that work, commercial or otherwise. In this sense, copyright law has always, at least implicitly, acknowledged not only the commercial value of rights to copy—because copyright can be bought, sold or assigned to others—but also the 'moral rights' of copyright holders, a category of great significance for Aboriginal and Torres Strait Islander creators of written and/or recorded and published material, as we shall see below.

Authors' rights

The sense in which we think of 'copyright' today is inextricably linked with a sense of authors' rights, particularly in the arena of written works, although Australian copyright law covers the rights of all generators of original works in material form, including literary, artistic, musical and dramatic works, films, sound recordings, published editions (that is, typesetting and typographical arrangements) and broadcasts. But copyright did not always protect the rights of the author.

Indeed, the construct of the 'author' was a highly marginalised, virtually irrelevant figure in the great copyright wars that marked the emergence of book culture and the expansion of printing industries in the sixteenth and seventeenth centuries.[9] The term 'author' itself derives from the French *auteur* by way of the Latin *auctor*, the past participle of *augere*, meaning to 'increase or enlarge'. It is also related to the Greek word *autor*, meaning 'creator'.[10] Both 'copy', from the Latin *copia*, and 'author', from the Latin *auctor/augere*, are thus linked with notions of amplitude and increase, an apt illumination of the cultural significance ascribed to both writing and authorship in Western cultures.

It was not until 1755 that Johnson's dictionary defined the 'author' as: 'The first beginner of any thing'; 'the first writer of any thing'; 'he that produces or effects anything'; 'a writer in general'.[11]

Johnson's definition of an 'author' signified a crucial moment in the cultural history of ideas and definitions of authorship, for it both established the idea of the author as the **primary originator or creator** of a work—not merely its 'amplifier' or 'enlarger'—and also creates a tighter association between the category of authorship and the specific activity of writing,

---

[9] For an excellent discussion of this period in the history of the book trade, see Maurice Couturier, *Textual Communication: A Theory of the Novel* (Routledge, London, 1991) 1–50.

[10] Ibid, 3.

[11] Samuel Johnson, *A Dictionary of the English Language* (Printed by W. Strahan for J. and P. Kneaton *et al.*, 1755) 'Author', as cited in Maurice Couturier, above n 9, 4.

an association previously only latent or marginal in the transitional period between manuscript and print culture. There is no question that this tightening of the cultural meanings of 'authorship' in relation to the written word has created problems for contemporary Australian authors, both Indigenous and non-Indigenous, whose contributions towards and interests in material published in textual form may not always be written, and may be 'original' only in the limited sense of the term employed by copyright law. The 'originality' of a work under the copyright law means something that has been created as 'original', or for the first time, **in material form**: printed, written, recorded, sung, danced. It does not refer to the 'originality' of an idea, a style, a theme, or to knowledge, information, memory or narrative. Moreover, Aboriginal and Torres Strait Islander authors have historically faced exclusion from Western cultural and legal definitions of authorship. For example, Stephen Muecke and Adam Shoemaker have commented, in relation to the copyright abuse and appropriation of David Unaipon's writing in the 1920s, that 'at the time when David Unaipon was first writing, the notion of an Indigenous person being an author was literally unheard of'.[12]

While I am specifically concerned here with copyright as it relates to and affects Aboriginal and Torres Strait Islander authors of written or published works, I should point out that Australian copyright law covers a wide range of creative works including music, composition, broadcast, artistic, typographic and recording. I should also point out that my use of 'author' rather than 'writer' is a deliberate one. The Australian Copyright Council (ACC) defines an author as a 'creator' of the kinds of original material covered by the *Copyright Act*. An 'author' in this expanded sense of 'creator' **may** be, but need not necessarily be, a writer, since under the Act, the category of 'author' covers all those who create original works including sculptures, visual works, compositions, recordings, designs etc.

The current state of Australian copyright law, as based on the *Copyright Act* and its interpretation in the courts, poses particular dilemmas for the authors and creators of Indigenous Australian works that are published in book form. The history of English copyright law demonstrates the extent to which contemporary notions of copyright and authorship are bound up with the legacies of Enlightenment-based approaches to economic value, individual rights and commodity culture. The right to copy—both in the sense of rights over content and rights over reproduction—is essentially viewed as an economic right, one bound up with the commercial realisation of writing as a commodity form rather than, as at common law, an

---

[12] See 'Introduction: Repatriating the Story' in David Unaipon, *Legendary Tales of the Australian Aborigines* (Melbourne University Press, edited and introduced by Stephen Mueke and Adam Shoemaker, Carlton, Victoria, 2001) xi, xvi.

intangible form of personal property. The 'copyright' to which authors are subject, and from which they seek protection of their rights, is based in a system designed to regulate and ensure an equitable distribution of the financial return on the capital and labour investments not only of authors but also of the publishers and distributors of written works; in this sense, the author, like the publisher with whom he or she contracts, is primarily conceived of as an economic unit rather than as a social entity.

It is only in the assertion of moral rights as part of copyright and intellectual property law that we see some return to the idea of the author as constituted by and bounded within a network of social and cultural relations that both precede and exceed the economic paradigms in which copyright law achieves the full force of its historical logic. Yet, the most common criticism levelled at copyright law by Australian Indigenous writers and commentators is the extent to which it fails to recognise, value and adjudicate on moral rights and intellectual property issues of great concern to Indigenous producers of written or published cultural material. These concerns fall roughly into two categories. The first category is that of Indigenous authors who fail to benefit from existing forms of mainstream copyright agreements because they have been excluded or limited in relation to their rights in those agreements. The second category is that of Indigenous authors who find that existing copyright laws and agreements place them, and their work, in serious tension with the competing claims, rights and obligations of Indigenous Australian customary law, a form of law that is not recognised by Australian courts and is thus a largely unenforceable aspect of Aboriginal and Torres Strait Islander legal and moral rights over the creation, maintenance and transmission of their cultural heritage.

Aboriginal and Torres Strait Islander authors and existing copyright law

As noted above, modern copyright law extends rights and protection to the creators of works only when that work has been realised or made concrete; that is, it recognises only those rights that attach to works that may be considered forms of commodity or property, a state of affairs sometimes referred to as an instance of 'tangible' cultural production. It may protect a work that 'uses' a particular technique or style, or 'expresses' a particular idea, or theme, but it cannot protect the technique, style, theme or idea itself. Most significantly, it does not necessarily protect the rights of those authors who deliver their work orally or who collaborate with others—such as anthropologists or editors—who are involved in the transcription, structuring and textual realisation of an Aboriginal or Torres Strait Islander author's oral material. For Indigenous authors who create new works of imagination, history or memoir, and who write down their own work, the standard protections afforded by current copyright law to all authors apply: the general rule under the *Copyright Act* is that 'the person who creates a work owns copyright', and 'writing it down' is seen as tangible evidence both of creation and of originality. But what of those Indigenous authors who create new works, say, of history or memoir, but who do not write down the work themselves? The ACC interprets copyright law in relation to oral histories as follows:

> It's not clear whether the person who tells their story will own copyright. The person recording the story may be just a 'mere scribe'—like a secretary taking dictation—but in other cases, the person writing down the story may have such a hand in constructing the report that he or she is an 'author', at least in the version that is written down.
>
> An example might be someone who records or writes down stories. If the person just pushes the button on a tape recorder, or just writes down the stories word for word, then the person who tells the story is more likely to be the only 'author'. However, if the person structures or edits these stories and puts them in his or her own words, then both the person telling the story and the person writing it down may be 'authors', and therefore, generally, joint copyright holders.[13]

The ACC goes on to observe that the law in Australia is unclear in this situation, and that it is best to have 'a written agreement about who will own copyright in oral histories'.[14]

An unorthodox resolution of this dilemma, however, may revolve around the use of the tape recorder in oral history interviews conducted between Indigenous Australian authors and non-Indigenous editors and researchers. Under the *Copyright Act*, sound recordings are automatically covered by the terms of the Act, since this lodges the work in the 'material form' required by law.[15] The claims of a number of editors of Indigenous works to joint authorship of texts in the past have been based on the face-to-face collection of oral material recorded by the editor, so that it was impossible to say that a recording belonged exclusively to the Indigenous creator because the editor controlled the materialisation of the stories and knowledges by writing them down and/or recording them. Aboriginal and Torres Strait Islander authors who are thinking of publishing their memoirs, histories or life stories based on oral accounts might consider making their

---

[13] Australian Copyright Council, above n 1, 25.
[14] Ibid.
[15] Ibid, 10.

tape recordings first, whether individually or in conjunction with families or communities, so that the editor is presented with pre-recorded material to work from. In this way, the editorial role in shaping and preparing that material for publication is very different to what it would be under the more traditional system of face-to-face interviews and compilations. Automatic copyright, under the *Copyright Act,* for Indigenous authors in the sound recordings would also allow those authors to negotiate from a position of strength about inclusions, alterations or exclusions of recorded material in the final published version.

The absence of clear and unambiguous laws relating to the legal and cultural ownership of Indigenous Australian oral narratives has inevitably created a series of uneven relationships between Indigenous authors and their editors, and also between Indigenous authors who participate in academic research projects in which their authorial contributions ultimately form part of a published work down the track. Yet, it is extremely rare in general for editors to receive copyright entitlements to an author's work. Why does this picture change with the disproportionate number of editors who have come to assume the status of 'co-authors' of Indigenous-authored texts?

One answer lies in the historical perception of Aboriginal and Torres Strait Islander writing and storytelling as 'lacking' both the formal and cultural literacy necessary to produce a 'publishable' version of a text. As is the case with oral histories produced in other social domains—for example, working-class memoir—the authors of such works are perceived to have a plenitude both of 'story' and of what social anthropologists and other scholars term 'verbal arts',[16] but a deficiency of the literacy based skills required to render that story serviceable in a print-based culture. In these cases, the editor's activities are understood to surpass those of a mere textual 'enhancer', 'improver' or 'mender': the editor becomes perceived as a 'collaborator', in the sense that their productive labour is awarded equal status by publishers and by the law with that of the creator–author of the work.

In her illuminating doctoral study of Aboriginal and Torres Strait Islander writing and publishing, Anita Heiss writes:

> *The Copyright Act* as it stands is unsuited to protecting Indigenous culture, because it is 'focused legally on individualistic commercial concepts, rather than notions of communal ownership or the cultural integrity of a work'.[17]

---

[16] See, for example, Ruth Finnegan, *Literacy and Orality: Studies in the Technology of Communication* (Basil Blackwell, Oxford and New York, 1988); Walter Ong, *Orality and Literacy: The Technologizing of the Word* (Methuen, London, 1982).

[17] Anita Heiss, *Dhuuluu Yala: To Talk Straight: Publishing Indigenous Literature* (Aboriginal Studies Press, Canberra, 2003) 83, citing Terri Janke, 'Protecting Australian Indigenous Arts and Cultural Expression: A Matter of Legislative Reform or Cultural Policy?' (1996) *Cultural Policy* 7(3), 14.

The Act also fails to accommodate the fact that Indigenous cultures, stories, information and knowledge are passed from generation to generation by oral means ... Generally, under the *Copyright Act*, once these stories are published in books and other documents, the person responsible for translating the oral story into written form is recognised as having copyright over the text. Similarly, when a performance of a previously unpublished story or dance is recorded on film or audiotape, the maker of the recording is acknowledged legally as owning the film or tape. In this way, copyright only protects the material medium rather than the idea or concept. It is also the case that the person who first reduces an oral literature to material form is recognised as the author of the ensuing work, and can exercise the exclusive rights granted to authors under the *Copyright Act* to reproduce the work in material form or to broadcast the work.[18]

Aboriginal and Torres Strait Islander authors and 'moral rights'

The problems this has created for Aboriginal and Torres Strait Islander authors of narrative are legion, and most of them arise under the heading of the 'moral rights' of authors to their work. Moral rights within the framework of copyright law:

> are based on the idea that a person who creates a work has a special connection with that work. 'Moral rights' are rights which always belong to the creator of the copyright material. A creator owns these rights whether or not they also own copyright.[19]

The *Moral Rights Act*

Despite Australia being a signatory to the *Berne Convention*, until the end of 2000, Australian copyright law had been extremely slow in recognising the moral rights of people who create things. Before the *Copyright Amendment (Moral Rights) Act 2000* (Cth) (*Moral Rights Act*) came into force at the end of that year, the moral rights for creators available under the existing *Copyright Act* included:

- the right not to have the wrong name affixed to your work or on copies of your work
- the right to object to commercial dealing with your work or its copy where that work is known to have the wrong name on it

---

[18] Anita Heiss, above n 17.
[19] Australian Copyright Council, above n 1, 18.

- the right to object to your work being claimed as an 'original version' when it has been altered by someone else
- the right to object to a claim that your work has been made by you when somebody else has made a copy of your work based on your work but not made by you.

In addition to these rights, two further categories of moral rights were introduced by the *Moral Rights Act* in 2000:

- the right to attribution of authorship
- the right to integrity of authorship.

The first of these additions means that, as well as claiming moral rights in circumstances in which someone else is falsely attributed as the creator of your work, you now have the right to be explicitly identified as the creator of your work: for example, your work may no longer be published anonymously, as the previous version of the Act allowed.

The second of these, from the vantage point of Aboriginal and Torres Strait Islander authors and all authors, really, is the critical change. It allows legal action to be taken when a work has been modified, mutilated or altered in a way that is considered derogatory to the author's reputation and to the integrity of their work. This might include, hypothetically, legal action against a publisher who has modified or distorted an author's work without obtaining their written consent to the modifications. It is less clear, however, what actions might be possible in relation to collaboratively authored works. It affords both protection and exposure for each party to a co-authorship agreement, especially when a dispute as to the integrity of each author's contribution becomes apparent. But it can also be a source of strength for Indigenous authors and their collaborators in the event that a joint authorship action needs to be mounted against a publisher.

Most importantly, however, the moral rights legislation now in force allows a greater capacity for Aboriginal and Torres Strait Islander authors to exercise rights in relation to their work even where this work has been written down, edited or structured by someone else. It enshrines the idea of a work's integrity as an artistic creation, and offers some protection for Indigenous creators who may previously have been coerced or misled by editors and publishers about the kind of changes 'necessary' to ensure that their work achieved a status considered publishable by industry standards. Moral rights legislation also enables the assertion and exercise of rights at law that were previously unrecognised by the economic focus of copyright law, which offered insufficient protection of Indigenous authors' interests in the social and cultural sphere. It makes inroads into the rigid separation under copyright law between 'culture and commerce'.[20] The challenge is the translation of moral rights legislation into concrete agreements between publishers and authors, so that the contractual nature of publishing is underpinned by an awareness of, and just consideration for, the moral rights of the Indigenous creators of published material.

Moral rights of families and communities

This is all well and good for those to whom the *Moral Rights Act* applies, namely, **individual** authors and creators of published material. But what of published material whose copyright owners and moral rights claimants are, or should be, Aboriginal or Torres Strait Islander families or communities? During parliamentary discussion of the Bill that became the *Moral Rights Act*, Australian Democrats Senator Aden Ridgeway proposed a further amendment to the Bill that would have allowed moral rights to be owned and exercised by Aboriginal and Torres Strait Islander communities over Indigenous cultural works and heritage. While the proposal was initially rejected by Parliament, in May 2003 Senator Richard Alston, Minister for Communications, Information Technology and the Arts, and The Honourable Daryl Williams, Attorney-General, announced new legislation to amend the *Moral Rights Act* by enshrining **communal** moral rights for Indigenous communities wishing to protect their knowledge and creations from inappropriate, derogatory or illegal use by others.[21] The new legislation, currently scheduled for introduction in Parliament sometime in 2004, offers some recognition and protection of the ways in which Indigenous authors may be embedded in social and customary relations that are at odds with traditionalist European notions of 'individual' authorship and ownership, and reflects the continuing struggle to use current legislation and agreements to serve the interests of Indigenous authors of all forms of creative works covered by the *Moral Rights Act*.

Moral rights and Indigenous customary law

The second area of difficulty for Aboriginal and Torres Strait Islander authors is in relation to laws governing their rights over published work: the incommensurabilities of existing copyright law with Indigenous customary law.

---

[20] Terri Janke, 'Network News Editorial' (1998) 1 *Queensland Community Arts Network: Network News Journal* 4.
[21] Senator Richard Alston, Minister for Communications, Information Technology and the Arts and The Hon. Daryl Williams AM QC MP, Attorney-General, 'Indigenous communities to get new protection for creative works' (Press Release, 19 May 2003) IPS 031/2003.

The most compelling of these are, as we have seen, those elements of copyright law which favour individual rights and entitlements over those of a group or community, and which fail to recognise at law the rights, obligations and responsibilities that Indigenous authors may have in relation to customary law. One of the most trenchant problems arising for Indigenous authors involves who retains copyright in their work once they have died. Under current laws, copyright is part of an individual's legal estate, and may be inherited by, or bequeathed to, nominated beneficiaries as part of a person's will. Should an author die intestate, however, the courts decide, usually on the basis of surviving next of kin, who should inherit the copyright in a particular work. Under this arrangement, it is possible for copyright quite literally to fall into hands that are wrong or inappropriate under customary law. While the inheritor of copyright can assign his or her rights, it can be difficult to re-assign copyright to an entire community or clan group.

Part of the problem revolves around the question of exclusive versus non-exclusive rights. 'Under copyright,' says the ACC, 'rights are generally "exclusive", and the copyright owner can choose' whether or not to exercise those rights. 'Under Indigenous customary law', however, 'rights are often non-exclusive, and often the person who is entitled to deal with things has obligations to use the work to maintain the life of the community', obligations which may nevertheless conflict with the restrictions and limitations of copyright law itself.[22] Beyond this, it is not difficult to contemplate the legal complexities occasioned when the copyright interest in published works, when joint copyright is held by Aboriginal or Torres Strait Islander authors and their editors or researchers, collides with those of the community, who may under customary law—and increasingly under moral rights law—be considered the rightful owners, custodians and proprietors of such work.

Probably the most comprehensive survey of the issues facing Indigenous Australian artists, creators, individuals and communities in relation to Indigenous cultural and intellectual property law, including the challenges posed by the failure of Australian courts to recognise customary law, has been produced by Terri Janke in a 1998 report titled *Our Culture, Our Future: Report on Australian Indigenous Cultural And Intellectual Property Rights*, prepared for the Australian Institute for Aboriginal and Torres Strait Islander Studies and the Aboriginal and Torres Strait Islander Commission.[23] In this ground-breaking report, Janke outlines the cultural and intellectual property

---

[22] Australian Copyright Council, above n 1, 61.
[23] Terri Janke, *Our Culture, Our Future: Report on Australian Indigenous Cultural and Property Rights* (Michael Frankel and Company, Solicitors, Sydney, 1998).

rights that Indigenous people want, based on wide consultation throughout the report's preparation. Not surprisingly, the following rights were listed in relation to Indigenous cultural property, heritage and intellectual property:[24]

1. the right to own and control
2. the right to control commercial use
3. the right to benefit commercially
4. the right to full and proper attribution
5. the right to protect sacred, secret and significant knowledge and sites
6. the right to own and control management [of lands]
7. the right to prevent derogatory, offensive and fallacious use
8. the right to have a say in preservation and care
9. the right to control the use of traditional knowledge.

Almost all of these rights, existing and desired, have some relevance in the sphere of Indigenous authorship and publishing, and many of them reflect the imperatives of customary law. Further rights related to defining what constitutes Indigenous cultural and intellectual property and/or heritage, the duty of care in relation to maintaining and developing Indigenous culture and knowledge, and the communal ownership of cultural and intellectual property were also identified drawing on the United Nations *Draft Declaration on the Rights of Indigenous Peoples*.[25] These, similarly, reflect the ways in which current copyright and moral rights laws fall short of the needs of Indigenous people and communities to fulfill their obligations and protect their interests under the principles of self-determination and cultural sovereignty.

Additional options for protecting Indigenous rights and interests

Recognition of Indigenous folklore

Some critics have made the effort to examine whether existing moral rights and copyright laws can be further amended to better accommodate the rights and interests of Indigenous authors, both individual and communal. One of these alternatives involves a legal framework for incorporating recognition of Indigenous folklore within the framework of copyright law, an issue given some discussion in Janke's report and by a number of other scholars

---

[24] Ibid, ch 4, 43–8.
[25] United Nations, *Open-Ended Inter-Sessional Working Group on the Draft Declaration on the Rights of Indigenous Peoples* http://www.unhchr.ch/indigenous/groups-02.htm at 17 November 2003.

such as Dieter Dambiec in *Indigenous Peoples' Folklore and Copyright Law.*[26] Dambiec notes that in New Zealand, Maori people have available to them (under Article 2 of the 1840 *Treaty of Waitangi 1840)* unequivocal recognition of customary rights, including rights and privileges relating to the possession and retention of Maori 'cultural treasures' and customs, which includes Maori languages. Dambiec's argument is that, if language is a 'cultural treasure' worthy of protection by the Crown (a protection recently reaffirmed by the Privy Council in 1994),[27] then other creative 'treasures', including folklore, must by extension also fall under the protection of the treaty. A similar clause that builds on and improves where necessary the terms of the *Treaty of Waitangi* relating to the protection and maintenance of cultural customs, treasures and practices would certainly be worthwhile in any future treaty or agreement made between Indigenous peoples and an Australian government.

Payment for works in the public domain

A few other possibilities are available in the present for the further protection and compensation of Indigenous authors and creators in relation to rights over their work. These include *domain public payant*, or payment for public domain works. Such works include those for which copyright has expired, works by unknown authors, traditional works, works by foreign people whose home states are not signatories to any of the international copyright conventions, and works owned by the state on the basis of intestacy at the time of death of the original copyright holder. Such payments, in circumstances in which they operate in other countries, are essentially a form of 'cultural levy'. People wishing to use such work pay a fee, usually in the form of royalties, if they want to use the work commercially. The significance of a public domain royalty system is that it can be used to benefit existing Indigenous communities by collecting money based on the works of long-gone authors. Such payments can be used to support new generations of authors and artists, whose works 'in turn produce income for the livelihood of future generations of authors'.[28]

Resale royalty rights

Another scheme is *droit de suite*, or resale royalty rights, a feature of copyright law in many European countries. A resale royalty provides an author or artist with the right to share in any profits their work may generate if the work is later resold. While it has most immediate relevance for Indigenous

---

[26] See Dieter Dambiec, *Indigenous Peoples' Folklore and Copyright Law* (2002) http://members. ozemail.com.au/~dambiec/indigenous-llm-essay.html at 31 January 2002.

[27] Ibid, 35.

[28] Australian Copyright Council, above n 1, 64.

visual artists—a number of whom have been victims of horrific instances of exploitation at the hands of gallery owners and private collectors—it has clear application to the rights of Indigenous authors, particularly in circumstances in which an author chooses to sell or otherwise assign his or her copyright, and the royalties that flow from this, in exchange for a set fee or other financial consideration.

The politics of cultural ownership

Australian publishing agreements have been slow to take up and explore options that enhance the rights and standing of Aboriginal and Torres Strait Islander authors of published material. This is so, in part, because of entrenched biases about what constitutes legitimate forms of 'authorship', 'rights' and 'copy' as part of a broader historical framework of Western discourses of knowledge, attitudes that are only now beginning to shift. In an article entitled 'Mabo and Museums: The Indigenous (Re)appropriation of Indigenous Things',[29] Sandra Pannell explores the complex relationship between Indigenous cultural re-possession and institutional practices in a post-*Mabo* context.[30] In her discussion of the politics of cultural ownership and the concept of inalienable rights to possession, Pannell contends that rather than being the 'fortunate recipients' of repatriation, restitution or the return of cultural objects/property held by institutions, Indigenous people are instead the agents of the (re)appropriation of museums' holdings in such transactions. Her argument, while too nuanced to do justice to it here, effectively dismantles the Western logic of ownership and possession based on phenomenological (that is, tangible) custodianship, and re-frames this logic in line with the inalienability of Indigenous ownership of cultural heritage that persists despite the colonial contexts and practices in which that heritage may be 'held' by institutions or the state.

By analogy, the idea that Aboriginal and Torres Strait Islander authors have inalienable rights to their stories, even when these stories have been written down and prepared for publication by others, suggests a fundamental shift in how we conceive of Indigenous ownership and cultural property in ways that recent moral rights legislation has only barely begun to touch upon. The intangibility of Indigenous words as a form of cultural property needs to be understood as inalienable in the same way that more tangible, material cultural property is currently understood. If that happens,

---

[29] Sandra Pannell, 'Mabo and Museums: The Indigenous (Re)appropriation of Indigenous Things' (1994) 65 *Oceania* 18.

[30] *Mabo v Queensland (No 2)* (1992) 175 CLR1.

we might have the beginnings of an ethical basis for laws, agreements and contracts that are defined by the standards of 'keeping-while-giving'[31] in the realm of Aboriginal and Torres Strait Islander authorship. And we might then truly be able to approach something that begins to look like an Indigenous Australian 'sovereign' text.

---

[31] See Annette B. Weiner, *Inalienable Possessions: The Paradox of Keeping-While-Giving* (Berkeley, University of California Press, 1992).

Chapter 18

Evaluating Agreements between Indigenous Peoples and Resource Developers

Ciaran O'Faircheallaigh[*]

Introduction

Agreement making between Indigenous peoples and non-Indigenous interests has become widespread in Australia during recent years, particularly since the introduction of the *Native Title Act 1993* (Cth) (*NTA*). There is broad and politically bipartisan support for agreement making as the preferred method by which to address conflicts or issues surrounding the recognition of native title.[1] Reflecting this fact, Indigenous peoples and their organisations, all levels of government and industry are devoting very substantial

[*] I am grateful to Chris Athenasiou, Tony Corbett, Paul Hayes, Deanna Kemp, Michael Neal and David Ritter for comments on earlier drafts of this paper. The views expressed and any errors or omissions remain solely my responsibility.

[1] See, for example, Peter Beattie in James Cook University, 'New Director to Practice "Practical Reconciliation"' (Media Release, 15 September 2003) http://media.jcu.edu.au/story. cfm?id=222 at 4 December 2003, 1; Patrick Dodson, 'Welcome on Behalf of the Organisers' in Gary Meyers (ed.), *The Way Forward: Collaboration and Cooperation 'In Country': Proceedings of the Indigenous Land Use Agreements Conference 26–29 September, Darwin, NT, Australia* (National Native Title Tribunal/Australian Government Publishing, Perth, 1996) 4; Robert French, 'Pathways to Agreement' in Gary Meyers (ed.), *The Way Forward: Collaboration and Cooperation 'In Country': Proceedings of the Indigenous Land Use Agreements Conference, 26–29 September 1995, Darwin*, (National Native Title Tribunal/Australian Government Publishing, Perth, 1996) 16; Darryl Manzie, 'Welcome by Northern Territory Government Minister' in Gary Meyers (ed.), *The Way Forward: Collaboration and Cooperation 'In Country': Proceedings of the Indigenous Land Use Agreements Conference, 26–29 September 1995, Darwin*, (National Native Title Tribunal/Australian Government Publishing, Perth, 1996) 2; Paul Wand, 'Negotiating with Aboriginal People for Land Access' (Paper presented at the Symposium on Native Title: Facts, Fallacies and the Future, Sydney, 30 May 1998).

financial and other resources to the negotiation of agreements. Support for agreement making results from a conviction that in comparison to the alternatives (essentially litigation or a resolution involving political conflict), negotiation of agreements is less time consuming, less costly, and more likely to permit 'win–win' situations that allow benefits to be channelled to Indigenous people without creating a backlash from competing interests that have incurred a commensurate loss.

But what are the outcomes or results of agreement making in practice? Is a negotiation-based approach actually offering win–win situations and an equitable distribution of costs and benefits between Indigenous and non-Indigenous interests? What benefits are being delivered to Indigenous Australians by agreements, and are those benefits being experienced equally by different Indigenous groups? Does agreement making represent an equitable and sustainable basis upon which to address native title issues? Or are agreements essentially a rhetorical and ideological device designed by non-Indigenous interests to create the impression that Indigenous concerns are being addressed, while in reality they constitute a vehicle for continuing dispossession of Indigenous peoples?

The fact that numerous agreements have been signed during recent times does not, of itself, allow us to address these questions. It is necessary to examine and assess the actual outcomes of agreements before reaching any conclusions about their role and significance. It is entirely possible, for example, that an agreement might in fact leave an Indigenous party worse off than before, as in the example in which the agreement involves extinguishment or impairment of native tile or other rights and allows activities that are destructive of Indigenous lands, yet at the same time creates few substantial benefits for Indigenous people.

Preliminary indications are that, in the area of resource development, outcomes from agreement making are, in fact, highly variable. In some cases, Indigenous groups are achieving substantial economic benefits and innovative provisions to minimise the impact of commercial activities on their traditional lands. In other cases the benefits gained by Indigenous groups are negligible, impact minimisation provisions are similar to those already provided in general legislation, while in some cases restrictions are placed on the exercise of rights that Indigenous parties possess under general legislation.[2] These (albeit preliminary) findings highlight the need for a thorough analysis of outcomes from agreements for Indigenous interests.

---

[2]   Ciaran O'Faircheallaigh, and Rhonda Kelly, 'Corporate Social Responsibility and Native Title Agreement Making' in *Development and Indigenous Land: A Human Rights Approach* (Human Rights and Equal Opportunity Commission and Griffith University, Sydney, 2003) 9.

Such an analysis has yet to occur in Australia. A substantial body of literature has developed on agreement making.[3] However, most of this literature deals with frameworks within which to conduct agreement making and, in particular, with provisions of the *NTA*; with the relationship between native title and Indigenous law, culture and society; with negotiation processes; and with strategies for pursuing agreements. Little of it deals with the

[3] See, for example, Parry Agius *et al.*, 'Negotiating Comprehensive Settlement of Native Title Issues: Building a New Scale of Justice in South Australia' (Issues Paper No 20, Native Title Research Unit, AIATSIS, 2002); Mary Edmunds (ed.), *Regional Agreements: Key Issues in Australia* (Native Title Research Unit, AIATSIS, Canberra, 1999); Marcus Holmes, *Native Title Negotiation in the New Legislative Environment* (Deacons, Perth, 2001); Bryan Horrigan and Simon Young (eds), *Commercial Implications of Native Title* (The Federation Press, Leichardt, NSW, 1997); Indigenous Support Services and ACIL Consulting, *Agreements between Mining Companies and Indigenous Communities: A Report to the Australian Minerals and Energy Environment Foundation* (ACIL Consulting, 2001), http://www.acilconsulting.com. au/pdf/ISSReport Indigenous agreements.pdf at 4 December, 2003; Bryan Keon-Cohen (ed.), *Native Title in the New Millenium: A Selection of Papers from the Native Title Representatives Bodies Legal Conference, 16–20 April 2000: Melbourne, Victoria* (Aboriginal Studies Press and Native Title Research Unit, AIATSIS, Canberra, 2001); Marcia Langton and Lisa Palmer, 'Modern Agreement Making and Indigenous People in Australia: Issues and Trends' (2003) 8(1) *Australian Indigenous Law Reporter* 1–31; Siobhan McKenna, 'Negotiating Mining Agreements under the Native Title Act 1993' (1995) 2(3) *Agenda* 301; Gary Meyers (ed.), *The Way Forward: Collaboration and Cooperation 'In Country': Proceedings of the Indigenous Land Use Agreements Conference, 26–29 September 1995, Darwin* (National Native Title Tribunal/Australian Government Publishing, Perth, 1996); Gary Meyers (ed.), *Implementing the Native Title Act: First Steps; Small Steps* (National Native Title Tribunal, Canberra, 1996); Ciaran O'Faircheallaigh, 'Negotiating with Resource Companies: Issues and Constraints for Aboriginal Communities in Australia', in Richard Howitt, John Connell and Philip Hirsch (eds), *Resources, Nations, and Indigenous Peoples: Case Studies from Australasia, Melanesia, and Southeast Asia,* (Oxford University Press, Melbourne, 1996) 184; Ciaran O'Faircheallaigh, 'Negotiating Major Project Agreements: The "Cape York Model"' (Discussion Paper No 11, AIATSIS, 2000) http://www.aiatsis.gov.au/rsrch/rsrch dp/negotiating.htm at 4 December, 2003; Diane Smith, 'Valuing Native Title: Aboriginal, Statutory and Policy Discourses About Compensation' (Discussion Paper No 222, Centre for Aboriginal Economic Policy Research, Australian National University, 2001); Margaret Stephenson, 'Negotiating Resource Development Agreements with Indigenous People: Comparative International Lessons', in Brian Horrigan and Simon Young (eds), *Commercial Implications of Native Title* (The Federation Press, Leichardt, NSW, 1997) 320. See also numerous papers published under the auspices of the National Native Title Tribunal http://www.nntt.gov.au and the Australian Institute of Aboriginal and Torres Strait Islander Studies (AIATSIS) http://www.aiatsis.gov.au.

[4] For some partial exceptions see Ciaran O'Faircheallaigh 'Mineral Development Agreements Negotiated by Aboriginal Communities in the 1990s' (Discussion Paper No. 85, Centre for Aboriginal Economic Policy Research, Australian National University, 1995) http://www.anu.edu.au/caepr/Publications/DP/1995 DP85.pdf at 4 December 2003; Ciaran O'Faircheallaigh, *A New Approach to Policy Evaluation: Mining and Indigenous People* (Ashgate Press, Aldershot, England, 2002); Frances Flanagan, Helen Lawrence and James Fitzgerald, 'The Burrup Agreement: A Case Study in Future Act Negotiation' (Paper presented at the National Native Title Conference: Native Title on the Ground, Alice Springs, 3–5 June, 2003); Clive Senior, 'The Yandicoogina Process: A Model for Negotiating Land Use Agreements' (Regional Agreements Paper No 6, AIATSIS, 1998) http://www.aiatsis.gov.au/rsrch/ntru/ ra/RAIP6.pdf at 4 December 2003.

outcomes of agreements.[4] There has certainly been no systematic attempt to evaluate such outcomes. More specifically, there are currently no benchmarks or criteria for assessing the terms of negotiated agreements.[5]

This paper contributes to the development of such benchmarks or criteria. It emerges from a research project that seeks to document and explain outcomes from agreements negotiated between Indigenous peoples, mining companies and (in some cases) government. The paper identifies criteria for assessing outcomes in relation to key issues commonly addressed in such agreements, as they affect Indigenous interests. These criteria are not meant to be definitive, but rather to provoke discussion and debate among researchers and Indigenous and non-Indigenous people involved in negotiating agreements.

Identifying criteria by which to assess outcomes of agreements involves significant challenges, which we discuss later. However, unless those challenges are addressed it is very difficult for Indigenous people to gauge whether agreement making represents an effective way to protect and promote their interests and those of their children and grandchildren. It is also difficult for non-Indigenous groups to determine whether the current large investment of resources in agreement making is appropriate, and impossible for researchers to reach informed judgments about the political, economic, social or cultural significance of agreement making in contemporary Australia. In the absence of systematic criteria for assessing the outcomes of agreements, there is also a danger that an 'ideology of agreement making' will dominate, with the achievement of agreements as such—rather than the creation of substantive outcomes for Indigenous peoples—taking central place.

The contents of agreements represent only one dimension of 'outcomes' from agreement making, a point addressed in the next section. We then discuss some of the issues involved in developing criteria for assessing the content of agreements. Subsequent sections identify criteria that could be applied in evaluating particular aspects of agreements between Indigenous peoples and resource developers, as they relate to Indigenous interests. In concluding the paper, we briefly discuss the question of how the criteria outlined below might be viewed by resource developers.

Defining 'outcomes' from agreement making

In terms of agreement making, there are four basic ways in which outcomes arise. These are:

---

[5]   Smith, above n 3, 44.

1. From the process of seeking an agreement. Outcomes in this sense may arise before an agreement is signed and, indeed, may occur even if the parties fail to reach agreement. Such outcomes could result, for instance, from the need to define the Indigenous parties to a proposed agreement and so to delineate land-owning groups and their boundaries; from debates within an Indigenous community about what would constitute an acceptable agreement; or from greater interaction between Indigenous and non-Indigenous interests.

2. Outcomes in terms of the content or provisions of an agreement. For example an agreement may provide that certain sums of money be paid annually, that specific numbers of apprenticeships be provided for Indigenous people, or that a particular cultural heritage protection regime be put in place.

3. Outcomes in terms of the putting into effect of provisions contained in agreements; that is, the actual payment of money, the filling of apprenticeships, the application of a cultural heritage protection regime. It is important to identify this as a separate dimension of 'outcomes', because agreement provisions, even when they are legally binding, are not always put into effect.[6] Given this fact, agreements might be evaluated quite differently if assessed from a 'post-implementation' perspective. An agreement that offered limited benefits to Indigenous parties but had been fully implemented might be judged more favourably than an agreement that offered much more extensive benefits that had not been put into effect.

4. Outcomes in terms of the final impact of provisions that are implemented; for example, the effects of financial payments on the economic, social and cultural well-being of recipients and on social relations in an Indigenous community; or the impact of employment and training programs on the skill levels and labour force status of community members.

This chapter focuses on outcomes in the second sense, the provisions or contents of agreements. This is not to suggest that other dimensions of outcomes are less important. However, we focus on the content of agreements for the following reasons. First, while agreement provisions do not of themselves determine outcomes in the third and fourth senses, they do **determine the range of possible outcomes**. For example, the financial provisions of an agreement directly determine what financial flows can

---

[6] See Susan Phillips, 'Enforcing Native Title Agreements: *Carriage v Duke Australia Operations Pty Ltd*' (2000) 5(3) *Indigenous Law Bulletin*, 14; Ciaran O'Faircheallaigh, 'Implementation: The Forgotten Dimension of Agreement Making in Australia and Canada' (2002) 5(20) *Indigenous Law Bulletin*, 14.

actually occur. Second, they also have a critical role in shaping the ultimate impact of these flows on recipients and communities, by determining the quantum of payments, the form in which they accrue and also, in many cases, to whom they will accrue in the first instance and how they will be spent. Third, whether an agreement contains provisions designed to ensure its subsequent implementation is a critical factor in determining whether implementation actually occurs.[7] Finally, people's assessment of agreement-making processes is not independent of the content of agreements that emerge from particular processes. Thus, the content of agreements is of central relevance to the other three dimensions of outcomes from agreement making.

Assessing the content of agreements

Assessing the content of agreements creates substantial challenges, in part because it is an inherently political process at a range of levels. Any agreement involves an allocation of costs and benefits to different (Indigenous and non-Indigenous) parties, and interpretations or understandings of particular outcomes depend very much on whether or not one is a beneficiary of those outcomes. For example, an outcome that results in a small number of Indigenous people receiving the major share of financial benefits from an agreement is unlikely to be regarded poorly by the recipients, but is almost certain to face criticism from other community members. In addition, political actors may seek to ensure that outcomes with which they are identified are regarded in a positive manner, and are likely to criticise any approach that defines these outcomes as negative. Finally, as in all communities, there are underlying differences between individuals and groups depending on factors such as personal values, age, gender, and kin affiliations and, for example, stereotypes that represent all Indigenous people as primarily interested in conserving natural and cultural heritage are misleading. It follows that various groups within an Indigenous community may differ greatly, for example, in their assessments of an agreement that creates strong protection for cultural heritage values but does little to generate additional economic activity.

Assessing agreement outcomes is inherently political for another reason. As indicated above, Australian politicians and policy makers have a substantial and public commitment to agreement making, and agreement making provides a basic rationale for the existence of a number of influential

---

[7] O'Faircheallaigh, 'Implementation: The Forgotten Dimension' above n 6.

institutional actors, in particular the National Native Title Tribunal (NNTT). It also provides a mechanism for the orderly and timely grant of mining interests that are critical to industry, and generates substantial financial benefits for legal and other professionals, Indigenous and non-Indigenous. If an assessment of agreement outcomes indicated that they are not generating significant benefits for Indigenous people, this would threaten a substantial political and economic status quo. It is revealing, for example, that the NNTT's emphasis appears to be overwhelmingly on the processes used in securing agreements, rather than on evaluating their outcomes.[8]

Another key issue involves the context within which individual agreements are made, particularly the goals being pursued by particular Indigenous groups, the nature of specific projects, the legal position of the native title parties, and the policy and legislative frameworks of specific states and territories. An outcome that might be regarded as strongly positive in one context might be considered a poor outcome in another. For example, a particular financial outcome might be highly regarded if the project concerned is economically marginal and if the legal position of the Indigenous people concerned is weak, for instance because the developer holds granted mining leases or because their chances of achieving a favourable native title determination through the courts are slim. The same outcome could be regarded as poor in relation to a project expected to be very profitable in a legal context that places Indigenous landowners in a stronger bargaining position.

If careful attention is not paid to context, Indigenous leaders or/and professional negotiators may be unjustly accused of negotiating deals that undermine Indigenous interests.

A final point arises from the fact that in the real world negotiation usually requires trade offs for each party between individual objectives. Concessions are made on issues of lesser importance in order to achieve gains in relation to issues of critical importance. The latter, given the diversity of Indigenous Australia, may vary from one community to another. Thus, an agreement that achieved a 'poor' outcome in relation to some specific issues might reflect a positive achievement overall and could be highly valued by Indigenous participants who have made carefully calculated concessions in order to get a positive outcome on issues of central importance to them.

---

[8] See the contributions of Tribunal members and staff to Meyers, *The Way Forward*, above n 3; Meyers, *Implementing the Native Title Act*, above n 3 and Keon-Cohen, above n 3. See also the NNTT's web site at http://www.nntt.gov.au.

Why gauge outcomes?

Yet, despite the difficulties it is essential to try to assess outcomes in a systematic manner. Otherwise, how are Indigenous people to gauge whether a proposed agreement is likely to generate positive results for them? How are they to hold accountable negotiators who act on their behalf unless there is some basis on which to assess performance? How can Indigenous leaders and professional negotiators demonstrate that they have achieved optimum outcomes in specific contexts, and so avoid the personal and political conflict arising from criticisms of their roles? How can Indigenous people evaluate the extent of concessions being proposed in one area or the gains being offered in another? For example, if less favourable employment and training provisions are being considered in order to achieve a desired cultural heritage protection regime, how large a concession is actually being made on the former? It is impossible to address this issue unless we have some independent benchmark for evaluating employment and training provisions.

In addition, researchers cannot gauge the impact on outcomes of system-level influences such as the character of native title or land rights legislation, or of specific factors such as the effectiveness of Indigenous organisations or negotiating teams unless there is some basis on which to assess those outcomes.

A core argument of this chapter is that it is feasible to develop standard criteria for assessing individual aspects of agreements, given what is known about the general objectives of Indigenous groups involved in negotiating agreements. Focusing on individual components of agreements acknowledges that the overall outcome generated by an agreement will be influenced by key contextual factors. At the same time, more transparency can be created in relation to what is being offered, achieved or conceded on each individual issue. This, in turn, can be useful in allowing Indigenous organisations and communities to assess what they are being offered by developers, how this compares with what has been achieved elsewhere and what degree of compromise will be involved if they make concessions in one area in order to make gains in another. In addition, criteria for gauging individual components of an agreement may facilitate an overall evaluation of whether an agreement represents a positive outcome for Indigenous parties. For example, if application of relevant criteria indicate that Indigenous people are expected to accept serious impairment of their native title rights, to give open-ended support to a project, but are offered financial, employment and training and cultural heritage provisions that rank poorly, there are serious doubts as to whether they should enter an agreement.

This chapter outlines preliminary work on developing criteria for assessing eight critical components of agreements that deal with resource development projects. The first three components are **environmental management, cultural heritage protection** and **rights and interests in land**. These are crucial in minimising negative cultural and social impacts and in allowing Indigenous parties to fulfil their responsibilities to look after country and to protect and promote their cultural integrity and social vitality. The next three components, **financial payments, employment and training** and **business development** are, along with rights and interests in land, critical in gaining economic (and associated social and cultural) benefits for Indigenous people from development on their country. The seventh component, **Indigenous consent and support**, represents a crucial issue for developers and a major area in which they seek a 'consideration' or *quid pro quo* in return for benefits they offer to Indigenous parties under an agreement. The final component, **implementation measures**, has a critical bearing on whether provisions related to the other seven are actually put into effect.

It is not assumed that these eight components encompass all the important facets of mining agreements. However, the eight components analysed below do represent critical aspects of agreements for many Indigenous groups, and so are an appropriate starting point for evaluating the contents of agreements.

Different sorts of criteria are developed to address each component, depending on the nature of the issue involved and the way in which it is dealt with in agreements. With financial provisions, the payments provided in individual agreements can be recalculated to a standard measure (total expected payments over the life of a project as a percentage of the expected value of project output), allowing comparison across agreements. In other cases (for example, environmental management, rights and interests in land) a scale is employed, with each step in the scale reflecting an increase in the likelihood that Indigenous goals will be achieved. A third alternative (applied to employment and training, business development and implementation) is to adopt a cumulative approach. A series of relevant initiatives is identified, with the prospect that Indigenous goals will be achieved increasing the more of these initiatives are included in an agreement. The way in which these approaches operate is set out in detail in the following sections. Our assumptions regarding Indigenous interests in relation to relevant provisions of mining agreements are also outlined.

Environmental management

For many Indigenous groups entering mining agreements in Australia, a central goal is to use the agreement to help minimise adverse impacts on 'country', a term that generally refers to the totality of the biophysical environment, areas and sites of cultural or/and religious significance associated with it.[9] Three sets of provisions commonly found in mining agreements are relevant here: those dealing with environmental management, with cultural heritage protection and with Indigenous rights and interests in land. These three issues are dealt with separately in virtually all mining agreements in Australia, reflecting the fact that separate legal and regulatory regimes apply to each issue under Australian law. The same approach is followed here. However, it is acknowledged that for many Indigenous people such a separation has little validity, because distinctions are not made between the biophysical environment and areas or sites of cultural significance associated with it, and because they regard recognition of their rights as landowners as integral to their capacity to look after country.

For Indigenous people, environmental management provisions in agreements should maximise the ability of Indigenous landowners to ensure that adverse effects on country are minimised, by allowing them to influence the way in which mining companies and regulatory authorities define and manage environmental issues and impacts.

A significant number of agreements contain no provisions in relation to Indigenous involvement in or responsibility for environmental management of the projects concerned. These agreements could be regarded as achieving a score of zero on a scale designed to measure the efficacy of provisions in this area (with zero being least efficacious).

In this case it is, in fact, possible for an agreement to achieve a negative (that is, worse than zero) score, for the following reason. Indigenous people have rights under general environmental management legislation; for example, the right to object to a development, to request a higher level of environmental assessment, to demand modifications to a proposed project or to sue for damages arising from environmental impacts. An agreement may limit the ability of Indigenous people to exercise those rights. A number of Australian agreements, for example, prohibit Indigenous parties from undertaking any action that would delay development of a project, and this might preclude their ability to lodge objections to the grant of environmental approvals. Inclusion of such provisions may leave Indigenous people worse off than in the absence of an agreement.

A scale against which environmental management provisions can be assessed could be constructed as follows (see Figure 18.1). A score of –1 would indicate the inclusion of provisions that limit exercise of existing rights under general legislation. A score of **0** would indicate the absence of any relevant provisions. Positive provisions would be ranked from **1** to

---

[9]   As noted above it is not assumed that this goal is held equally by all Indigenous people.

6 as indicated below, with each step in the scale reflecting an increase in the likelihood that Indigenous parties will be able to substantially influence environmental management and impacts. It is not assumed that each step involves an **identical** increase in this likelihood.

Figure 18.1: Criteria for assessing environmental management provisions

– Provisions that limit existing rights
0 No provisions.
1 Developer commits to Indigenous parties to comply with environmental legislation.
2 Developer undertakes to consult with affected Indigenous people.
3 Indigenous parties have a right to access information, and to evaluate independently, information on environmental management systems and issues.
4 Indigenous parties may suggest enhanced environmental management systems; project operator must address.
5 Joint decision making on some or all environmental management issues.
6 Indigenous parties have the capacity, within specified limits, to act unilaterally to prevent potential environmental damage.

The positive steps on the scale are:

1. The developer makes a commitment to the Indigenous parties to comply with environmental legislation, regulations and management plans. This allows the Indigenous parties to take legal action if any breach of legislation or regulations occurs, because such a breach constitutes breach of the agreement.

    However, such a provision on its own does not allow traditional owners to play a **positive** role in avoiding negative impacts in the first place, except to the extent that a company might apply higher environmental standards in the expectation that traditional owners might take legal action if damage occurs.

2. The project operator undertakes to consult with affected Indigenous people regarding major environmental management issues, and structures (such as consultative committees) are put in place to ensure that this happens. While such provisions potentially allow Indigenous people to contribute in a positive way to environmental management, there is no guarantee that the operator will accept their perspectives or respond to their suggestions.

3. Indigenous parties have a right to access, and independently evaluate, information on environmental management systems and activities. Access to information and technical expertise can place traditional owners in a stronger position, both because it may provide a firm basis

314 Honour Among Nations?

for threatening or taking legal action, and because the information obtained may support traditional owners' concerns or positions and make it harder for the company to ignore these.

4. Indigenous parties may suggest ways to enhance environmental management systems, and the project operator undertakes to implement these or some agreed alternative. This approach addresses the possibility that project operators might ignore proposals put forward by Indigenous parties through consultative structures.

5. There is provision for joint decision making in relation to some or all aspects of environmental management. The project operator no longer makes unilateral decisions, possibly after consultation with or input from traditional owners. Rather, traditional owners are incorporated into decision-making processes in a structural and permanent fashion.

6. Indigenous parties have a capacity under specified conditions to act unilaterally (for example, by suspending mining operations) in circumstances in which they believe that environmental damage is occurring or may occur. Such a provision can have powerful effects, but not necessarily because it is regularly (or, indeed, ever) invoked. Rather, it creates a compelling incentive for the project operator to work closely with traditional owners in order to avoid the possibility of environmental damage or risk that might lead them, for example, to suspend production. Provisions of this sort have been included in one mining agreement in Queensland and one in Alaska.

A number of general points should be made in relation to this scale.

First, each point on the scale represents a broad approach, and there is scope for variation in outcomes **within** each of these approaches. For example, in relation to point 5—joint decision making—the role of Indigenous parties may be restricted to some nominated and very specific aspects of a project (for instance, release of water into a particular creek), or could extend to the whole of a project's environmental management system.

Second, the different approaches are not mutually exclusive. For example, it may be that an Indigenous party seeks a commitment to comply with environmental legislation so that it can take legal action if adverse impacts do occur (point 1), while at the same time wishing to contribute to enhancing environmental systems (point 4) in order to minimise the chances that environmental damage will happen.

On the other hand, however, the scale does represent a clear hierarchy in terms of the potential for allowing Indigenous influence in relation to environmental management, and a commitment to provisions further up the scale would often also result in adoption of points lower on the scale. For example, it is most unlikely that a developer would not consult with

Indigenous parties in relation to environmental management issues (point 2) if those parties have a capacity to halt project operations should they believe that environmental damage is likely to occur (point 6).

Cultural heritage protection

Any approach to protection of cultural heritage has two critical components: the level of protection that is sought and the means (activities, processes, resources) available to secure that protection. The two are inextricably linked. For example, avoidance of any damage to areas or sites of cultural significance may be specified as the required level of protection. However, if the processes used to pursue this goal make it difficult or impossible to involve the Indigenous people who hold relevant cultural knowledge, important sites or areas may be left unprotected or managed inappropriately and the goal cannot be achieved.

Each jurisdiction in Australia has legislation that purports to offer protection to Indigenous cultural heritage. Agreement provisions are of value to Indigenous people to the extent that they provide **additional** protection to that contained in legislation. This can occur in circumstances in which the degree of protection required by an agreement is higher than in legislation, or in which additional means of securing protection are provided through an agreement, or in which both of these occur. One implication of this situation is that an evaluation of cultural heritage provisions in agreements must take the nature of relevant state or territory cultural heritage legislation into account. The same set of agreement provisions might provide substantial additional protection in a state with weak cultural heritage protection legislation, but little or no additional protection in a state with strong legislation.

Potential negative outcomes of cultural heritage protection agreements

The manner in which agreements can create positive outcomes for Indigenous people in relation to protection of their cultural heritage is discussed in detail below. However, it must be remembered that, as with environmental management, agreements can leave Indigenous people worse off in this regard, for a number of reasons.

First, when cultural heritage legislation creates rights for Indigenous people whose exercise is discretionary, an agreement can involve a commitment not to exercise some or all of those rights.

Second, under some agreements Indigenous parties undertake that site protection measures will not add significantly to the cost of project development. This may exclude from consideration options for site protection that could be available under general heritage protection legislation in the absence of an agreement.

Third, an agreement may create additional obstacles to the effective operation of Indigenous law and custom, in a way that results in less effective protection of sites or areas of significance. For instance, some agreements require that Indigenous parties indicate whether or not heritage clearance work is required or/and conduct clearances within very short periods (as little as seven days). Such provisions can render it impossible to involve the range of Indigenous people required to determine whether sites or areas of significance might be affected by project activities and, if so, how appropriate and effective protection could be achieved.

Potential positive outcomes of cultural heritage protection

Looking first at the **level** of cultural heritage protection, five general approaches can be identified, and can be seen as points along a spectrum that reflects increasingly positive outcomes for Indigenous parties. These are presented in Figure 18.2, in ascending order according to the level of protection offered to Indigenous cultural heritage.

Figure 18.2: Levels of protection in relation to Indigenous cultural heritage

---

1 Sites or areas of significance may be damaged or destroyed by project development without any reference to Indigenous people.

2 Sites or areas of significance may be damaged and destroyed, and Indigenous parties only have an opportunity to mitigate the impact of the damage; for example, by removing artefacts or conducting ceremonies.

3 The developer must 'minimise' damage, to the extent that this is consistent with commercial requirements; for example, by re-routing infrastructure to avoid areas of significance.

4 The developer must avoid damage, except where to do so would make it impossible to proceed with the project (for instance, when a major site is co-located with the ore body to be developed).

5 There is an unqualified requirement to avoid damage.

In assessing agreement provisions on the basis of this spectrum we must also consider, as indicated earlier, the level of protection already available under legislation. In Western Australia, for instance, state legislation allows the relevant government minister to permit the destruction of sites as part of project development work. It can therefore be regarded as falling at point 1 on the spectrum outlined in Figure 18.2. An agreement in Western Australia that required the developer to avoid damage except where this would involve abandoning a project (point 4 on the spectrum) would represent a significant increase in the level of protection relative to that provided by state laws.

Turning to the activities, processes and resources applied to actually securing a desired level of protection, mining agreements can include a number of approaches that are outlined in Figure 18.3. As with environmental provisions discussed earlier, each general approach can encompass a number of 'gradations'. The benefits created for Indigenous parties by relevant agreement provisions depend on two factors: (i) the degree to which elements provided through an agreement are already mandated by cultural heritage protection legislation, and (ii) how many of the elements listed in Figure 18.3 are present in an agreement. In other words, the list is **cumulative**. The more provisions are included, the higher the 'score' an agreement would earn and the greater the level of effective protection likely to be afforded. This is in contrast to Figures 1 and 2, which present **alternative** approaches organised in a hierarchy.

Figure 18.3: Activities, processes and resources applied to securing protection of Indigenous cultural heritage

- Provisions that maximise Indigenous control of site clearance and heritage management processes; for example, by allowing them to choose technical staff who assist in surveys, organise field trips, receive reports from technical staff and control the flow of information to the developer.
- Provision of financial and other resources to support cultural heritage clearances, facilitating the effective participation of the appropriate Indigenous people.
- Explicit protection of any cultural knowledge provided by Indigenous people as part of the cultural heritage protection regime.
- Measures to enhance an Indigenous community's internal capacity for cultural heritage protection; for example, by supporting a ranger program or funding activities to promote cultural vitality.
- Provisions that allow traditional owners to, at least temporarily, stop project activities where sites or areas of significance are threatened or damaged, so as to allow protective or remediation measures to be put in place.
- General measures designed to reinforce the **system** of cultural heritage protection (as opposed to specific protection of individual sites); for example, cultural awareness training for mining company employees and contractors to make them aware of the need for cultural heritage protection and of the protection measures in place.

Drawing these points together, an agreement would generate large net benefits for Indigenous parties if it sought a high level of protection for Indigenous cultural heritage on the scale presented in Figure 18.2, included provisions covering most or all of the elements listed in Figure 18.3, and was located in a state with weak cultural heritage legislation.

Rights and interests in land

In a minority of cases (most importantly, Aboriginal freehold land in the Northern Territory) Indigenous people are recognised under Australian law as owners of land subject to development. In such cases, Indigenous rights and interests in land do not arise as an issue in negotiations. However, for most Indigenous groups in Australia a key goal in negotiating agreements is to be recognised by the developer and government as the owners of their ancestral lands, and to have title to these lands recognised, or conferred on them, under Australian law. This may involve recognition of native title, or grant of freehold or other title under relevant state or territory legislation. Typically, an agreement will relate only to land covered by mining interests dealt with in that agreement. However, some agreements (for instance, that for the Century zinc/lead mine) provide for the transfer to Indigenous people of tenure to other areas of land held by the mining company.

Any legal recognition or conferring of title requires the support of the relevant state or territory government, as developers have no power to deal in title. This support may be expressed as an obligation accepted by government as a party to an agreement, or it may arise from a policy decision by a government that is not a party. Destruction or diminution of existing Indigenous rights in land can also only be effected by government.

At a general level, provisions of agreements that deal with rights and interests in land create benefits for Indigenous parties to the extent that they recognise and protect any existing rights and interests; increase the possibility of a future recognition or grant of rights or interests; or have the immediate effect of recognising or creating rights or interests. Recognition or conferring of rights or interests as an integral part of an agreement is preferable to commitments by non-Indigenous parties to promote such an outcome in the future, given the uncertainty that inevitably surrounds the realisation of those commitments.

Agreement provisions are contrary to Indigenous interests when they destroy, reduce or require the surrender of existing rights in land; deny the existence of Indigenous rights in land; require that the exercise of such rights be limited or suspended during project life; or lessen the possibility that rights or interests will be recognised in the future, for example by leaving the developer free to oppose a future application for determination of native title.

On the basis of this discussion, Figure 18.4 sets out possible criteria in relation to Indigenous rights and interests in land. These cover a spectrum from comprehensive extinguishment or surrender of existing rights and interests, at one end, to the immediate recognition or grant of new rights or interests at the other. For consistency, all provisions that represent any diminution of Indigenous rights or interests, or reduce the possibility that such rights and interests may be recognised in the future, are given a negative sign. This does not mean that inclusion of any provision designated as negative would, in the overall context of an agreement, represent a poor outcome for Indigenous parties. It is difficult to envisage, for example, how a mining project could proceed and so generate benefits for Indigenous people in the absence of any suspension or limitation of Indigenous rights or interests in land.

Figure 18.4: Criteria for assessing agreement provisions related to Indigenous rights or interests in land

- −5 Provisions that have the **general** effect of extinguishing or requiring the surrender of existing rights or interests in land.
- −4 Provisions that extinguish or require surrender of **specific** rights or interests in land (for example, rights in minerals).
- −3 Provisions that define Indigenous rights or interests in a narrow or restricted manner (for instance, by specifying a native title determination that defines native title rights more narrowly than might occur under Australian law).
- −2 The exercise of Indigenous rights or interests is suspended or restricted during project life.
- −1 There is no immediate effect on Indigenous rights or interests, but non-Indigenous parties reserve the right to oppose any future determination of native title or the grant of another form of title.
- 0 There are no provisions in relation to Indigenous rights and interests in land
- 1 While no recognition of Indigenous rights or interests is made or proposed, there is an explicit statement that the agreement is not intended to extinguish any rights or interests that do exist.
- 2 Developers undertake not to oppose any future determination of native title or grant of other title.
- 3 Indigenous people are recognised as having rights or interests under Indigenous law and custom, but there are no provisions in relation to recognition of such rights or interests under Australian law. (While such recognition may lack legal consequences, it may hold symbolic value for some Indigenous people).

4 Developers or/and governments make positive commitments in relation to a future recognition or grant of rights or interests to Indigenous parties; for example, by setting out a process intended to lead to such an outcome.
5 The agreement has the effect of recognising or conferring Indigenous rights or interests in land; for example, through an Indigenous Land Use Agreement (ILUA) that involves a determination of native title.

Financial payments

At least in principle, financial payments represent the least complex of the areas in terms of establishing benchmarks. As long as details of the payments and of the actual or likely economic scale of the project are available, it is possible to establish a common measure against which to assess individual agreements. For instance, total annual payments (regardless of the basis on which they are imposed) can be aggregated and calculated as a proportion of annual sales revenue, and the resulting ratio used to compare different agreements. This approach has the advantage that it takes into account a critical contextual factor: project scale. For example, it will rate highly an agreement that provides for small payments in absolute terms if those payments are substantial relative to the earning capacity of the project.

This discussion relates solely to the quantum of payments to Indigenous interests provided for in agreements, and assumes that the larger the share of sales revenue accounted for by such payments, the more favourable the agreement for Indigenous interests. It is acknowledged that matters are more complex if one considers the impacts that ultimately arise from expenditure of payments under agreements (that is, outcomes in the fourth sense identified earlier). From this perspective, a critical issue is how payments are utilised, and it is conceivable that, if payments are used in ways that are socially destructive, a larger quantum of money might actually generate **less** favourable 'outcomes' for Indigenous parties.[10]

Employment and training

Mining generates relatively few jobs relative to the investment involved. However, in the regions in which many Indigenous people live, mining represents one of the few sources of wage employment. In addition, wages

---

[10] Colin Filer, 'The Bougainville Rebellion, the Mining Industry and the Process of Social Disintegration in Papua New Guinea', in Ronald May and Matthew Spriggs (eds), *The Bougainville Crisis* (Crawford House Press, Bathurst, 1990) 73; O'Faircheallaigh *A New Approach to Policy Evaluation*, above n 4 (Ashgate Press, Aldershot, England, 2002).

in the mining industry are considerably higher than the national average. Employment in mining can help people develop skills that can be used in establishing small businesses, in other industrial employment and in community development work. For these reasons, Indigenous communities usually wish to use agreements to help achieve a high level of Indigenous participation in a project's workforce.

Until the 1990s, agreements in Australia tended to include only a general commitment by the developer to maximise opportunities for Indigenous employment on the project, a commitment unsupported by any specific initiatives or resources. A typical provision would require the project operator to 'employ as many Aboriginal people as is practicable where those Aboriginal people have the skills required to perform the work involved'. In assessing the employment and training component of an agreement, this sort of approach could be regarded as a minimum or 'base' case. A cumulative approach can then be adopted, with provisions being regarded as more favourable to the extent that they also include commitments to the other measures outlined in Figure 18.5.

An agreement containing substantial measures under each of the categories below could be regarded as being at the other end of a spectrum from agreements that contain no relevant provisions.

Figure 18.5: Provisions to encourage Indigenous employment and training

- A general commitment is made to maximise opportunities for Indigenous employment and training.
- Specified resources are committed to Indigenous employment and training; for example, in dollar terms or in the form of numbers of apprenticeships or dedicated training staff. The extent of such commitments, relative to the scale of the project, represents an important basis for comparison in this area.
- Concrete goals are specified for employment and training programs (for instance, specific and rising proportions of Indigenous employees), and incentives (or sanctions) are created for the achievement (or non-achievement) of these goals.
- In relation to recruitment to training positions and jobs, an explicit statement of preference is made in favour of Indigenous people who are suitably qualified or capable of becoming so, and resources are committed to ensuring that such people are made aware of employment opportunities.
- An explicit developmental component is included, by setting out a staged progression through levels of skill and responsibility for Indigenous trainees/ employees.
- Measures are required to make the workplace conducive to recruitment and retention of Indigenous workers; for instance, cross-cultural awareness training for non-Indigenous employees and supervisors, or adjustment to rosters or rotation schedules in order to acknowledge cultural obligations.

Business development

Many Indigenous groups are keen to take advantage of business opportunities associated with a mining project, because of the employment and income they generate. Such opportunities are also valued because they can allow creation of sustainable enterprises that can continue after a specific mining project has ended, by selling goods and services to other mines or to other industrial or commercial customers. However, most Indigenous communities and organisations face serious constraints in pursuing available business opportunities, because of (i) the high transaction costs that can be involved in standard tendering and contracting arrangements; (ii) scarcity of capital for business investment; (iii) lack of relevant skills; and (iv) their competitive disadvantage in relation to large, well-established non-Indigenous businesses.

In developing criteria for business-development provisions, the need to overcome these barriers should be considered. There may, however, be different ways to overcome each barrier. On this basis, criteria have been established as follows. The absence of any provisions relating to business development attracts a score of zero. An agreement that expresses general support for Indigenous business development but contains no specific provisions designed to overcome the barriers listed above attracts a score of 1. An additional point is obtained for each provision or set of provisions that address a barrier in a specific and substantive manner. Thus, an agreement that contains such provisions in relation to two barriers would obtain a score of 3; an agreement that addressed all four barriers would earn a score of 5. This approach is outlined in Figure 18.6. It should be noted that in some cases the examples provided of specific initiatives represent alternatives, while in others a combination of the initiatives might be required to achieve the desired effect.

Indigenous consent and support

A critical component of agreements from the perspective of both developers and Indigenous peoples involves the provision by the latter of consent for the issuing and exercise of project or other related rights and more generally their support for a project. The former usually involves the issue and renewal of licences and associated grants of interests to allow resource exploitation and operation of associated infrastructure. The concept of 'support' for a project is less specific, but in general involves undertaking activities that promote the efficient development and operation of a project or/and refraining from activities that might hinder the development or efficient operation of a project. Indigenous consent and support represent a critical part of the 'consideration' that a developer receives from Indigenous parties to an agreement.

Figure 18.6: Criteria for assessing business development provisions

> **0** No relevant provisions.
>
> **1** General commitments to promote Indigenous business opportunities.
>
> **2** Contains specific initiatives designed to minimise transaction costs for Indigenous businesses; for example, by:
>   - 'unbundling' large contracts into smaller contracts that are more easily managed by Indigenous businesses
>   - offering contracts to Indigenous businesses on a 'cost plus margin' basis, as an alternative to competitive tenders.
>
> **3 Also** contains specific initiatives designed to overcome paucity of relevant expertise; for example, by:
>   - giving Indigenous enterprises access to the business expertise of staff employed by the developer
>   - funding Indigenous people to undertake business management training, possibly by providing them with preferential access to relevant public programs (where government is a party to the agreement).
>
> **4 Also** contains specific initiatives designed to overcome paucity of business capital; for example, by:
>   - providing 'bankable' long-term contracts to Indigenous enterprises in order to assist them in obtaining finance from commercial lenders
>   - providing capital via joint ventures between the developer and Indigenous businesses during their start-up phase.
>
> **5 Also** contains specific initiatives designed to overcome disadvantage of Indigenous enterprises relative to large, well-established non-Indigenous businesses; for example:
>   - including a preference clause for competitive Indigenous businesses
>   - specifying a margin in favour of Indigenous businesses in assessing tenders.

It should be stressed that our focus is on **what an agreement requires of Indigenous people** in terms of consent and support, not on the actual level of political support for a project within the relevant Indigenous community or group. It is entirely possible that an Indigenous community strongly supports a project, but that the relevant agreement demands little by way of consent or support. The converse is also possible. An agreement may require extensive consent and support, but may face underlying opposition within a community; for example, because Indigenous people felt they had little choice but to enter the agreement.

It is difficult to understand why a developer would enter a legally binding agreement that offers significant benefits to Indigenous parties unless the agreement entitles the developer to some degree of Indigenous consent or/and support. Thus, the provision of such consent or support does not, of itself, represent a negative outcome for Indigenous parties. Rather, it represents a requirement that must be fulfilled if they are to achieve positive outcomes that they value.

However, the nature of Indigenous consent and support can vary considerably. Critical to any overall evaluation of an agreement is an awareness of this point, and an ability to weigh up the extent of consent and support offered to a company against the benefits offered to Indigenous parties. At one end of the spectrum, Indigenous parties may be asked to do nothing other than indicate that **they** accept the validity of specified mining interests granted under Australian law. At the other end of the spectrum, Indigenous people may be asked to give open-ended support to all of a developer's activities on their traditional lands. Agreements that include an identical package of benefits could be assessed very differently depending on where they fall along this spectrum.

Figure 18.7 lists a range of alternative approaches, with the extent of Indigenous consent and support (and so the extent of benefit accruing to the developer) increasing as one progresses through the list from 1 to 7. Distinguishing features between the various approaches include: (i) whether recognition or approval or interests or project support is or is not qualified, for instance, to ensure the operation of cultural heritage legislation; (ii) whether the support Indigenous parties provide is passive, for example by requiring them not to oppose a project, or demands that they actively support the developer's activities; and (iii) whether the consent or support is restricted to specific interests identified in an agreement or extends more widely to other potential interests or activities.

Figure 18.7: Criteria for assessing agreement provisions related to Indigenous consent and support

---

1 The Indigenous parties recognise the validity of, and undertake not to challenge, identified mining or other related tenements already granted to the developer.

2 The Indigenous parties consent to and undertake to facilitate the issue of identified mining or other related tenements.

3 The Indigenous parties undertake not to impede or prevent the developer from the enjoyment of existing or newly granted mining tenements or related interests. However, such a commitment is qualified, for example, by not precluding the application of cultural heritage or environmental protection legislation.

4 The Indigenous parties have a positive obligation to support development once mining tenements or interests are granted. However, such a commitment is qualified, for example, by not precluding the application of cultural heritage or environmental protection legislation.

5 Indigenous people make an unqualified commitment that they will do nothing to hinder the efficient development or operation of a particular project.

6 Indigenous people consent to the grant of unspecified interests to the developer beyond those identified in an agreement.

7 Indigenous parties make an open-ended and general commitment to support the developer's activities.

Implementation measures

Implementation of agreements is a complex field that deserves extensive and separate discussion.[11] However, given the critical importance of implementation, a brief and general discussion is offered here and relevant criteria for assessing implementation provisions are identified.

The prospect that an agreement will actually be put into effect is influenced by a range of factors. Many of these relate to the wider economic, political and social context within which an agreement operates, rather than to the provisions of an agreement itself. A critical issue involves the general human and organisational capacities of Indigenous and other parties, which shapes their ability to sustain commitments they have made under agreements. Other important factors include, for instance, the degree of political support mobilised for an agreement; prevailing conditions in regional, national and corporate economies; and broader policy and legislative frameworks within which agreements operate.

However, the prospects for success are also greatly influenced by the degree to which agreements contain the means for its own implementation. It is on this latter issue that we focus here.

Research on implementation of agreements and on policy implementation generally[12] highlight the critical need to allocate human and financial resources **specifically** to the task of implementation, including in some cases to developing general organisational capacity. Yet, many mining agreements fail to do this.[13] Thus, a critical component in evaluating agreements

---

[11] See O'Faircheallaigh, *A New Approach to Policy Evaluation*, above n 4; O'Faircheallaigh, *Implementation: The Forgotten Dimension*, above n 6; Phillips, above n 6.

[12] O'Faircheallaigh, *A New Approach to Policy Evaluation*, above n 4; O'Faircheallaigh, *Implementation: The Forgotten Dimension*, above n 6.

[13] O'Faircheallaigh, *Implementation: The Forgotten Dimension*, above n 6.

in this context is the extent of human and financial resources allocated to implementation, relative to the size of the task involved.

This and other critical matters related to implementation are listed in Figure 18.8. A cumulative approach applies in this case also. The more of these matters that are addressed in an agreement, the greater the likelihood of successful implementation.

Figure 18.8: Criteria for assessing implementation provisions of agreements

---

- The extent of human and financial resources allocated to implementation, relative to the size of the task involved.
- Creation of structures (such as monitoring and management committees) whose **primary** purpose is implementation of the agreement.
- Establishment of processes that require senior managers in each signatory organisation to focus on implementation on a systematic and regular basis.
- Clear and explicit statements of each party's obligations, with specific incentives for parties to fulfil these obligations and/or credible and appropriate sanctions and penalties for non-performance.
- Regular and systematic monitoring of relevant activities and initiatives to provide reliable information on the extent of implementation or non-implementation.
- Periodic and adequately resourced review processes to establish whether specific measures are creating the outcomes anticipated by the parties and to address any implementation failures, where necessary by amendment of agreements.

Conclusion

The criteria developed in this chapter are not intended to allow an overall quantitative, numerical assessment of an agreement by simply adding up scores for each component of an agreement. This is impossible because the issues dealt with in an agreement are different in nature (for example, financial payments, cultural heritage, employment, Indigenous consent and support) and so different criteria must be adopted in addressing various issues. It is also undesirable because, as noted earlier, context is critical in assessing agreements, and a comparison of agreements on the basis of single numerical scores might detract from a focus on context. However, the criteria can be used in a number of ways that are useful to Indigenous parties, to their advisers and to developers.

In particular, the criteria represent a standard against which individual components of agreements can be gauged, and so against which Indigenous people and their advisers, and in some cases developers (see below), can assess offers or demands they are proposing to put to other negotiating parties, or which they have received from other parties. In addition, the criteria allow Indigenous parties to be better informed in assessing the potential trade-offs that inevitably arise in negotiations, because they can be used to assess what will be sacrificed by making a concession in one area, and what will be gained in another area. The criteria can also offer a clear basis on which Indigenous groups can assess proposed agreements in their entirety, and on which non-Indigenous advisers can base advice to their clients.

The criteria can also be useful in broadly assessing the relative performance of organisations and negotiators; for example, on the basis of a comparison of outcomes contained in agreements negotiated in similar legal and economic contexts. They can thus promote accountability. They can also be of considerable help to researchers who wish to examine, for example, the outcomes generally associated with negotiation-based approaches or who wish to compare the sorts of negotiated outcomes being achieved under different legislative regimes.

In sum, the criteria can help support a more rigorous and transparent approach to negotiation of agreements between developers and Indigenous parties, and so enhance the net benefits gained by Indigenous peoples from development on their land.

A final issue involves the degree to which developer and Indigenous evaluations of particular agreement provisions would converge or diverge. It should certainly not be assumed that a 'developer perspective' would be achieved by inverting the scales discussed above; that is, that a '6' for Indigenous people is a '1' for developers and vice versa. For example, if a mining company wishes to achieve excellence in environmental management, it might share with Indigenous parties a preference for provisions that ensure active Indigenous participation in its environmental programs. A project operator moving from a fly-in/fly-out to a residential workforce for technical and economic reasons might face strong commercial incentives to quickly increase recruitment from long-term residents of a region, most of whom might be Indigenous. The operator might therefore wish to adopt employment and training provisions that would be rated highly by Indigenous parties to an agreement.

On the other hand, in some cases the developer's perspective will certainly diverge from that of Indigenous parties. For example, a company planning a short-life mine on a fly-in/fly-out basis might find extensive commitments to Indigenous training and employment unacceptable.

The degree of divergence or convergence between Indigenous and developer perspectives will be affected by a range of factors, including corporate policies and organisational cultures; the time frames employed in corporate decision making; legislative and policy regimes in certain jurisdictions; and the technical and economic characteristics of individual projects. Extensive and detailed analysis is required to identify how these variables would interact and affect corporate assessment of alternative agreement provisions, and to identify approaches that would maximise support from both Indigenous and developer interests in specific contexts.

Chapter 19

Creative Conflict Resolution: The Timor Sea Treaty between Australia and East Timor

Gillian Triggs

Introduction

Few issues strike so profoundly at the heart of national sovereignty than disputes over the ownership of offshore oil and gas resources on the continental shelf. When the dispute also involves an impoverished nation emerging from colonial and illegal occupations and a relatively resource-rich nation, prospects for legal settlement appear to be dim. The historical inability of Indonesia and Australia, and more recently East Timor, to delimit the seabed boundary between them in the Timor Gap remains unresolved. It is thus a significant diplomatic achievement that Australia and East Timor have recently agreed upon a new *Timor Sea Treaty,* which entered into force on 2 April 2003,[1] and also upon an *International Unitisation Agreement* for the oil and gas deposit known as Greater Sunrise.[2]

It is the purpose of this chapter to consider how legal and diplomatic skills can be employed to ensure that any such potential international conflicts can be either avoided or better managed. The central argument is that if states can set aside, even temporarily, seemingly intractable problems of

---

[1] *Timor Sea Treaty Between the Government of East Timor and the Government of Australia,* opened for signature 20 May 2002, [2003] ATS 13 (entered into force 2 April 2003) (*Timor Sea Treaty*).

[2] *Agreement Between the Government of Australia and the Government of the Democratic Republic of Timor-Leste Relating to the Unitisation of the Sunrise and Troubador Fields,* opened for signature 6 March 2003, [2003] ATNIF 6 (*International Unitisation Agreement*).

sovereignty raised by national boundaries, then they can move forward to manage other issues of mutual concern, such as access to petroleum resources, regional security, the environment and people-smuggling. By working together on defined and achievable goals, it becomes possible to build confidence and trust between states. Such a piecemeal and functional approach to international problem solving thus offers states a means of resolving other more fundamental and damaging issues dividing them.

The Timor Gap issue, the focus for this chapter, is but one of several regional examples of potential conflict over offshore territories and seabed boundaries. Creative diplomatic and legal skills are needed to defuse and resolve differences including overlapping claims in the continental shelf of the Gulf of Thailand and in the areas north, west and east of the Natuna Islands in the East Asian Seas.[3] Sovereignty disputes over islands with related maritime claims include the Spratleys, the Kuriles, and Senkuku or Diayutai and more recently Pulan Batu Puteh.[4] These disputed claims variously involve all major nations in the Asia Pacific region including Russia, China, the Philippines, Brunei, Japan, Thailand, Vietnam, Indonesia, Cambodia, Korea, Taiwan, Australia, Singapore and Malaysia.

The *Timor Sea Treaty* and the *International Unitisation Agreement* demonstrate how potentially damaging impediments to neighbourly relations can be managed and how creative thinking, flexible diplomatic negotiations and innovative legal drafting can provide solutions to some kinds of international conflicts.

Political and legal background

In order to understand the differing legal perspectives of Australia, Indonesia and East Timor regarding their rights to the petroleum resources of the Timor Gap, it is useful to revisit the history of negotiations and political developments over the past thirty years or so.[5] A starting point is the *1972 Seabed Agreement*[6] between Australia and Indonesia on seabed boundaries

---

[3] Jonathan Charney and Lewis M. Alexander, *International Maritime Boundaries* (M. Nijhoff, Dordrecht, 1993) vols 1, 2; Jonathan Charney, 'Central East Asian Maritime Boundaries and the Law of the Sea' (1995) 89 *American Journal of International Law* 724, 739.

[4] Ibid.

[5] For a legal background see Gillian Triggs and Dean Bialek, 'The New Timor Sea Treaty and Interim Arrangements for Joint Development of the Timor Gap' (2002) 3 *Melbourne Journal of International Law* 322.

[6] *Agreement Between the Government of the Commonwealth of Australia and the Government of the Republic of Indonesia Establishing Certain Seabed Boundaries in the Area of the Timor and Arafura Seas Supplementary to the Agreement of 18 May 1971*, opened for signature 9 October 1972, 974 UNTS 319 (entered into force 8 November 1973) (1972 Seabed Agreement).

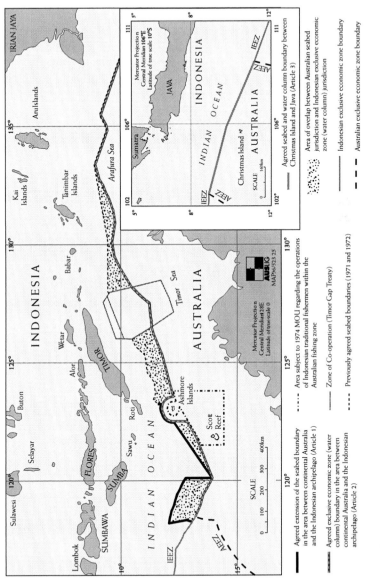

Figure 19.1: Consolidated depiction of all Australian–Indonesian maritime boundaries after entry into force of the Treaty.
Source: Geoscience Australia. © Commonwealth of Australia, reproduced by permission, all rights reserved

in the Arafura and Western Timor Seas—an agreement that is the source of the current discord (see Figure 19.1).

A glance at these boundaries will immediately illustrate the problem— the seabed delimitations on either side of the Timor Gap (see Figure 19.2) are significantly closer to the coast of Indonesia than that of Australia. The gap between the two parts of the 1972 line reflects the role of the colonial power, Portugal, as the United Nations-appointed Administrative Authority over the territory of East Timor. It was not possible for the Australian Government to delineate a seabed boundary between itself and the territory of East Timor unless and until it had engaged in negotiations with Portugal itself. The political upheavals in Portugal in the early 1970s rendered any such negotiations impossible. The Timor Gap was thus left to be resolved on another day.

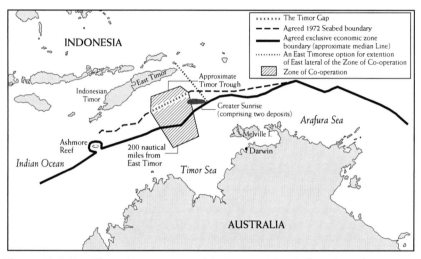

Figure 19.2: East Timor (map not to scale). Source: School of Anthropology Geography and Environmental Studies (SAGES), University of Melbourne, reproduced by permission

When the *1972 Seabed Agreement* was reached with Indonesia, interna- tional law appeared to be relatively clear. Under the 1958 *Convention on the Continental Shelf*, a coastal state has sovereign rights over the continental shelf as the natural prolongation of its land territory up to the depth of 200 metres or to the depth at which exploitation of the natural resources is technically possible.[7] Australia has consistently maintained that the natural prolongation of its north-western continental shelf extends, as a geomor-

---

[7]   *Convention on the Continental Shelf*, opened for signature 29 April 1958, 499 UNTS 311, art 1(a) (entered into force 10 June 1964).

phological fact, up to the Timor Trough. The Timor Trough is approximately 40 nautical miles from East Timor, is 250–350 nautical miles from the closest part of Australia (Melville Island) and is up to 3000 metres in depth. The *1972 Seabed Agreement* thus reflected Indonesia's acceptance at the time that the Timor Trough differentiates the Australian continental shelf from the seabed claimed by Indonesia.

The respective rights of Indonesia and Australia were thus relatively clear at international law as it was recognised in 1972. Since that time, however, there has been a period of dramatic legal and political change. With the withdrawal of Portugal from East Timor in 1975, civil war broke out in the territory, prompting the illegal invasion of East Timor by Indonesia in December 1975.[8] By 1976 Indonesia, through its *Statute of Integration*, had absorbed East Timor into the State of Indonesia. In 1978 and 1979 respectively, Australia recognised Indonesia as the *de facto* and *de jure* sovereign over East Timor. Whatever the legal and ethical merits of Australia's recognition of Indonesian effective control over East Timor, it facilitated closer relations between these nations and led to renewed attempts to close the Timor Gap. Prompting these efforts to agree upon a permanent seabed boundary were the exploratory findings of international petroleum companies that indicated the presence of oil and gas resources. Any such resources could be exploited only if there was legal stability and security of tenure for concessions and licenses in order to attract the financial investment that is required to unlock the wealth of the area.

By the early 1980s, however, international law, and most particularly Indonesia's understanding of it, had changed. The 1982 *United Nations Convention on the Law of the Sea* had been concluded, under which new principles had evolved.[9] One of the most important of these new principles is the concept of a 200-nautical mile Exclusive Economic Zone dealing with water rights and resources and the principle of equitable delimitation of overlapping claims to an Exclusive Economic Zone and continental shelf.[10] Indonesia now argued that, as there are fewer than 400 nautical miles between the opposite coasts of East Timor and Australia and, as it also argued, contrary to Australia's view, that there was a common continental shelf between them, a starting point for negotiations for a permanent seabed boundary should be a median line. In short, Indonesia was no longer prepared to draw the line across the Timor Gap directly between the two boundary lines agreed in

[8] See Department of Foreign Affairs and Trade, *East Timor in Transition 1998–2000* (2001).
[9] *United Nations Convention on the Law of the Sea*, opened for signature 10 December 1982, 1833 UNTS 3 (entered into force 16 November 1994).
[10] *United Nations Convention on the Law of the Sea*, opened for signature 10 December 1982, 1833 UNTS 3, arts 55, 74, 83 (entered into force 16 November 1994).

1972. Rather, Indonesia demanded that any final boundary should be closer to a median line between it and Australia (see Figure 19.2).

In response to Indonesia's claim, Australia repeated its long-maintained legal position, that the Australian continental shelf extends to the Timor Trough. Australia argues that the legal requirement for an 'equitable solution' to delimitation of a shared continental shelf does not apply if the disputing states do not, in fact, share a common shelf.[11] Geomorphologically Australia's continental shelf finishes at the Timor Trough, being co-existent with the Timor Gap. Neither Indonesia nor Australia was prepared to negotiate on their views of the international rules on delimitation of the seabed boundary between them. In these circumstances of opposing legal positions, each of which is credible, there was an impasse. It was in this diplomatic gridlock that information was confirmed that significant oil and gas deposits lay within the area of the Timor Gap. The governments of Indonesia and Australia now recognised that some form of compromise was needed, for otherwise neither state could benefit from the lucrative potential of the petroleum resources. Representatives of both states then embarked upon negotiations for the conceptually innovative *Timor Gap Treaty* that was agreed between Indonesia and Australia in 1989.[12]

Timor Gap Treaty

The most notable feature of the *Timor Gap Treaty* is that it adopted the principle of 'sovereign neutrality', enabling resource exploitation to proceed jointly, on the grounds that no activities would prejudice the legal positions of either Indonesia or Australia. Under Article 2(3):

> Nothing contained in this Treaty and no acts or activities taking place while this Treaty is in force shall be interpreted as prejudicing the position of either Contracting State on a permanent continental shelf delimitation in the Zone of Cooperation nor shall anything contained in it be considered as affecting the respecting sovereign rights claimed by each Contracting State in the Zone of Cooperation.

Such a clause will be effective at international law to protect the legal rights of both states and has the signal advantage of enabling them to exploit the

---

[11] *United Nations Convention on the Law of the Sea*, opened for signature 10 December 1982, 1833 UNTS 3, art 83 (entered into force 16 November 1994). Art 83 deals with 'delimitation of the continental shelf between States with opposite or adjacent coasts'.

[12] *Treaty Between Australia and the Republic of Indonesia on the Zone of Cooperation in an Area Between the Indonesian Province of East Timor and Northern Australia*, opened for signature 11 December 1989 [1991] ATS 9 (entered into force 9 February 1991) (*Timor Gap Treaty*).

resources of the area without fearing a prejudice to their long-term rights to negotiate a permanent boundary in the future.

The *Timor Gap Treaty* also established a zone of co-operation (ZOC) within which the joint petroleum exploitation could take place under the regulatory control of the Joint Authority.[13] All benefits of exploitation were to be shared equally between Indonesia and Australia. In this way, employing a 'without prejudice' clause, it became possible to unlock the resources of the ZOC, making them available to both states, even though permanent delimitation of the continental shelf remained to be resolved at some stage in the future.

The *Timor Gap Treaty* proved to be successful in facilitating petroleum activities over the following ten years, with revenue first becoming available in July 1998. Nonetheless, the unavoidable fact remained—the Treaty was founded on Indonesia's illegal annexation of territory under Portuguese and United Nations administrative control. With the resignation of President Suharto and the assumption of the presidency by Dr Habibe, the political position in East Timor underwent yet another change. To international surprise, Indonesia agreed to a plebiscite to determine the future governance of East Timor. The convincing vote of the peoples of East Timor for full independence led to the termination of Indonesia's authority in the area in October 1999. The United Nations Transitional Administration in East Timor (UNTAET)[14] then assumed authority over East Timor—this being the first time that a United Nations body had sole responsibility for managing a territory during its transition to nationhood. The mandate for UNTAET also included a power to conclude international agreements.

Interim period under UNTAET

One of the many concerns of UNTAET during this interim period was to ensure that the legal security for investments in petroleum activities in the Timor Gap could continue, for it had rapidly become clear that East Timor needed an economic foundation if it was to survive in the future. The diplomatic and legal problem with maintaining the regime for joint exploitation, however, was that the *Timor Gap Treaty* was viewed by the representative

---

[13] *Timor Gap Treaty*, opened for signature 11 December 1989 [1991] ATS 9, art 2 (entered into force 9 February 1991).

[14] United Nations Security Resolution 1272, UN SCOR, 54th Sess, 4057th mtg, [1], UN DOC S/RES/1272 (1999), provides UNTAET with power to 'exercise all legislative and executive authority'.

of the East Timorese as an illegal or 'tainted' agreement.[15] Some alternative resolution to the boundary issue or to ensure a stable legal environment for continued petroleum activities was needed. For the interim period it was agreed between UNTAET and Australia that while the *Timor Gap Treaty* itself was not acceptable, the 'terms' of the agreement would be.[16] By employing the notion that the terms of the *Timor Gap Treaty* would continue to apply, the embarrassing illegality of the original agreement could be avoided, at least insofar as the East Timorese were concerned.

The technique of using the terms of the *Timor Gap Treaty* rather than continuing the agreement itself—something of a diplomatic nicety—proved, nonetheless, to be a successful means for ensuring that resource activities could be maintained during the interim period. There had, however, been no resolution of what would happen on the full independence of East Timor. It was at this pre-independence stage that new legal arguments were introduced. The representatives of East Timor now claimed that the median line principle of equidistance was, as Indonesia had earlier argued, the valid principle of international law for establishing a seabed boundary between East Timor and Australia.[17] Complicating discussions was the discovery of the Greater Sunrise fields, 20 per cent of which straddles the eastern lateral of the ZOC.[18] They also argued that the lateral boundaries of the ZOC needed to be expanded, both to the west and east, to enlarge the area to which East Timor was entitled. The practical effect of this argument was that many of the resources of the ZOC under the *Timor Gap Treaty* would now be within the sovereign jurisdiction of East Timor, including the resources of the Greater Sunrise deposit (see Map 2).

The Greater Sunrise deposit has emerged as the most valuable resource in the area, with a projected gross value of approximately $30 billion.[19] The Greater Sunrise fields straddle the eastern lateral of the ZOC, the eastern

---

[15] Dr Mari Alkatiri, currently the Prime Minister of East Timor, is reported to have said, 'We are not going to be a successor to an illegal treaty'. See Karen Polglaze, 'Timor Gap Treaty in Doubt', *The Canberra Times* (Canberra) 30 November 1999, 2.

[16] *Exchange of Notes Constituting an Agreement between the Government of Australia and the United Nations Transitional Administration in East Timor (UNTAET) Concerning the Continued Operation of the Treaty between Australia and the Republic of Indonesia on the Zone of Cooperation in an Area Between the Indonesian Province of East Timor and Northern Australia of 11 December 1989* [2000] ATS 9 (entered into force 10 February 2000, with effect from 25 October 1999) (*Exchange of Notes*).

[17] A median line approach relies on state practice and the 1958 *Convention on the Continental Shelf*, opened for signature 29 April 1958, 499 UNTS 311, art 1(a), (entered into force 10 June 1964).

[18] The Greater Sunrise resources area is estimated to contain recoverable gas reserves valued at approximately A$30 billion: Department of Foreign Affairs and Trade, *Government Press Kit: Timor Sea Treaty*, 20 May 2002.

[19] Ibid.

part of the deposit lying within an area that, on the basis of the *1972 Seabed Agreement*, lies within Australian sovereignty. The legal problem had thus dramatically expanded from dealing with the Timor Gap to assessing the legal rights to resources of a much more valuable deposit that straddles the demarcation line of the ZOC. Dr Mari Alkatiri, on behalf of the peoples of East Timor, argued that the whole of the Greater Sunrise field should lie within the seabed jurisdiction of East Timor. Following independence, Dr Ramos Horta[20] has more dramatically noted that 'anyone of average IQ can look at the map and observe that the Greater Sunrise field lies wholly within the maritime jurisdiction of East Timor'.[21]

While the battle lines were thus drawn for the purposes of negotiations between Australia and the shortly-to-be independent East Timor, there was another legal issue to be resolved. Any negotiations with the East Timor transitional administration could not bind any future government of East Timor. On its independence, East Timor would be free to decide at that time whether any pre-negotiations remained in its national interests.[22] It was in this context that the Australian Government and representatives of East Timor began negotiations to map out a workable solution to this range of problems.

Negotiation of the Timor Sea Treaty

The first stage of the new negotiations in anticipation of East Timor's independence was a *Memorandum of Understanding* under which a new *Timor Sea Arrangement* could be adopted.[23] This tentative *Arrangement* was agreed to be 'suitable for adoption' and created a capacity for continuing joint development of the resources of the ZOC once independence was achieved. Under these arrangements, however, joint development was to be on the basis that the revenues gained from exploitation should be split so that East Timor would receive 90 per cent of the product and Australia would receive 10 per cent. This is a significant departure from the earlier position of 'sovereign neutrality' that had been reflected in part on the 50–50 share of production under the *Timor Gap Treaty*. The question thus arises whether a 90/10 split of production can effectively preserve the respective legal positions of the

---

[20] Currently the Minister for Foreign Affairs for East Timor.

[21] Ramos Horta, 'Experience with the United Nations' (Speech delivered at the International Peace and Reconciliation Conference, University of Melbourne, 14 July 2003).

[22] For a discussion of the international legal principles applicable on independence see Gillian Triggs, 'Legal and Commercial Risks of Investment in the Timor Gap,' (2000) 1 *Melbourne Journal of International Law* 98, 106–8.

[23] *Memorandum of Understanding of Timor Sea Arrangement,* 5 July 2001 http://www.austlii. edu.au/au/other/dfat/special/MOUTSA.html at 5 March 2004.

two states as to their continental shelf rights. For many, a 90/10 split seems to be as close to recognising the weakness in Australia's legal position as it is possible to move without conceding sovereignty entirely. As a matter of law, however, as both states have agreed to joint development with a 90/10 revenue split on a non-prejudicial basis, they are entitled to resume their earlier legal positions on boundary delimitation if, in the future, they agree not to continue with joint activities.[24] As was the case in the *Timor Gap Treaty*, the *Timor Sea Treaty* includes a provision (art 2(b)) that:

> Nothing contained in this Treaty and no acts taking place while this Treaty is in force shall be interpreted as prejudicing or affecting Australia's or East Timor's position on or rights relating to a seabed delimitation or their respective seabed entitlements.[25]

Such a 'without prejudice' clause has proved to be one of the most important legal techniques in the armory of international law, enabling states to put their sovereignty disputes to one side in the interests of functional problem solving. Were an international tribunal to rule upon the validity and effect of art 2(b), it is probable that such a 'without prejudice' clause would be enforced, thereby protecting Australia from any negative implications that might otherwise have been drawn from the terms of the *Timor Sea Treaty*.

A 'without prejudice' clause cannot, however, overcome all impediments to agreement. A further difficulty emerged during negotiations for the *International Unitisation Agreement*, an agreement providing for legal certainty in the commercial exploitation of Greater Sunrise. Despite an original provision in the *Memorandum of Understanding* that resolution of the Timor Gap issue would not be dependent upon negotiation of some form of unitisation of Greater Sunrise,[26] Australia reneged on this understanding. Australian negotiators adopted the strategy that the Government could not agree to ratification of the *Timor Sea Treaty* unless and until East Timor had agreed to the terms of the *International Unitisation Agreement* for Greater Sunrise. As the Greater Sunrise deposit was proving to be by far the more important source for future income for East Timor, the linking of the two agreements was potentially disadvantageous to East Timor, as indeed, the present government of East Timor believes it to be.

Complex legal arguments were developed to support the position of the representatives of East Timor to the effect that the western and eastern laterals of the ZOC should be extended and that any boundary line should

---

[24] See Triggs and Bialek, above n 5, 332.
[25] *Timor Sea Treaty*, opened for signature 20 May 2002, [2003] ATS 13 art 2(b) (entered into force 2 April 2003).
[26] *Memorandum of Understanding of Timor Sea Arrangement*, above n23.

be a median line. The outcome of these proposals would be to place Greater Sunrise exclusively within East Timor's sovereign jurisdiction. To this the Australian Government would not agree. The principles upon which the western and eastern laterals of the ZOC were drawn for the *Timor Gap Treaty*, appear to be valid at international law.[27] The legal validity of the laterals is not, however, the subject of this analysis. Effective conflict resolution depends at least as much on the perceptions of the strength of the legal arguments as it does on the technical jurisprudential position. The legal arguments consistently made by Australia that the continental shelf would conclude at the Timor Trough are credible and reasonable at international law.[28] Similarly, East Timor can also credibly argue that international law is dynamic and that, increasingly, state practice supports the adoption of a median line if the distance between opposite states is less than 400 nautical miles.[29] No resolution of the legal issues can be achieved in the absence of willingness to reach agreement by the states themselves, other than through some form of mediation, arbitration or judicial determination. Any resolution of the Timor Gap dispute by the International Court of Justice (ICJ) was eliminated when Australia, six weeks prior to the independence of East Timor, amended the terms of its acceptance of the compulsory jurisdiction of the ICJ, withdrawing all matters relating to maritime delimitation.[30] While a withdrawal in these circumstances appears to have been made in the absence of good faith, it remains acceptable at international law for the government of any nation to decide that negotiation of permanent boundaries is a matter for negotiation rather than judicial determination.[31] For this reason, a challenge to Australia's withdrawal before an international tribunal is unlikely.

In these evolving circumstances, it was clear to both states that any resolution of differing judicial positions on the Timor Gap and Greater Sunrise fields was going to be dependent upon negotiations, and ultimately upon their goodwill, rather than upon any imposed adversarial judicial resolution. The strategic positions of both states at this stage in negotiations should be understood. If Australia were to ratify the *Timor Sea Treaty* without being sure of prior agreement on unitisation on the basis that only 20 per cent

---

[27] For a fuller discussion of the legal principles see Triggs and Bialek, above n 5.

[28] See Triggs and Bialek, above n 5.

[29] Ibid; *Libya–Malta Case* [1985] IJC Rep 13.

[30] *Declaration Under the Statute of the International Court of Justice Concerning Australia's Acceptance of the Jurisdiction of the International Court of Justice*, [2002] ATS 5 (entered into force 21 March 2002).

[31] Australia defended its action by arguing that it had been considering the withdrawal 'for quite some time', Hamish McDonald, 'Timor Gas Billions All at Sea', *The Sydney Morning Herald* (Sydney), 27 March 2003, 6.

lies within the Joint Petroleum Development Area (JPDA) (being largely the ZOC under the *Timor Gap Treaty*) and that the balance of 80 per cent lies within Australian jurisdiction, it would have 'given away' 90 per cent of revenues from the JPDA (as the area is now known in the *Timor Sea Treaty*), with no assurances that exploitation of Greater Sunrise could proceed. Australia would thus have lost its 'bargaining chip' in safeguarding its more valuable Greater Sunrise interests. If the parties could not agree on the *Timor Sea Treaty* or on Greater Sunrise, East Timor would have no revenue stream from either of these fields. Moreover, were Australia to 'give way' to seabed boundary claims made by East Timor this could well stimulate other nations such as Indonesia, Papua New Guinea, New Caledonia and New Zealand[32] to claim the benefit of an asserted 'contemporary' approach to seabed boundary delimitation. If existing boundaries were to be challenged, the possible consequences both to those boundaries and to others that remain to be agreed, would be far more significant for Australia than any that might flow from any continuing failures to agree a boundary with East Timor. Agreement upon the *Timor Sea Treaty* was also economically of greater importance to East Timor than to Australia.

In these circumstances, East Timor was persuaded to accept the linkage between the *Timor Sea Treaty* and the *International Unitisation Agreement* for Greater Sunrise on the grounds required by Australia, thereby ensuring the receipt of some revenues under both agreements. Understanding the strategic positions that underlie final agreement on these two agreements is useful because it explains why their future success may prove to be vulnerable. East Timor may choose to revisit its claims to sovereignty in the greater area of the Timor Sea than is currently included in the JPDA. Indeed, Dr Ramos Horta has stated that he hopes to continue discussions with Australia on a permanent boundary that fully recognises East Timor's claim.[33] Any significant risk to its revenue is, however, contrary to East Timor's interests. It is this balance of interests that favours legal stability for petroleum activities and the opportunity for co-operation and confidence building that could be provided as better outcomes of both agreements.

The legal and political aspects of negotiations of the *Timor Sea Treaty* and the *International Unitisation Agreement* have been unusually complex and difficult. East Timor agreed to the terms of the *International Unitisation Agreement* under which the 20 per cent of revenue from within the JPDA will be split 90/10, while all the revenue from the 80 per cent that lies within Australian sovereignty will go to Australia. While the *International Unitisation Agreement* does not meet East Timor's demands for a larger share,

[32] Negotiations between Australia and New Zealand are currently underway (August 2003).
[33] Triggs and Bialek, above n 5.

or indeed, the whole of Greater Sunrise, it is a unique international compromise that successfully combines joint development of the resources of the disputed seabed area with unitisation of a deposit that straddles part of the joint development area.

On independence, East Timor ratified the *Timor Sea Treaty,* which has now entered into force both for it and Australia. As has been noted, however, the *International Unitisation Agreement,* while agreed by East Timor and Australia, has not yet entered into effect. It is, moreover, entirely possible that the *International Unitisation Agreement* will not come into force at all if East Timor decides to pursue its legal claims. If so, the result will be that Australia has agreed to share the resources of the Timor Gap on a 90/10 basis, without ensuring that exploitation of the vastly more lucrative resources of Greater Sunrise can proceed on a stable legal basis. So, too, East Timor will have gained the primary share of the resources of the Timor Gap but will not be able to benefit from any resource exploitation of Greater Sunrise, primarily because, in the absence of unitisation, the relevant petroleum companies will not proceed to exploitation. If this analysis is correct, the interests of both states indicate that ratification of the *International Unitisation Agreement* would be to their mutual advantage.

Conclusion

The *Timor Sea Treaty* provides an opportunity to build upon the original *Timor Gap Treaty* of 1989 by maintaining a relatively stable legal environment for petroleum activities. Most importantly, the *Timor Sea Treaty,* hopefully to be consolidated by the *International Unitisation Agreement,* has the potential to form the foundations upon which Australia and East Timor can build a fruitful partnership for the future. Australia now has the legislative authority to ratify the *International Unitisation Agreement,* though the prospects of ratification by East Timor remain unclear (*The Greater Sunrise Unitisation Agreement Implementation Act 2004* (Cth) has now been passed by the Senate). It is for these reasons that the two agreements can be seen as examples of creative problem-solving that puts sovereignty to one side, enabling the states to provide legal security for investment in oil and gas exploitation. As a practical outcome, both state parties could receive petroleum revenues from the Timor Gap and Greater Sunrise fields to their mutual advantage.

The advantages of joint development as a technique for dispute resolution is that the parties can benefit from production revenues and have the opportunity to develop mutual confidence to focus on other issues such as fisheries management, the environment, maritime navigation and questions of people smuggling, slave trading and drug trafficking. There are thus strategic advantages in problem-solving through negotiating techniques that preserve the juridical positions of the parties but that also enable them to go forward in the short-term in the hope that, ultimately, in the future, the legal issues can be resolved on a non-confrontational basis. It must be acknowledged, however, that, despite these agreements, the underlying international boundary disputes remain unresolved. Thus, the proof of success of the new *Timor Sea Treaty* and *International Unitisation Agreement* will depend upon their ability to provide significant benefits to both Australia and East Timor in the near future.

Index

Bold page numbers refer to a page containing a map or illustration related to the item.